Parallel Algorithms and Architectures

Parallel Algorithms and Architectures

Michel Cosnard
Denis Trystram

INTERNATIONAL THOMSON COMPUTER PRESS

I(T)P An International Thomson Publishing Company

London • New York • Bonn • Boston • Johannesburg • Madrid • Melbourne • Mexico City
• Paris • Singapore • Tokyo • Toronto • Albany, NY • Belmont, CA • Cincinnati, OH • Detroit, MI

Parallel Algorithms and Architectures

British Library Cataloguing-in-Publication Data
A catalogue record for this book is available from the British Library

Library of Congress Cataloging-in-Publication Data
A catalog record for this book is available from the Library of Congress

First printed 1995

Translated and typeset by Logotechnics C.P.C. Ltd., Sheffield

Commissioning Editor: Samantha Whittaker

Printed in the UK by: Clays Ltd., St Ives plc

ISBN 1-85032-125-6

International Thomson Computer Press   International Thomson Computer Press
Berkshire House   20 Park Plaza
High Holborn   14th Floor
London WC1V 7AA   Boston MA 02116
UK   USA

http://www.thomson.com/intlitcp.html

Imprints of International Thomson Publishing

PWS Publishing Company, 20 Park Plaza, Boston, MA 02116

Contents

1

Introduction

Two parallels intersect at infinity
Anonymous

1.1   General description

1.1.1   Motivations

Resorting to parallelism in order to speed up computation is not a recent idea. Even in the earliest years of computing, computer designers thought about making several processors work simultaneously to resolve the same problem. However, hardware constraints imposed the use of a single processor. Technical developments in the 1980s reduced the costs of producing computer components while at the same time increasing performance in terms of processing time, the quantities of data processed and reliability. The technological level reached is such that it is now possible to build multiprocessor architectures and to use them efficiently, using several processors for general systems (tens of units) and many more for specialized machines (thousands of units).

The decline in the increase in speed of electronic circuits (only a factor of three in cycle time between 1976, Cray 1, and 1986, Cray 2) has led to a search for new techniques that will increase power, either at the algorithm level or at the architecture level. The concept of parallelism is a departure from the traditional approach, which consists of reducing computing time by carrying out each operation faster. In parallel computing, time is saved by carrying out several operations simultaneously. Parallel algorithms have been studied for a long time, in particular the complexity of certain parallel problems. However, the various parallel architectures have forced algorithm designers to impose new constraints on their models in order to bring them closer to reality.

Owing to the ever-increasing demands for computing power, the parallel computing area has developed considerably since 1985. Most present-day computers use this concept in one form or another. Parallelism can be very specialized and transparent to the user; on the other hand, it can require great effort if it is to be really efficient. In every case, better results will be obtained from the machines if you have a thorough knowledge of the basic mechanisms, and this is what we aim to provide in this book. Engineers and researchers who have not specialized in parallel computing will have to use it more and more frequently, but they often find it hard to understand the basics. We will try to tease out the main ideas and illustrate them with simple examples, both at a theoretical level and in terms of implementation.

Making a method parallel involves several stages. It is useful to start with the different ways the method can be written in algorithmic form, and then study its complexity theoretically in order to discover its intrinsic parallelism. After choosing the best version(s), you can look at implementation, that is, how the instructions can be executed on a target machine. This poses the particular problems of where to locate instructions, data circulation, the efficient use of communications, and so on.

The development of parallel computers has led to a re-evaluation of the most common algorithms in the light of new viability and performance criteria. In order to make an algorithm parallel, you first divide the problem into sub-tasks. Then you draw up a task graph in order to define the time constraints on the execution of tasks. The last thing to do is to assign the tasks to processors, taking into consideration both the precedence constraints and the hardware constraints imposed by the machine's architecture. The latter are used to select the most efficient parallel version for the machine in question. Generally these constraints are of two types: limited access to data and processor synchronization problems.

1.1.2   From sequential to parallel

Nowadays, the history of computing is usually divided into five generations characterized by their technological level, their mode of operating and processing, the languages used and the objects processed.

First generation (1938–53)

- 1938: First electrical analog computer
- 1946: First electrical digital computer, ENIAC
- 1950: First computer with a recorded program
- Mechanical and electro-mechanical technology
- Sequential ALU
- Binary language

Second generation (1954–63)

- 1954: First computer with transistors, TRADIC (800 transistors)
- Magnetic memory
- Developed ALU
- Assembly language, then Fortran and Algol
- Batch processing of a single program
- Purely scientific use

Third generation (1964–73)

- Integrated circuits
- Intelligent compilers for high-level languages
- Multiprogramming
- Vector processors
- Time sharing with multiprogramming
- Virtual machines
- From data processing to information processing

Fourth generation (1974–present)

- Large-scale integrated circuits (LSI)
- Large memories
- Languages that allow vector processing
- Parallel and pipeline ALUs
- Several processors
- From information processing to knowledge processing (expert systems)

Present and near future

- Specialized very large-scale integrated circuits (VLSI)
- Parallel multiprocessors
- Massive parallelism
- From knowledge processing to intelligence processing

1.2   Parallel processing

1.2.1   General points

Parallel processing is a form of information processing which uses concurrent events during execution. These events are at several levels: at program, procedure and instruction levels or even inside an instruction.

At the highest level, parallel processing can execute several independent programs simultaneously. It uses multiprogramming, time sharing and multiprocessing. It is used in mainframes and is handled at operating system level.

Parallelism can be introduced inside a program at procedure level. The program is broken down into tasks, the dependency relations between those tasks found and independent tasks programmed in parallel. It can be handled at operating system level (programs made parallel automatically, by intelligent compilers) or at algorithm level.

The parallel processing of independent instructions uses the vectorization technique. It is handled at system level (vectorizer), at programming language level (HP Fortran) or at algorithm level.

The pipeline technique is used to introduce parallelism at instruction level. This involves splitting an instruction into several successive steps and executing different steps of several instructions at the same time. This type of parallelism is handled at hardware level.

Large computers now make use of all these techniques. The increase in their numbers is astonishing. New systems are appearing with comparable performance and greatly reduced prices, giving credence to the idea of the personal supercomputer (the power of a Cray on your desk).

1.2.2   Parallelism in single processor machines

Generally, single processor architectures have the same basic structure: a main memory, a central processor and a set of communication components. The relations between these three units can be implemented in different ways, for example using a shared bus (VAX-11/780) or by concentrating everything on the processor (IBM 370). Parallelism can be introduced in several ways:

- several functional units

- parallel ALU

- simultaneous operation of the three units

- multiprogramming and time sharing.

The first computers only had one arithmetic and logic unit (ALU). The ALU could only execute one operation at a time. Later, the various functions of an ALU were distributed to separate units which operated in parallel. The CDC 6600 has ten functional units (addition, multiplication, division, logical shift and so on) in its ALU. The IBM 360/91 has two parallel arithmetic units: one for fixed point operations, one for floating point operations, divided into two functional units (additions and multiplications).

ALUs now have parallel adders with carry forward lookahead and integrated multipliers. They carry out pipeline processing. The simultaneous operation of the basic units is made possible by the use of local buses: transfers from memories to registers, processes in the processors' internal registers, input/output operations.

Multiprogramming means that various resources (generally the input/output unit and the processor) can be used in parallel by several processes of one or more programs. The most interesting case is when two programs are being executed, one of which mainly calls on the input/output unit (such a program is said to be *I/O-bound*) and the other on the processor (*compute-bound*). It involves considering the two programs as a series of tasks which are assigned to the functional units with the aim of maximizing their busy time and therefore reducing the total execution time.

The yield from multiprogramming is low when a process occupies a unit for a long time. Time sharing provides a solution to this problem. It means limiting the time the units are occupied. Therefore, the processes are divided into tasks whose duration is less than the limits for the units. By multiprogramming these tasks you get a total execution time which is less than that of a program or several programs executed without multiprogramming.

1.2.3 Parallelism in multiprocessor machines

In Chapter 2, we describe in detail the main parallel architectures and their models. In contrast to the parallelism of single processor machines, which is hidden from the user, when you use multiprocessor machines you must actually program the individual processors. Therefore, a computer is parallel if it has more than one processor for processing a single program. The Cray 2 has four very powerful processors and the Connection Machine has 65 536 1-bit processors. How can we construct and analyse algorithms and programs for such different machines? Can we think of a universal programming method? Are there any automatic parallelism tools and on what principles are they based? Are some problems intrinsically sequential? Does massive parallelism have a future and can it be used efficiently? These are some of the questions we will be trying to answer.

1.2.4   The applications

Numerous domains require increasing computing power:

- modelling and simulation: weather forecasting, oceanography, astrophysics, macroeconomics

- engineering: aerodynamics, nuclear engineering, chemical engineering, robotics and artificial intelligence, image processing and synthesis, micro-electronics

- energy resources research: oil, mineral and geological exploration

- medical, military and basic research.

The measurement of computer power is the capacity to execute a million floating point operations per second on real numbers represented in 64 bits: *megaflops (Mflops)*. All the above problems require powers greater than a thousand Mflops (*gigaflops (Gflops)*). The supercomputers of the early 1990s are only capable of about a few hundred Mflops. In order to obtain the power required, the cycle times of the processors must be reduced and their numbers multiplied. But the corresponding volumes of data must also be transferred from the memory (or memories) to the processors. The transfer unit is one million bytes (*Megabyte (Mbyte)*) per second. If the operations implemented are binary operations on 64-bit words, each one of them will require two data items to be read and a result to be written, which represents three eight-byte transfers. In order to obtain a megaflop of power, 24 Mbytes per second are used. The volume of data which can be transferred from the memory to the processors is called the memory's *bandwidth*. It is therefore very important that the bandwidth is large enough to allow the power of the functional units to be used effectively.

1.3   Summary of the following chapters

In Chapter 2 we survey the different parallel architectures: pipeline and vector processor architectures, multiprocessor machines with shared or local memories, data-flow architectures, and systolic and cellular architectures. We give an introduction to the various models and the main paradigms of parallel programming. Then we show how to measure the performance of these architectures.

In Chapter 3, we tackle the problem of the parallel organization of memory shared between several processors. Such memories are divided into banks, and only one data item in each bank can be read or written simultaneously. There is a conflict when two processors want to access the same bank or when a processor needs two data items located in the same bank. We study the question of organizing the data in these banks in order to minimize access conflicts. Then we look at an essential component of shared memory architectures: the network of interconnections between processors and memory banks. Generally, dynamic networks are used to link the processors to the various banks that make up their shared memory.

Chapter 4 is a general description of interconnection networks and their properties. Static networks are used to connect processors to each other according to a certain topology (ring, hypercube, grid, and so on). We mainly study regular topologies with fixed numbers of processors. At the end of the chapter, we describe the main tools for implementing algorithms on these networks (Hamilton paths, spanning trees, and so on).

General considerations about the complexity of parallel algorithms are discussed in Chapter 5. The main models are described (PRAM, exclusive and concurrent reads, Boolean circuits, and so on). A whole section is devoted to the problem of the evaluation of arithmetic expressions and their relationship to labelled binary trees. Some theoretical results for linear algebra and the problem of parallel sorts are given.

In Chapter 6 we start the algorithmic part of the book. In this chapter we study the pipeline principle and the basic techniques used to design pipeline operators and to implement them in software. Traditional tools such as reservation tables and collision vectors are explained.

Vector computing itself is discussed in Chapter 7. After presenting a general model of an architecture with registers, we examine how to vectorize an algorithm, with special emphasis on linear algebra algorithms (scalar multiplication, matrix multiplication and, more generally, basic linear algebra procedures (BLAS)).

Chapter 8 implements the algorithms discussed in the preceding chapter in order to vectorize linear algebra algorithms. We briefly summarize the Gaussian elimination algorithm, for which we propose an algorithmic analysis that does not consider the problems of numerical stability. Sequentially, this algorithm corresponds to three nested loops. A combination of these three indices gives us six versions whose performance is different on a vector architecture. The principle of cyclic reduction is described. This method can be used to break the dependencies between different instructions for linear recursion.

The next part deals with machines with shared memory. In Chapter 5, the architectural aspect was not taken into account: it was simply a question of looking for the maximum parallelism inherent in an algorithm, that is, all the operations that could possibly be executed at the same time. In Chapter 9, the architectural aspect is integrated into the hypotheses: the model is a multiprocessor machine with data sharing. We present a methodology for making algorithms parallel which can be used to construct several parallel algorithms from a sequential algorithm and to test their performance. This analysis is based on the notion of a task precedence graph. After constructing the graph by dividing a sequential algorithm into tasks, the creation of the parallel algorithm is the equivalent of ordering the tasks on the processors. A specific graph is used to illustrate this in detail.

The problem of ordering tasks is central to methods for applying parallelism and to the analysis of parallel complexity. Chapter 10 summarizes the general results, from both a theoretical and a practical point of view, and give some specific heuristics. At the end of the chapter, we show how communication times can be taken into account.

Chapter 11 uses the methodology described above to solve dense linear systems by diagonalization (Jordan's method) and by triangularization (Gaussian method and variations). As in Chapter 6, we construct several parallel algorithms from several versions of the same sequential algorithm, study their ordering and analyse their performance.

Chapter 12 is devoted to parallelizing QR factorization by Givens' method on a computer with shared memory. This study allows us to discern the limits of the methodology proposed in Chapter 9 and illustrated in Chapter 11. We also show how to evaluate the complexity of a class of parallel algorithms completely.

Chapter 13 continues the study started in Chapter 11 by including the cost of communication between shared memory and processors. We compare a points method and a blocks method. A different approach, based on the concept of overheads, is discussed using the same example of Gaussian elimination.

From Chapter 14 onwards, we study parallel algorithms on a processor network with distributed memory, operating by exchanging messages. Firstly, we describe the additional problems caused by these architectures and, mainly, the problem of mapping processors in the network. We show the close link to the ordering of tasks and demonstrate the main heuristics.

Chapter 15 deals with global communications algorithms. The main models are presented and the main communication schemes (diffusion, total exchange, distribution, and so on) discussed for static topologies (essentially hypercube, ring and grid). We also introduce the problem of communication by routing, and in particular the computation of permutations corresponding to structured movements of data. The example of transposing a matrix on grid and hypercube networks is discussed.

Chapter 16 summarizes some implementations on synchronous machines. After introducing the general problem of how to allocate regular data (vectors and matrices), we discuss the general principles for designing parallel numerical algorithms. Then, we study parallel algorithms for the distributed processing of vectors, matrix problems and sorting problems.

In Chapter 17, we discuss how to implement parallel algorithms for the solution of linear systems on networks of processors. Mainly, we study the implementation of parallel Gaussian elimination, triangular system solution, and the implementation of parallel Gauss-Seidel iterative and conjugate gradient methods. We also demonstrate synchronous and asynchronous algorithms for calculating roots of polynomials.

Finally, before giving an extensive bibliography on this vast subject, we discuss the prospects for development and the main outstanding questions, both in terms of software and hardware and from a theoretical point of view.

1.4   Reminders and notations

There are no particular prerequisites for reading this book. All we assume is that the reader has some basic understanding of computing: the basic structure of a computer, the basic principles behind algorithms, and how algorithms are expressed in a standard language (such as Pascal) and evaluated in terms of arithmetic operations and memory space. Below we remind the reader of a few concepts and present some notations which are essential to the understanding of this book.

The structure of sequential computers is based on the *Random Access Machine* model, usually known as *RAM*. These machines are made up of:

- a *computing unit*, also known as an *arithmetic and logic unit* (ALU), which carries out the basic computations;

- a *control unit* which executes the program and, in combination with the ALU, constitutes the *processor*;

- a set of registers which make up a *memory*, access to which, for reading or writing, is direct, in the sense that a data item is read or written in a time which is independent of its position in memory.

An *algorithm* is a set of operations defined in a rigorous and unambiguous way, such that each of the operations is effective, that is, can effectively be carried out by a RAM. A *program* for such a machine is used to describe an algorithm and is a sequence of instructions expressed using constructions like those in *Pascal*. The main ones, for a sequential algorithm, are the assignment constructions, the loops `for` and `while` *condition* do *instructions*, and the conditional `if` *condition* `then` *instructions* `else` *instructions*. Later, we will study parallel extensions to these instructions, but we will limit ourselves to those strictly necessary for expressing correctly and unambiguously the parallel algorithms whose design and analysis is the main aim of this book. We will not actually be writing real parallel programs, but only algorithmic schemes. Here is an example of a sequential program for calculating the product of two matrices:

```
for i ← 1 to n
    for j ← 1 to n
        C(i, j) ← 0
        for k ← 1 to n
            C(i, j) ← C(i, j) + A(i, k) * B(k, j)
```

Notice that the ← symbol is used to represent assignment; there are no **begin** and **end** delimiters marking the blocks – indentation is used instead; and there are no declarations and no semicolons terminating statements.

We will call the number of arithmetic operations the *computation time* or *execution time*. In the matrix multiplication example, the computation time is $2n^3$ operations. Therefore we will assume from now on that an arithmetic operation takes a unitary execution time. In certain cases, we consider that the execution of the expression c+ab takes a unitary time. This is justified by the fact that many computers have arithmetic units that have a multiplication operator as well as an addition operator. For most of our complexity studies we will use the traditional notation defined by the letters O, o, Ω and Θ [Knu73]. Let us remind ourselves of their definitions. We assume f and g to be two monotonic functions mapping from N (the set of natural integers) onto itself (or sometimes the set of real numbers):

- $f(n) = O(g(n))$ if $\exists\, c > 0$ and m / $\forall\, n \geq m$, $f(n) \leq c\, g(n)$

- $f(n) = o(g(n))$ if $\forall\, \varepsilon > 0$, $\exists\, m$ / $\forall\, n \geq m$, $f(n) \leq \varepsilon\, g(n)$

- $f(n) = \Omega(g(n))$ if $\exists\, c > 0$ and m / $\forall\, n \geq m$, $f(n) \geq c\, g(n)$

- $f(n) = \Theta(g(n))$ if $\exists\, c_1$ and $c_2 > 0$ and m / $\forall\, n \geq m$, $c_1\, g(n) \leq f(n) \leq c_2\, g(n)$

In the last case we say that f and g are of the same order. We will use these notations to study the algorithmic complexity of the parallel algorithms described in the rest of the book. In the case of matrix multiplication, we would say that the algorithm is in $O(n^3)$, to express the fact that it takes a number of arithmetic operations of the order of a constant times n^3 (we could also say that the execution time is in $O(n^3)$). It is a well-known fact that it is impossible to multiply two matrices in less than n^2 arithmetic operations. Consequently, the time taken to solve this problem is in $\Omega(n^2)$.

An algorithm will be said to be *optimal* if there is no other algorithm with a lower computation time that can be used to solve the same problem. Actually, this notion can only be applied correctly to sets of problems that are indexed by a parameter which measures the size of each instance of the problem. Generally, this parameter is represented by n. In order to show that an algorithm is optimal, we start by evaluating its execution time, and then we show that we cannot do better. Therefore we have an upper limit and a lower limit on the computation time taken to solve the problem. When these limits are the same, any algorithm whose time is equal to the limit is said to be optimal and we also say that the limit represents the complexity of the problem. We then use the notation $f(n)=\Theta(g(n))$. For example, it is well known that the complexity of the evaluation of any polynomial whose size is n is $\Theta(n)$ (it takes at least n operations because there may be n non-null coefficients and Horner's algorithm is in $O(n)$). When the two limits are different no conclusion can be drawn. This is true in the case of matrix multiplication (even though we know that there are more efficient algorithms than the one described above, we do not know the complexity of the problem).

Essentially, we will be studying how to make polynomial problems parallel, that is, problems for which there is a sequential algorithm whose execution time is a polynomial of the problem's size. In very special cases, we refer to NP-complete problems. We will not define this class of problem here, as we do not wish to overload this section, but we refer the reader to specialist books on the complexity of algorithms, such as [Wol91].

Finally, let us define the basic mathematical notations. We will write:

- $\lfloor x \rfloor$ the (lower) integer part of x, that is, the integer n such that $n \leq x < n+1$,

- $\lceil x \rceil$ the (upper) integer part of x, that is, the integer n such that $n-1 < x \leq n$.

Now we can get to the heart of the matter.

2

Classification of parallel architectures

In this chapter, we review the various concepts on which parallel architectures are based.

The distinction between synchronous and asynchronous architectures leads to a classification which ranges from pipelines through vector processors, SIMD machines, systolic networks, and MIMD machines with shared memory to processor networks.

We define two theoretical models which are important for studying algorithmic complexity: PRAMs and Boolean and arithmetic circuits. Finally we describe how the performance of parallel computers is measured.

2.1   The classes of parallel computers

2.1.1   An informal description of parallel computers

As we emphasized in the introduction, parallel computing has developed considerably recently. This has not only affected the field of architecture but also the fields of connection technology, environments (languages, systems, and so on), algorithms and programming.

The notion of parallelism covers numerous concepts, from a very fine grain level (bit manipulation) to a coarser level (the division of programs into independent complex procedures). And, of course, all the stages in between. Several classification systems have been proposed in the literature. The most popular, Flynn's system [Fly66], is based on the ways data flows and instruction flows are organized. However, it is generally agreed that there are many factors that this classification does not take into account, such as the operational mode of processors, memory organization and the granularity of processors. Taking actual machines as our starting point, we can distinguish three large classes of parallel machines: the general-purpose machines with shared memory, the networks of asynchronous processors with distributed memory and the massively parallel synchronous distributed machines with fine-grain parallelism (general-purpose or specialized). After a short preliminary on vector computing, we will discuss each model in detail.

2.1.2   The main forms of parallelism

Increasing the number of processors alters the basic structure of the machine enormously. Memory access problems become crucial because a flow of data at the processors' operating speed must be provided. Similarly, the problems of communication between processors are important. Many solutions to these problems have been proposed and several architectures have been realized. For simplicity, we will describe the classification most frequently used, Flynn's [Fly66]. The selection criterion it uses is the control mode for the sequences of basic operations carried out by the different processors. Other classifications have been proposed: they are based on the instruction and execution flows [Kuc78], on different computational models and their implementations [TBH82] or on specific architectural characteristics [Sch83].

The essential process in a computer is the execution of a sequence of instructions on a set of data. Therefore, generally, computers can be classified according to the multiplicity of the instruction flows and data flows actually available [Fly66], [Dun90]. Essentially, we get the following architectures:

- SIMD: single instruction flow, multiple data flows

- SPMD: each processor has the same program

- MISD: several successive instructions process the same data

- MIMD: multiple instruction flows, multiple data flows

An instruction flow is a sequence of instructions transmitted from a control unit to one or more processors. A data flow is a sequence of data items coming from a memory area to a processor or going from a processor to a memory area.

2.1.3   Synchronous architectures

The principle of the sequential computer

Let us briefly summarize the principle of the von Neumann sequential computer. The instructions are executed sequentially but can be pipelined (which is what actually happens in most present-day machines in this category). This structure is shown in Figure 2.1. It includes a memory which contains the program and which the control unit (CU) and the arithmetic and logic unit (ALU) both access.

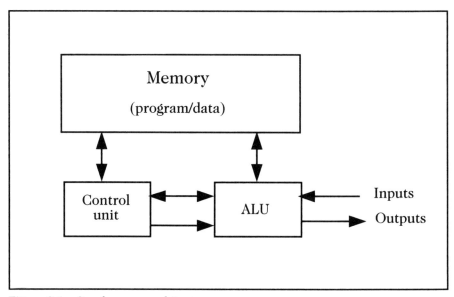

Figure 2.1   Synchronous architecture

Pipeline and vector architectures

The principle of pipeline architectures is as follows [HwB84], [Her87]: the operation to be carried out is divided into steps of equal duration which are executed one after the other. The inputs to one stage are the outputs of the preceding one. The pipeline is a hardware unit which reflects that division. Therefore, it is made up of stages separated by the registers required for the storage of intermediate data. In terms of Flynn's classification, these architectures belong to the MISD class. In reality the same data item is processed by a flow of successive elementary instructions.

A vector is an ordered set of n elements. Each element can be a scalar, a real floating point number, an integer, a Boolean or a character. A vector processor is a unit that can process vectors. It is made up of storage registers and one or more pipeline units. It handles vector instructions which provide all the useful vector–scalar combinations.

SIMD architectures

This structure is shown in Figure 2.2. Several processing units are supervised by the same control unit. All the processing units receive the same instruction (or program, in which case we talk of an SPMD structure) from the control unit, but operate on distinct data sets, which come from different data flows. As each processing unit executes the same instruction at the same time, the processors are operating synchronously. The shared memory can be divided into several modules, in which case the processing units access the different modules using an interconnection network, which we will study in the next chapter. A SIMD computer can be seen as a single processor machine which executes instructions on slices of data composed of several elements. Therefore, it is particularly well adapted to vector processing. For example, the ILLIAC IV, BSP, STARAN, MPP machines and, more recently, DAP from AMT, Connection Machine CM2 from TMC Corp., MP-1 and MP-2 from Maspar (marketed by DEC) and the ZEPHIR from WaveTracer are all SIMD machines. However, OSPILA [Au86] and the FPS T series hypercubes [GHS86] are SIMD/SPMD machines. Note that most current MIMD machines can be used in SPMD mode. Cellular and systolic networks, which we will describe later, are also included in the category of SIMD machines (synchronicity means that the same sequencer can control a very large number of processors).

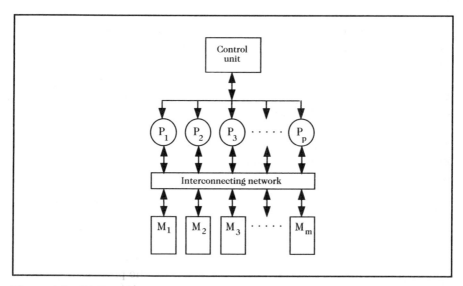

Figure 2.2   SIMD structure

Systolic networks

The complexity of the integrated circuits now being made means that it is possible to manufacture low-cost specialized operators, on condition that the number of computations to be executed is very much larger than the number of data transfers to be carried out.

Systolic networks, introduced by Kung and Leiserson [KuL80], are made up of basic cells which operate synchronously: at instant t they receive, as inputs, variables which come from neighbouring cells, and, after having carried out basic transformations on these variables, they send them, at instant t+1, to neighbouring cells as outputs. These networks have a local, regular, planar interconnection graph.

- In dimension 1, every cell i communicates with cells i–1 and i+1.

- In dimension 2 there can be orthogonal, hexagonal and other types of network.

The cells operate in parallel, in principle under the sole control of a global clock: several computations are carried out simultaneously on the network, and you can pipeline the solution of several instances of the same problem on the network. The name systolic comes from the analogy between the circulation of data flows on the network and that of blood in the body, the clock which ensures overall synchronization being the 'heart' of the system.

2.1.4   Asynchronous MIMD architectures

The first parallel computers to be really commercially successful were shared memory machines. Let us consider p processors linked to a large shared memory. The processors operate in MIMD mode, that is, each processor can operate independently of the others. Exchanges of information between the processors are carried out via the memory. Generally, access is by simultaneous reads and exclusive writes (CREW; *see* Section 2.2.2 on PRAMs). Machines belonging to this class have a relatively small number of processors (a dozen at the most), but each of them is quite powerful. Several attempts have been made to increase this number by introducing several hierarchical levels of memory.

The decrease in execution times is not the users' only aim. They would also like to have more memory available for processing more complicated problems. These two aspects are obviously linked, because access to large memories is slow. As the basic speed of processing units is continually increasing, the memories must be organized so that accesses are fast. There are almost always small very fast memory areas, local to the processors (registers or cache memories), for anticipated data transfers (pipeline) and for limiting memory accesses. Furthermore, the large memory is divided into distinct modules, each with its own input/output channel (*memory banks*). These banks are linked to the processors by a bus or an interconnection network. The first of these is a rapid resource, but blocks, whereas the second generally allows any access from the processors to the banks, with occasional blocks.

The scheme is that shown in Figure 2.3. The great difference between this structure and the preceding one is that, in this case, each processor has its own control unit. Therefore, the processors operate independently (and in particular, asynchronously) and execute different programs. An 'intrinsic' MIMD structure implies interactions between the p processors, because all the memory flows come from the same unit assigned to the data. If p data flows came from unconnected sub-units of the shared memory the structure would be called 'multiple SISD', which is the same thing as the juxtaposition of p independent single processor SISD systems.

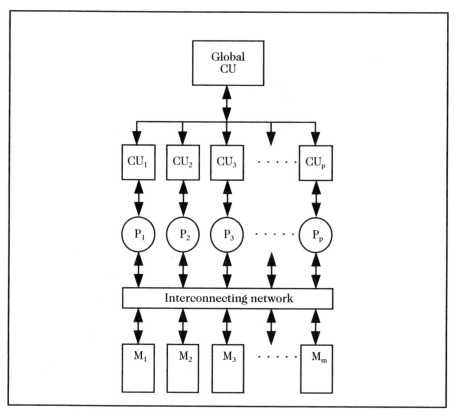

Figure 2.3   MIMD structure

Another classification can be obtained if we consider how processors communicate. In the models of parallel machines from the 1970s, the basic architecture is made up of a large common memory shared by several processors. The architectural problems mainly concern the difficulties of accessing that memory. Many solutions have been proposed for improving the flow from the memory to the processors: splitting the memory into several memory banks, introducing caches and making the memory hierarchical, generalizing the use of 'pipeline' operators and designing efficient interconnecting networks, which we will look at in Chapter 3. There are several supercomputers available that use all these solutions. The constraints imposed by the memory and the connecting network are such that interactions between the processors are important. These are called *strongly coupled* computers. Among the strongly coupled MIMDs we find the Cray-2, the Cray X-MP and Y-MP series, the IBM 3090 and the Alliant FX series and Convex [Bab87] mini-supercomputers.

Distributed MIMD architectures

The difficulties of accessing the memory limit the number of processors: once there are more than about ten processors, the performance of the interconnecting network degrades. In order to build massively parallel machines, designers have resorted to architectures in which the memory is decentralized and connections are limited: each processor has a local rapid access memory and is only connected to a certain number of neighbouring processors. The basic principles of this type of architecture are not new [HwB84]. Many prototypes have been built and systolic networks are directly descended from this approach [KuL80]. However, the first supercomputers built according to this principle have only recently appeared. The connection topologies most commonly used are the ring, the toric grid and the hypercube. In Chapter 4, we will look at the various types of connection. Generally, these multiprocessor machines are said to be weakly coupled. In this category we find the Intel Personal Supercomputer (iPSC) [TrW91] and the many parallel computers based on Inmos transputers, such as the TNode and MegaNode from Telmat [MuW90], [Fli90], the Computing Surface from Meiko [TrW91], the Concerto from the European consortium of Meiko–Parsys–Telmat [Bab87], and the VolVox from Archipel [RoT90].

In the first model, the processors work by sharing the data in common memory. Each processor reads the data it needs from memory, does its processing and then writes the results back to memory. In the second model, the processors operate by exchanging messages. Each processor reads the data it needs, which comes from other processors via one or more communication channels, does its processing and then transfers the results to other processors that need them. In this case, the execution time for a sequence of tasks no longer depends solely upon the execution time of each task, but also upon the location in the network of the processor that executes that task.

2.1.5   Data flow architectures

The conventional single or multiprocessor architectures which we have described are based on the principle of the execution of a sequence of instructions processed by the control unit whose basic component is the instruction counter. Even in the case of multiprocessor systems, these instructions are executed sequentially by each of the processors.

Data flow architectures attempt to exploit the parallelism of an algorithm to the maximum by freeing themselves from the constraints linked to the execution order of instructions. The basic principle is to allow an instruction to be executed immediately its operands are available. The start of an instruction therefore depends solely on the availability of data and not on its place in the program: program execution is linked to dependency constraints between data items. In this sense, systolic networks can be seen as data flow machines.

A program for such architectures is represented as a data flow graph. Figure 2.4 shows the graph corresponding to the computation of the expression z = (x+y) * (u+v). Therefore, an instruction is part of the graph, made up of a node (the operator), input arcs (the operands) and output arcs (the results). An instruction is activated immediately the operands have values.

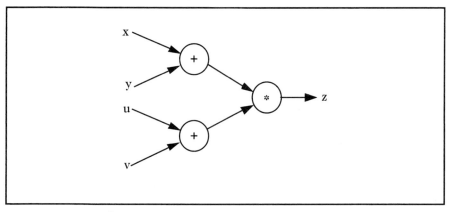

Figure 2.4   Graph for the expression z = (x+y) * (u+v)

The general organization of a data flow computer is shown in Figure 2.5. It includes:

- a memory unit containing the operands and the inactive instructions;
- a unit for searching for the active instructions;
- a queue of active instructions waiting for execution;
- a processing unit with several processors;
- an update unit whose role is to assign values to the operands at the end of processing.

We have already touched on some of the problems arising from traditional parallel architectures and these can also be found, in part, in data flow architectures: complicated and centralized control, which makes synchronization difficult, and frequent memory access conflicts. All these problems seriously affect the performance expected from parallelism.

Furthermore, the main part of an algorithm's execution time often involves repeated basic operations which require simple control, such as, in scientific programming, the computation of a scalar product, a matrix product or a fast Fourier transform (*FFT*), the search for paths in a graph, and so on. These operations could advantageously be carried out by a specialized operator such as a systolic network.

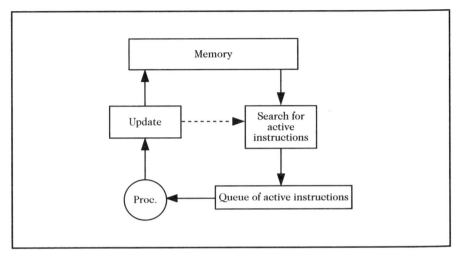

Figure 2.5   General organization of a data flow machine

2.1.6   Current architectural trends

All computer scientists know how difficult it is to sum up the trends embodied by the different computers at any given time. This is even more difficult in the field of parallelism where the lifetimes of machines are short.

Current general developments

After concentrating almost exclusively on a market for scientific parallel supercomputers with shared memory, manufacturers are now turning towards less architecturally sophisticated machines which are often built out of commercially available hardware. At present, the 'distributed' option is certainly the most promising from an economic point of view. All the economic studies show that the market for high performance computers is growing rapidly. The market share of distributed computers is increasing all the time. Today it only represents a few percentage points in a total market of several billion dollars but, with a growth rate estimated at 37% a year, it will reach 10% by 1995!

However, distributed programming environments are still rudimentary. These machines are reserved for experts in parallel processing and special efforts will no doubt have to be concentrated on this area before non-specialists can use them.

The processors

The 1980s saw the arrival of RISC architectures (Reduced Instruction Set Computer) [CiV87]. The idea behind the creation of RISC processors is based on the observation that only a small percentage of a processor's basic instructions are used in the majority of cases. So it is better to build processors where those instructions are implemented efficiently on simplified, and therefore faster, hardware even if you have to spend more time decoding the others (in reality, RISC architecture was mainly a reaction against the development of increasingly complicated processors).

These ideas can be found at many levels in current architectures:

- pipeline processors based on the segmentation of functional units and lookahead mechanisms for loading data (which we will look at in Chapter 6);

- superscalar processors where several instructions can be started at the same time;

- vector processors, natural extensions of pipelines and superscalars for regular data structures;

- VLIW (Very Large Instruction Word) processors, whose principles are based on the duplication of certain processing units for parallel operation.

The trend, for the future, seems to be in the direction of processors with great computing power (tens of Mflops) and communication facilities. The processors which are the basic units of present-day distributed machines are of this type and are mainly the following [Rum92], [TrW91]:

- i860 from Intel: this is a very powerful 64-bit RISC processor (the improved version has a 50 MHz clock speed which gives it a peak performance of around 75 Mflops). Along with the traditional features, it also has separate floating point and graphics units.

- The processors in the Inmos transputer family: these are processors with a communication system, made up of four two-way links, integrated into the component itself. The T800 processor has a 32-bit arithmetic unit and a floating point unit. It has a fast local cache memory and communication channels linked to direct memory accesses which allow direct inter-processor links, without buffering. Its successor, the T900, has built on experience with the T800 to achieve high computing performance (more than ten Mflops), simplicity of use and low cost for constructing networks of processors. This superscalar type processor is compatible with the present range of T800s. It is available with a component called the C104, which is used to link the transputers to each other and organizes the routing of messages very efficiently and, most importantly, in a way which is transparent to the user.

- There are some other processors which are used in workstations and also found in several parallel machines (Sparc from Sun, RS6000 from IBM, and others). They generally have RISC type architectures and their own specific characteristics. In order to build parallel machines, they have to be combined with specialized components that manage communication. Also note that many processors have been specially developed for parallel machines, such as those from Cray [Bab88] and nCube [TrW91]. The list would be incomplete if we did not mention specialized processors, such as the TMS320C40 from Texas Instruments which is dedicated to signal and image processing applications. This component has six communication links, which makes it an important candidate for the building of parallel machines (designed to solve regular numerical problems).

- The Alpha processor from DEC was announced as being one of the fastest on the market. This component is the successor to the MIPS RISC architectures, it is of the RISC/64-bit type and the manufacturers estimated that its peak performance would be more than a hundred Mflops with a high clock speed. It has many registers and 32-bit instructions covering four different formats.

Descriptions of some machines

We do not describe here large parallel machines with vector processors linked by a shared memory, such as the Cray XMP and YMP range, Cray2, IBM 3090 VF, NEC SX series, Fujitsu VP and Alliant FX series.

Let us examine the main machines with distributed memory. There are many massively parallel synchronous machines (SIMD). The most famous is undoubtedly the Connection Machine CM-2 from TMC [TrW91]. The CM-2 is a machine that can take up to 2^{16} 1-bit processors. Each group of 32 basic processors is linked to a floating point unit. These modules communicate using a hypercube 11-degree network.

Among the other SIMD machines [HoJ88], [TrW91] we will mention the MP series from Maspar (marketed by DEC under the name MPP), which has several thousand 4-bit processors, the DAP from AMT (which has implemented many dedicated applications, particularly military applications for optimal control), and the ZEPHIR from WaveTracer which is a three-dimensional grid.

The CM-5 is the new machine from TMC. The aim is to build a machine that achieves performance higher than a teraflop (Tflop). It is a MIMD machine with distributed memory which has three networks (one for data, one for control and one for error detection): this network is a four-way tree in which each node has two parents (a fat tree). The basic processor is based on a Sparc and has a local 32 Mbyte memory. Each basic processor is linked to four floating point units each of 32 Mflops, which means that vectors can be processed efficiently.

The Paragon machine from Intel is the commercial version of the *Touchstone* project. This is the range that supersedes the iPSC hypercubes, which succeeded in making some impact on the market. It is a distributed MIMD machine which can contain several thousand processors connected by a grid. Peak performance is around 300 Gflops. Naturally the basic processors are made by Intel (i860 SXs). They have a large local memory (128 Mbytes). A second i860 processor is used to manage message transmission and reception: it is attached to a dedicated communications processor (PMRC – Paragon Mesh Routing Chip). Each PRMC has four two-way communication links, used to route the messages in wormhole mode.

As we said previously, the transputer is a very popular European component. Its main attraction is the modularity it provides for connecting processors (4-degree topologies can be built). Many machines have been built using this component: the FPS T series hypercubes, the Telmat TNode and MegaNode, the Archipel VolVox, the Meiko Computing Surface and more recently, the Concerto which is the result of a collaboration between Meiko, Parsys and Telmat.

Note that several of these machines are heterogeneous; the transputer is used for communication and the actual computations are done by 'faster' processors, such as the i860.

The nCube-2 is a network of processors linked in a hypercube operating in MIMD mode. In its maximum configuration it contains 8192 processors. The basic processors are made specially for the machine by nCUBE. Each processor is directly linked to the outside world, to facilitate input/output.

KSR (Kendal Square Research) is a MIMD machine with a hierarchical structure which can contain a thousand processors. Groups of 32 processors connected in a ring are themselves connected in a ring by controllers. Its originality lies in the programming mode. It is an all-cache machine, that is, the memory is virtually shared by all the processors and managed like a cache. The basic processor (a 64-bit RISC chip) is made by Sharp: it is combined with a floating point unit, an ALU and a coprocessor for managing input/output.

To terminate this description of the main machines, let us mention the BBN machine, which has a distributed virtual memory, the iWARP, whose processors are VLIWs connected in a grid, the SP1 from IBM and the CS2 from Meiko–Parsys–Telmat, constructed from multi-layered networks.

2.2   Introduction to the models

2.2.1   General description

In order to study the complexity of parallel algorithms we have to define a computational model, which we will call the *machine model*, for executing the algorithms. However, there are many models for parallel computers. Therefore, there are different notions of algorithmic complexity depending on the model used. In this section we look at two of them: *PRAMs* (Parallel Random Access Machines) and *Boolean and arithmetic circuits*. This will allow us to start to justify the 'parallel computation thesis', which is used a lot both in complexity theory and for classifying machine models.

The parallel computation thesis

The parallel computation thesis is based on the intuitive idea of a relationship between the computing time of parallel machines and the computing space (size of memory) of sequential machines. Naturally, you must be careful because this thesis cannot be applied just as it stands to all possible models of parallel and sequential machines. One possible formulation is the following:

Parallel computation thesis
Any problem that can be resolved on a reasonable sequential machine using a polynomial-sized space can be resolved in polynomial time on a reasonable parallel machine, and vice versa.

The invariance thesis

It is not a simple task to define reasonable computers, whether sequential or parallel. Theoreticians have agreed on a consensus which is based on the 'invariance thesis'.

Invariance thesis
Reasonable machines can simulate each other with, at the most, a polynomial increase in time and a constant multiplication of space.

One way of constructing reasonable models is to consider the class of reasonable machines, including the Turing machine.

2.2.2   The PRAM model

Definition

The reference sequential model which we use in this chapter is the Random Access Machine (RAM) [AHU74].

Definition 2.1
A Parallel Random Access Machine (PRAM) is a set of independent sequential processors, RAMs, which each have a private (or local) memory and which communicate with each other using a global memory which they share.

Basic operations

Let us consider a PRAM made up of p processors numbered P_0 to P_{p-1} and m memory locations M_0 to M_{m-1}. A processor can find out the contents of a memory location M_i using the instruction $Read(M_i)$, and modify that memory location using $Write(M_i)$. Each processor can carry out atomic operations, which therefore take one unit of time. These operations have the following forms:

```
Read(M_i)
Compute(f)
Write(M_i)
```

All these atomic operations are executed synchronously. In other words, all the processors read, compute and write at the same time. Some restrictions may be imposed on computation. The most traditional is to assume that only arithmetic operations can be executed in atomic time.

Variations on PRAMs

The memory can be accessed in various ways. Snir [Sni82] proposed classifying memory accesses according to whether a single processor or several processors could read or write to the same memory cell.

If only one processor can read a memory cell at a given time it is called Exclusive Read *(ER)* and if several processors can read a memory cell at the same time it is called Concurrent Read *(CR)*. It is obvious that we are talking about the same memory cell, and that in both cases different memory cells can be read simultaneously by different processors.

A similar classification has been proposed for write accesses. Write access is exclusive (Exclusive Write, *EW*) if only one processor can write to a memory cell at a given instant and concurrent (Concurrent Write, *CW*) if several processors can write the contents of the memory cell. In the latter case, the processors may have different data, which will cause a conflict. Several models have been proposed to resolve this conflict. Here are the three main ones:

- common model: all the processors must write the same value in the same cell.

- random model: any processor can succeed in writing, but whatever happens the algorithm must execute successfully.

- priority model: the processors are classified according to an order of priority and only the processor with the highest priority, amongst all the processors that want to write to the memory cell, will access the memory.

By combining the various read and write options, we get different models. Generally, we differentiate between the EREW PRAM, the CREW PRAM and the CRCW PRAM, with, in the last case, three different models, one for each write strategy.

Going from one PRAM model to another

An algorithm for a PRAM is the sequence of atomic operations that each processor must execute. The initial data for the algorithm is located in shared memory and the results are returned there after processing. It is evident that an algorithm that satisfies the constraints of the EREW PRAM model will execute without any changes on a CREW PRAM model. Similarly for those with concurrent write strategies: if all the processors want to write the same value who cares which one writes it! Is the converse true? We shall see in Chapter 5 that it is not. To be more specific, the various PRAM models form a hierarchy, from the least powerful (we will clarify this later) to the most powerful. In order, they are EREW, CREW, CRCW common, CRCW random and CRCW priority.

If a processor is inactive, we say it is executing the *nop* (no operation) instruction. Therefore, all the processors execute the same number of instructions (but a different number of operations). This number of instructions is the algorithm's execution time. The notion of space is more subtle. Clearly, the number of processors is an important factor. You can also take the sizes of the shared memory and the local memories into account.

Extensions

In the case of distributed memory, the PRAM model must be modified to take memory accesses into account. Cosnard and Ferreira [Co91] suggested generalizing the PRAM model by modelling access to local memories using an interconnection network.

Definition 2.2
    A DRAM (Distributed RAM) is a set of p processors P_i, m memory locations M_i and a family of pairs X=(i, j). We write X_i for the set of pairs (i, .). Processor P_i can only access memory areas M_j for any j in X_i.

X is the interconnection network of the DRAM. In order to read a data item located in a memory cell to which it is not directly connected, a processor must obtain the help of other processors which, by reading and writing, will move the data item from the initial memory cell to a cell that can be accessed by the processor that requires the data item. In Chapter 5, we shall come back to the relationship between DRAMs and PRAMs, and the quality of the modelling.

2.2.3 Boolean and arithmetic circuits

General description

The Boolean circuits model is mainly used to define classes of complexity. This model is based on the combinatorial circuits used in computer architecture. To be more specific, a Boolean circuit is a directed acyclic graph (DAG). Each node in the graph belongs to a class of Boolean functions and therefore executes the function in that class. Traditionally, we consider the basic Boolean functions: *input, constant, and, or, not* and *output*.

An *input* node receives one of the problem's data items and transmits it to its neighbouring nodes, whereas a *constant* node always transmits the same value. Both have zero fan-in. The *and* and *or* nodes calculate the corresponding Boolean functions from their respective inputs (fan-in equal to 2) and transmit the computed value to their neighbouring nodes. A *not* node inverts its input, and an *output* node contains the result of the computation carried out by the circuit (fan-in equal to 1). An output node has zero fan-out. All these nodes are linked by arcs. Their directions correspond to the information transfers between neighbouring nodes. Variations can be introduced into the model by discussing the number of output links from each node. For simplicity, we will not hypothesize about this number (unbounded fan-out).

The computational model in this case is also synchronous. Each node (also called a gate by analogy with models of electronic circuits) atomically reads its inputs, evaluates its Boolean function and transmits on its output links in one unit of time.

A Boolean circuit with n input nodes and m output nodes computes a Boolean function f of $\{0, 1\}^n$ in $\{0, 1\}^m$, assuming, naturally, that the input and output nodes are ordered. The general problem that arises is how a Boolean circuit can carry out (synthesize) a given function. Obviously, this problem is the same as designing an algorithm for a PRAM.

Relationship to the PRAM model

Boolean circuits are characterized by two parameters: surface area and time. The number of arcs in the graph is called the circuit's size and the length of the longest path between an input node and an output node its depth. The circuit's size corresponds to the amount of hardware required to construct it and its depth is a measure of the function's computation time. Therefore, they are equivalent to the number of processors and the computation time of a PRAM model respectively.

If we do not restrict the *and* and *or* functions to two inputs, we get a new class of models (unbounded fan-in Boolean circuits). Arithmetic circuits are constructed from Boolean circuits by replacing the Boolean functions with arithmetic functions (or adding them).

NC classification

As in the sequential context, we introduce an order relation in order to classify problems by level of difficulty. Thus we define the NC class of problems as those problems that can be solved in polylogarithmic time with a polynomial number of processors. If we take the equivalence between models into account, this class is independent of the underlying parallel model.

We can easily show that the NC class is included in the class of problems that can be solved sequentially in polynomial time (the converse has still to be proved...).

More precisely, we define the classes NC^k of problems of size n that are solved in time $O(\log_2^k(n))$ with a polynomial number of processors. Then we have the following equality:

$$NC = \bigcup_k NC^k$$

2.3   Performance

2.3.1   Speed-up

Let us consider an algorithm that executes on a parallel computer with p (identical) processors in a time t_p and let t_1 be its sequential execution time (that is, on a computer with only one processor). The speed-up is defined by the ratio:

$$Sp = \frac{t_1}{t_p}$$

We can make two comments about this notion. Firstly, we must specify what we mean by the sequential execution time. In the preceding definition, we assumed implicitly that the algorithm is independent of the number of processors, which is generally false. Therefore, it seems more realistic to consider the execution time of the best sequential algorithm. Furthermore, an algorithm's execution time depends on the size of the problem, that is, the number of data items. We will look at this parameter in the paragraph on superlinear speed-ups. Theorem 2.1 shows the speed-up's limits.

Theorem 2.1
    For any p, $1 \le S_p \le p$.

Proof
    As a parallel computer can be used with only one processor, the execution time with p processors is at most equal to the sequential time.

Conversely, a single processor machine can simulate a multiprocessor machine in the following way: for each time unit of the multiprocessor machine, the single processor machine uses p time units to simulate the execution carried out by each of the processors.

There is no specific reference for this theorem, which is generally used without any justification being given. In this sense it is part of the folklore of parallelism. The formulation of this theorem is very imperfect, because some hypotheses have not been specified. In particular, there is an important point about the resources available to the processors. It is evident that p processors can store p times more data than one can. Theorem 2.1 therefore assumes sufficient resources for each processor.

2.3.2   Limitations of the speed-up

Amdahl's law

Various authors have attempted to specify the speed-up's limits. Amdahl [Amd67] proposed considering the inherent quantity of sequential program, which can only be executed by a single processor.

If

$$t_1 = t_{seq} + t_{par}$$

we deduce that

$$t_p = t_{seq} + \frac{t_{par}}{p}$$

Consequently:

$$S_p = t_{seq} + \frac{t_{seq} + t_{par}}{t_{seq} + \frac{t_{par}}{p}} \leq \frac{t_1}{t_{seq}}$$

and therefore the speed-up is, for any p, less than the proportion of sequential code. For example, if 10% of the program is sequential, then for any p, the speed-up will be less than 10. This result is known as Amdahl's law (1967). It expresses the fact that the speed-up is limited by a limit which is independent of the number of processors and the structure of the machine.

This law was generalized by Lee [Lee80], who considered, for i varying from 1 to p, the quantity of program which could be executed with i processors. Let $q_i t_1$ be that quantity. We then have:

$$t_1 = \sum_{i=1}^{p} q_i t_1 \qquad t_p = \sum_{i=1}^{p} \frac{q_i}{i} t_1 \qquad s_p = \frac{1}{\displaystyle\sum_{i=1}^{p} \frac{q_i}{i}}$$

If all these proportions are equal, so that

$$q_i = \frac{1}{p}$$

for all i, we get

$$S_p \le \frac{p}{\log_2(p)}$$

Minsky's law

Minsky [KaF90] ([MiP71]) considered the execution of programs with branch points on a SIMD structure. If a program has a conditional branch with branches of equal length, half the processors will be inactive when it is executed. Each branch can itself contain a conditional branch point. In the ideal case where each branch of the program has p binary branches of the same length, the program has a tree structure. We can easily deduce the following relations (the total sequential time is called t_1 which gives $t_1/\log(p)$ for each of the $\log(p)$ steps in the program, then we say that the ith step can be executed with 2^i processors):

$$t_1 = \sum_{i=1}^{\log(p)} \frac{t_1}{\log_2(p)} \qquad t_p = \sum_{i=1}^{\log(p)} \frac{t_1}{2^i \log_2(p)} \le \frac{t_1}{\log_2(p)} \qquad S_p \le \log_2(p)$$

This relation, known as Minsky's law, shows that the speed-up is limited by $\log_2(p)$.

Stone's table

In any case, the best we can hope for is of course $S_p = p$, but it is obviously illusory. Stone [Sto73a] proposed the following table, which evaluates S_p (empirically!) for some common problems:

S_p	Examples
$\alpha\, p$	Matrix computations Discretization
$\dfrac{\alpha\, p}{\log_2(p)}$	Sorts Three-dimensional systems Linear recursions Evaluation of polynomials
$\alpha \log_2(p)$	Search for an element in a set
α	Certain non-linear recursions Program compilation

In this table, α is a positive number smaller than 1 which depends on the machine.

Efficiency

The speed-up is a global measurement of the quality of a parallel algorithm. The *efficiency* of a parallel algorithm is the ratio:

$$e_p = \frac{S_p}{p}$$

Using Theorem 2.1, we can immediately deduce that e_p is less than 1. In fact, e_p is the equivalent of an efficiency indicator. It is used to measure the average usage of the processors, and the better the parallelism of the algorithm the nearer e_p is to 1. The preceding table shows that a constant value of e_p when p tends towards infinity can only be obtained for particular problems.

Superlinear speed-ups

The preceding approach is reasonable in the case of 'traditional' parallel machines; however, in the case of massively parallel machines with distributed memory, this approach is insufficient. The speed-up thus defined is generally not very good because of the cost of communication between processors and does not take into account the fact that the size of the problems processed can be much larger (which is often crucial in many real applications). We can then define a new speed-up by referring to the largest possible size of problem that can be solved using the set of processors [Gus88]. Similarly, we calculate the ratio between sequential time and parallel time, by extrapolating the sequential time on an ideal processor with a memory whose size is equivalent to that of all the processors.

The theorem which demonstrates a linear limit on the speed-up is based on the hypothesis that you can choose the best algorithm, that is, that this choice is made after you know the instance of the problem that needs to be processed. For some algorithms (in linear algebra for example) the choice is independent of the instance. It is different in other cases (traversing graphs for example). In this latter case, it may seem more reasonable to choose the sequential and parallel algorithms for a whole class of instances of the problem. You can then get superlinear speed-ups by using additional processors to find a correct solution rapidly, particularly in combinatorial problems where you do not really solve the same problem in sequential and parallel algorithms (for example, Branch-and-Bound where parallelism allows you to combine the depth and breadth traversal). Often you obtain superlinear speed-ups because you compute the correct solution faster by exploring different strategies. This is generally the case with all greedy algorithms (lists).

3

Basic components of parallel machines

New ideas based on parallelism have led to components being specially designed to extract maximum benefit from various architectures. This chapter looks at the main components of parallel machines – forms of parallel memory and interconnection networks.

3.1   Memory

First, we look at how efficient concurrent access can be enabled by general memory organization and at the problems involved. Then, we look in detail at static interconnection networks linking processors to various memory modules.

3.1.1 General memory organization

Introduction

The performance characteristics of traditional memory are measured by its bandwidth, that is, the number of words that can be accessed per second. This can be improved by:

- reducing cycle time,
- increasing word length,
- duplicating modules so that several data items can be accessed simultaneously.

The first type of memory is called random access memory (RAM), in which any word can be accessed in the same time. At the opposite end of the spectrum are sequential access forms of memory, which from a technological point of view are accessed faster, but which, on average, are slower.

All processors in a parallel computer must be able to access global memory when an instruction to read or write is executed, and the performance of parallel architectures is directly related to fast access to data.

Increasing access speed

There are two main ways in which computer memory can be organized – horizontally and vertically. The larger the memory, the more time is required to access randomly data items stored in it. But the higher cost incurred by fast memory means that it should be structured hierarchically – into small, very fast, direct access memory (sometimes called registers), primary storage (more often than not, there is a cache between these two types of memory) and, finally, slow access storage units. When parallel access to primary storage is required, memory has to be organized vertically and is partitioned into several independent modules (see Figure 3.1).

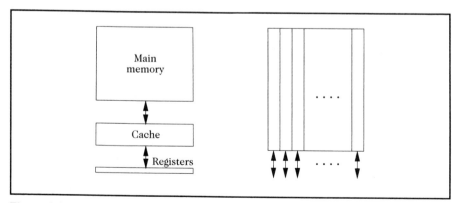

Figure 3.1 Vertical and horizontal memory organization

3.1.2   Caches

A cache's capacity is usually a few dozen kilobytes and performance characteristics are in the order of 50–100 nanoseconds.

Definition

The idea behind caches is similar to that behind virtual memory – several active data areas are stored by duplicating them in a faster module. The way this works is simple: data requests are first addressed to the cache, and then, if the cache is unable to respond, to main memory.

The main difference lies in how storage operates in these different devices. With a cache, data is managed by the hardware.

Physically, cache memory is organized into globally managed blocks of data. When a read request is sent from the central unit to main memory, a complete block is transferred to the cache. Of course, mapping between main memory and cache blocks has to be made explicit, and at the same time the cache has to be updated as comprehensively as possible. A *cache miss* means access to data items that are not located in the cache. Sometimes the *cache-miss ratio* is used; this is the probability that an item will *not* be in the cache.

A search for a data item in a cache is executed in two steps (*see* Figure 3.2). First, the address of the block's reference where the data may be located is searched for; then, if the reference exists, the data item is searched for in the block. If the reference does not exist, main memory is searched.

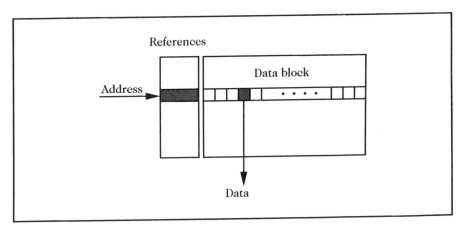

Figure 3.2   How cache memory works

Mapping

There are several possible solutions to the problem of mapping blocks from main memory onto those in the cache. We will use a 16-bit address from main memory and a cache consisting of 128 blocks as an example:

- **Direct mapping:**
  This is the simplest solution. The address in cache memory is obtained by taking modulo 128 of the address in main memory. The first 12 bits of a complete 16-bit address are the block's address, and the last 4 are the address of the word in the block. The 12 bits are then broken down into 5 and 7 bits, with the first 5 being the block's cache address (modulo quotient). When a memory request is generated, the 7 low-order bits in the 12 specify the cache block, the 5 high-order bits the block label and, when the block is in the cache, the 4 low-order bits provide the address of the word being searched for.

- **Associative mapping:**
  Any mapping operation applies here. A block from main memory can be associated with any reference in the cache. The first 12 bits of the address are then the block's label. When a request is made, the 128 labels are searched to see if the request can be met.

- **Associative mapping of sets of blocks:**
  Blocks in the cache are grouped together. The 12-bit address is divided into two parts, with one designating a group of blocks and the other a block within a group (searches for labels at this level are associative). For example, if the 12-bit address is divided into two parts of equal length, each group contains two blocks and each label is checked against two 6-bit labels.

Updating cache memory

Caches have to be updated as their storage capacity is relatively small, and it has to be decided which block should be replaced.

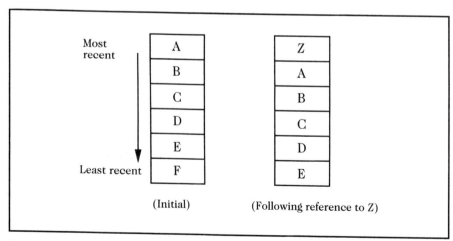

Figure 3.3   LRU replacement strategy in a cache

The majority of cache replacement algorithms in present-day machines are based on an LRU (least recently used) strategy, in which the least recently used block is removed, so that rows of data blocks in the cache can be reorganized. Assume that the cache is full and that references are stored from top to bottom, in LRU order (A, B, C, and so on). When a new request arrives and a cache miss occurs, the oldest data block (F in Figure 3.3) is removed, and the new request becomes the most recently used block.

The way a cache is managed clearly has an influence on algorithm efficiency. Writing numerical matrix algorithms using block decomposition (BLAS-3 nodes, defined in Chapter 7) is often more efficient than writing the usual algorithms.

3.1.3   Parallel memory

Let us now look at partitioning memory vertically.

Definitions

Generally speaking, memory is partitioned into subsets, commonly referred to as memory banks. They are connected to processors by networks of connections which enable processors to gain fast access to memory. However, partitioning memory into banks does not by itself ensure that access is fast, because it fails to solve conflicts, such as when several processors need to access data stored in the same memory bank. For example, if each column of a matrix is stored in a different memory bank, the processors can gain parallel access to data items by rows, diagonals and off-diagonals, but not to data items in the same column.

We will go into parallel memory organization and the storage rules related to it later on.

Definition 3.1

A memory bank M is a subset of M with its own input/output channel. M consists of the set of the memory banks. All the input/output channels can be accessed independently of each other.

Memory in the ILLIAC IV parallel computer (designed by the University of Illinois in 1970) was partitioned into 64 synchronous access memory banks, with one bank for each processor. Nowadays, storage is organized differently – parallel and independent memory banks are connected to processors via fast switching systems. We will look at interconnection networks later in this chapter.

Some examples

Before we look in detail at memory partitioning, we provide some examples that illustrate the problems associated with storing vector data.

• Consider the numerical solution of Poisson's Equation $\Delta u = f$, where Δ is the Laplacian operator. When the problem is discretized, instructions of the following form have to be executed:

$$A(i,j) = \frac{A(i-1,j) + A(i,j-1) + A(i,j+1) + A(i+1,j)}{4}$$

Assume that access to memory is slow in terms of arithmetic operations, as for example in pipeline execution. It is desirable that for all the pairs (i, j), the values $A(i-1, j)$, $A(i, j-1)$, $A(i, j+1)$ and $A(i+1, j)$ should be stored in different memory banks so that they can be read quasi-simultaneously, or at least pipelined.

• Now, assume that we have a SIMD system with three processors P_0, P_1, P_2, and with memory divided into three banks M_0, M_1, M_2. If the elements $A(i, j)$ of a 3×3 matrix are stored as in Figure 3.4, a parallel instruction on the columns cannot be randomly executed. For example, for each value of i, the three operands of the instruction below are in the same memory bank and require memory to be accessed three times consecutively.

```
for i ← 1 to 3
    A(1, i) ← A(2, i)*A(3, i)
```

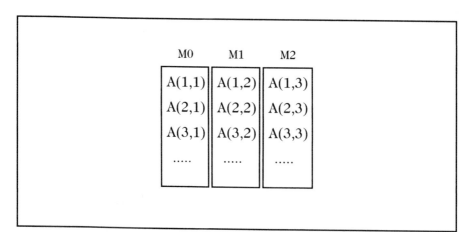

Figure 3.4   Storage by columns

By contrast, if the coefficients are stored as shown in Figure 3.5, rows, columns and diagonals (but not off-diagonals) can be accessed.

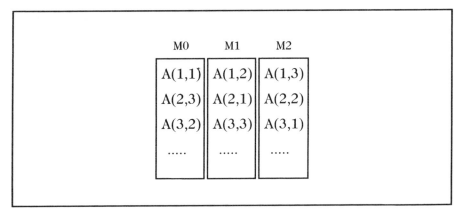

Figure 3.5   Individual storage

3.1.4   Storing data in memory

General aspects of storage rules

We will represent all indices as $Z \times Z$ in order to avoid problems with edges. This in no way detracts from the general nature of the problem.

Definition 3.2
A *template of the order p* is a subset of $Z \times Z$ with p elements including $(0, 0)$:

$P = \{ (0, 0), (x_1, y_1), ..., (x_{p-1}, y_{p-1}) \}$

P is *linear* if $x_i = ix$ and $y_i = iy$. P is written as $[x, y]_p$ in this case. The *P-cut* around (i, j) is the subset:

$P(i, j) = P + (i, j) = \{ (i+x, j+y) / (x, y) \in P \}$

The template associated with the discretized Laplacian is:

$P = \{ (0, 0), (0, 1), (1, 0), (-1, 0), (0, -1) \}$

It is of the order 5.

The linear templates $P_1 = [0, 1]_p$, $P_2 = [1, 0]_p$, $P_3 = [1, 1]_p$, $P_4 = [1, -1]_p$ are, respectively, the matrix's rows, columns, diagonals and off-diagonals.

Definition 3.3

A *storage rule* of size m is an application:

$$R: \mathbf{Z} \times \mathbf{Z} \to \{\, 0, 1, ..., m-1 \,\}$$

The index element (i, j) is stored in bank R(i, j).

Example: the rules R_1 and R_2, which are illustrated in Figures 3.4 and 3.5, are:

$$R_1(i, j) = j - 1 \text{ modulo } 3 \qquad R_2(i, j) = i + j - 2 \text{ modulo } 3$$

Storage rules that are compatible with templates

The problem we will turn to now is as follows: given a matrix of data (here $\mathbf{Z} \times \mathbf{Z}$) and a set of parts of the matrix (its templates and the corresponding cuts), how can the matrix's elements be stored (that is, how can a storage rule be defined) in such a way that each of the parts can be accessed in one cycle? In other words, we are seeking to store the matrix so that elements of each of its parts are in different memory banks – and thus to establish a rule that is compatible with the matrix's template or templates.

Definition 3.4

A storage rule R of size m is compatible with a template P if the restriction of R to P(i, j) is injective for all (i, j) of $\mathbf{Z} \times \mathbf{Z}$.

If R is compatible with P, the elements of a P-cut are ordered in different memory banks and they can be accessed in parallel. Note that p must be lower than or equal to m for a rule to be compatible with a template of the order p. With a SIMD machine, this implies that the number of processors is less than or equal to the number of memory banks. In the ILLIAC VI, each processor has a local memory, and the number of memory banks and processors is the same.

General results

In this section, we prove that the existence of a storage rule that is compatible with a template for a matrix of bounded size is equivalent to the existence of a rule that is compatible with the same template in $\mathbf{Z} \times \mathbf{Z}$.

Definition 3.5

All the definitions above are extended by replacing $Z \times Z$ with:

$$\left\{ -\left\lfloor \frac{q-1}{2} \right\rfloor, \ldots, -1, 0, 1, \ldots, \left\lfloor \frac{q}{2} \right\rfloor \right\} \times \left\{ -\left\lfloor \frac{q-1}{2} \right\rfloor, \ldots, -1, 0, 1, \ldots, \left\lfloor \frac{q}{2} \right\rfloor \right\}$$

where $\lfloor x \rfloor$ denotes the integer part of x. A storage rule is then said to be *of the order q*.

It is important not to confuse a storage rule's order with its size. The order characterizes its departure space while the size characterizes its arrival space.

$$R: \left\{ -\left\lfloor \frac{q-1}{2} \right\rfloor, \ldots, -1, 0, 1, \ldots, \left\lfloor \frac{q}{2} \right\rfloor \right\} \times \left\{ -\left\lfloor \frac{q-1}{2} \right\rfloor, \ldots, -1, 0, 1, \ldots, \left\lfloor \frac{q}{2} \right\rfloor \right\} \to \left\{ 0, 1, \ldots, m-1 \right\}$$

Definition 3.6

A storage rule R of the order q is compatible with a template P, if $R(a, b) = R(c, d)$ implies for different (a, b) and (c, d) that (a, b) and (c, d) do not belong to the same P-cut:

$$(a, b) \in P(i, j) \Rightarrow (c, d) \notin P(i, j)$$

In concrete terms, this corresponds to the intuitional idea that two data items located in the same memory bank must not be accessed simultaneously. The problem we will look at now is the existence of such rules and how they are constructed. The theorem below enables the problem to be put into a general framework and studied much more easily.

(Generalization) theorem 3.1

Let P be a template. For each q, there exists a storage rule of the order q that is compatible with P, if and only if a storage rule that is compatible with P exists.

Proof

Note that if R is a storage rule that is compatible with P, the restriction of R to $\{0, 1, \ldots, q-1\} \times \{0, 1, \ldots, q-1\}$ is compatible with P. The same argument proves that, if R is a storage rule that is compatible with P, for all $i \leq q$, the restriction of R to $\{0, 1, \ldots, i-1\} \times \{0, 1, \ldots, i-1\}$ is a rule of the order i that is compatible with P.

A tree in which each node is a storage rule that is compatible with P, defined on $\{-1, -i+1, \ldots, i-1, i\} \times \{-i, -i+1, \ldots, i-1, i\}$, is constructed. An arc exists between a node at level i and a node at level i+1, if the rule that is on level i+1 and is restricted to {−1, −i+1,..., i−1, i}x{−i, −i+1,..., i−1, i} is the rule linked with the level i node. The tree's root is the level −1 node which is the only rule that is compatible with the null matrix.

Let us consider the rule R_{2i+1} of the order 2i+1, which is compatible with P and which is assumed to exist. The storage rule R', defined as:

$$R'_i(a, b) = R_{2i+1}(a+i, b+i)$$

is compatible with P and has {−i, −i+1,..., i−1, i}x{−i, −i+1,..., i−1, i} as its domain.

By construction, R_i is a node of the tree. The beginning of the proof shows that a path connecting R_i to the root node exists. Furthermore, each node has only a finite number of descendants. The lemma below (which is proved in [Knu73]) shows that a path of infinite length exists.

König's lemma 3.1

In a tree with an infinite number of vertices, in which each vertex has a finite number of successors, a path of infinite length exists.

To conclude the proof, let the nodes of the tree be called R_{-1}, R_0,..., R_i. Let a storage rule R be defined by:

$$R(a, b) = R_i(a, b) \text{ where } i > \max(|a|, |b|)$$

R is well defined, as it is possible to move along the path by means of successive restrictions. By construction, R is compatible with P, and that concludes the proof.

Characterizing compatible rules

We now describe a theorem for characterizing compatible rules with a given template. It will be seen that the existence of a compatible rule does not depend solely on templates' geometry. All the storage rules we shall look at from here onwards will be defined on Z×Z.

Lemma 3.2

Let P be a template of the order p and R a storage rule of size m. R is compatible with P if and only if all the P-cuts around points with the same storage do not have a common point:

$\forall \, k \in \{0, 1,..., m-1\}$ and $\forall \, (a_1, b_1)$ and (a_2, b_2)
such that $R(a_1, b_1) = R(a_2, b_2)$

we have

$$P(a_1, b_1) \cap P(a_2, b_2) = \emptyset$$

Proof
$\Leftarrow$ Let $P = \{x_0, y_0) = (0, 0), (x_1, y_1),..., (x_n, y_n - 1)\}$
Assume that (a_1, b_1) and (a_2, b_2) exist, such that $R(a_1, b_1) = R(a_2, b_2)$
and that $P(a_1, b_1)$ and $P(a_2, b_2)$ share a common element:

$$(a_1 + x_i, b_1 + y_i) = (a_2 + x_j, b_2 + y_j)$$

Then consider $P(a_1 - x_j, b_1 - y_j)$. Its ith element is equal to:

$$(a_1 - x_j + x_i, b_i - y_j + y_i) = (a_2, b_2)$$

Its jth element is equal to (a_1, b_1). Just as by assumption, $R(a_1, b_1)$
$= R(a_2, b_2)$, R is not compatible with P, which is a contradiction.
$\Rightarrow$ Now assume that R is not compatible with P. Let (a, b) be such
that $R(a + x_i, b + y_i) = R(a + x_j, b + y_j) = k$. The ith element of
$P(a + x_j, b + y_j)$ is equal to the jth element of $P(a + x_i, b + y_i)$.

We have seen that a necessary condition for the existence of a storage rule
is for the number of memory banks (m) to be greater than the template's
order (p). Where m is very large compared with p, access conflicts are rare,
but the interconnection network is complex. We shall look at the extreme
case which brings about optimal storage rules.

Definition 3.7
A template P is said to *cover* Z×Z, if a set of P-cuts exists such that all
points of Z×Z are in one and only one P-cut.

Figures 3.6 to 3.8 describe templates of the order 3 and 5. Some cover
Z×Z while others do not. This is basic to our purposes here and the idea
enables the existence of a rule that is compatible with a template to be
characterized, as the theorem below proves.

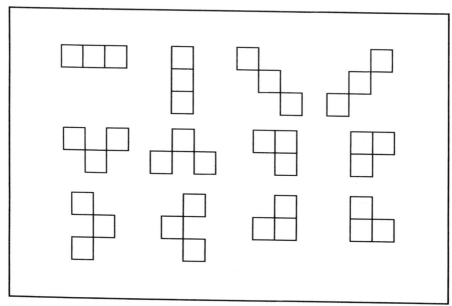

Figure 3.6   Templates of the order 3 that cover **Z**×**Z**

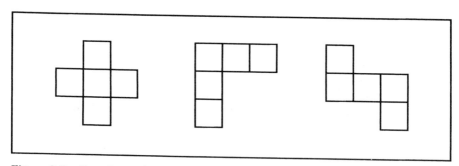

Figure 3.7   Templates of the order 5 that cover **Z**×**Z**

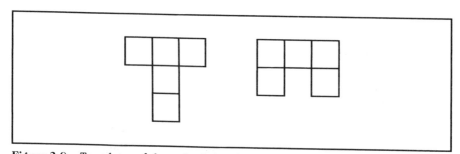

Figure 3.8   Templates of the order 5 that do not cover **Z**×**Z**

Theorem 3.3

Given a template P of the order p, a storage rule R of size p that is compatible with the template exists, if and only if P covers **Z**×**Z**.

Proof

⇐ Assume that $P=\{(x_0, y_0)=(0, 0), (x_1, y_1),..., (x_{p-1}, y_{p-1})\}$ tiles the template. All elements (a, b) of $Z \times Z$ belong to one and only one P-cut. Let k be the row of (a, b) in the P-cut. $R(a, b)=k$ is written down.

Lemma 3.2 is applied to show that R is compatible with P. The set of partitions corresponding to $k=0$ is the tiling associated with P and the lemma's condition is satisfied by defining the tiling. Where $k \neq 0$, the set of partitions $P(a, b)$ such that $R(a, b)=k$ is a tiling that is translated from the original. The lemma's condition is still satisfied.

⇒ Let R be a storage rule that is compatible with P. It will be shown that the set of partitions $P(a, b)$, where $R(a, b)=0$, tiles $Z \times Z$.

Lemma 3.2 implies that two partitions of the set do not cover each other. We will show now that all points (a, b) belong to a partition of the set. Let $P(a_0, b_0),..., P(a_{p-1}, b_{p-1})$ be the p partitions that contain (a, b). If where $i \neq j$ we have $R(a_i, b_i)=R(a_j, b_j)$, then Lemma 3.2 is contradicted, since (a, b) belongs to $P(a_i, b_i)$ and $P(a_j, b_j)$. Thus, all the $R(a_i, b_i)$ are different and an i exists where $R(a_i, b_i)=0$. (a, b) is covered by $P(a_i, b_i)$.

The theorem can be extended in order to characterize rules that are compatible with a finite set of templates.

Theorem 3.4

Given r templates of the order p, $P_1,..., P_r$, a storage rule R of size p that is compatible with the set of the templates exists, if and only if the tilings T_1 around $P_1,..., T_r$ around P_r of $Z \times Z$ exist, such that the partitions that each of the tilings consists of are around the same points.

$$\forall\ i, j\ P_i(a, b) \in T_i \Leftrightarrow P_j(a, b) \in T_j$$

Proof

⇐ By using T_1, a storage rule R of size p that is compatible with P_1 is defined, in accordance with the proof of Theorem 3.3: (a, b) belongs to only one P-cut and its row in the P-cut is k; $R(a, b)=k$ is written down.

Lemma 3.2 is used to show that R is compatible with P_1. For $k=0$, the P-cuts around the points (a, b) such that $R(a, b)=0$, constitute T_i. $P_i(a, b)$ belongs to T_i, if and only if $P_1(a, b)$ belongs to T_1, in which case $R(a, b)=0$. For $k \neq 0$, each point (c, d) such that $R(c, d)=k$ is obtained by translating from point (a, b) where $R(a, b)=0$, that is, from T_1. The set of P-cuts around points (c, d) thus covers $Z \times Z$. Lemma 3.2 can then be applied.

⇒ If R is compatible with each P_i, let the set T_i of the P-cuts around the points (a, b) be such that R(a, b)=0. T_i then tiles $\mathbf{Z} \times \mathbf{Z}$. The condition on the T_i is satisfied, since P_i(a, b) belongs to T_i if and only if R(a, b)=0.

Note that, for a given family of templates, template tilings for which the theorem's condition is satisfied may or may not exist, as shown by Figures 3.9 and 3.10, which illustrate storing by rows and columns of the order 3.

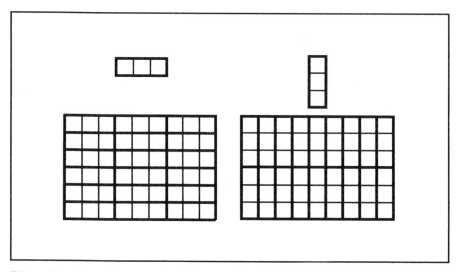

Figure 3.9   Poor tilings in which there is no compatible rule

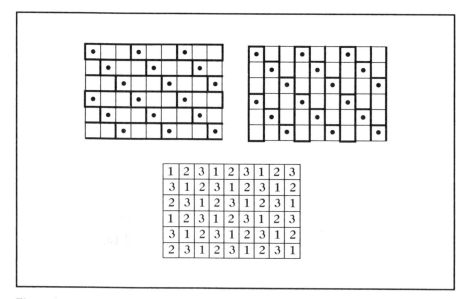

Figure 3.10   Good tilings and associated compatible rule

3.1.5   Rules and regular templates

So far we have looked at the issue generally and we have not gone into the problem of computing storage rules, which in terms of some complex templates or rules may prove costly. In this section, we look at some regular rules and templates.

Definition 3.8

A storage rule R is *periodic*, with period n, if R(i, j)=R(i+kn, j+nl) for all i, j, k, l.

Theorems 3.3 and 3.4 are much simpler when storage rules are periodic.

Theorem 3.5

Given a template of the order p, a periodic storage rule R of size p with period n that is compatible with this template exists, if and only if P covers $\mathbf{Z}/n\mathbf{Z} \times \mathbf{Z}/n\mathbf{Z}$.

Theorem 3.6

Given r templates of the order $p: P_1, \ldots, P_r$, a periodic storage rule R of size p with period n that is compatible with all the templates exists, if and only if tilings T_1 around $P_1, \ldots, T_r$ around P_r of $\mathbf{Z}/n\mathbf{Z} \times \mathbf{Z}/n\mathbf{Z}$ exist such that the P-cuts that each of these tilings consists of are around the same points:

$$\forall\, i, j\ P_i(a, b) \in T_i \Leftrightarrow P_j(a, b) \in T_j$$

Definition 3.9

A storage rule R of size m is *linear* if u and v exist such that R(i, j)=ui+vj modulo m.

Linear storage rules are sometimes described as *helicoidal*, as they operate in $\mathbf{Z}/p\mathbf{Z}$. They are a particularly simple form of periodic rules.

Theorem 3.7

The linear storage rule of size m R(i, j)=ui+vj modulo m is compatible with the linear template $[x, y]_p$ if and only if:

$$m \geq p\ \text{pgcd}(ux+vy, m)$$

Proof

R is compatible with $[x, y]_p$ if and only if for all (a, b) such that $0 \leq b < a < p$ we have:

$$uax + vay \neq ubx + vby \text{ modulo } m$$

This is equivalent to:

$(a - b)(ux + vy) \neq 0$ modulo m where $1 \leq a-b < p$

Let $\partial = \text{pgcd}(ux + vy, m)$. We then have:

$ux + vy = r\partial$ m=s∂ pgcd(r, s) = 1

This condition is the same as:

$kr\partial \neq 0$ modulo $s\partial$ where k=1,..., p−1

---

that is:

$kr\partial \neq 0$ modulo s

---

and similarly:

$p - 1 < s$, that is, $p \leq s = m/\partial$

One particular situation that is important is obtained when m = p. The theorem is simpler:

Corollary 3.8

The linear storage rule of size p, R(i, j)=ui+vj modulo p is compatible with the linear template $[x, y]_p$ if and only if ux+vy and p are relatively prime.

Corollary 3.9

A linear storage rule of size p that is compatible with linear templates $[0, 1]_p$, $[1, 0]_p$ and $[1, 1]_p$ exists if and only if p is odd.

Corollary 3.10

A linear storage rule of size p that is compatible with linear templates $[0, 1]_p$, $[1, 0]_p$, $[1, 1]_p$, $[-1, 1]_p$ exists if and only if p is odd and not divisible by 3.

In other words, if p is not a multiple of 2 or 3, a linear storage rule exists which enables rows, columns, diagonals and off-diagonals to be accessed in parallel.

3.2   Interconnection networks

Since the advent of parallelism, the problem of how units are interconnected has been of paramount importance. Interconnection may be between processors (or more simply processing units) and memory modules, or as we will see in Chapter 4, between a number of processors.

3.2.1   Static and dynamic networks

The main forms of parallelism

Machines can be initially classified according to whether connections between processors are direct or through common, shared-memory banks. If the former, the interconnection network is generally static. If the latter, it is dynamic and a routing algorithm has to be used.

Whether the processors function synchronously or asynchronously is the second important parameter. In SIMD (synchronous) systems, data interchange is governed by a global clock. The network is easier to control in comparison with a MIMD structure in which data is interchanged asynchronously.

The number of connections is the third parameter. One processor may be connected by means of fixed connections to all the others or to all the memory banks (fixed complete network). One processor may be linked to any other or any memory bank with a connection that depends on the two communicating units (rearrangeable complete network). There are only a certain number of permutations between processors (or between processors and memory banks), so several passes through the network are required to achieve some connections.

An interconnection network establishes relations between input and output units. It is most frequently used for exchanging data between these units, but it can also be used for executing duplication or compression operations.

Dynamic networks

In static networks, all processors are, generally speaking, connected to each other, in which case each processor has a local memory. It is helpful to use notation from graph theory to compare the different types of network. Processors are represented by nodes. Connections, which are assumed to be bidirectional, are represented by the edges between these nodes [Rum92].

The following chapter is dedicated to describing the main forms of network and studying their characteristics, and the reader is referred to it for details on connection topologies.

This chapter looks more specifically at dynamic networks. We describe connections by means of buses and then go into the various forms of dynamic network, following with the logic behind the development of their characteristics. First, we describe crossbar matrices, in which input and output nodes can be simultaneously connected, then rearrangeable networks and finally blocking networks.

3.2.2   Buses and arbitration

The simplest way of connecting several functional units is to group them around a bus. This communication unit is shared by all the units and a bus controller must therefore assign the bus to a given unit. Here we look briefly at some algorithms for allocating buses to units (arbitration). Note that such algorithms are normally carried out by hardware.

Fixed priority daisychaining

Functional units that share a bus are given a fixed priority and are ordered according to their size. When several units require access to the bus, the unit with the highest priority uses it. Generally speaking, the arbitration device and the functional units are grouped around the bus in such a way that their order of priority is the same as their geography (daisychaining).

The algorithm is simple to implement and optimizes resource utilization. But it is not symmetrical and on some occasions a unit can wait for an infinite amount of time before accessing the resource.

Time slicing

In time slicing, each functional unit is given a period of time in which to use the bus according to an unchanging order. If the bus is not used by a unit, it remains unused throughout the time period. This type of arbitration is called symmetrical, as all units are allocated the same amount of time to use the bus.

The main advantage of this algorithm is that the time each unit has to wait is limited. The major disadvantage is that its utilization rate is poor. Both explain why the algorithm is usually implemented in synchronous structures.

Dynamic priorities

Here, the bus is allocated according to the order of priority described in the paragraph above on fixed priority daisychaining, but the order can be changed over time, so that each unit can access the bus. One way of changing the order of priority is to group functional units in a ring. When a unit has finished using the bus, it assigns it to the nearest (predetermined) unit requesting access to the bus.

First come, first served

This is a rather unusual way of allocating dynamic priorities. The bus is allocated to the first unit to request access to it. This algorithm is symmetrical, as no unit is given priority over another. It minimizes waiting time, but it is difficult to implement, because the order in which requests for access are made has to be retained.

3.2.3   Crossbar matrices

Crossbar networks

Crossbar matrices are the simplest form of dynamic network. All the input lines cross all the output lines and there is a switch at each point of intersection. Crossbar matrices are such that any given input line can be connected with any given output line.

We have assumed in the following example of a 4×4 crossbar matrix (Figure 3.11) that processor 1 is requesting access to memory bank 2 and processor 3 access to memory bank 1. The switch at the intersection of the 2nd row of the 2nd column is used by the message from processor 1 in step 2 and by the message from processor 3 in step 4.

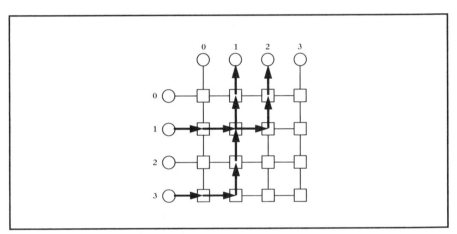

Figure 3.11   Example of a crossbar matrix

c_{22} switches

We shall adopt Lenfant's terminology by calling the hardware variant of a switch c_{22} as shown in Figure 3.12. It has two input and two output lines.

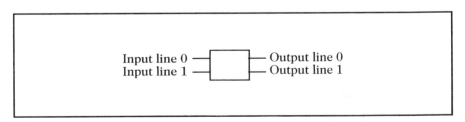

Input line 0 —☐— Output line 0
Input line 1 —☐— Output line 1

Figure 3.12 c_{22} switch

In control state 0, the lines are connected directly; in control state 1 they are connected by crossing each other (Figure 3.13).

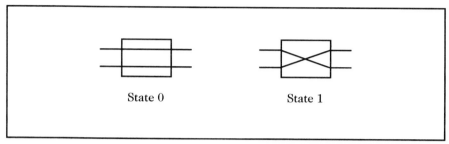

State 0   State 1

Figure 3.13   Main states possible with a c_{22} switch

Its implementation in hardware is based on inverse switches, as shown in Figure 3.14 [Len82].

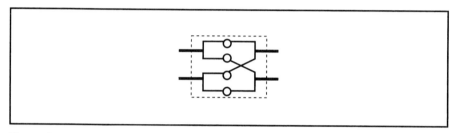

Figure 3.14   Detail of hardware implementation of a c_{22} switch

Exchanges, multiplexing, broadcasting and permutation are all easily implemented using the switch.

Implementing a crossbar using a c_{22} switch

First, some definitions.

Definition 3.10

A finite set of switches establishes a link between input line i and output line j, if a state of the switches exists such that a data item entering through i passes through the switches and exits through j.

Definition 3.11

A network maps a bijection b between some of its input and output lines, if a relationship between i and b(i) can be established for all i belonging to the output lines concerned.

Finally, a crossbar matrix C_{nm} with n input and m output lines can be designed with c_{22} switches. The two output lines of $c_{22}(i, j)$ are connected with input line 0 of $c_{22}(i, j+1)$ and 1 of $c_{22}(i+1, j)$ (Figure 3.15).

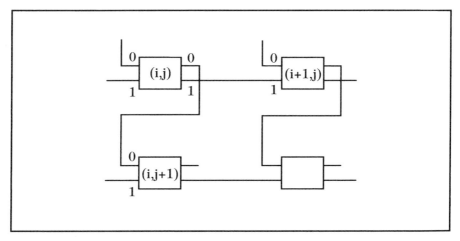

Figure 3.15   Connections between c_{22} switches

Theorem 3.11

Let C_{nm} be a crossbar matrix, with c_{22} switches and n input and m output lines.

1   If: $c_{22}(i, j) = 1$ and $\forall\ k{>}i,\ \forall\ r{<}j\ c_{22}(i, r) = c_{22}(k, j) = 0$, a link between input line i and output line j can be established.

2. C_{nm} enables all bijections of a part of $[0, n{-}1]$ to be mapped onto $[0, m{-}1]$.

Proof

Assume that the theorem's condition is satisfied. We then have

$$\forall\ r{<}j,\ c_{22}(i, r) = 0$$

and therefore the input lines 1 of $c_{22}(r, j)$ are linked to each other. As $c_{22}(i, j)=1$, output line 1 of $c_{22}(i, j{-}1)$ is connected to input line 0 of $c_{22}(i{+}1, j)$. The condition $(\forall k{>}i\ c_{22}(k, j)=0)$ means that data can be propagated vertically to output line j.

The second part of the theorem follows on directly from the first.

The control states of the network are the applications of C_{nm} in $\{0, 1\}$ and can be represented by Boolean matrices (Figure 3.16).

As can be seen from Figure 3.16, a number of the switches' input and output lines are not used and bijections can be mapped between some input lines and some output lines.

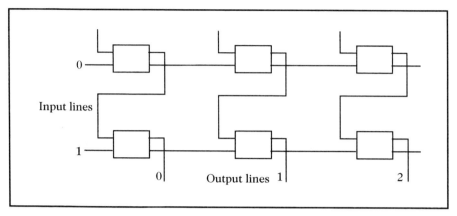

Figure 3.16   Illustration of C_{23}

3.2.4   Operations on networks

In this section, we consider an interconnection network as a pair (i, o), representing input and output lines. Such networks can be crossbar or other types of network.

Definition 3.12

Let R_k(k=1, 2) be two interconnection networks R_k=(i_k, o_k). The *product of R_1 and R_2 is $R_1 \times R_2$* defined by:

- i_2 copies of R_1,

- o_1 copies of R_2,

- the jth output line of the ith copy of R_1 is linked to the ith input line of the jth copy of R_2 (Figures 3.17 and 3.18):

$$i_{R1 \times R2} = i_2 i_1$$
$$o_{R1 \times R2} = o_1 o_2$$

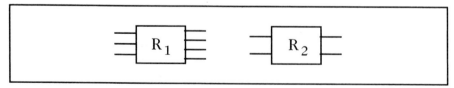

Figure 3.17   Interconnection networks R_1 and R_2

Proposition 3.12

The product of networks is an associative law:
$$R_1 \times (R_2 \times R_3) = (R_1 \times R_2) \times R_3$$

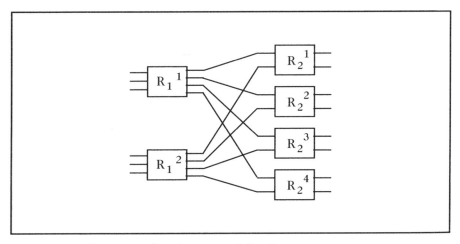

Figure 3.18   Illustration of product network $R_1 \times R_2$

Definition 3.13

Let R_k (k=1, 2, 3) be three interconnection networks $R_k = (i_k, o_k)$ such that $o_1 = i_3$. The network $[R_1, R_2, R_3]$ defined by:

- i_2 copies of R_1,

- o_1 copies of R_2,

- o_2 copies of R_3,

- the restriction of $[R_1, R_2, R_3]$ to its first two steps is equal to $R_1 \times R_2$,

- the restriction of $[R_1, R_2, R_3]$ to its last two steps is equal to $R_2 \times R_3$,

is called a *composite* of R_1, R_2, R_3.

Figure 3.19 shows the network $[c_{22}, c_{22}, c_{22}]$. It can be seen that $[c_{22}, c_{22}, c_{22}] \neq (c_{22} \times c_{22}) \times c_{22}$ which is shown in Figure 3.20. It could be proved that the latter is equal to $c_{22} \times (c_{22} \times c_{22})$, if the switches were reorganized.

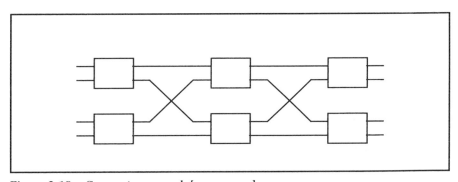

Figure 3.19   Composite network $[c_{22}, c_{22}, c_{22}]$

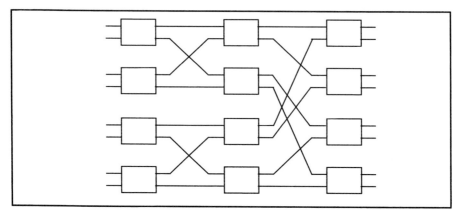

Figure 3.20   Network product $(c_{22} \times c_{22}) \times c_{22}$

3.2.5   Nonblocking networks

Some definitions

Definition 3.14

Let there be a set of connections $L_k = (i_k, o_k)$ such that $k = 1, 2, \ldots$ An input (or output) line is said to be *inactive* if it does not belong to $\{i_k\}$ (or $\{o_k\}$). An inactive input line i is said to have access to an inactive output line o if a control state enabling connections between i and o exists, without changing the connections L_k.

Note that here, both the extremities that are connected and the connections between them remain unchanged. The network is dynamic but does not need to be reconfigured to take the connection (i, o) into account. The number of intersection points (c_{22} switches) is called the *size of the network*.

Definition 3.15

A network is *nonblocking* if, for all sets of connections that are established, all inactive input lines have access to all inactive output lines. Nonblocking networks permit maximum throughput between various input and output units.

Properties of nonblocking networks

In a nonblocking network, a bijection of any of its input lines is mapped onto any of its output lines. The crossbar matrix C_{nm} is nonblocking for all n and m.

Now let's look at space complexity (that is, the minimum size $T(n)$ of nonblocking networks with n input and n output lines).

Theorem 3.13

The complexity of a nonblocking network with n input and n output lines is equal to:

$$T(n) = n\log_2(n) + o(n\log_2(n))$$

Proof

A nonblocking network enables n! permutations between its input and output lines. The number of points of intersection p must therefore prove $2^p \geq n$!

Consequently,

$$T(n) \geq n\log_2(n) + o(n\log_2(n))$$

Bassalygo and Pinsker [Len 82] [Len84] show that networks of size $n\log_2(n) + o(n\log_2(n))$ exist.

It can be seen that crossbar matrices are far from being optimal, as their size is n^2. Unfortunately, Bassalygo and Pinsker's networks are extremely complex and controlling them is so difficult that it is almost impossible to use them.

Clos (nonblocking) networks

Let's use the operations that were defined on the above networks to construct nonblocking networks whose size is less than n^2. One of the most well-known networks with this characteristic is the *Clos network*, which we shall now describe.

Theorem 3.14

Let $R_k = (i_k, o_k)$ (k=1, 2, 3) be three nonblocking networks, such that $o_1 = i_3$. The network $[R_1, R_2, R_3]$ is nonblocking if and only if $o_1 \geq i_1 + o_3 - 1$.

Proof

$\Leftarrow$ Assume that $o_1 \geq i_1 + o_3 - 1$. Let o be an inactive input line of the ith copy of R_1, written as R_{1i}, and o an inactive output line of the jth copy of R_3, written as R_{3j}. There are at most $i_1 - 1$ other connections from input lines of R_{1i} and $o_3 - 1$ to output lines of R_{3j}, and the number of copies equals o_1. It is strictly greater than $(i_1 - 1) + (o_3 - 1)$. Consequently, at least one copy of R_2 exists which is not on any connection from R_{1i} or to R_{3j}. Let's look at this copy. Because it is assumed to be nonblocking, a connection between i and o can be established.

$\Rightarrow$ If $o_1 < i_1 + o_3 - 1$, a counterexample can easily be obtained.

Clos [Clo53] proved the following theorem. His proof is the same as above. It is described here as a corollary of the theorem.

Corollary 3.15 [Clos' theorem]

Let p, q and r be three strictly positive integers. The network $[C_{qp}, C_{rr}, C_{pq}]$ is nonblocking if and only if $p \geq 2q-1$.

If we try to use the above construction to design a nonblocking network with a lower cost, the network's size has to be reduced:

$$T = o_1(i_1 i_2 + i_2 o_2 + o_2 o_3)$$

under the following constraints:

$i_1 i_2 = n$ (number of input lines)
$o_2 o_3 = n$ (number of output lines)
$o_1 \geq i_1 + o_3 - 1$ (nonblocking condition)

Corollary 3.16

A single, minimum size, nonblocking network with n input lines and n output lines in the form $[R_1, R_2, R_3]$, in which R_k are crossbar matrices, exists for sufficiently large n. The network is the following Clos network:

$$\left[C_{\sqrt{\frac{n}{2}}, \sqrt{2n-1}}, C_{\sqrt{2n}, \sqrt{2n}}, C_{\sqrt{2n-1}, \sqrt{\frac{n}{2}}} \right]$$

Its size is $4n\left(\sqrt{2n} - 1\right)$

Proof

$$T = o_1(2n + i_2 o_2) = o_1\left(2n + \frac{n^2}{i_1 o_3}\right)$$

has to be minimized.

The minimum is obtained for $o_1 = i_1 + o_3 - 1$, which results in a problem with two variables:

$$\text{minimize} \quad T = (i_1 + o_3 - 1)(2n + \frac{n^2}{i_1 o_3})$$

Asymptotically, i_1 and o_3 must be of the order $\sqrt{n}$. Let's write $i_1 = a\sqrt{n}$ and $o_3 = b\sqrt{n}$. We then have

$$T = (a\sqrt{n} + b\sqrt{n} - 1)(2 + \frac{1}{ab})n$$

For large values of n, the problem is again one of minimizing:

$$(a + b)(2 + \frac{1}{ab})$$

For $(a+b) = S$ fixed, the minimum is obtained for $a = b = \frac{S}{2}$. Hence:

$$T_{min,\infty} = S(2 + \frac{4}{S^2}) = 2S + \frac{4}{S}$$

It is not difficult to show that a single optimum exists for $a = b = \frac{1}{\sqrt{2}}$. The values of i_k and o_k can be deduced from this. The network obtained is this Clos network:

$$\left[C_{\sqrt{\frac{n}{2}}, \sqrt{2n}-1}, C_{\sqrt{2n}\sqrt{2n}}, C_{\sqrt{2n}-1}\sqrt{\frac{n}{2}} \right]$$

Note that this network is much better than a crossbar matrix, but it is far from being optimal. The theorem can be constructed recursively. The result below is obtained.

Theorem 3.17

Let k be a non-null integer and $q_1, \dots, q_k$ a set of k positive integers whose product divides n. We write $d = \frac{n}{q_1 q_2 \cdots q_k}$. The network

$$[C_{q_1, 2q_1-1}, [\dots [C_{q_k, 2q_k-1}, C_{dd}, C_{2q_k-1, q_k}] \dots], C_{2q_1-1, q_1}]$$

is nonblocking and has n input and n output lines.
Its size is:

$$T = 2n \sum_{i=1}^{k} \left[\prod_{j=1}^{i-1} \frac{2q_i - 1}{q_i} \right] (2q_i - 1) + n^2 \prod_{i=1}^{k} \frac{2q_i - 1}{q_i^2}$$

Proof

The proof is obtained by recursively applying the theorem above.

Finally, note that finding the set of q_i that minimizes T is an open problem.

3.2.6   Rearrangeable networks

Definition

Nonblocking networks are large and it is difficult to reduce their size without diluting the concept behind such networks. This explains why few of them are designed in practice (except perhaps in telephony).

Where the number of input and output lines is the same, assuming that the network functions synchronously, nothing is lost by recomputing all the connections at this stage. The only constraint is that it should be possible to map all permutations of input and output lines.

Definition 3.16

An interconnection network is *rearrangeable*, if bijections can be mapped between some of its input lines and some of its output lines.

Note that a rearrangeable network can be blocking, since existing connections may have to be changed to connect inactive input and output lines.

Rearrangeable Clos networks

Let's take another look at how the above Clos networks are constructed. Obviously, for the network [R_1, R_2, R_3] to be rearrangeable, the condition $o_1 \geq i_1 + o_3 - 1$ is not necessary. By taking the proof of Theorem 3.14, it can be shown that it is necessary for $o_1 \geq \max(i_1, o_3)$.

This condition is also sufficient.

Theorem 3.18

Let $R_k = (i_k, o_k)$ (k=1, 2, 3) be three rearrangeable networks such that $o_1 = i_3$. The network [R_1, R_2, R_3] is rearrangeable if and only if $o_1 \geq \max(i_1, o_3)$.

A generalization of Clos's theorem is obtained.

Corollary 3.19

Let p, q, and r be strictly positive integers. The network of the integers $[C_{qp}, C_{rr}C_{pq}]$ is rearrangeable if and only if $p \geq q$.

If we attempt to use the proof above to design a nonblocking network with a lower cost, its size has to be minimized:

$$T = o_1(i_1i_2 + i_2o_2 + o_2o_3)$$

with the constraints:

$$i_1i_2 = n \qquad \text{(number of input lines)}$$
$$o_2o_3 = n \qquad \text{(number of output lines)}$$
$$o_1 \geq \max(i_1, o_3) \quad \text{(rearrangeability condition)}$$

Corollary 3.20

A single, minimum size, rearrangeable network with n input and n output lines in the form $[R_1, R_2, R_3]$ exists for sufficiently large n. The network is the following Clos network:

$$\left[C_{\sqrt{\frac{n}{2}},\sqrt{\frac{n}{2}}}, C_{\sqrt{2n},\sqrt{2n}}, C_{\sqrt{\frac{n}{2}}\sqrt{\frac{n}{2}}} \right]$$

Its size is:

$$\left[2n(\sqrt{2n} - 1) \right]$$

Proof

The result is obtained by minimizing

$$o_1(2n + \frac{n^2}{i_1o_3})$$

It can be seen that, in comparison with the optimal Clos nonblocking network, the size of the above network has been halved. But the cost of this is that control complexity has increased – a price that is generally too high.

Existing connections must be changed to establish a new connection. But connections in asynchronous multiprocessors (MIMDs) cannot be reconfigured. As a result, a connection can only be added when established connections permit. By contrast, all connections can be reconfigured at each point of synchronization in a synchronous system. Control of a Clos network is consequently different in each case. The reader is referred to [Len82] for an in-depth analysis of such controls.

Benès networks

The above techniques can be applied to obtain rearrangeable networks whose size is smaller than Clos networks. Let's take the example of a network with n input and n output lines, with $n=2^p$.

Consider the Clos network $[c_{22}, C_{n/2,n/2}, c_{22}]$. It is obviously rearrangeable, as the median step can be rearranged. $C_{n/2,n/2}$ can be replaced by the rearrangeable Clos network $[c_{22}, C_{n/4,n/4}, c_{22}]$. By repeating this construction, a rearrangeable network consisting of $(2n-1)$ steps of $n/2$ c_{22} switches – called a *Benès network* [Ben65] – is obtained. The following theorem has therefore been proved:

Theorem 3.21
    Let n be a power of 2. The size of the Benès network with n input lines and n output lines is $n\log_2(n) + o(n\log_2(n))$.

For example, the size of the network in Figure 3.21 is 20. It can be seen that the Benès network is asymptotically optimal, as not all permutations can be mapped with a smaller size network. Control of this network is deduced from Clos network control.

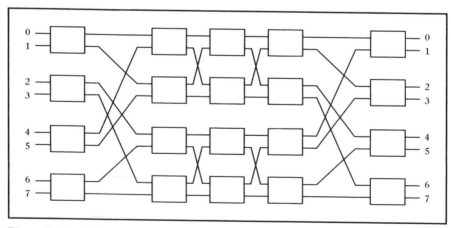

Figure 3.21   Benès network with eight input lines

3.2.7   Blocking networks

Where the rearrangeability condition is not validated, a network is blocking. In other words, an input line cannot always be connected to an output line, and the resulting conflict is irreducible. Generally speaking, the idea of blocking is linked to the time it takes to establish a connection in the network (given that established connections modify its properties). The level of blocking depends on both the network's topology and its control algorithm. We describe these networks below.

Omega networks

An *omega* network with n input and n output lines consists of $\log_2(n)$ steps that are identical to those of a *perfect shuffle* [Law75]. It should be recalled that this transformation is defined as follows: output line MP(i) is associated with an input line i such that:

$$MP(i) = 2i \text{ if } i < \frac{n}{2}$$

$$MP(i) = 2i{-}n{+}1 \text{ if } i \geq \frac{n}{2}$$

The result is illustrated in Figure 3.22.

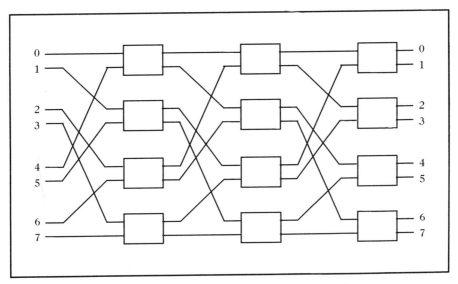

Figure 3.22   Omega network with eight input and eight output lines

Figure 3.23 shows an irreducible conflict on this network. Input lines 0 and 4 cannot be linked simultaneously to output lines 1 and 2.

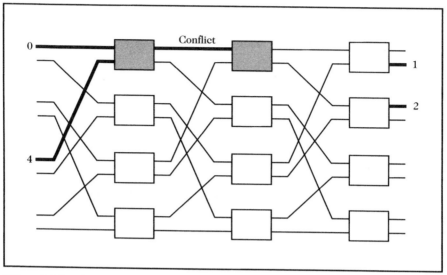

Figure 3.23   An example of irreducible conflict

Butterfly networks

Another very common blocking network is the *butterfly* network. It has a natural recursive definition – an n-dimensional butterfly template is obtained from two (n–1)-dimensional butterfly templates. The 2-dimensional butterfly network is illustrated in Figure 3.24.

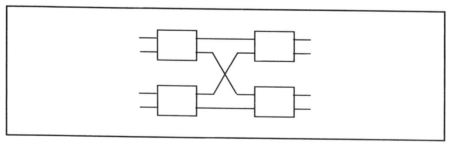

Figure 3.24   2-dimensional butterfly network

To obtain an n-dimensional network, the two (n–1)-dimensional butterfly templates are placed together and a step is added as shown in Figure 3.25.

Comments

Butterfly and omega networks are equivalent (the switches have simply to be given new indices) [Rum92].

If two symmetrical butterfly networks are placed end to end, a Benès network is obtained and the network becomes rearrangeable.

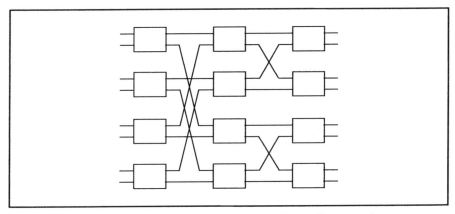

Figure 3.25   Recursive template of a 3-dimensional butterfly network

3.2.8   Network control

Controlling simple, nonblocking networks such as Clos networks is simple to implement, but a few synchronization problems arise when controlling blocking networks.

Controlling Clos networks

Let's assume we want to link the input and output line of a given switch. The control shown in Figure 3.26 is centralized. A Boolean vector that shows whether a connection is busy or not (using the convention that the ith component is equal to 1 if the ith line is free) is associated with each switch at input and output. The input switch in Figure 3.26 is associated with the vector $(1, 0, 1, 1)$.

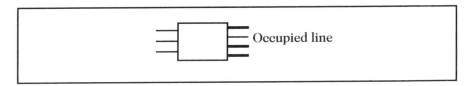

Figure 3.26   Vector associated with an input switch

To find a free connection in the network, an AND operation has to be implemented between the input and output switches. Any 1 in the result is a free connection.

With rearrangeable networks, the control algorithm that we have just described can still be used. Where there is no path (that is, there is no 1 in the AND operation of the vectors associated with the input and output switches), the network's existing connections have to be changed.

Asynchronous control of blocking networks

Let's assume that, as above, we want to link an input line (a processor) with an output line (a memory bank). The switches are c_{22}. The operation is based on *routing vectors*, which are associated with each input line. Each input line sends its own routing vector into the network in an attempt to establish a connection with the output line. Figure 3.27 illustrates this.

Definition 3.17

The binary representation of an output line is called a *routing vector*. A network switch at level i uses bit (n–i–1). If it is 0, the connection is made with the top output line, if not, the bottom output line. Higher binary elements are transmitted at output without being changed.

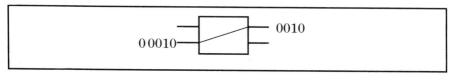

Figure 3.27   Local progression of a routing vector

We shall provide an example of this, based on an 8×8 omega network. Let's assume we want to connect input line 2 with output line 5. The binary coding of the output line is 101. When the switch corresponding to input line 2 has been chosen, the first step is to make the bottom connection, the second step is to make the top connection and the third, the bottom (Figure 3.28).

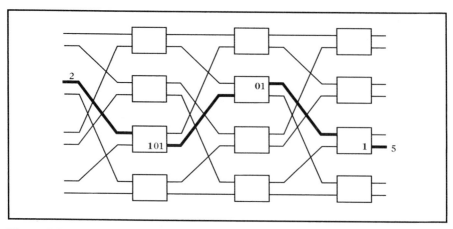

Figure 3.28   Establishing connections in an omega network

3.3   Conclusion

In this chapter, we looked at the ideas behind two essential components of parallel architectures – parallel memory and dynamic interconnection networks. They are integral parts of shared memory architectures, but can also be used for distributed memory architectures. In Chapter 4, we look at static networks, their specific components and the communication problems associated with them.

4

Topologies of static networks

Here we describe the main forms of topology – and their properties – of static networks.

A processor network is usually represented by an undirected graph, in which edges represent communication links and vertices (nodes) represent processors. We shall be using normal graph theory terminology [Ber83] [GoM79]. In an undirected graph, the degree of a node is the number of its adjacent edges. The degree of a network is defined as the maximum of the degrees of all its nodes. All nodes have the same degree in regular networks, such as rings, toric grids and hypercubes. If not, we speak of the average degree, and denote this by Δ. The eccentricity of a vertex is the largest distance from that vertex to any other in the network. The diameter, which is denoted D, is defined as the maximum of the eccentricities of the nodes. D and Δ are used to describe the properties of messages passed across static networks. Let's look first at the main forms of network topology, before we describe their properties. Further reading on the subject is to be found in [Lei91] and [Rum92].

4.1   Description of various forms of topology

Most architectures, whether shared-memory (multistage interconnection networks) or distributed-memory (processor networks) architectures, are based on regular, static topologies. Here we describe the most popular forms [MoS88].

4.1.1   Meshes

Linear networks and rings

Since distributed-memory multiprocessors first appeared, linear network and ring topologies have been very popular, at least in terms of theoretical work, due to both their simplicity and the fact that complex results can be obtained by using them.

In a linear network, nodes are ordered in ascending order of their numbers, from 0 to p–1. Each node has two neighbouring nodes, its *predecessor* and its *successor*. The neighbours of node i for i=1, 2,..., p–2 are $V(i) = \{i-1, i+1\}$, except for the first and last nodes which only have one neighbour, $V(0) = \{1\}$ and $V(p-1) = \{p-2\}$ respectively. The diameter of a linear network is p–1 (Figure 4.1).

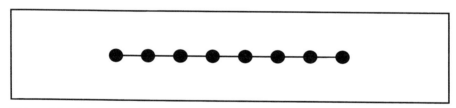

Figure 4.1   8-processor linear network

In a ring, all nodes have exactly two neighbours, with the first and the last linked to each other: $V(i) = \{i-1 \text{ modulo } p, i+1 \text{ modulo } p\}$ for all i=0, 1,..., p–1. A ring's diameter is $\lfloor \frac{p}{2} \rfloor$ (Figure 4.2).

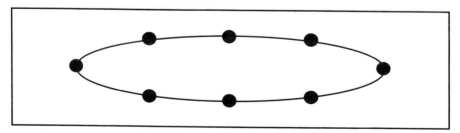

Figure 4.2   8-processor ring

Meshes and toric grids

A *mesh* of size $q_1 q_2$ consists of q_1 rows of q_2 processors. Each processor has four neighbours, except those on the first and last rows and columns. If the pair of indices (i, j) denotes the jth processor on the ith row (starting from (0, 0)), the following is obtained:

- For interior vertices, i=1, 2,..., q_1–2 and j=1, 2,..., q_2–2:
  V(i, j) = {(i–1, j), (i+1, j), (i, j–1), (i, j+1)}

- For vertices on the first row:

  V(0, 0) = {(1, 0), (0, 1)} and V(0, q_2–1) = {(1, q_2–1), (0, q_2–2)}
  for $1 \leq j \leq q_2$–2   V(0, j) = {(1, j), (0, j–1), (0, j+1)}

- For vertices on the last row:

  V(q_1–1, 0)={(q_1–1, 1), (q_1–2, 0) and
  V(q_1–1, q_2–1) = {(q_1–2, q_2–1), (q_1–1, q_2–2)}
  for $1 \leq j \leq q_2$–2   V(q_1–1, j) = {(q_1–2, j), (q_1–1, j–1), (q_1–1, j+1)}

- For vertices on the first column:

  For $1 \leq i \leq q_1$–2   V(i, 0) = {(i, 1), (i–1, 0), (i+1, 0)}

- For vertices on the last column:

  For $1 \leq i \leq q_1$–2   V(i, q_2–1) = {(i, q_2–2), (i–1, q_2–1), (i+1, q_2–1)}

$q_1 + q_2 - 2$ links have to be traversed for two vertices on opposite sides of the mesh to communicate with each other.

A toric grid is obtained by linking processors on the first and last rows and the first and last columns to each other, and this is defined as a Cartesian ring product [Ber83]. The topology is attractive, because its algorithms are very easy to implement (especially when it comes to manipulating tables) and because of its implementation on hardware. Its degree is 4 and its diameter is $\lfloor \frac{q_1}{2} \rfloor + \lfloor \frac{q_2}{2} \rfloor$ (Figure 4.3). In practice, toric grids are almost invariably used, rather than meshes.

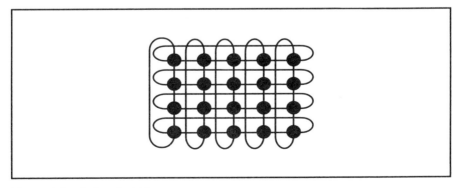

Figure 4.3   4×5 toric grid

More generally, an n-dimensional hypermesh is a topology with

$$\prod_{k=1}^{n} q_k$$

nodes, consisting of q_k nodes on each dimension k (for k = 1, 2,..., n). Each processor has exactly 2n neighbours.

4.1.2   Hypercube

Definition

A *hypercube* of degree d (or *d-cube*) is a network of 2^d nodes, in which each node has exactly d neighbours and which can be constructed recursively, as Figure 4.4 shows: a d-cube can be obtained from two (d–1)-cubes, in which each node of one cube is connected to a node in the same position in the other cube (a hypercube of degree 0 being a single, isolated node). Figure 4.5 is an illustration of a 4-cube, or a degree 4 hypercube.

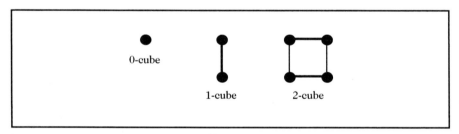

Figure 4.4   Recursive construction of hypercubes

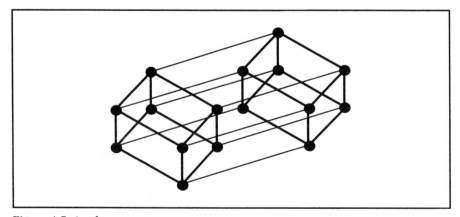

Figure 4.5 4-cube

Hypercubes can be defined in other ways. For example, a d-cube is the Cartesian product of a d–1-cube with a complete graph with two vertices, or the Cartesian product of two $\lfloor \frac{d}{2} \rfloor$ and $\lceil \frac{d}{2} \rceil$-cubes.

Gray codes

There is a convenient way of denoting nodes, based on *Gray codes*, in which each node on a network is an integer coded in d bits, with neighbours obtained by complementing each bit successively [SaS85]. For example, node 1 of a 3-cube (001 in binary code) is linked to nodes 0, 3 and 5 (000, 011 and 101 respectively). Each bit position corresponds to a *direction* (Figure 4.6).

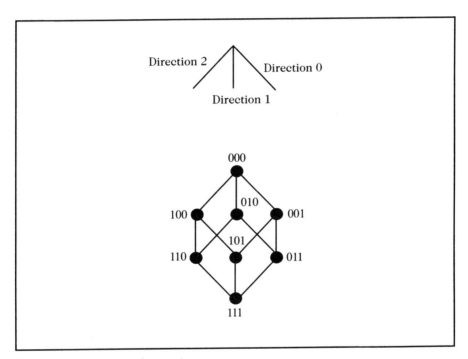

Figure 4.6   Gray code for 3-cube

Definition 4.1
A *level* is defined by the number of 1-bits in its Gray code. (A *family relation* is said to exist between nodes on the same level.)

Each level k of a d-cube contains C_k^d (for k=0 to d). The set of level k nodes is denoted C_k. Each of the nodes is related to (d–k) nodes on the next level. A node has several *children*, which are defined as the node's neighbours on the level above it (except of course 11...1) and, by analogy, several *parents*, which are neighbours on the level below (except 00...0). By definition, the node obviously has no neighbours on the same level.

Multiprocessors based on hypercubes are of interest in that they do not have a large diameter, with the largest distance between any two nodes in a d-cube being at most d. However, a hypercube's degree depends on d and, if a network with a large number of processors is required, the links differ in length, which means that it is difficult to build such machines in hardware.

One of the basic problems of network topology is to find networks of bounded degree – because most of the available components have a fixed, usually small, number of connectors – and, so far as possible, small diameter.

Cayley graphs

All the topologies we have just described (rings, toric grids and hypercubes) are *regular*, that is, all their nodes have the same degree and, by definition, they are able to perform the same tasks in the network. As will be seen in Chapter 15, this is important in implementing some communication schemes. Rings, toric grids and hypercubes are also *Cayley graphs*, with very important generic properties. For example, it is thought that all Cayley graphs are probably Hamilton cycles [Rum92].

Definition 4.2

Let a group Γ and a set S of generators of Γ be such that the neutral element does not belong to S. G is a Cayley graph associated with Γ, if and only if the following is proven:

- $\forall s \in S$, its inverse $s^{-1} \in S$,

- the vertices of G are the elements of Γ,

- the neighbouring vertices of all vertices x of G are the vertices x.s, $\forall s \in S$.

For example, a ring is a Cayley graph that is connected with a circular permutation group moving one position to the right (and, inversely, to the left). Readers who wish to know more about this should consult [Ber92].

4.1.3   De Bruijn networks

Constructing de Bruijn networks

De Bruijn networks are a good compromise – the diameter increases only logarithmically with the total number of vertices in the network, whilst the degree is independent of this number. Alphabets are used as the basis for constructing De Bruijn graphs. Generally speaking, a relation of some kind is established between two nodes. Note that a hypercube is also a graph that can be constructed over a binary alphabet and the edges between its nodes, based on bit complementation.

Definition 4.3

A (d, D) de Bruijn network is a directed graph, constructed with words of length D over an alphabet of size d. By definition, it is a directed network. The relation between its nodes is as follows: two nodes are connected, if the last (D–1) letters of one coincide with the first (D–1) letters of the other.

On most occasions, de Bruijn networks are considered as being over binary alphabets, and we then have $p=2^D$, where p is the number of processors. Another simple way of looking at a de Bruijn network in this example is as follows: at node i, nodes 2i and 2i+1 modulo p are connected.

It can be quite easily proven [BeP89] that the diameter of the networks is D. The indegrees and outdegrees are d in a directed network. For undirected links, the degree is $\Delta=2d$.

In a 2×3 de Bruijn network, for example, node 001 is connected with 010 and 011 and, conversely, nodes 000 and 100 are connected with 001 (Figure 4.7).

Apart from having all the useful properties described above, not all the nodes in the network have the same degree and this may be considered an advantage, as it means that links can be reserved for external communication (loops at the vertices 000 and 111 of a 2×3 de Bruijn network can be used as outgoing connections).

Finally, it should be noted that a de Bruijn network with $\Delta=D=8$ has 65 536 nodes whereas a hypercube of the same order only has 256.

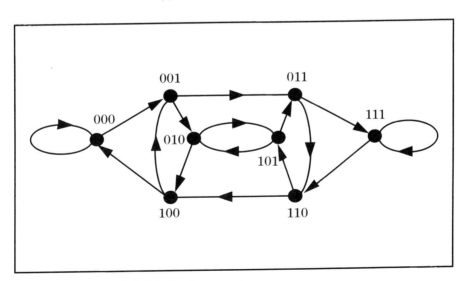

Figure 4.7   Directed 2×3 de Bruijn network

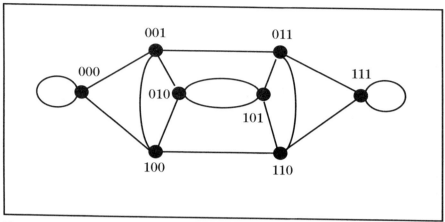

Figure 4.8   Undirected 2×3 de Bruijn network

Perfect shuffle

Perfect shuffles are quite common. As we shall explain later on, there is a close relationship between them and de Bruijn networks.

Definition 4.4

A *perfect shuffle* is based on the function that links node i to node 2i if i < p/2 and node 2i−p+1, if it is not (Figure 4.9).

Leaving aside the orientation of the network, the relation can be directly expressed in code: let $(x_0 x_1 \ldots x_{n-1} x_n)$ be the binary code of any given node $x_i \in \{0, 1\}$. Nodes $(0 x_0 x_1 \ldots x_{n-1})$ and $(1 x_0 x_1 \ldots x_{n-1})$ are linked to it.

However, the relation is insufficient to the extent that it does not bring about a connected graph. Another connection has to be added – possibly a ring (*see* Figure 4.10), or a relation called an *exchange*, that links node $(x_0 x_1 \ldots x_{n-1} x_n)$ to node $(x_0 x_1 \ldots x_{n-1} \bar{x}_n)$.

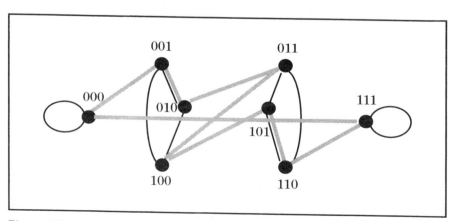

Figure 4.9   8-processor ring-perfect shuffle

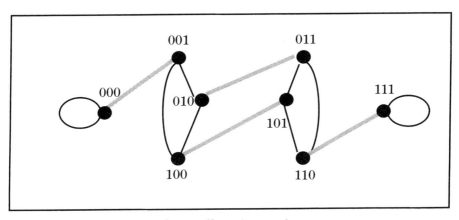

Figure 4.10   8-processor perfect shuffle with an exchange

This is a very useful transformation in terms of algorithms, because, for example, it serves as the basis for fast Fourier transforms [Fox88]. Note also that the transformation can be represented by de Bruijn networks and hypercubes (*see* Section 4.2.4).

4.1.4   Binary trees

Definitions and properties

Trees are logical structures that are commonly used in designing parallel programs, especially in centralized strategies, such as those for processor farms, master–slave systems, and so on. Loading the code of a parallel system is a case in point. Trees can be used to represent hierarchical machines.

Definition 4.5

First, it should be recalled that a tree is an acyclic connected graph. A *complete binary tree* has 2^n-1 vertices and all its non-terminal nodes have exactly two children (Figure 4.11).

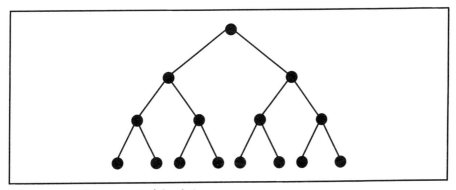

Figure 4.11   Binary tree of depth 3

The average degree of the processors in a complete binary tree is 3, the root is of degree 2 and the terminal nodes (*leaves*) have a degree of only 1. The diameter of a complete binary tree is $2\lfloor\log_2(p)\rfloor$ where p is the number of vertices. The distance of all nodes from the root is less than $\log_2(p)$.

The processors of a complete binary tree can be notated in several convenient ways. The two most popular are illustrated in Figures 4.12 and 4.13. The most useful feature of the first method (in which the notation of a node's two children is simply a matter of keeping the same prefix and adding a 0 on the right for a left child and a 1 for a right child) is that, at any given level, notation in ascending order from left to right is retained. In the second, all the left vertices of a given vertex have lower numbers than the right vertices, which enables some algorithms to be written simply.

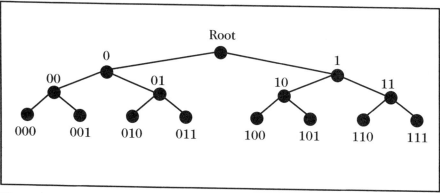

Figure 4.12   Binary notation

The low degree of the leaves can be used to improve communication at the lowest level of the tree, and a regular graph of degree 3, as illustrated in Figure 4.14, is obtained. Because the root has only two connections, a third can be added for external connections (for input and output).

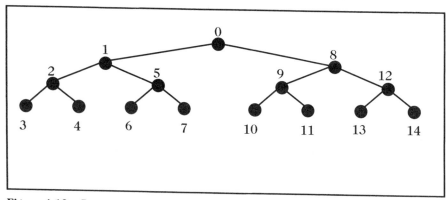

Figure 4.13   Binary tree notated with integers

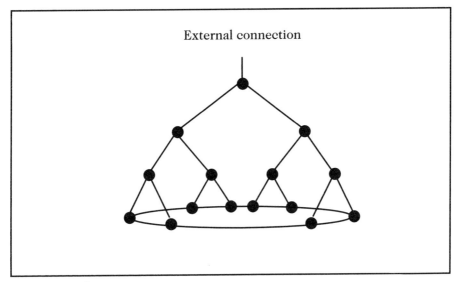

External connection

Figure 4.14   Binary ring tree

4.1.5   Initial summary

The topology of shared-memory architectures may be fixed or it may be possible to reconfigure them; if the latter is the case, one has to be in the best position to choose the most appropriate topology for implementing a given algorithm. Table 4.1 compares the characteristics of the main topologies. The networks in the table are undirected, with single connections between one node and another. The various topologies are all of the order of a power of 2 and have more or less the same number of nodes – this does not have to be the case, but it simplifies comparison. The mesh is a square and the de Bruijn network is written over a binary alphabet.

To complement the table, readers should also study which networks enable standard algorithms to be easily represented (the subject of Section 4.3).

	d-cube	Ring	2-D Mesh	Binary tree	De Bruijn
No. of nodes	2^d	2^d	2^d	2^d-1	2^d
No. of links	$d\,2^{d-1}$	2^d	2^{d+1}	2^d-2	$2^{d+1}-2$
Diameter	d	2^{d-1}	$2^{d/2}$	$2(d-1)$	d
Degree	d	2	4	3	4

Table 4.1   Comparison of the main networks' characteristics

4.1.6   Modular forms of topology

As we have just indicated, in practice, processor networks often have bounded degrees, which are generally rather low. Because a considerable number of algorithms for regular structures that do not impose limits on the number of processors involved have already been elaborated, it is important that a given topology can be created on the basis of a physical network with a low degree.

Cube connected cycles

A great deal of research has been conducted on networks which connect in a hypercube groups of processors that are already linked by other networks, such as linear networks, meshes or even trees. The most well-known topology is without doubt the *cube connected cycle* (CCC), that is, a d-cube in which each vertex is a ring of length d (as illustrated in Figure 4.15). Each processor is linked to one of the hypercube's dimensions.

A CCC's diameter is of the order $D=\frac{3d}{2}$, so if the network is of degree 3, only a 24-vertex network can be obtained.

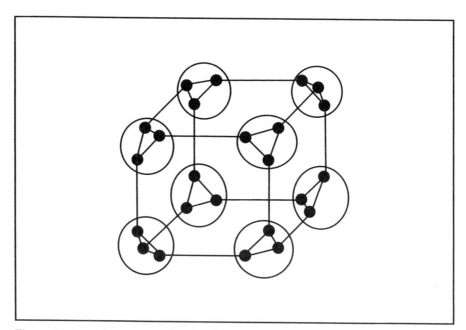

Figure 4.15   Cube connected cycle of degree 3

Figure 4.16 illustrates a 4-cube built with processors of only degree 3. A 'meta-processor' consists of two basic processors connected in a linear network. The 'meta-processor' has 32 vertices. The network's diameter is 6.

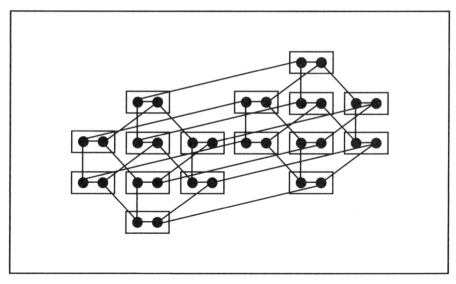

Figure 4.16   4-cube with processors of degree 3

Variations on trees and meshes

Binary trees and meshes have important properties, and the two topologies can be combined in several ways.

One possible solution is a *mesh of trees*. For integer n, consider two series of n binary trees whose leaves are organized in a mesh. One leaf belongs to both a vertical and a horizontal tree. Figure 4.17 illustrates such a topology where n=4. The mesh's processors are shown in white.

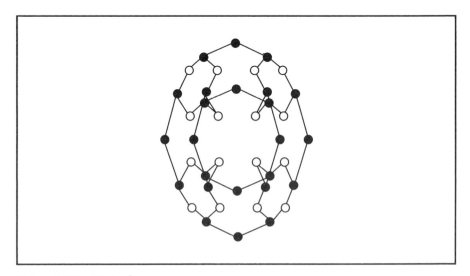

Figure 4.17   Mesh of trees

The number of vertices is easily determined: it is the number (n^2) in an $n \times n$ square mesh plus 2n times the number (n–1) in a binary tree of depth $\log_2(n)$: this gives a total of $3n^2 - 2n$. The leaves are of degree 2, as are all the roots of the 2n trees. The other processors are of degree 3. The diameter is $4\log_2(n)$ [Lei91].

Figure 4.18 shows another mesh of trees, which on this occasion is recursive, of the order n and based on four meshes of trees of the order n/2. Note that a mesh of trees is a subgraph of a hypercube.

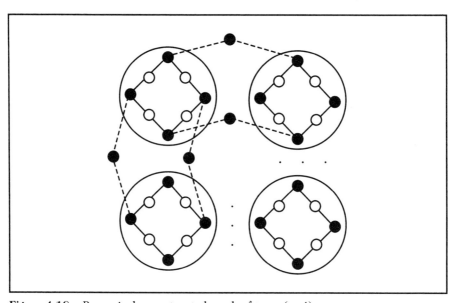

Figure 4.18   Recursively constructed mesh of trees (n=4)

Pyramids, a natural generalization of the ring-binary trees described in Section 4.1.4, provide another possible solution for combining meshes and trees. Pyramids consist of 4-ary trees with meshes on each level.

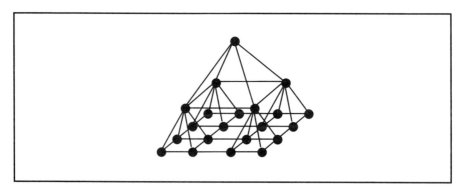

Figure 4.19   Pyramid network

Some more unusual topologies

Any network can be attached to the nodes of a processor network. In particular, it is quite possible to consider a Petersen graph to this end; it is the best compromise, in that it has the smallest diameter and the largest number of nodes for a fixed degree of 3. If a degree 4 is considered, there is one link per processor left over for connecting all the processors to each other. It is also quite possible to construct hypercubes with a Petersen graph (a graph with 10 vertices, as illustrated in Figure 4.20) as nodes. A 320-processor topology which has a very good diameter can be obtained on a 5-cube. But it should be noted that such solutions are very rare in practice.

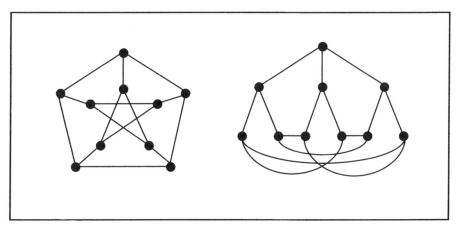

Figure 4.20   Two Petersen graphs

4.2   Sub-topologies and embedding

4.2.1   Introduction to the problem of embedding

General description

In terms of algorithms, the tree is one of the most popular data structures. Similarly, many numerical algorithms use a mesh logic structure, while hypercubes lend themselves naturally to divide and conquer algorithms. Some algorithms, such as the computation of the fast Fourier transform, use a very regular structure (perfect shuffles). Whether a network has a fixed topology, or whether the user can configure to suit the particular application, it must be possible to change from one topology to another efficiently. This problem is known in graph theory as *embedding* one graph in another. More specifically, it involves finding a mapping of the vertices of the source graph (representing the algorithm) to the target graph (representing the network) such that chains in the target graph are linked to the edges of the source graph. In practice, embedding denotes mapping graphs onto other graphs [Lei91] [Rum92].

Some definitions

The main criteria for assessing the quality of an embedding are dilatation and congestion.

Dilatation is a measure of the extent to which neighbouring vertices in the source graph become separated in the target graph. For example, in Figure 4.21 the images in G' of the two neighbouring vertices in G are separated by a chain of length 3, giving a dilatation of 3 for these source vertices. The dilatation for the source graph as a whole is the maximum of the dilatations for all its edges.

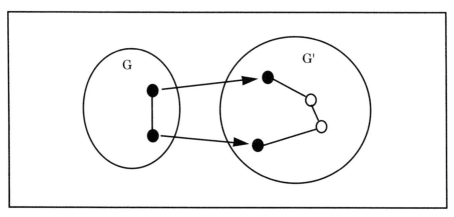

Figure 4.21   Dilatation of an edge

The *congestion* of an embedding is the maximum, over all all the edges of the target graph, of the number of chains to which any specified edge belongs. The example in Figure 4.22 has a congestion-2 embedding, as the edge in bold in graph G' belongs to the two image chains of the edges in G.

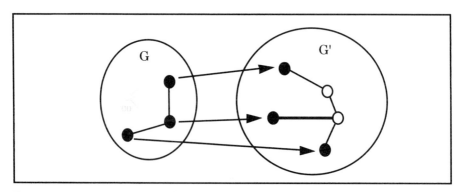

Figure 4.22   Congestion-2 embedding

The term *expansion* of an embedding is often used. This is the ratio of the number of vertices in the target graph to the number in the source.

Here, we look at the problem of embedding in relation to the main graphs that we described above. Generally speaking, attempts are made to minimize dilatation, so that neighbouring vertices are not 'too far away' from each other in the target graph. Limiting expansion is also important because the target graphs representing networks have a limited number of processors.

4.2.2 Rings and meshes

Ring into hypercube

A ring is easily derived from a hypercube. A ring whose number of vertices is a power of 2 is a partial graph of the hypercube it is being mapped onto (that is, it has a dilatation-1 embedding).

The idea is to start with any given vertex (node 0 in Figure 4.23, which has been chosen to simplify this description) and to specify its successors in the ring by bit complementation. The position of the bits is determined by the directions of the *reflected Gray code*.

The set of 2^d-1 successive directions is constructed recursively by the following formula:

$d(1) = 0$
$d(m+1) = (d(m)md(m))$ where $1 \leq m \leq d-1$

To obtain a ring, the connection has to be wrapped around d at the end.

In more concrete terms, $((010)2(010))$ is written to denote successive directions in a 3-cube, $((0102010)3(0102010))$ in a 4-cube and so on.

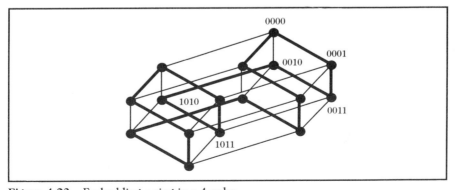

Figure 4.23 Embedding a ring in a 4-cube

Toric grid into a hypercube

One of the most useful embeddings is mapping a toric grid onto a hyper-cube. With square grids, where the number of processors is a power of 2, the proof that the grid is a partial graph of the hypercube is easy. This can be done by chaining Gray codes on each of the grid's directions, as shown by Figure 4.24 for 16 processors; note that the 4×4 grid and the 4-cube in this example are equivalent.

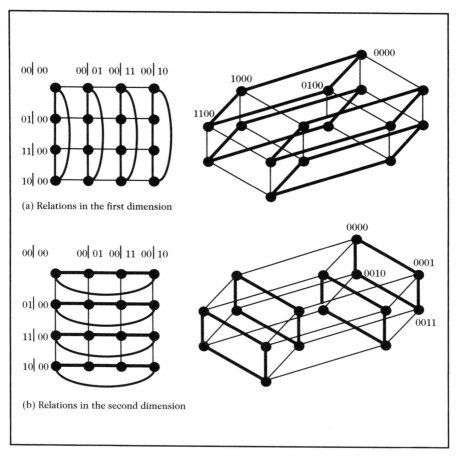

(a) Relations in the first dimension

(b) Relations in the second dimension

Figure 4.24   Embedding a 4×4 toric grid into a hypercube

Rectangular meshes are more difficult to deal with. It can be demonstrated that a dilatation-1 embedding does not necessarily exist. However, it is possible to embed a mesh with p processors into a hypercube of degree $\lceil \log_2(p) \rceil$ with a dilatation of 2. Figure 4.25 illustrates this, in an embedding of a 5×3 mesh into a 4-cube [Lei91].

Note that a similar result exists for 3-dimensional meshes which can be embedded into a hypercube with minimal expansion and dilatation 7.

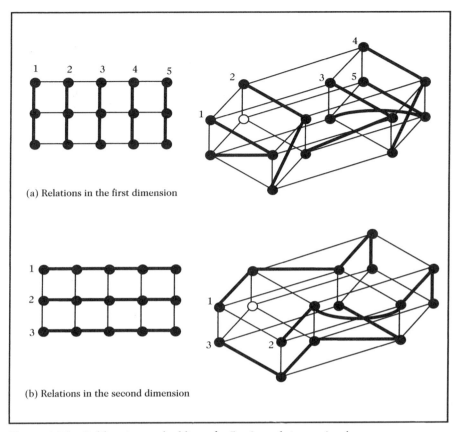

(a) Relations in the first dimension

(b) Relations in the second dimension

Figure 4.25   2-dilatation embedding of a 5×3 mesh into a 4-cube

de Bruijn networks

Now consider a $(2, d)$ de Bruijn network. The ring whose number of processors is a power of 2 is a partial graph of the de Bruijn network.

A de Bruijn graph has several types of cycle – those that link successive nodes whose code has a number of ascending, then descending 1-bits and cycles that link vertices with the same number of 1-bits in their code. So, with the 2×3 de Bruijn graph, we have an initial cycle (000–001–011–111–110–100) and two cycles of length 3 (110–101–011 and 001–010–100). A ring is obtained by following the first cycle to 110 and then by taking part of the others without returning to a processor that has already been used. The result is the solution illustrated in Figure 4.26.

The problem of embedding meshes into a de Bruijn network is still open and it is thought that any solution to it would have a poor dilatation. This is probably the most important point in understanding why de Bruijn networks are not very popular, as it explains why the efficiency of linear algebra algorithms on such networks is poor.

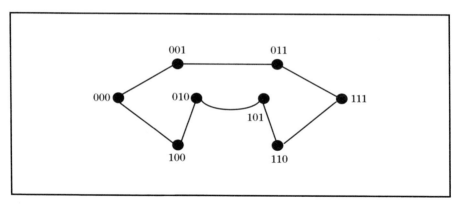

Figure 4.26   Ring into 2×3 de Bruijn network

4.2.3   Binary trees

Binary trees and hypercubes

Binary trees can be obtained from hypercubes in two distinct ways. Figure 4.27 shows the first solution: obtaining a binary tree by splitting the root, with the new root having two nodes.

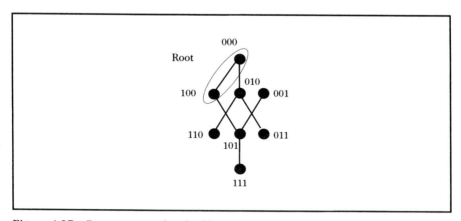

Figure 4.27   Binary tree with a double root in a 3-cube

The general method of constructing this is recursive and can be easily extended to higher dimensions. Two trees with (n–1)-dimensional hypercubes are considered and the nodes x00...0 are linked to each other, thus forming the new double root. Clearly, edges have to be removed, so that a binary tree is retained, and others have to be added for the purposes of connection, as illustrated in Figures 4.28 and 4.29. The new edges are in bold and those that have been removed are represented by dashed lines.

This leaves unsolved the problem when the trees are other than binary, but this appears to be of less interest for parallel algorithms.

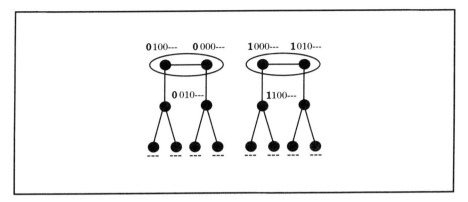

Figure 4.28   Two double-rooted binary trees

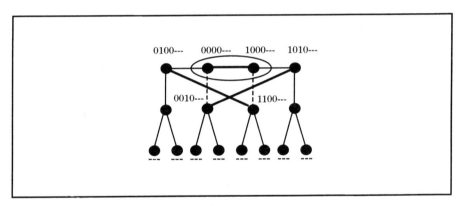

Figure 4.29   Recursively constructed binary tree in a hypercube

Binary trees and meshes

The problem of coherently constructing binary trees on rings or toric grids is complex. But some optimal results and heuristic methods do exist [HKM91] [Rum92]. Below, we use a simple example to illustrate embedding a binary tree into a linear network, but do not go into its generalization. An optimal result with dilatation $\lceil \frac{2^n-1}{n} \rceil$ exists, where n is the tree's depth.

With a complete binary tree with 15 vertices, the nodes are grouped into packets of three, from left to right and from bottom to top (left and right groupings are symmetrical), as illustrated by Figure 4.30. The packets of nodes are then distributed in turn along the ring, maintaining the left to right order of the nodes in each packet. The proof that a dilatation of 3 is obtained (the size of the packets is $\lceil \frac{2^3-1}{3} \rceil = 3$) is easy.

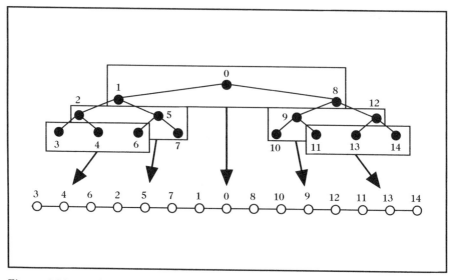

Figure 4.30 Embedding of a complete binary tree with 15 vertices in a ring

The generalization is based on the same principle of grouping and distributing the nodes.

Binary trees and de Bruijn networks

Finally, note that binary trees can be obtained by direct proof from de Bruijn networks and this seems natural enough given the latter's construction. As shown in Figure 4.31, the connection that links the nodes coded $(x_1x_2...x_n0)$ and $(x_1x_2...x_n1)$ with the node coded $(x_0x_1...x_{n-1}x_n)$ defines a double-rooted tree $00...00$ and $00...01$. Similarly, another binary tree with no common edge with the above tree is obtained from the double root $11...10$ and $11...11$.

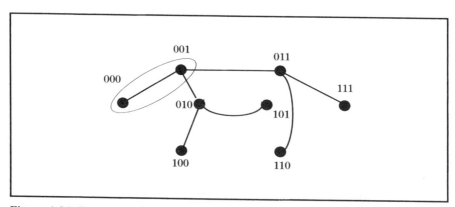

Figure 4.31 Binary tree from a de Bruijn network

4.2.4   Perfect shuffles

Consider that the number of processors p is a power of 2. First, the definition of a perfect shuffle should be recalled: 2i is linked to node i, if i < p/2 and, if not, 2i–p+1. A perfect shuffle is a partial graph of a de Bruijn network.

Where p=8, a perfect shuffle relation brings about two cycles of length 3 and two loops, which are illustrated in Figure 4.32. The proof that the cycles belong to de Bruijn networks is easy and it is easily generalized by applying the definition of de Bruijn networks.

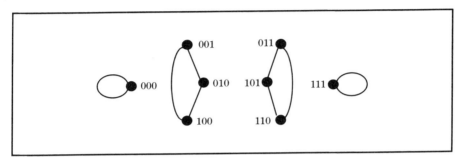

Figure 4.32 Perfect shuffle for 8 processors

A perfect shuffle is embedded with dilatation 2 into a hypercube. The computation is the same for the cycles of a perfect shuffle. Each cycle has only nodes whose code contains the same number of 1-bits. All the nodes in a cycle are on the same level of the hypercube and, as a result, cannot by definition be direct neighbours. But the proof that the distance between two nodes on the same level is 2 is easy. Figure 4.33 illustrates one solution for this property where p=8 and the cycle of the level is 1 (this and the other cycle are symmetrical).

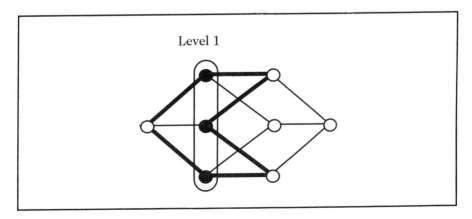

Figure 4.33   Perfect shuffle for the cycle (001–010–100) in a 3-cube

4.2.5   Introduction to network emulation

As highlighted earlier, embedding enables an algorithm, represented by a graph whose vertices are tasks and whose edges are relations between the tasks, to be executed on a network of processors that is also represented by a graph. Embedding a graph into a network means specifying which processor will execute the tasks and the paths along which communication between them will be established. Assume that it is known how to execute an algorithm efficiently according to a particular scheme – a hypercube for example – and that there is a new toric grid network on which the algorithm is to be executed. The problem is one of a toric grid *emulating* a hypercube.

The *slowdown* factor, defined as the ratio between the time taken to execute the algorithm on the network G' and time taken on the network G is used to measure emulation of graph G by graph G'. We will discuss this point when implementing communications is discussed in Chapter 15. Further in-depth reading is to be found in [Lei91].

4.3   Analytical tools

4.3.1   Spanning trees

Spanning trees are one of the basic tools for studying communication diagrams. They are trees that contain all the nodes of a processor network. In this section, we describe how they can be used to implement some communication procedures.

Hypercubes

Spanning trees can be mapped onto hypercubes in several different ways. There are three main types: binomial, balanced, and edge disjoint spanning trees – trees are by definition directed but, obviously, their direction can be omitted. We shall look at each of these categories in turn.

A *binomial* tree mapped onto a d-cube is constructed recursively by connecting the roots of two binomial trees spanning (d–1)-cubes, as the 4-cube in Figure 4.34 shows.

Binomial trees clearly follow the structure of a hypercube very closely. However, each of the root's sub-trees has a different number of nodes; it can even be stated that the sub-tree i has 2^{i-1} nodes for i=1,..., d. Note also that there exist d different binomial trees by construction, depending on the order in which successive dimensions are considered.

In many cases, the fact that the number of children in a node is balanced may be useful. Below, we describe a simple way of constructing balanced trees, which is based on the *base* of a binary number [HoJ89]. But first let's define a node's *period*. It is the minimum number of cyclical rotations to the right that have to be carried out over the number's binary representation in order to obtain the same representation. A *cyclical node* is a node whose period is strictly lower than the number of bits in its representation (d for a d-cube). The smallest number of cyclical rotations to the right on the binary representation of a node that is necessary to obtain the smallest value possible is referred to as the *base* of the node. For example, 1001 has 3 as its base because 0011 (3 in binary) is the smallest of the numbers generated by the cyclic shifts – 1001, 1100, 0110 and 0011.

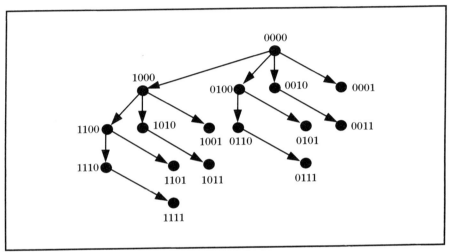

Figure 4.34   One of four binomial spanning trees on a 4-cube

A *balanced* tree is constructed by putting all elements that belong to the same base in each branch of the tree. The nodes 000...0 and 111...1 belong to all bases and are dealt with separately. Problems do not arise where a hypercube's degree is a prime number, as the only cyclical numbers are 000...0 and 111...1. Conversely, cyclical nodes exist that have to be distributed as evenly as possible to avoid disturbing the balance of the tree; for example, they are all distributed globally, when all the non-cyclical nodes have been distributed. A detailed description is to be found in [Del93]. Note that another, more sophisticated way of constructing balanced trees was put forward in [BOS91].

Figures 4.35 and 4.36 show one way in which nodes can be distributed on a 4-cube. Three of its branches have four nodes and the fourth has only three.

Obviously, trees such as these can be obtained from any root (apart from 0, which was chosen for simplicity of description). To move from one tree with a root of 0 to a tree with any other root, an XOR simply has to be executed on all the vertices with the root that has been selected.

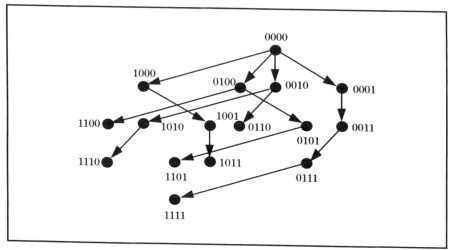

Figure 4.35 Balanced tree in a 4-cube

Base 0	Base 1	Base 2	Base 3
0001	0010	0100	1000
0011	0110	1100	1001
0101*	1010*	0101*	1010*
0111	1110	1101	1011
1111	*1111*	*1111*	*1111*

Figure 4.36 Distribution of nodes according to their bases. * indicates cyclical nodes

Edge disjoint spanning trees are the last type of spanning tree of a hypercube of degree d. The main concern here is to obtain a number of spanning trees that is equal to the degree.

The main result is that how to construct d trees of depth (d+1) is known. Once again, the construction of the trees is recursive (*see* Figure 4.37): consider a given dimension and a binomial tree on a (d–1)-cube constructed on the basis of (d–1) other dimensions. The root of the tree is connected to the root of this binomial tree and all the other nodes are obtained by projection of the vertices. (d–1) other trees are obtained by reviewing all the dimensions in turn.

Figures 4.38 and 4.39 illustrate two of four possible edge disjoint spanning trees in a 4-cube. Note that at any given moment, the same link can be used in different directions; the assumption has to be made that the links are bidirectional (in the example, a path exists from 0011 to 0111 in the first tree and another from 0111 to 0011 in the second).

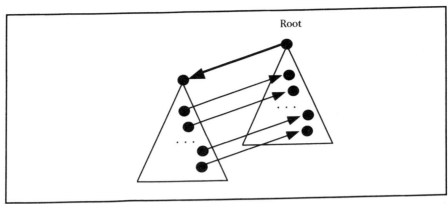

Figure 4.37 Edge disjoint spanning tree

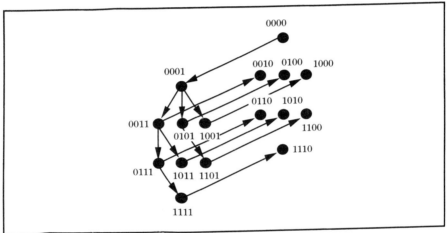

Figure 4.38 One of four possible edge disjoint spanning trees in a 4-cube

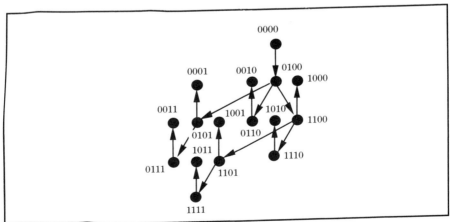

Figure 4.39 Another edge disjoint spanning tree of the four possible in a 4-cube

Toric grids

A tree that spans all the processors of a p-processor ring can be easily obtained. Assuming that the links are unidirectional, a tree whose depth is equal to its diameter D is obtained and, of course, only one exists (Figure 4.40). Where the links are bidirectional, two edge disjoint spanning trees of depth p–1 can be easily found (Figure 4.41).

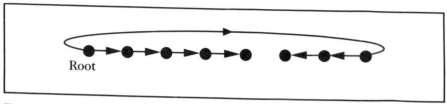

Figure 4.40 Spanning tree for a ring

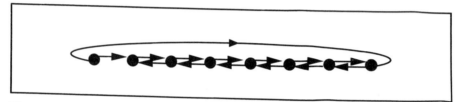

Figure 4.41 Two edge disjoint spanning trees in a bidirectional ring

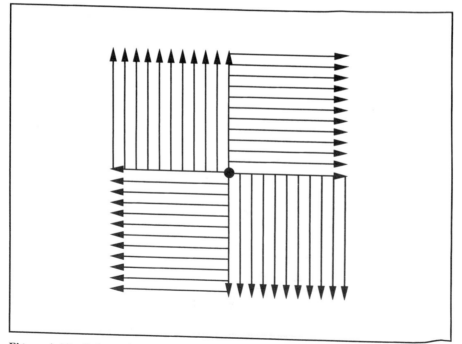

Figure 4.42 Balanced spanning tree mapped into a mesh

Meshes are 4-degree networks. Figure 4.42 illustrates one of several ways of constructing a balanced tree whose depth is equal to its diameter. Figure 4.43 illustrates the levels of the tree shown in Figure 4.42.

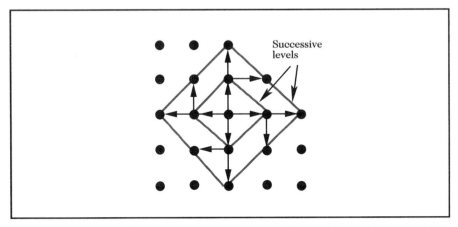

Figure 4.43   Levels of vertices that are all the same distance from the root node in a toric grid

Assuming that the links are bidirectional, edge disjoint spanning trees can be constructed on meshes.

The first solution is to be found in [SaS89]. Four edge disjoint spanning trees exist whose depth is double their diameter. This was recently improved by making the above construction symmetrical and by taking only one of two rows (and columns) into account, which enables a family of four edge disjoint spanning trees of only depth D+2 to be obtained [MTV92]. Figure 4.44 illustrates the principle of how an east tree is constructed. The three other trees can be derived directly from this by three rotations in turn – north, west and south.

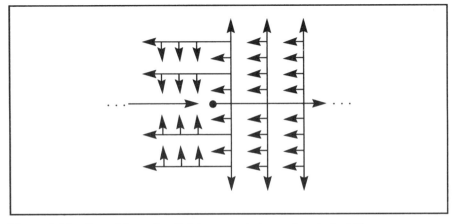

Figure 4.44   One of four edge disjoint spanning trees in a toric grid

Construction is simple in the case of (4k+1)×(4k+1) and (4k+3)×(4k+3) meshes (k integral), since these can be partitioned into four quadrants with the same number of processors in each. Extending this to other meshes (4k)×(4k) and (4k+2)×(4k+2) is a little more tricky, as they cannot be divided into four equal quadrants (*see* [MTV92]). The same applies to rectangular toric grids. In the simple square toric grid (4k+1)×(4k+1), the result illustrated in Figure 4.45 is obtained, in which the root is at the centre of the grid.

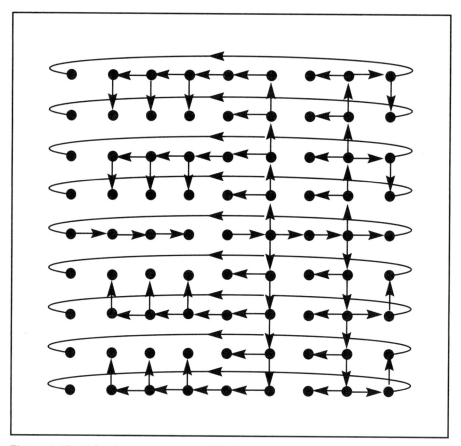

Figure 4.45   Edge disjoint east tree of depth D+2 on a 9 × 9 toric grid

The above construction is very regular. With a few extra touches on the bounds, a family of four trees can be obtained, whose depth is exactly D+1 and which can be proved to be optimal. It is easy to prove, by means of a global argument on the number of arcs, that four edge disjoint spanning trees of depth D cannot be obtained.

A similar result was obtained for unidirectional toric grids [BMT92]. Based on much the same principle, it can be shown that a family of two edge disjoint spanning trees of minimal depth n exists for an n × n square toric grid (Figure 4.46).

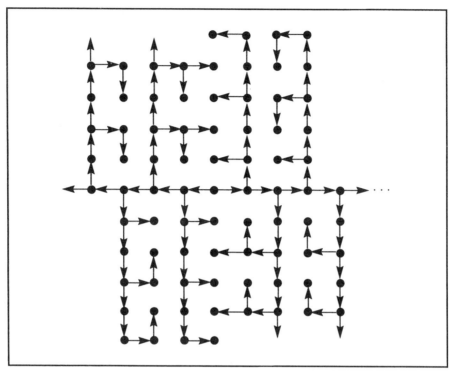

Figure 4.46   Mapping two edge disjoint spanning trees onto a unidirectional grid

de Bruijn network

Consider a (d, D) de Bruijn network. It can be shown that (d–1) edge disjoint spanning trees exist whose root is at the vertex (αα...α) for α ∈ {0, 1,..., d–1}. Where the root is written on another vertex, the tree's depth is at most $D + \lfloor \frac{d}{2} \rfloor + 1$. The general construction of this is very complex and the reader is referred to [BeF91] for further details. Note, however, that (2, D) de Bruijn networks are more common in practice and that, given what was said on page 92, the network can be spanned by a complete double-rooted binary tree.

4.3.2   Hamilton cycles

Hamilton cycles, that is, cycles of a graph in which each vertex is visited once and once only, are basic tools for implementing communication algorithms on distributed architectures. The problem of finding several disconnected Hamilton cycles on a given graph is important and, in general, difficult.

Meshes and toric grids

Consider a mesh (n, m). Where at least one of the two integers n or m is even, obtaining a Hamilton cycle from a circuit that visits all the nodes in one dimension before visiting the other (that is, the even dimension) is straight-forward, as shown in Figure 4.47, an example of a 6×9 mesh. Where the two dimensions n and m are odd, the above is adapted slightly and a Hamilton cycle is obtained (*see* the example of a 7×9 mesh in Figure 4.48). Note that two other disconnected Hamilton cycles can be obtained [Ber83].

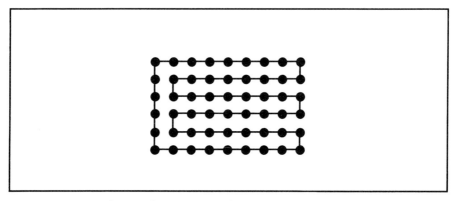

Figure 4.47   Hamilton cycle in a 6×9 mesh

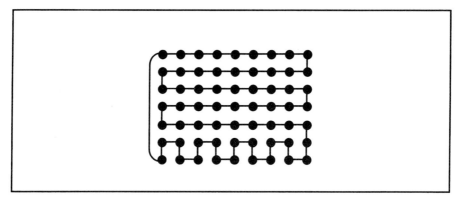

Figure 4.48   Hamilton cycle in a mesh where dimensions are odd

Hamilton cycle hypercubes

The construction of a Hamilton cycle on a hypercube can be derived directly from the method given in Section 4.2 for extracting a ring, based on reflected Gray codes. In a hypercube of degree d, $\lfloor \frac{d}{2} \rfloor$ disconnected cycles can be obtained. And as Figure 4.49 shows in the case of a 4-cube, there are two disconnected Hamilton cycles.

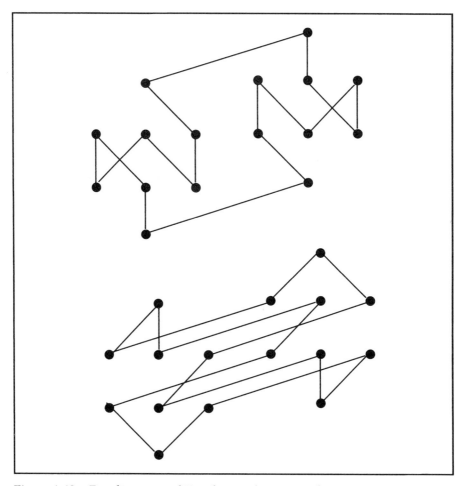

Figure 4.49   Two disconnected Hamilton cycles in a 4-cube

de Bruijn network

The problem of finding a Hamilton cycle in a de Bruijn network is easy. The result is based on the following property.

Property 4.1
The line-digraph of the $(2, D)$ de Bruijn network is the $(2, D+1)$ de Bruijn network.

It should be recalled that a line digraph is obtained by taking the arcs of the initial network as vertices and the initial vertices as arcs. If a little thought is given to how the vertices are to be numbered, a de Bruijn network is obtained by direct proof. Let's take a small example so that this property is more easily grasped. The eight arcs of the 2×2 de Bruijn network (Figure 4.50) become the vertices of the 2×3 de Bruijn network.

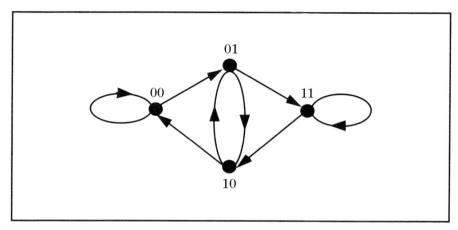

Figure 4.50   2×2 de Bruijn network

A code of a vertex (an arc in the initial digraph) is obtained by chaining the codes of the initial digraph. So, for the vertex that corresponds to arc a, with code 00, the code becomes 0000. As the two mid-point bits are always the same, they are contracted into one bit, so that the code is 000. Similarly, arc b becomes 0001 which is contracted to 001 (Figure 4.51), and so on, until it can be proved easily that a 2×3 de Bruijn network has been obtained.

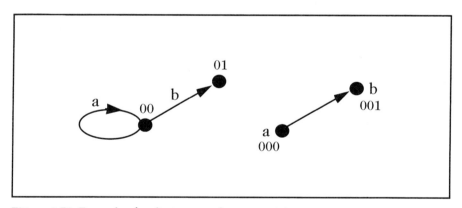

Figure 4.51 Example of coding, as arcs become vertices

Using this property, the problem of finding a Hamilton cycle in a (2, D) de Bruijn network reduces to that of finding an Eulerian cycle – a cycle that includes each edge exactly once – in a (2, D+1) de Bruijn network and this is known to be simple [Ber83]. Because of the regularity of the graph, the problem can be solved in a time that is linear in terms of the number of links. The problem of finding several disjoint cycles is difficult, but solutions have been found for some slightly modified de Bruijn networks [RoB91].

Octopuses

This section would be incomplete if octopuses were not mentioned. An octopus is a kind of spanning tree whose branches are linear networks and which can be used to describe some communication procedures (Figure 4.52).

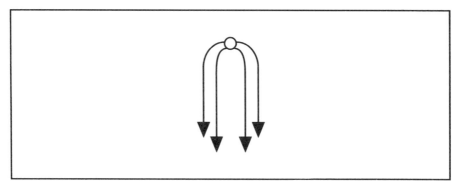

Figure 4.52 Octopus

In a bidirectional toric grid with p processors, each processor is connected with its neighbours by the four directions north, east, west and south (NEWS). Covering balanced areas of a mesh with an octopus consisting of four unconnected Hamilton paths is useful. Figure 4.53 illustrates one solution.

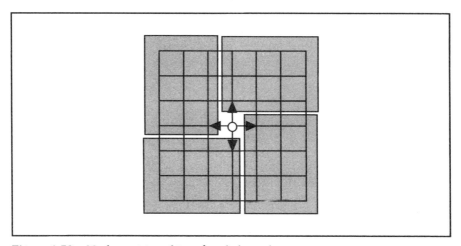

Figure 4.53   Mesh partitioned into four balanced areas

How areas are to be travelled around still has to be determined. There are several strategies that can be used to describe the sub-areas, which are also meshes. Figure 4.54 illustrates one suggestion. Finally, note that partitioning the mesh into sub-area meshes is not necessarily the wisest course of action, particularly if the meshes are to be extended to higher dimensions [PIT92]. It would be better for meshes to be partitioned into elementary triangular areas, in which case the cycle obtained would look like the second example in Figure 4.54 below.

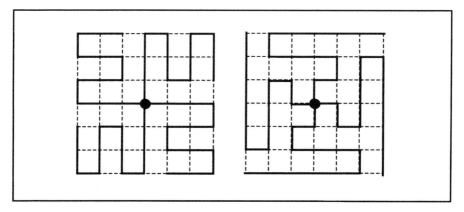

Figure 4.54   Octopus contained in a square toric grid

4.4   Conclusion

In this chapter, we have described the main topologies of static networks and their basic properties, and on this basis, we shall, in Chapter 15, execute global communication algorithms on these networks.

5

Complexity of parallel algorithms

In this chapter, we introduce the main concepts of parallel complexity. The PRAM model and those derived from it form the main model. We look at the parallel complexity of a number of basic algorithms for both numerical analysis and non-numerical problems.

5.1 Introduction

5.1.1 General description

Description of assumptions

In this chapter, we look at parallel algorithms proper. Except where otherwise stated, a SIMD or MIMD computer with a common shared memory will be used. We derive the theoretical complexity bounds of the main algorithms of linear algebra. Results from parallelizing Gaussian and Gauss-Jordan elimination are elaborated in Chapters 10 and 11. In the later chapters of the book we look at some of the specific features of processor networks that communicate by means of message exchange.

We assume that our model has an unbounded number of processors. The basic unit of measurement is the time taken to execute an operation and we ignore communication time between processors. To the extent that what we are suggesting is essentially theoretical, the assumption of zero communication time has no effect on the results obtained, as data transfer on shared-memory architectures takes a constant amount of time, irrespective of the processor and memory bank involved. Clearly, we also assume that there are no memory access (that is, read or write) conflicts.

Aims of the study of parallel complexity

We shall try to find the maximum parallelism contained in various algorithms. We shall take arithmetic operations as the level of granularity for parallelization, and this involves finding those operations in the algorithms that can be executed simultaneously. Several issues can then be addressed in this context.

First, consider a given problem, such as computing the scalar product of two vectors of size n. A standard problem involves seeking the sequential complexity of the product [Win70], that is, the minimum computation time in which the problem can be solved. The problem is solved in two stages – first the lower bound of the problem is sought and then a sequential algorithm whose execution time is equal to the bound is constructed. The algorithm is said to be *optimal*.

In parallel algorithms, there is a further parameter – the number of processors, denoted by p. By assuming that the number of processors is unbounded – the algorithms we shall look at are executed in a finite number of operations, which is 2n–1 for the scalar product of two vectors, so this amounts to assuming that the number of processors is the same as the number of operations – the parallel complexity of the problem can be sought. The same method is adopted for sequential complexity, but with the further assumption that two independent operations that do not modify any common variable can be executed simultaneously.

5.1.2   Some basic definitions

We shall consider the PRAM model that we defined in Section 2.2.2. The list of computations executed by each processor in successive time units is called a *parallel algorithm* with p processors. We assume that, at any given moment, at least one processor is active.

Atomic operations

Consider a PRAM consisting of p processors, numbered from P_0 to P_{p-1} and m memory addresses M_0 to M_{m-1}. A processor can discover the content of a memory address M_i by executing the instruction $Read(M_i)$ and modify it by executing $Write(M_i)$. Each processor executes atomic operations, which take one time unit. The operations are as follows:

```
Read(M_i)
Compute(f)
Write(M_i)
```

All these operations are executed synchronously.

Relations between execution time and number of processors

A parallel algorithm with p processors (parallelism of width p) is optimal, if its execution time $t_{opt}(p)$ is minimal. $t_{opt}(p)$ is the time complexity of the problem with p processors. t_{opt} is the minimum of the $t_{opt}(p)$. Several algorithms executed in t_{opt} may exist and each requires a different number of processors. We call the minimum number of processors required to solve the problem in optimal time p_{opt}. Using one processor, $t_{opt}(1)$ is the sequential complexity of the problem. Theorem 2.1 on speed-up limitation implies that the upper bound of the product $p.t_{opt}(p)$ (called the cost of the algorithm) is $t_{opt}(1)$. Where the cost of a parallel algorithm is the same as that of an optimal sequential algorithm, the parallel algorithm is said to be cost optimal. The first step in establishing the complexity of a parallel algorithm is thus to determine $t_{opt}(p)$, t_{opt} and p_{opt}.

Now consider a sequential algorithm – standard Gaussian elimination for solving a dense linear system, for example. Even where the number of processors used is fixed, there may be several parallel algorithms that correspond to Gaussian elimination. Analysing the parallel algorithms would lead to the same questions being posed as for a given problem. So, where this is the case, we shall use the same notation as above, if there is no risk that this will lead to confusion: t_{opt} ($t_{opt}(p)$ respectively) is the time complexity (with p processors respectively) of the parallel algorithm. p_{opt} is the minimum number of processors required for the problem to be solved in optimal time. Note that it is easier to determine $t_{opt}(p)$, t_{opt} and p_{opt} here than it was in the case above and that complexity measures of parallel algorithms associated with a sequential algorithm are higher than those of all the algorithms associated with the problem they relate to.

5.1.3   Granularity of parallelism

As we have just seen, there are different problems according to whether the number of processors p is fixed or not. *Fine granularity* is the term used if the number of processors is greater than or equal to the number of data items; if not, *coarse granularity* is the term used. Granularity is a simple, rather than a strictly mathematical, method of classifying algorithms. We shall use granularity in Chapter 12, in which we extend our study of complexity by taking memory access into account, where it is an important parameter.

One result that is now part of the folklore of parallel algorithms was proved by Brent [Bre73]. It enables a parallel algorithm with p processors to be constructed from a parallel algorithm with a greater number of processors. A coarse-grain algorithm can thus be deduced from a fine-grain algorithm. Known as Brent's lemma, it can be applied to any algorithm and any PRAM model.

Lemma 5.1

Let there be a given PRAM model. If a parallel algorithm requires t time units and q operations to solve a given problem, a parallel algorithm with p processors that solves the problem and whose execution time is less than or equal to $t + \frac{q-t}{p}$ does exist.

Proof

Assume that q_i operations are executed at time i by the initial algorithm and therefore that:

$$\sum_{i=1}^{t} q_i = q$$

With p processors, the ith step can be subdivided into $\lceil \frac{q_i}{p} \rceil$ steps. An algorithm whose execution time is as below is obtained:

$$\sum_{i=1}^{t} \left\lceil \frac{q_i}{p} \right\rceil \leq \left(1 - \frac{1}{p}\right) t + \sum_{i=1}^{t} \frac{q_i}{p} = t + \frac{q-t}{p}$$

Note that the number of processors is not specified for the initial algorithm, although it is very important for the algorithm. Operation is understood to mean that a processor is active – a processor is either inactive or it is executing an operation. Thus the number of operations gives the total active time for all the processors.

An important application of the lemma is when the execution time of the initial algorithm is negligible in relation to the number of operations. The time of the algorithm using p processors is then t+q/p. If q is the number of operations for the optimum sequential algorithm (that is, the length of time that this algorithm takes), optimal parallel algorithms can be obtained.

5.2   Evaluation of arithmetic expressions

5.2.1   Basic assumptions

In this section, we look at the complexity of parallel evaluation of any given arithmetic expression. It is assumed that each processor can execute only unary or binary operations in one time unit. It is also assumed that the model is a CREW PRAM, in other words, that concurrent reads are allowed, but several processors writing simultaneously to the same memory address is not. We describe how a lower bound for the optimal computation time of a problem which has n data items and which provides a single result is constructed. The problem requires at least n − 1 binary operations. In the case of addition of n data items, for example, n − 1 computation units are sufficient to obtain the sequential result. In other words, it involves establishing how many operations can be executed in parallel.

First, we look at the relations between algorithms for evaluating expressions and labelled binary trees. A lower bound, $t_{opt}(p)$, is obtained for the problem. Finally, proof is provided that the bound is attained in a number of simple expressions. We then go on to construct algorithms for obtaining an upper bound in general expressions.

5.2.2   Arithmetic expressions and labelled binary trees

First, we provide a formal definition of an arithmetic expression, then go on to describe the relations between labelled binary trees and evaluation algorithms.

Definitions

Definition 5.1

An expression of size n is a problem that contains n data items (variables or atoms), provides a single result and consists entirely of binary operations.

The expression is *simple* if each of the variables is used as an operand only once. E is a simple expression if it satisfies one of the following conditions:

1. $E = x_i$, where x_i is a variable.

2. $E = \circ\, G$ where G is a simple expression and $\circ$ belongs to $\{\,+\,,-\,\}$.

3. $E = G \circ D$ where G and D are simple expressions involving unconnected sets of variables and $\circ$ belongs to $\{\,+\,,-\,,*\,,/\,\}$.

Condition 2 of the definition is such that any subtraction can be replaced by an addition preceded by a change of sign. Since sign changes can be executed in parallel at the beginning of an algorithm, we shall ignore them.
Examples:

- $x_i * x_j * x_k$ is a simple expression,

- x^3 is not simple,

- $a_1 + x_1 * (\, a_2 + x_2 * (\, a_3 + x_3\,))$ is simple,

- $a_1 + x * (\, a_2 + x * (\, a_3 + x\,))$ is not simple,

- $x_1 + \frac{x_3}{x_2}$ is simple,

- $x_1 + \frac{1}{x_2}$ is not simple.

We now define *labelled binary trees*. The definition is based on an integer p, which denotes the number of processors. The labelled tree leads to an evaluation algorithm with p processors, with each node representing an operation and the node's label representing the date the operation was executed.

Definition 5.2

Let p be a positive integer. We denote by A(p) the set of labelled binary trees constructed as follows:

1. The tree consisting of a single node labelled 0 belongs to A(p) and its depth is 0.

2. For $d \geq 0$, an element of A(p) of depth d+1 is obtained from an element of A(p) of depth d by adding 1 to all the labels and by replacing at most p of its leaves by the binary tree with three vertices whose leaves are labelled 0 and whose root is labelled 1.

The binary tree with three vertices whose leaves are labelled 0 and whose root is labelled 1 is called a base tree.

Example

Let p=3. The trees illustrated in Figure 5.1 belong to A(3).

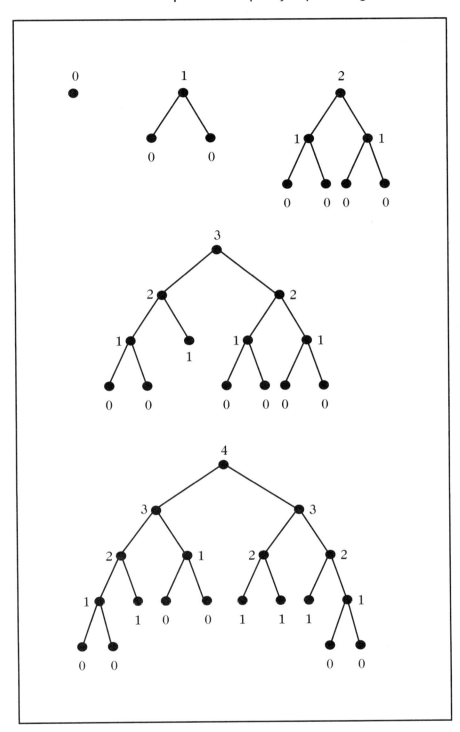

Figure 5.1 Elements of A(3)

Relations between expression evaluation and binary trees

Lemma 5.2

1. Any parallel evaluation algorithm for evaluating an expression of size n with p processors can be represented by an element of $A(p)$ that has at least n leaves.

2. Any simple expression of size n can be represented by an element of $A(p)$ that has n leaves. The tree specifies a parallel evaluation algorithm of the expression using p processors.

3. For any tree of $A(p)$ of depth d and with n leaves, there exist a simple expression of size n and an evaluation algorithm of the expression, represented by the tree.

Proof

1. The operations executed by the processors are binary. Consider the tree for the execution of the algorithm. Put in each interior node a label equal to the time when the relevant operation is executed. The labelled binary tree that results is an element of $A(p)$ and has at least n leaves, because the algorithm has n data items and no more than p operations can be executed simultaneously.

2. The proofs just need to be recurrent. The property is true for n=1. Assume that it has been proved for m<n. The expression E of size n is written $E = G \circ D$, where G and D are simple expressions relating to unconnected sets of variables. G and D can be represented by elements A_G and A_D of $A(p)$ of depths d_G and d_D. Add $d_G + 1$ to all the labels of A_D and let the tree that is obtained be called A'_D. Let A_D be the labelled binary tree of depth $d_D + d_G + 2$ whose two main sub-trees are A_G and A'_D. The parallel evaluation algorithm of E is obtained by executing the evaluation algorithm of G, then that of F and lastly by applying the operation $\circ$ to these two results.

3. Consider, by way of an example, the addition of n variables. The labelled binary tree has the following algorithm – at time t, the nodes labelled t act as operands in the computation which results in the nodes labelled t+1. The n data items are the leaves of the tree, with the interior nodes representing binary operations.

One useful way of representing algorithms for labelled binary trees is to put the relevant operation next to the label of the interior nodes; when the algorithm is executed, the operation is executed at the time specified by the label and has the two successors of the relevant node as its operands. The depth of an element $A(p)$ is therefore the time taken by the relevant algorithm. Generally speaking, the time taken is different from its height (the number of branches between a tree's root and leaves), but is always greater than or equal to the height.

Definition 5.3

F(p, d) is the maximum number of leaves of an element of A(p) of depth d, and D(p, n) is the minimum depth of an element of A(p) with n leaves.

Lemma 5.3

We then have the following relations:

1. $F(p, 0) = 1$

2. $F(p, d+1) = F(p, d) + \min(p, F(p, d))$

3. If n is such that $F(p, d-1) < n \leq F(p, d)$, then $D(p, n) = d$.

   If k is the ceiling of $\log_2(p)$, $k = \lceil \log_2(p) \rceil$,
   and if $m = \min(k, d)$:

4. $F(p, d) = 2^m + p.\max(0, d-k)$

5. $D(p, n) = \min(k, \lceil \log_2(n) \rceil) + \max(0, \lceil \frac{n-2^k}{p} \rceil)$
   $= \log_2(n) + n/p + o(\log_2(n) + n/p)$

Proof

1, 2 and 3 follow directly from the definitions.

4. While $d \leq k$, the tree with the maximum number of leaves is a complete binary tree and, therefore, $F(p, d) = 2^d$. Where $d > k$, the maximum number of leaves is obtained for a tree which has been constructed from the complete binary tree of depth k by replacing each of the p leaves by the base tree – hence the formula.

5. $F(p, d)$ increases strictly with d. Let $n_d = F(p, d)$; solving the equation for d we get:

$$d = \min\left(k, \log_2(n_d)\right) = \max\left(0, \frac{n_d - 2^k}{p}\right)$$

It follows from 4. that if n is such that $n_{d-1} < n \leq n_d$, then d is given by the above formula. The proof of the result is easy

Lower bounds in general expressions

Using the above two lemmas, a general lower bound can be obtained for the evaluation of any expression. Note that the complexity of an expression is always greater than or equal to that of a simple expression of the same size. One method of associating a simple expression with any other expression (*see* the definitions in Section 5.2.2) is to replace all occurrences of variables other than the first with new variables.

Theorem 5.4 (Munro and Paterson)

1. The minimum number of steps required to evaluate an expression of size n with p processors is D(p, n):

$$\log_2(n) + \frac{n}{p} + o\left(\log_2(n) + \frac{n}{p}\right) = D(p, n) \le t_{opt}(p)$$

2. The minimum number of steps required to evaluate an expression of size n is $\lceil \log_2(p) \rceil$, that is: $\lceil \log_2(p) \rceil \le t_{opt}$

Proof

1. Lemma 5.2 shows that an evaluation algorithm for the expression can be represented by an element of A(p) with at least n leaves. The conclusion follows from the definition of D(p, n).

2. Follows directly from Lemma 5.3.

Similarly, by using the same argument and the results for F(p, n), it can be shown that, whatever the number p of processors, a result from $2^n + 1$ data items cannot be obtained in fewer than n steps.

5.2.3   Particular expressions

Clearly, if more precise lower bounds or complexity results are required (equality of lower and upper bounds) then the general expressions have to be particularized in some way. An initial approach to this would be to assume that the same operation is repeated in the expression.

Single operation expressions

Theorem 5.5

Let o be an associative operation. D(p, n) is the complexity of the evaluation, with p processors, of the simple expression $A_n = a_1 o a_2 o \ldots o a_n$:

$$t_{opt}(p) = D(p, n) = \log_2(n) + \frac{n}{p} + o\left(\log_2(n) + \frac{n}{p}\right)$$

If $p \le O(n/\log_2(n))$, the algorithms obtained are cost optimal.

Proof

A parallel algorithm can be constructed on the basis of a labelled binary tree of depth $D(p, n)$, by executing the operation o at the relevant time of each label of an interior node on the two relevant operands.

In order to show that the algorithms are cost optimal, it is sufficient to state that if $p \leq O(\frac{n}{\log_2(n)})$, then $p.D(p, n) = O(n)$.

Note that, with this kind of expression, any element of $A(p)$ of depth $D(p, n)$ is a cost optimal (associative fan-in) algorithm.

Example

The computation of A_{10} with p=3 processors has a complexity of 4:

$$D(p, n) = \min(k, \lceil \log_2(n) \rceil) + \max(0, \lceil \frac{n - 2^k}{p} \rceil)$$
$$D(3, 10) = \min(2, 4) + \max(0, 2) = 4$$

Figure 5.2 illustrates an element of $A(3)$ of depth 4. The corresponding optimal algorithm is described in the accompanying table:

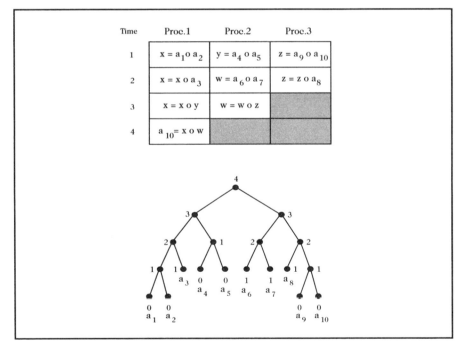

Figure 5.2   Tree of the computation of A_{10} with three processors

Corollary 5.6

1. The complexity of the sum of n numbers is $\lceil \log_2(n) \rceil$. The minimum number of processors required to evaluate the sum of n numbers in optimal time is less than or equal to $\lfloor \frac{n}{2} \rfloor$:

$$t_{opt} = \lceil \log_2(n) \rceil \qquad P_{opt} \leq \lfloor \tfrac{n}{2} \rfloor$$

2. The complexity of the product of n numbers is $\lceil \log_2(n) \rceil$. The minimum number of processors required to evaluate the product of n numbers in optimal time is less than or equal to $\lfloor \tfrac{n}{2} \rfloor$:

$$t_{opt} = \lceil \log_2(n) \rceil \qquad P_{opt} \leq \lfloor \tfrac{n}{2} \rfloor$$

3. The complexity of the sum and product of n numbers on a CREW PRAM model of p processors is $D(p, n) = \log_2(n) + \tfrac{n}{p} + o(\log_2(n) + \tfrac{n}{p})$.

Proof

The proofs follow directly from the theorems above.

Note that n numbers can be added in $\lceil \log_2(n) \rceil$ steps with less than $\lfloor \tfrac{n}{2} \rfloor$ processors, for some values of n.

Example

$A_6 = a_1 + a_2 + a_3 + a_4 + a_5 + a_6$ can be computed in three steps with two processors. Figure 5.3 illustrates the computation tree of an optimal algorithm for this.

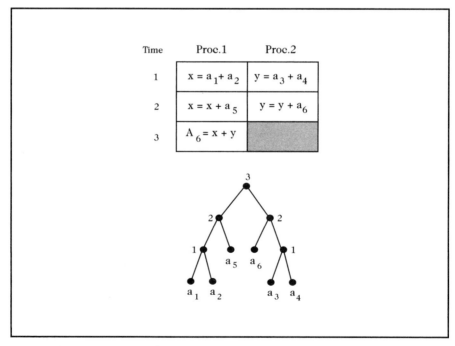

Figure 5.3   Computation of A_6

Minimum number of processors

Muraoka [Mur71] studied the minimum number of processors and proved the following theorem.

Theorem 5.7

Let o be an associative operation. To evaluate $A_n = a_1 o a_2 o \ldots o a_n$ in $t_{opt} = \lceil \log_2(n) \rceil$ steps, the minimum number of processors is:

$$
P_{opt} = \begin{cases} \left\lceil \dfrac{n - 2^{\lceil \log(n) \rceil - 2}}{2} \right\rceil & \text{if } 2^{\lceil \log(n) \rceil - 1} < n \leq 3.2^{\lceil \log(n) \rceil - 2} \\[2mm] & \text{if } 3.2^{\lceil \log(n) \rceil - 2} < n \leq 2^{\lceil \log(n) \rceil} \\[2mm] n - 2^{\lceil \log(n) \rceil - 1} \end{cases}
$$

Extensions

The results hold for any associative operation. In particular, the complexity of the computation of the maximum (or minimum) of n numbers of processors is D(p, n). The fundamental importance of the assumptions below must be stressed:

- the elementary operations are binary

- the model is CREW PRAM

If either of these is not satisfied, the result is not true. It can be shown that if k-ary operations are allowed, most of the above results can be extended by replacing base 2 logarithms with base k logarithms. On the other hand, it is more difficult to describe the role played by concurrent writes.

It should be recalled that the common model of writing in CRCW PRAM allows processors to write the same value to the same memory address.

Theorem 5.8

The maximum of n numbers can be computed in constant time with a common CRCW PRAM model with $\frac{n^2 - n}{2}$ processors.

Proof

To simplify description of the algorithm, assume that the processors have double subscripts, P_{ij} for $1 \leq j < i \leq n$ and that the n numbers are stored in addresses M_{i1}. n backing store addresses AM_i, initialized to 0, are also used. The maximum is written to address M_0. The algorithm proceeds as follows. Each processor P_{ij} compares the contents of the addresses M_{i1} and M_{j1}. If the content of M_{i1} is less than that of M_{j1}, then P_{ij} writes 1 to address AM_i. Only one of the addresses AM_i contains

0 corresponding to AM_i – the index of the maximum, whereas all the others contain 1. The processor P_{i1} reads from address A_i; and the processor that reads 0 writes the content of M_{i1} to M_0.

A third basic assumption is that the result depends on all the data items. At first sight, this assumption may appear strange – the maximum of n numbers depends on the n numbers. But this is not true. More specifically, if the maximum of n bits (0 or 1) is sought (in other words if an OR operation is computed) the maximum is known when a 1-bit is read, in which case the maximum does not depend on the subsequent numbers. Cook, Dwork and Reischuk [CDR86] use the argument very cleverly to prove the result below. The reader is referred to the original article or to Lakshmivaharan and Dhall [LaD90] for details.

Theorem 5.9.1

The maximum of n bits can be computed in $0.72 \log n + O(1)$ time on a CREW PRAM with n processors.

Theorem 5.9.2

To compute the maximum of n bits, at least $0.44 \log n + O(1)$ time units are required on a CREW PRAM.

The above results can be put into a more generalized context. Consider an associative operation $*$ on the values of field E, an array $[x_1, x_2,... x_n]$ of elements E and a PRAM with p processors. Assume that the memory cell M_i contains x_i at the beginning of the algorithm. The problem of computing its prefixes is to compute $S_i = x_1*...*x_i$ and store it in M_i. This general problem may be applied directly when using the operation $*$ and the set E with individual operations: addition, multiplication, maximum, minimum, computing OR and AND, broadcasting, merging two lists, rank computation and so on.

The sequential complexity of the problem is $\Theta(n)$: the S_i are computed iteratively by the recurrence $S_i := S_{i-1} + x_i$. A description of how the problem is parallelized can be found in [LaF80].

Theorem 5.10

On an EREW PRAM with p processors, prefix computation can be executed in the time:

$$t_{opt} = O(\log_2(n)) \text{ if } p = O\left(\frac{n}{\log_2(n)}\right)$$

$$t_{opt}(p) = O\left(\frac{n}{p}\right) \text{ if } p \leq O\left(\frac{n}{\log_2(n)}\right)$$

Proof

The following algorithm can be used to compute the prefixes in logarithmic time with n processors by executing a total of n $*$ operations. The proof of the result is obtained by directly applying Brent's lemma (Lemma 5.1).

We now give a special version of the algorithm which we shall use in Section 5.5.2. We assume that in addition to the memories M_i we have a further set R_i, and that when the algorithm terminates, each R_i contains the total combination of the x_i. The principle is this: neighbouring processors start by computing their prefixes, then processors a distance 2 apart, then 4 and so on. Let i_d be the dth digit in the binary representation of i and $i \oplus d$ the index i in which the dth digit has been complemented.

```
{computation of prefixes: Processor Pᵢ}
write (Mᵢ) in Rᵢ
for d ← 0 to logn-1 do
        if  i_d = 1 then Mᵢ ← Mᵢ * R_{i⊕d}
        Rᵢ ← Rᵢ * R_{i⊕d}
```

5.2.4   General arithmetic expressions

In this section, we describe the results obtained by Brent [Bre74], Winograd [Win75] and Muller and Preparata [MuP76] for evaluating simple general expressions. The results can be directly generalized, because an expression can always be considered as being simple if the various occurrences of the same variable are interpreted as different variables. The proofs are very complex and we shall not go into them here. They are based on rearranging the expression that is to be evaluated. For example, Brent rearranges the expression so that it has the form $E_1 x + E_2$, where E_1 and E_2 can be evaluated simultaneously, but only at the cost of an increase in the number of arithmetic operations executed. Initially, we look at cases where the number of processors is not given *a priori*.

Any number of processors

Theorem 5.11.1

Let E be a simple expression of size n, in which there are no divisions. The complexity of its evaluation satisfies the following inequalities:

$t_{opt} \leq 2 \log_2(n) + O(1)$	with $O(n^{1.82})$ processors	[Kos86]
$t_{opt} \leq 2.08 \log_2(n) + O(1)$	with $O(n^{1.82})$ processors	[MuP76]
$t_{opt} \leq \lfloor 4 \log_2(n-1) \rfloor$	with $n-1$ processors and $2(n-1)$ operations	[Bre74]
$t_{opt} \leq O(\log_2^2(n))$	with $\frac{3(n-1)}{2}$ operations	[Win75]

Theorem 5.11.2

Let E be a simple expression of size n, in which there are divisions. The complexity of its evaluation proves the following inequalities:

$t_{opt} \leq 2.88 \log_2(n) + O(1)$	with $O(n^{1.44})$ processors	[MuP76]
$t_{opt} \leq \lfloor 4 \log_2(n-1) \rfloor$	with $3(n-1)$ processors and $10(n-1)$ operations	[Bre74]
$t_{opt} \leq O(\log_2^2(n))$	with $5(n-1)/2$ operations	[Win75]

The most that can be said [MuP76] is that the complexity of the parallel evaluation of an expression lies between $\log_2(n)$ and $2.88\log_2(n)$ and this holds good whatever the expression. However, the number of processors in not linear in n. Brent's algorithm is the most efficient of the three, since it is in $4\log_2(n)$ with a linear number of processors. Note, in conclusion, that Winograd's algorithm is in $O(\log^2(n))$, but executes fewer arithmetic operations.

Results with fixed number of processors

If Lemma 5.1 is applied to the results of Theorem 5.11, the following is obtained:

Theorem 5.12.1

Let E be a simple expression of size n, in which there are no divisions. The complexity of the evaluation satisfies the following inequalities:

$$t_{opt}(p) \leq \lfloor 4\log_2(n-1) \rfloor + \frac{2(n-1)}{p} \qquad \text{[Bre74]}$$

$$t_{opt}(p) \leq O\left(\log_2^2(n)\right) + \frac{3(n-1)}{2p} \qquad \text{[Win75]}$$

Theorem 5.12.2

Let E be a simple expression of size n in which there are divisions. The complexity of the evaluation proves the following inequalities:

$$t_{opt}(p) \le \left\lfloor 4\log_2(n-1) \right\rfloor + \frac{10(n-1)}{p} \qquad \text{[Bre74]}$$

$$t_{opt}(p) \le O\!\left(\log_2^2(n)\right) + \frac{5(n-1)}{2p} \qquad \text{[Win75]}$$

It is noticeable that the bounds obtained by Winograd are better than those obtained by Brent when p is of order less than $\frac{n}{\log^2(n)}$. In the previous section we showed that $D(p, n)$ is a lower bound for $t_{opt}(p)$ and when p is of order less than n, $D(p, n) = \frac{n}{p} + o(\frac{n}{p})$. For an expression in which there are no divisions and in which p is of order less than $\frac{n}{\log^2(n)}$, Winograd's bound is near to being asymptotically optimal:

$$\frac{n}{p} + o\!\left(\frac{n}{p}\right) \le t_{opt}(p) \le 1.5\frac{n}{p} + o\!\left(\frac{n}{p}\right)$$

Parallel polynomial evaluation

A great deal of research has been conducted on the complexity of sequential algorithms. The result below can be used to deduce the lower bound of a parallel algorithm from the complexity of a sequential algorithm. The result should be seen in relation to Brent's lemma (5.1).

Theorem 5.13

If n operations are required to evaluate an expression, at least $D(p, n+1)$ steps are needed to evaluate it with p processors.

Proof

$F(p, d) - 1$ is the maximum number of operations that can be executed in d steps with p processors.

Let t be an integer such that $F(p, t - 1) - 1 \le n \le F(p, t) - 1$. Lemma 5.3 implies that $t = D(p, n + 1)$. It follows that n operations cannot be executed in fewer than $t + 1$ steps.

Evaluating a polynomial of degree n is an example of how the above theorem is applied. It is well known that 2n operations are necessary and sufficient in sequential evaluation – Horner's method is optimal. With p processors, at least $D(p, 2n+1)$ steps are required to evaluate the polynomial. Horner's method obviously does not bring about an optimal parallel algorithm. The following result shows that the lower bound is almost reached.

The reader is referred to the bibliography for proofs of this and to Lakshmivaharan and Dhall on which the following is based.

Theorem 5.14.1 [Mar73] [MuP73]

The complexity of the evaluation of a polynomial of degree n satisfies:

$$t_{opt} \leq \log_2(n) + \sqrt{2\log_2(n)} + O(1)$$

Theorem 5.14.2 [MuP73]

The complexity of the evaluation of a polynomial of degree n with p processors satisfies:

$$t_{opt}(p) \leq D(p, 2n+1) + O(1) = \frac{2n}{p} + \log_2(n) + o(\log_2(n))$$

Proof

1. Let P(x) be a polynomial of degree n and $q = \lceil \log_2(n+1) \rceil$. Let m be the greatest integer such that $m(m-1) < 2q-2$ and $k = q-m$. P(x) is expressed as follows:

$$P(x) = P_0(x) + P_1(x)\, x^{2^k} + P_2(x) \ldots + P_{2^m-1}(x)\, x^{(2^m-1).2^k}$$

Then, by recurrence, P can be computed in q + m + 1 time units. This is true for a polynomial of degree 1, since then q=1, m=0 and a+b.x can be evaluated in two time units. Suppose it is true for all polynomials of degree less than n. As P is of degree n, each P_i is of degree less than 2^{q-m}, so it follows from the definition of m that:

$$(m-1)(m-2) < 2(q-m) - 2 \leq m(m-1)$$

Then by recurrence, each of the P_i can be evaluated in parallel in:

$$(q-m) + (m-1) + 1 = q \text{ units of time}$$

The x^i can be computed in q time units for $1 \leq i \leq n$ (Theorem 5.5). When the P_i and the x^i have been computed, P(x) can be evaluated in m+1 time units (Corollary 5.6). In total, q+m+1 time units are obtained, which proves the result, as m is of the order $q^{1/2}$.

2. This follows by applying Brent's lemma (Lemma 5.1) with $\log_2(n)$ as parallel time and $2n$ as number of processors.

   In practice, the above is a complexity result. Kosaraju [Kos86] proved that:

$$t_{opt}(P) \geq \log_2(n) + \sqrt{2\log_2(n)} - \sqrt[4]{\log_2(n)} - O(1)$$

It can be deduced from this that the algorithm we have just described is asymptotically optimal.

5.2.5   Scalar products and matrix multiplication

Winograd [Win70] showed that n multiplications and n–1 additions are necessary and sufficient to compute the scalar product $u^t.v$ of two vectors of size n sequentially. The above results imply that $D(p, 2n)$ time units are required, using p processors.

Where both multiplications and additions can be executed (on a MIMD architecture), $D(p, 2n)$ steps are sufficient. Where they cannot both be executed (on a SIMD architecture), $\lceil \frac{n}{p} \rceil + D(p, n)$ steps are required.

This can be applied to computing $u = \max |u_i|$. $\lceil \frac{n}{p} \rceil$ steps are necessary and sufficient for computing the $|u_i|$ and $D(p, n)$ to write the maximum, as max is an associative operation. The same applies to computing the Euclidian norm of a vector:

$$\|u\|_2^2 = \sum_{i=1}^{n} u_i^2$$

Note that the product of a matrix and a vector and the product of matrices can be seen as several independent scalar products.

Theorem 5.15

1. The complexity of the scalar product of two vectors is $\lceil \log_2(n) \rceil + 1$. The minimum number of processors required to evaluate the scalar product in optimal time is less than or equal to n:

$$t_{opt} = \lceil \log_2(n) \rceil + 1 \quad p_{opt} \leq n$$

2. The complexity of the product of a (q, n) matrix and an n-element vector is:

$$t_{opt} = \lceil \log_2(n) \rceil + 1 \quad p_{opt} \leq n \, q$$

3. The complexity of the product of a (q_1, n) matrix and an (n, q_2)-element matrix is:

$$t_{opt} = \lceil \log_2(n) \rceil + 1 \quad p_{opt} \leq n \, q_1 \, q_2$$

Apply Brent's lemma to the above and an optimal cost algorithm is obtained for the scalar product, and the number of processors is reduced without the execution time being increased to any great extent.

Corollary 5.16

1   The scalar product of two vectors can be computed in $2 \lceil \log_2(n) \rceil + 1$ steps with $\lceil \frac{n}{\log_2(n)} \rceil$ processors.

2. The product of a (q, n) matrix, multiplied by an n-element vector, can be calculated in $2 \lceil \log_2(n) \rceil + 1$ steps with $q \lceil \frac{n}{\log_2(n)} \rceil$ processors.

3. The product of a (q_1, n) matrix, multiplied by an (n, q_2) matrix, can be calculated in $2 \lceil \log_2(n) \rceil + 1$ steps with $q_1 q_2 \lceil \frac{n}{\log_2(n)} \rceil$ processors.

Similarly, the complexity of the three problems can be computed on a CREW PRAM with p processors.

Corollary 5.17

1. The scalar product of two vectors can be computed in $O(\frac{n}{p})$, using p processors.

2. The product of a (q, n) matrix and an n-element vector can be computed in $O(q \frac{n}{p})$, with p processors.

3. The product of a (q_1, n) matrix and an (n, q_2) matrix can be calculated in $O(q_1 q_2 \frac{n}{p})$, using p processors.

5.3   Solving linear systems

5.3.1   Solving triangular systems

General bound

Before looking at the general problem of solving dense linear systems, we shall look at a particular problem, the triangular system Lx=b. L is assumed to be an $n \times n$ lower triangular system.

Lemma 5.18

To find a parallel solution to the triangular system Lx=b, at least $2 \log_2(n) + o(\log_2(n))$ steps are required.

Proof

$x=L^{-1}b$, where L^{-1} is a lower triangular system. x_n depends on all the elements of L and b, around $\frac{n^2}{p}$. It follows from this that at least $D(p, n^2/2)$ steps are required, which, where p is large, is equal to $2\log_2(n) + O(\log_2(n))$ steps.

Whether the bound can be reached is not known. On the other hand, there are several algorithms in $O(\log_2(n))$ processors with $O(n^3)$ processors. It should be recalled that the sequential time is $O(n^2)$.

Elimination by diagonals

The algorithm we intend to look at, which was described by Chen and Kuk [ChK75], is based on Gaussian elimination. It involves eliminating sub-diagonal elements on the same diagonal, with the number of diagonals processed doubling at each step (*see* Figure 5.4). We assume that L is bordered by the vector b so that the algorithm terminates with the solution of the last column of L. L_i denotes the ith row of L.

```
{Elimination by diagonals}
L_i ← L_i / L_i, i  (1≤i≤n)
for  j ← 1  to n-1 by steps of j
             2j-1
    L_i ← L_i - Σ L_i, i-k L_i-k  (j+1≤i≤n)
            k=j
x_i ←L_i, n+1 (1≤i≤n)
```

Theorem 5.19

By using elimination by diagonals,

$$\frac{\left(\lceil \log_2(n) \rceil + 1\right)\left(\lceil \log_2(n) \rceil + 2\right)}{2} = \frac{\log_2{}^2(n)}{2} + O(\log_2(n))$$

---

steps are sufficient to solve Lx=b with $p=n^3/68 + O(n^2)$ processors.

Proof

We shall only compute the number of steps. The divisions can be executed in one step. For each value of j, all multiplications can be executed in parallel in 1 step and additions in $\lceil \log_2(j+1) \rceil$ steps by using a labelled binary tree. By writing $j=2^q$, the following is obtained:

$$1 + \sum_{q=0}^{\lceil \log(n) \rceil - 1} \left(1 + \lceil \log_2(2^q + 1) \rceil \right) = \frac{\left(\lceil \log_2(n) \rceil + 1\right)\left(\lceil \log_2(n) \rceil + 2\right)}{2}$$

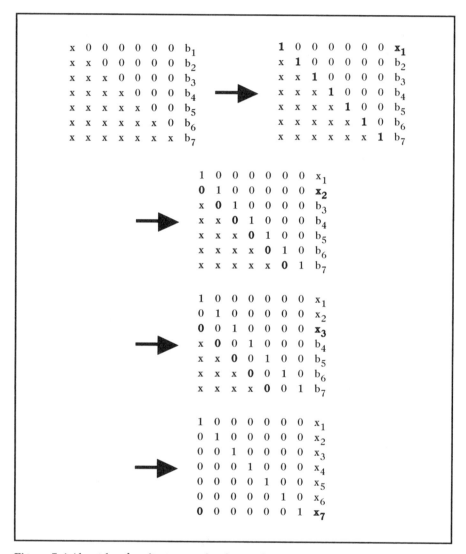

Figure 5.4 Algorithm for elimination by diagonals on a 7×7 system

Divide and conquer algorithms

Another algorithm (Heller [Hel78], Borodin and Munro [BoM75]) uses a *divide and conquer* technique to solve the triangular system Lx=b.

Consider the following decomposition of the lower triangular matrix L:

$$L = \begin{bmatrix} L_1 & 0 \\ L_2 & L_3 \end{bmatrix}$$

where L_1 and L_3 are two lower triangular matrices of size (q, q) and (n–q, n–q). The vector b is decomposed in the same way into b' of size q and b" of size n–q.

We then have:

$$L^{-1} = \begin{bmatrix} L_1^{-1} & 0 \\ -L_3^{-1} \ L_2 \ L_1^{-1} & L_3^{-1} \end{bmatrix}$$

It is assumed the number of processors is sufficient. To compute $L^{-1}b$, the algorithm begins by simultaneously computing $L_1^{-1}b'$ and $L_3^{-1}b"$ solving the systems $L_3 Y = L_2$. The complete value of $L^{-1}b$ is obtained by multiplying –Y by $L_1^{-1}b'$ and adding it to $L_3^{-1}b"$.

T(n) is the number of steps required to compute $L^{-1}b$. Computing $L^{-1}b'$ requires T(q) steps and computing $L_3^{-1}b"$, T(n–q) steps. Computing Y requires T(n–q) steps, as solving (n–q) linear systems requires the same number of steps as solving one. Thus, by using $O(n^3)$ processors,

$$T(n) = \min_{q=1,n} \ (\max(T(q), \ T(n - q)) + \lceil \log_2(n) \rceil + 1)$$
$$T(1) = 1$$

$\frac{n}{2}$ is the right choice of q and $T(n) = O(\log_2 n)$ is obtained.

5.3.2   Solving dense linear systems

The subject of this section is the complexity of algorithms for solving a linear system Ax = b, where A is a given matrix of size (n, n) with real coefficients and no particular structure. Clearly, if the problem can be solved in T time with p processors, linear systems AX=B, where B is a matrix of size (n, m), can be solved in T time with mp processors. The time complexity of solving a linear system is the same as that of a matrix inversion.

In the rest of this chapter, we look at the complexity of Gauss-Jordan elimination and Givens QR decomposition.

General bounds

First, we describe a general result that provides the best upper and lower bounds that are currently known for solving a general linear system.

Theorem 5.20

The complexity t_{opt} of a linear system of size n is such that:

$$2\log_2(n) \le t_{opt} \le \frac{3\log_2{}^2(n)}{2} + O(\log_2(n))$$

Proof

Lower bound:

Because matrix A is general, each component of the solution x depends on the n^2+n coefficients of A and b. It follows from this that $D(p, n^2+n)$ steps are required to compute each of the components with p processors. For large p,

$$D(p, n^2+n) = 2\log_2(n) + o(\log_2(n))$$

and thus,

$$T(n) \ge 2\log_2(n) + o(\log_2(n))$$

Upper bound:

This upper bound is due to Csanky [Csa76], who devised an algorithm that solves a general linear system in the corresponding time.

Let λ_i be the eigenvalues of a, and $P(z)$ the characteristic polynomial:

$$P(z) = \prod_{i=1}^{n}(z - \lambda_i) = z^n + c_1 z^{n-1} + c_2 z^{n-2} \ldots + c_{n-1} z + c_n$$

The Newton identities give the coefficients of the polynomial in terms of its roots:

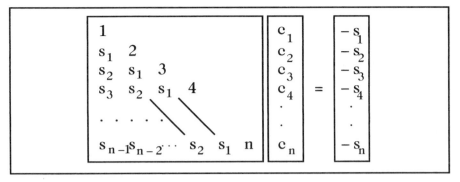

where the s_i are defined by:

$$s_i = \text{trace}(A^i) = \sum_{k=1}^{n} \lambda_k^i$$

Finally, by the Cayley-Hamilton theorem:

$$A^{-1} = \frac{A^{n-1} + c_1 A^{n-2} \ldots + c_{n-2} A + c_{n-1} \text{Id}_n}{c_n}$$

The algorithm is therefore as follows:

Phase 1:
Computing the powers of A^i for $1 \le i \le n$.
We have seen that all the z^i, $1 \le i \le n$ can be computed in $\lceil \log_2(n) \rceil$ steps with $n/2$ processors. It can be deduced from this that by computing in parallel all the scalar products, matrices A^i, $1 \le i \le n$ can be computed in $\lceil \log_2(n) \rceil.(\lceil \log_2(n) \rceil+1)$ steps with $n^4/2$ processors.

Phase 2:
Computing the s_i for $1 \le i \le n$.
As $s_i = \text{trace}(A^i)$, $1 \le i \le n$, the s_i can be computed in $\lceil \log_2(n) \rceil$ steps with n^2 processors.

Phase 3:
Computing the c_i for $1 \le i \le n$.
The c_i are solutions of a lower triangular system. We have seen that systems of this kind can be solved in $(\lceil \log_2(n) \rceil+1).(\lceil \log_2(n) \rceil+2)$ steps with $n^3/68$ processors.

Phase 4:
Computing $x = A^{-1}b$.

By applying the above formula, A^{-1} can be computed in $(\lceil \log_2(n) \rceil + 2)$ steps with n^3 processors. Computation of x can then be obtained in $(\lceil \log_2(n) \rceil + 1)$ steps with n^2 processors.

Csanky's upper bound is found by totalling the number of steps in the various phases and by taking the maximum of the numbers of processors.

Csanky's method is of some theoretical interest but is of no practical use since it is very unstable numerically. In practice, more classical methods have to be used; we shall look in turn at Jordan's method (also called Gauss-Jordan), Gauss's method (LU decomposition) and QR decomposition: notice that all three methods involve the solution of triangular systems.

Gauss-Jordan and Gaussian elimination

The problem is to solve a set of m linear equations with the same matrix A of order n. The right-hand elements of the equations are written as m extra columns of A, so that this becomes of order (n, m+m). A_i is the ith row of A.

```
{Gauss-Jordan elimination}
for  k ← 1  to  n
    for  i ← 1  to  n with i≠k
        A(i, .) ← A(k, k)*A(i, .) - A(i, k)*A(k, .)
{Solution of the m systems}
for  i ← 1  to  n
    for  j ← n+1  to  n+m
        x(i, j) ← A(i, j)/A(j, j)
```

The multiplications $A_{kk}*A_i$ and $A_{ik}*A_k$ can be executed in one time unit with $2(n-1)(n+m)$ processors, and subtraction in one time unit with $(n-1)(n+m)$ processors. Since the x_{ij} can be computed simultaneously, the algorithm can be computed in a total of $2n+1$ time units with $2(n-1)(n+m)$ processors.

The rows have to be exchanged (a technique known as pivoting) to obtain a numerically stable algorithm. Searching for the pivot (the maximum or the first non-null element) is the same as seeking the maximum element in n–k, and this can be executed optimally in $\lceil \log_2(n-k) \rceil$ time units. The total number of steps is:

$$\sum_{k=1}^{n} \lceil \log_2(n-k) \rceil = n\log_2(n) + O(n)$$

It follows from this that pivoting may have a higher overhead than the computation itself, in contrast with the sequential algorithm. From a practical point of view, the maximum element of the whole column does not have to be found – Sorenson [Sor84] demonstrated that pivoting with only two consecutive rows is numerically stable. Even here, finding pivots is of the order of the computation.

Theorem 5.21.1
Gauss-Jordan elimination without pivoting to solve m linear systems of the same matrix of size n can be executed in 2n+1 time units with $2(n-1)(n+m)$ processors.

Theorem 5.21.2
Gauss-Jordan elimination with finding the maximum pivot in each column requires the order of $n \log_2 n$ time units.

The principle behind Gaussian elimination is similar to the above method, but it eliminates only those elements in the lower triangle of A. It is followed by solving the resulting upper triangular system. Sequentially, the number of arithmetic operations $(2n^3/3)$ is lower than that in Gauss-Jordan elimination (n^3). Obviously, where parallelism is unbounded, Gaussian elimination will entail higher overheads, as the eliminations on n rows or n–k rows take the same time to execute. Chapter 8 describes the principle behind Gaussian elimination in detail. Chapters 11 and 12 are dedicated to parallelizing the methods on a shared-memory architecture with a fixed number of processors of the order n. Chapter 16 looks at parallelization of the methods on processor networks.

Givens decomposition

A great deal of research has focused on using Givens' plane rotation to parallelize QR decomposition. The method is stable in that it uses only orthonormal transformations [GoV83]. The number of arithmetic operations used in the method $(4n^3/3$ multiplications and additions and $n^2/2$ square root extractions) is greater than those used in the methods outlined above. However, pivoting is not required and, with an unbounded number of processors, it can be executed in a linear number of steps in n.

Givens' algorithm can be used to compute the orthogonal decomposition of A by plane rotations: that is, to find an upper triangular matrix R such that QA = R, where Q is an orthogonal matrix. In solving a linear system of m equations, A is bordered with the m columns of right-hand members. The rotation in the plane (i, j) that eliminates the element a_{ik} is called $rot(i, j, k)$, $i \neq j$, $1 \leq i, j \leq m$ and $1 \leq k \leq n$. For example, $rot(i, j, 1)$ combines rows i and j in such a way as to eliminate a_{i1}:

$$\begin{vmatrix} \alpha_{j1} & \alpha_{j2} & \cdots & \alpha_{jn} \\ 0 & \alpha_{i2} & \cdots & \alpha_{in} \end{vmatrix} = \begin{vmatrix} c & s \\ -s & c \end{vmatrix} \begin{vmatrix} a_{j1} & a_{j2} & \cdots & a_{jn} \\ a_{i1} & a_{i2} & \cdots & a_{in} \end{vmatrix}$$

It should be noted that the two rows used to perform the rotation are changed, by contrast with Gaussian elimination. In the sequential algorithm, the order of the rotations is such that an element that has already been reduced to zero is not subsequently removed, with elimination generally occurring from left to right and from bottom to top. Measured in terms of the number of rotations (of unit costs r) the cost of the algorithm is

$$\frac{n(n+1)}{2} r$$

which corresponds to the number of sub-diagonal elements of A.

There are two phases in performing a rotation:

(1) Computing the coefficients c and s, which requires four time units (including the square root):

$$c = \frac{a_{j1}}{\sqrt{a_{j1}^2 + a_{i1}^2}}$$

$$s = \frac{a_{i1}}{\sqrt{a_{j1}^2 + a_{i1}^2}}$$

(2) Applying the matrix to the vectors in order to compute the values of a (which, with a number of processors four times the size of the vector, requires two time units):

$$\alpha_{jk} = c \, a_{jk} + s \, a_{ik}$$

$$\alpha_{ik} = -s \, a_{jk} + c \, a_{ik}$$

Parallelizing the algorithm basically involves simultaneously performing independent rotations, that is, rotations affecting different rows. The problem of finding the number of groups of independent rotations is difficult: we take this up in Chapter 12. Specifically, it will be seen that the optimal number of groups of independent rotations is $2n-O(n)$. The optimal greedy algorithm ([CoR86b], [MoC84]) performs $\lfloor \frac{n}{2} \rfloor$ rotations in the first phase – on the vectors of size n+m−1. After that, the groups' cardinal is less than or equal to $\lfloor \frac{n}{2} \rfloor$, and executing the algorithm therefore requires 12n−O(n) time units with 2n(n+m−1) processors. The optimal number of processors required to execute the algorithm in optimal time is unknown. As Figure 5.5 shows, the basic purpose of the greedy algorithm is to execute the greatest number of independent rotations at any given moment. The figures in the illustration represent the numbers of the phases during which coefficients are eliminated.

```
*
3    *
2    5    *
2    4    7    *
1    3    6    8    *
1    3    5    7    9    *
1    2    4    6    8    10   *
1    2    3    5    7    9    11   *
```

Figure 5.5   Groups of independent rotations in the greedy algorithm

Sameh and Kuck's algorithm [SaK78], illustrated in Figure 5.6, performs 2n−3 groups of independent rotations and is therefore asymptotically optimal. The cardinal of the largest group is $\lfloor \frac{n}{2} \rfloor$, but its rotations zeroize one element of each of the first $\lfloor \frac{n}{2} \rfloor$ columns and therefore act on vectors of decreasing size. It follows that executing the algorithm requires 12n−18 time units, where the number of processors is:

$$p = \sum_{q=1}^{n/2} 4(n + m - q) = \frac{n(3n + 4m - 2)}{2}$$

Although the greedy algorithm is optimal, it is less efficient than Sameh and Kuck's algorithm.

```
*
7    *
6    8    *
5    7    9    *
4    6    8    10   *
3    5    7    9    11   *
2    4    6    8    10   12   *
1    3    5    7    9    11   13   *
```

Figure 5.6   Groups of independent rotations in Sameh and Kuck's algorithm

Theorem 5.22.1

The greedy method is optimal for parallel execution of Givens' method for computing the orthogonal decomposition of a matrix of size n with m elements. Its execution time is $t_{opt}=12n-O(n)$ with $2n(n+m-1)$ processors.

Theorem 5.22.2

Sameh and Kuck's algorithm is asymptotically optimal. Its execution time is $12n-18$, with $\frac{n(3n+4m-2)}{2}$ processors.

Of course, the m linear systems of the same matrix R still have to be solved, and this can be done in logarithmic time (Section 5.3.1).

We shall not describe parallelization of other linear algebra problems in detail, and the reader is referred to [Hel78] for a more detailed treatment of such problems. However, it should be pointed out that a parallel solution of a tridiagonal system is of the order $\log_2(n)$. Each part of the solution depends on $4n-2$ data items (the $3n-2$ coefficients of the matrix and the vector), and $D(n, 4n-2)$ time units are required, which is of the order $\log_2(n)$. Stone's algorithm [Sto73b] can be used to define an algorithm that can be executed in $O(\log_2(n))$, using n processors.

5.4   Parallel sort algorithms

5.4.1   Introduction

In this section, we look at the complexity of parallel sorting on a PRAM. Of course, the subject is far too vast to be discussed adequately in a few pages, and this is only an introduction to it. The section is based to a considerable extent on Gibbons and Rytter's book (Chapter 5 [GiR88]). The reader is referred to this and Akl's book [Akl85] for a more complete description. There are several models of parallel computation for sorting algorithms. The most well known, apart from the PRAM model, is the sorting network model, and this is due mainly to Batcher's work on sorting networks [Bat68] and to the work of Hungary's Ajtai, Komlos and Szemeredi [AKS84]. Sorting networks have played an important role in obtaining complexity bounds. Batcher's model is not optimal, but it is simple and has been widely used in practice as a result. The Hungarians' model is optimal, but its difficulty and the size of the constant in its greatest term mean that it cannot be used in practice. We describe Batcher's network and Cole's algorithm which is optimal for PRAMs [Col90].

We assume that the elements to be sorted are integers held in a 1-dimensional array Key[1..n], and for simplicity we take n to be a power of 2. We consider only methods that are based on comparisons; the basic operation is therefore *compare-exchange*, which involves comparing two elements of Key and swapping them if necessary. It can be described as follows:

```
compare-exchange (Key, i, j)
Key(min(i, j)) ← min(Key(i), Key(j))
Key(max(i, j)) ← max(Key(i), Key(j))
```

This will sort an array with two elements. We use the name *compare-exchange module* to mean a device with two inputs and two outputs, such that the outputs are the result of applying the compare-exchange operation to the inputs. A sorting network for an array of size n is built from a number of such modules.

5.4.2   Sorting networks and PRAMs

A sorting network is an acyclic directed graph with n input nodes and n output nodes. Each of the graph's interior nodes is the final point of two arcs (fan-in=2) and the initial point of two arcs (fan-out=2). A compare-exchange module is located in each interior node. The input nodes transmit input data, while the output nodes store results.

The nodes are distributed on levels, with the input nodes on level 0, and with those nodes whose predecessors are on the preceding levels, with at least one predecessor on level i–1, located on level i. The number of levels of the network is referred to as its depth and the largest cardinal of its levels, excluding the input and output levels, is the network's width – this will be compared with equivalent definitions in Chapter 9, in which task graphs are described. Networks operate synchronously, moving from one level to the next. At time i, each of the modules on level i reads the values from the input arcs, performs a compare-exchange operation and writes the results to the output arcs. The relation between sorting networks and PRAMs is very simple.

Lemma 5.23
A sorting network of width p and depth t can be simulated by a p-processor CREW PRAM in $O(t)$ time.

Proof
The n input values are assigned to the first n memory positions. The processors execute the module's program. Phase i of the network is simulated in constant time by the PRAM's processors, with each processor performing a compare-exchange operation.

5.4.3   Batcher sorting networks

In this section, we describe two sorting networks for obtaining a parallel algorithm whose time complexity is $O(\log_2 n)$. Both networks are based on the *parallel merge* operation, which merges two sorted lists into a single one. The two networks obtained can be considered as parallelizations of the sequential mergesort algorithm.

Odd-even merge

The first Batcher network is based on odd-even merges and using a binary tree of merges. The latter is constructed as follows:

- the leaves of the tree are the elements Key[i] that are to be sorted,

- the nodes of the tree are the operations of merging the two children of the node.

The tree is of depth $\log_2(n)$. Merges on one level can be performed in parallel. Odd-even merges should be defined in order to complete the description.

$Odd(Key)$ (or $Even(Key)$) is the set of odd (or even) elements of Key. Let S be a set of elements of cardinality n. The function *odd-even exchange* (S) changes S into a new set that is obtained by comparing and exchanging all the odd elements with the subsequent element. More specifically:

```
odd-even exchange (S)
for  i ← 1  to  n/2
    compare-exchange (S, 2i, 2i+1)
```

The function *interleave* (S, S') constructs a list whose *even* elements are in S and whose *odd* elements are in S'. Odd-even merge can now be described:

```
Odd-even merge (S, S')
if Card(S) = Card(S') = 1 then
    Odd-even merge ←compare-exchange (interleave (S, S'), 1, 2)
else
    S1 ← Odd-even merge (even(S), even(S'))
    S2 ← Odd-even merge (odd(S), odd(S'))
    Odd-even merge ← odd-even exchange (interleave (S1, S2))
```

We do not intend to prove the resulting algorithm, that is, that the merge leads to two sorted lists being sorted into one. The reader is referred to [GiR88]. Of course, S1 and S2 can be computed in parallel, as can *odd-even exchange*. The latter can be executed in constant time with n/2 modules. From this, it can be deduced that the execution time of the odd-even merge is $O(\log_2(n))$.

Theorem 5.24

The depth of Batcher's odd-even merge sorting network is $O(\log^2 n)$ and its width is n.

Bitonic merge

The second of Batcher's networks is based on *bitonic merge* and, as was the case with the first network described, on using a binary tree of merges. A set is said to be bitonic when it consists of two chained sets, with the first sorted in ascending and the second in descending order. A bitonic merge sorts a bitonic set. A bitonic set is created in a node on a tree of merges from two sorted children and a bitonic merge is performed on it.

We shall call the first sequence *beginning*(S) and the second *end*(S). The bitonic merge is as follows:

```
Bitonic merge (S)
repeat log(n) times
   S ← odd-even exchange (interleave (beginning(S), end(S)))
Bitonic merge ← S
```

Clearly, parallel odd-even exchanges can be performed in constant time with n/2 modules. The procedure's execution time is therefore $O(\log^2 n)$.

Theorem 5.25

The depth of Batcher's bitonic merge sorting network is $O(\log^2 n)$ and its width is n.

5.4.4   Reducing the number of processors

The existence of two sorting algorithms in time $O(\log^2 n)$ on a CREW PRAM with n processors is deduced by applying Lemma 5.23 to Theorems 5.24 and 5.25. The sequential complexity of the sort is $O(n \log^2 n)$, so the above algorithms are not cost optimal. Applying Brent's lemma is sufficient to obtain cost optimal algorithms.

Corollary 5.26

Parallel algorithms for odd-even and bitonic merges can be executed in time $O(\log^2 n)$ on a CREW PRAM with $\frac{n}{\log_2(n)}$ processors.

Proof

Brent's lemma is used with a sequential algorithm of complexity $O(n \log_2 n)$ and a parallel algorithm of complexity $O(\log^2 n)$ on a CREW PRAM with n processors. The lemma is used to deduce an algorithm in time $O(\log^2 n) + O(n \log_2 n)/p$ on a CREW PRAM with p processors. The result is obtained by writing $p = \dfrac{n}{\log_2(n)}$

5.4.5   Cole's algorithm

Batcher's algorithms are based on parallelizing the phases of a mergesort. Mergesort has $\log_2 n$ phases, with each phase taking time $O(\log_2 n)$. Even in the absence of further information about the sets that are to be merged, it can be shown that $O(\log_2 n)$ is optimal. However, successive merges are performed on a set of n elements. Cole [Col88] took advantage of this and devised a very sophisticated algorithm, which enables sets to be merged in constant time. The basic idea behind the algorithm is to use a third set that is a good sample of the two that are to be merged.

Let S be a sorted list. E is said to be a *good sample* of S if, for all k, there are at most $2k+1$ elements of S between $k+1$ elements of E: thus there are at most 3 elements of S between any pair of consecutive elements in E.

Let S, S' be two sorted lists that are to be merged and E a good sample of both: the function *merge by sample*, given below, will merge the two in a constant parallel time. It applies a sequential merge procedure to a constant number of elements and uses the standard operation of chaining.

```
Merge by sample (S, S', E)
for  i ← 1  to  Card(E)
   construct S(i) the list of elements of S between E(i) and
      E(i+1)
   construct S'(i) the list of elements of S' between E(i) and
      E(i+1)
   Merge by sample (i) ← merge (S(i), S'(i))
Merge by sample ← chaining (merge by sample (i))
```

As merges of a constant number of elements are performed in constant time, the lists S(i) and S'(i) must be constructed in constant time in order for the merge by sample to be performed in constant time. Cole's algorithm uses merge by sample on the nodes of a binary tree with n leaves. The tree is constructed is such a way that a good sample is preserved from level to level, as the final set is constructed. It is also such that the elements between the sample's two consecutive elements can be calculated in constant time.

Theorem 5.27
Cole's merge by sample algorithm is executed in time $O(\log_2 n)$ on an n-processor EREW PRAM.

5.5   Comparison of several models

So far in this chapter, our work has essentially been based on the CREW PRAM, but we have also described some results for EREW and CRCW PRAMs. In this section, we look at them again, as well as at the extensions to them that we described in Section 2.2. Our aim here is to study the power of each of the models, the possibility of moving from one model to another and the relations between them.

5.5.1   PRAM models

Before the various PRAM models can be compared, the criteria on which the comparison is made have to be defined. As far as the three main PRAM models are concerned, comparison will centre on computation time. More specifically, we shall use the following definitions.

Comparative power of the models

Definition 5.4
Given two models M_1 and M_2, M_1 is weaker in solving a problem P than M_2, if its time complexity for solving P on M_1 is higher than that for solving P on M_2. The relation is written $M_1 \propto M_2$.
M_1 is weaker than M_2, if $M_1 \propto M_2$ for any problem. Furthermore, if a problem P exists for which the time complexity for solving P on M_1 is strictly higher than that for solving P on M_2, M_1 is strictly weaker than M_2. The relation is written $M_1 \ll M_2$.

Theorem of differentiation between PRAMs

To simplify the description, we shall consider only one CRCW model and adopt the following writing policy – two processors writing the same value to a memory cell are allowed simultaneous access to it. Of course, an algorithm designed for a EREW PRAM can be executed on a CRCW PRAM and any algorithm designed for a CREW PRAM can be executed on a CRCW PRAM. Snir's theorem [Sni85], below, shows that the contrary is not true.

Theorem 5.28 (Differentiation theorem)

Assume that the three models have p processors. We have:

- EREW PRAM << CREW PRAM

- CREW PRAM << CRCW PRAM

Proof

Theorems 5.8 and 5.9 show that differentiation between CREW and CRCW PRAMs can be achieved on the basis of computing the maximum of n bits. The problem is solved in constant time on a CRCW PRAM and requires at least $O(\log n)$ steps, if concurrent writes are not allowed.

For the first part of the theorem, differentiation between the models is achieved by searching in a sorted set [Sni85].

PRAM simulation theorem

We shall now introduce the concept of simulation in order to look at the extent to which the models differ.

Definition 5.5

Given two models M_1, M_2, we say that M_1 can be simulated by M_2 in time t if a single computing step of M_1 can be performed on M_2 in time t. The relation is represented by $M_2 = t.M_1$.

Theorem 5.29 (Simulation theorem)

Assume that the three models have p processors. We have:

- EREW PRAM = $O(\log p).$CREW PRAM

- CREW PRAM = $O(\log p).$CRCW PRAM

- EREW PRAM = $O(\log p).$CRCW PRAM

Proof

We shall not describe the proof in detail; it can be found in [Vis83]. It is based on the following concept, which applies to both reads and writes. The first thing to be noticed is that simulating each computation step suffices. When several processors access the same memory cell, the value stored in the cell has to be duplicated to simulate the access. A broadcast algorithm that can be executed in logarithmic time can be used for this.

The above bound is reached. We have already seen that computing the maximum takes logarithmic time on a CRCW PRAM and can be solved in constant time on a CRCW PRAM. Our study of PRAM models is based on these two CREW theorems. It can be developed in a number of directions, particularly when relations between the various writing policies for CRCWs are being established. In the following section, the study is generalized to shared-memory computation models.

5.5.2   HypercubeRAM models

In Section 2.2, we described the DRAM model in terms of a generalization of the PRAM model. In this section, we look at differentiation and simulation problems for DRAMs. Recall that in Definition 2.2, a DRAM is defined as being based on a network X consisting of a family of X_i, the set of pairs (i, .). The processor P_i can access only the memory areas M_j, whatever j belongs to X_i. The processors P_j are called the neighbours of P_i. As is the case in PRAMs, time is discrete and at any time interval, all the processors of a DRAM operate synchronously and execute the following operations: $Read(M_j)$, *Compute*, $Write(M_k)$ for j and k that belong to X_i. Different models – EREW, CREW and CRCW DRAMs – can also be defined according to how memory is accessed.

Definition of a HypercubeRAM

The aim of this chapter is to show that assumptions about concurrent reading and writing exert an influence on the interconnection network. However, where the network has a constant degree (or is bounded by a constant), that is, where the cardinal of X_i is constant for all i, then concurrent access can be executed sequentially with a constant overhead. It follows that differences in power between the models will be hidden by the notation O. And that is why it is assumed that the interconnection network is a graph whose degree is a non-constant function of the number of processors. We shall consider a hypercube for the sake of simplicity (*see* Section 4.1.2).

> **Definition 5.6**
> A *HypercubeRAM* is a DRAM such that X is a hypercube interconnection network:
> $H_i = X_i = \{ j \in \{1,\ldots,p\} / $ binary representations of i and j differ by only one bit}.

HypercubeRAM algorithms

Before going on to generalize theorems for differentiating and simulating PRAMs, we shall look in a little more detail at the HypercubeRAM model by describing a few algorithms. Of course, this is not an exhaustive study of the subject.

The computation of prefixes on a PRAM was described in Section 5.2.3. We used Nassimi and Sahni's algorithm [NaS81], below, in proving Theorem 5.11:

```
{computation of prefixes: Processor Pᵢ}
write(Mᵢ) in Rᵢ
for  d ← 0  to  log(n-1)  do
    if  iₐ = 1  then  Mᵢ ← Mᵢ * R_{i⊕d}
    Rᵢ ← Rᵢ * R_{i⊕d}
```

The procedure is as follows: neighbouring processors begin by computing their prefixes, then processors at a distance of 2, then 4, and so on, with i_d being the dth bit of i and $i \oplus d$ the index i in which the dth bit has been complemented. Processor P_i writes to memory cells of indices $i \oplus d$ where $i \oplus d$ belongs to H_i. It follows that the same algorithm can be executed on a HypercubeRAM. We have therefore proved the result below.

Theorem 5.30

Computation of prefixes on an EREW HRAM HypercubeRAM consisting of n processors can be executed in time $O(\log n)$.

The result – and the algorithm that is used to obtain it – are very important in practice. Prefix computation is used on hypercube SIMD machines (Connection Machine, for example) as a basic operation. It is called Scan. We shall come back to this in Chapter 16.

However, Theorem 5.30 does not directly correspond to Theorem 5.11, as the operations carried out in it are fine-grain, whereas Theorem 5.11 relates to operations of any granularity (*see* Section 5.1.3 for a definition of granularity). To obtain an equally strong result on a HypercubeRAM, a tool based on Brent's lemma (Lemma 5.1) is needed – the lemma can be used to write coarse-grain algorithms on the basis of fine-grain algorithms. Unfortunately, directly generalizing from the result is false – only fine-grain computations carried out on a neighbouring processor can be grouped together in coarse grain on another processor, and it is not always possible to do this. However, where all the processors are working on the same computation, a natural extension of Brent's lemma is as follows.

Lemma 5.31

Let there be a given HypercubeRAM model. If a parallel algorithm requires t time units on a HypercubeRAM with m processors and executes mt operations to solve a given problem, there is an algorithm with p processors that solves the same problem and whose execution time is less than or equal to $O(\frac{mt}{p})$.

Proof

This is based on the recursive construction of a hypercube (*see* Section 4.1.2). Write $m = 2^r$ and $p = 2^q$ and consider the initial hypercube as a hypercube with 2^q computation nodes, each of which is a hypercube of size 2^{r-q}. It then suffices to simulate on a single hypercube of p processors the computations executed on the sub-cube of size

$m/p = 2^{r-q}$. Since, by hypothesis, every processor is active at every moment, the result follows.

The above lemma is applied in practice and corresponds to the concept of a *virtual* *processor* on the Connection Machine; an algorithm is written for virtual processors and when it is executed, the processors are grouped together on physical processors. However, when the lemma is applied to prefix computation, a cost optimal algorithm is not obtained, as the computation time is then

$$O\left(\frac{n \log n}{p}\right)$$

But a much better result is possible; an algorithm that is directly analogous to Theorem 5.11 can be obtained. All that needs to be done is for the computations on one processor to be executed efficiently – with the best sequential algorithm.

Theorem 5.32

Prefix computation on a EREW HypercubeRAM with p processors can be executed in time:

$$t_{opt} = O(\log n) \text{ if } p = O\left(\frac{n}{\log n}\right)$$

$$t_{opt}(p) = O\left(\frac{n}{p}\right) \text{ if } p \leq O\left(\frac{n}{\log n}\right)$$

Proof

Initially, we can assign n/p consecutive data items to each processor. Prefixes can then be computed locally on each of the processors using a sequential algorithm in time $O(\frac{n}{p})$ and, subsequently, by using Theorem 5.30, prefixes can be computed in time $O(\log p + \frac{n}{p})$ and this proves the theorem.

Batcher's bitonic sort algorithm (*see* Section 5.4.3) has the same property as prefix computation; reads and writes are executed on neighbouring processors for a HypercubeRAM. The result below is obtained by applying the results described in Section 5.4.3 and the method set out in Theorem 5.32.

Theorem 5.33

Batcher's bitonic sort algorithm can be executed on an EREW Hyper-cubeRAM with p processors in time $O(\log^2 n + n\log^2 n/p)$.

Note that this algorithm is not optimal. It was recently improved (theoretically) by Cypher and Plaxton [CyP90], who designed *sharesort*, an algorithm that can be executed in time $O(\log n \log^2 \log n)$ with n processors. Constructing an algorithm in time $O(\log n)$ to sort n data items on a HypercubeRAM with n processors is an open problem.

Theorem of differentiation between HypercubeRAMs

Our study of differentiation between PRAMs can be applied to HypercubeRAMs. Here, too, we shall consider only one CRCW and adopt the same writing policy; two processors are allowed to write simultaneously to a memory cell, if they both write the same value. Of course, an algorithm designed for an EREW HypercubeRAM can be executed on a CREW HypercubeRAM, and an algorithm written for a CREW HypercubeRAM can be executed on a CRCW HypercubeRAM. Theorem 5.28 is used to generalize the differentiation theorem.

Theorem 5.34 (Differentiation theorem)
Assume that the three models have p processors. We then have:

- EREW HypercubeRAM << CREW HypercubeRAM
- CREW HypercubeRAM << CRCW HypercubeRAM

Proof
We shall not provide a detailed proof and the reader is referred to [CoF91a]. Problems that can be used to differentiate between the models are similar to those used for PRAMs.

Simulation theorem for HypercubeRAMs

Now let's look at the extent to which the models differ, by using the simulation definition used above.

Theorem 5.35 (Simulation theorem)
Assume that the three models have p processors. We then have:

- EREW HypercubeRAM = $O(\log p)$.CREW HypercubeRAM
- CREW HypercubeRAM = $O(\log p)$.CRCW HypercubeRAM
- EREW HypercubeRAM = $O(\log p)$.CRCW HypercubeRAM

Proof
The proof of the simulation theorem for PRAMs can be adapted to the case of HRAMs. In contrast to the case for PRAMs, it is not known if the simulations are optimal; the best lower bound known is, in fact, $O(\log \log n)$.

Differentiation between HypercubeRAMs and PRAMs

Clearly, for the same reading and writing policies, a Hypercube is weaker than a PRAM; but this is not the case if that constraint is not applied.

Theorem 5.36 (Differentiation theorem)

Assume that all the models have p processors. We then have:

- EREW HypercubeRAM << EREW PRAM

- CREW HypercubeRAM << CREW PRAM

- CRCW HypercubeRAM << CRCW PRAM

- CREW HypercubeRAM and EREW PRAM cannot be compared

- CRCW HypercubeRAM and CREW PRAM cannot be compared

Proof

The first three inequalities can be proved by selecting problems in which information has to be exchanged between two distant processors on a hypercube. This can be done in constant time on a PRAM and requires $O(\log n)$ steps on a HypercubeRAM.

The truth of the fourth statement is established by stating a problem that can be solved in a shorter time on a CREW HypercubeRAM than on an EREW PRAM. It is left to the reader to show that searching a sorted list for a given element is such a problem. Correspondingly, the problem of finding the OR of all the children on the spanning tree of the Hypercube establishes the truth of the fifth statement.

PRAM simulation by HypercubeRAMs

Simulating a PRAM on a hypercube entails an overhead. At the very least, one has to be able to transfer a data item between the most distant processors, which requires time of the order of the network's diameter (see Chapters 4 and 15), that is, $\log p$. However, simulation algorithms are all based on using sorts and that leads to the result below:

Theorem 5.37

Assume that all the models have p processors. We then have:

- EREW HypercubeRAM = $O(\log p.\log^2\log p)$.EREW PRAM
- CREW HypercubeRAM = $O(\log p.\log^2\log p)$.CREW PRAM
- CRCW HypercubeRAM = $O(\log p.\log^2\log p)$.CRCW PRAM

5.6.   Conclusion

In general, all the studies in this chapter lead to algorithms characterized by very fine-grain structures and very large numbers of processors. These two features are contradictory. The greater the number of processors, the more complex must be the interconnection network and the structure of the shared memory; it follows that the communication times can no longer be neglected, and, therefore, that the amount of computation performed by each processor must be large compared with the amount of data on which it operates. We go into the details of this problem in Chapter 13.

Finally, whilst the complexity results that we have obtained are best-possible – they cannot be improved on – it is important to treat them as theoretical: results obtained in practice will be much poorer.

6

Pipelining – architecture and implementation

In this chapter, we look at pipelining and, more specifically, at the design of pipeline hardware operators and their implementation in software.

6.1 Pipeline architecture

6.1.1 General description

Basic principles

Pipeline architectures have been around in computing for 20 years or so. They are a fundamental form of parallelism and are based on dividing instructions and data into segments, or stages. While one stage is executing, another is being loaded and the input of one is the output of the previous stage. Data flows through the pipeline in a synchronized fashion. Pipelining

149

lends itself very naturally to operations executed on regular data structures such as vectors. The technique is used in one way or another in even the smallest microprocessors.

The term *pipeline* is also used to describe a hardware unit that mirrors the above-mentioned segmentation. It consists of a number of successive stages, separated by registers which save the results of the intermediate stages and data.

Example of a pipeline operator

Executing a set of arithmetic instructions provides an example of how pipelining works. For example, in floating-point addition, execution of the operation can be divided into three stages, each taking more or less the same time. First, the exponents are compared, then the mantissa of the smaller of the two numbers is aligned. Fixed-point addition of the two mantissas can then be performed. Then, the result is normalized and that ends the operation. Figure 6.1 illustrates how this works.

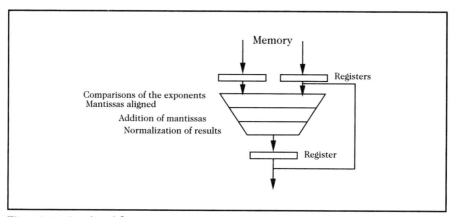

Figure 6.1 Pipelined floating-point addition

The example is unifunctional and static. Of course, pipelines used on supercomputers are more complex.

Formal description

Assume that a set of operations O_1, O_2, ..., O_n is to be executed on a pipeline operator with k stages and that the same operations are to be executed for different data sets. Let τ be the time taken for any particular stage to execute; this is generally the machine's cycle time. The operations are loaded into the pipe one after the other, with a gap of t time units between two consecutive operations, so that when the ith stage executes the ith phase of operation O_j, the $(i-1)^{th}$ stage executes the $(i-1)^{th}$ phase of O_{j-1}.

The first result is obtained after $k\tau$ time units – the initialization time the pipeline needs to begin operating. Other results are produced at the rate of one new result every τ time units.

The time taken to execute all the operations is $t = (k-1)\tau + n\tau$. $(k-1)\tau$ is called the *latency time*.

6.1.2   Performance characteristics of pipelining

Simple and regular operations

Definition 6.1
The speed-up S_k is the relation between execution time on a pipeline and the time taken to execute n operations on a usual scalar processor $(nk\tau)$:

$$S_k = \frac{t_1}{t_k} = \frac{nk}{k + n - 1}$$

Theorem 6.1, which explains the importance of pipeline architectures, can be deduced from the definition.

Theorem 6.1
The speed-up of a pipeline with k stages tends towards k, when n, the number of operations performed, tends towards infinity.

This may seem almost miraculous. Computations are executed k times faster (asymptotically) without any further elements being added. Theoretically, the more stages there are in the pipe, the greater the desired speed-up. Obviously, there is a limit to this. And there are two factors that limit performance – the fact that it is difficult to divide an operation into a set of consecutive sub-operations and the fact that the successive stages have to be synchronized.

Definition 6.2
A pipeline's efficiency is the relation between actual and ideal speed-up:

$$e_k = \frac{S_k}{k} = \frac{n}{n + k - 1}$$

Theoretically, the longer the sets of operations processed in the pipeline, the more efficient it is.

The *throughput* r, defined as the number of operations carried out per second, is a measurement of pipeline performance:

$$r = \frac{n}{t} = \frac{n}{\left(k + n - 1\right)\tau}$$

Asymptotically, the speed $r_\infty = \frac{1}{\tau}$ is achieved.
Establishing the number of data items at which mid-point performance is surpassed is also useful – the $n_{1/2}$ *factor*. It is easily computed [HoJ81]:

$$\frac{n_{1/2}}{\left(k + n_{1/2} - 1\right)\tau} = \frac{1}{2} \text{ which yields } n_{1/2} = \left(k - 1\right)\tau$$

Note that the $n_{1/2}$ factor is equal to the latency time. Figure 6.2 provides an illustration of this.

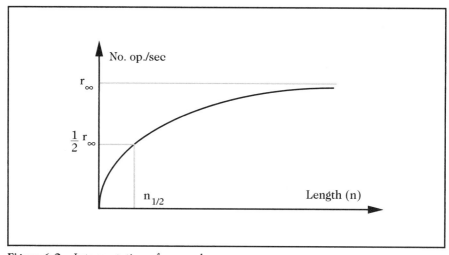

Figure 6.2   Interpretation of $n_{1/2}$ and r_∞

The effect that loading memory has on performance is also a very important parameter. The relation between the number of elementary operations and the number of memory references is defined as a pipeline's *computation intensity*. Solutions with the greatest possible intensity are sought.

Using pipelines with more complex operations

The pipelining technique described above was for a regular operation such as the sum of two vectors. In a more general operation, each stage does not necessarily take the same time to pass through the pipe. Let t_i be the time taken by the ith stage and t_e be the sum of all the time periods for all the stages. An additional period of time, t_r, in which the intermediary stages are completed, is also required. The maximum time that has to be considered in order for each stage to complete is $t_e + t_r$. The clock cycle in the pipeline can be selected as being $\tau \geq t_e + t_r$. Actual speed-up is:

$$S_k^n = \frac{n \sum_{i=1}^{k} t_i}{(k+n-1)(t_r + t_e)}$$

$$S_k^\infty = \frac{\sum_{i=1}^{k} t_i}{t_r + t_e} < k$$

In a pipeline such as this, speed-up is strictly less than k – and the more irregular the stages are, the more this is the case. In an ideal pipeline, speed-up is greater than 1 whatever the length of the vector. On the other hand, if the actual time for each stage to complete is taken into account, the vectors to be processed have a minimum length below which pipelining entails larger overheads than using a scalar functional unit that is not pipelined. The following formula yields the minimum length n:

$$n > \frac{(k-1)(t_r + t_e)}{\sum_{i=1}^{k} t_i - (t_r + t_e)}$$

The term 'superscalar'

Many current microprocessors are *superscalar*, that is, the number of functional units is duplicated, so that several instructions can be executed per clock cycle. The term 'superscalar' derives from the fact that the performance of such machines increases more than linearly with the relevant time period.

6.1.3   Chaining pipelines

Chaining without conflicts

In the same way that an operator can be pipelined, several operators can be chained in a pipeline. For example, the following describes what would happen if an algorithm for a multiplication followed by an addition had to be pipelined:

```
for  i ← 1  to  n
    Z(i) ← a*X(i) + Y(i)
```

Figure 6.3 illustrates one solution based on a very simple adder and multiplier, both of which take time τ. Transfers from registers to memory also last one time period. Loading and storing (written *ld* and *st* respectively) can be executed simultaneously, as long as they use different inputs. Below we provide a detailed description of how this operator is pipelined.

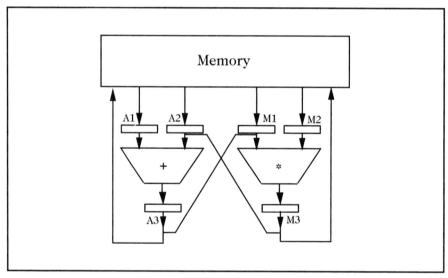

Figure 6.3   Chained multiplication and addition operators

First, the scalar a is loaded into one of the multiplier's input registers (M2, for example). The first element of the vector x is loaded into the other register, and the multiplication can then be carried out. The result a*x(1) is ready to receive y(1), which must already have been loaded in the adder's input register A1 (with the other input kept for the multiplier's output). The process is repeated, at maximum efficiency, until all the computations have been completed (Figure 6.4).

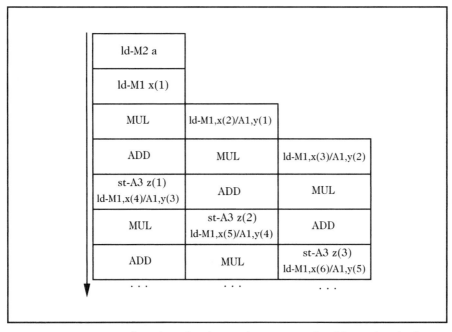

Figure 6.4 Execution of an algorithm for pipelining a simple adder and multiplier

Reduction operator

Now we want to pipeline a reduction algorithm:

```
s ← 0
for  i ← 1  to  n
    s ← s + X(i)
```

It is assumed that there is a hard-wired addition unit. The problem here lies in chaining a succession of computations. It can be seen from a detailed breakdown of the procedure (see the initial steps in Figure 6.5) that the problem cannot be pipelined in the same way as a usual operator can, because of the conflict on the variable s. X(1) is loaded during the first stage. The computation then begins to lead to the result s being partially updated, while X(2) is being loaded at the same time. The new computation should have s as its operand. But it is not yet available, because it has not yet left the pipe.

The solution lies at software level. Because there are three stages, the partial results are available once every 3τ. So the three results s1, s2 and s3 have to be calculated and inserted in the operator. This is referred to as *unrolling the loop*. If, for the sake of simplicity, it is assumed that n is a multiple of 3, the following algorithm is obtained:

```
s1 ← 0 and s2 ← 0 and s3 ← 0
for  i ← 1  to  n/3
    s1 ← s1 + X(3*i-2)
    s2 ← s2 + X(3*i-1)
    s3 ← s3 + X(3*i)
end for
s ← s1 + s2 + s3
```

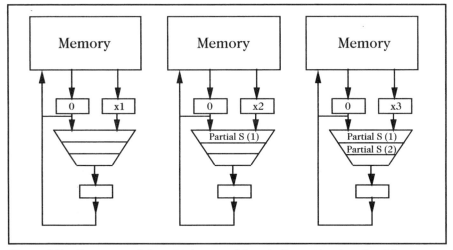

Figure 6.5   Execution of the initial steps of the pipeline reduction algorithm

Some machines have a hard-wired operator to compute, for example, scalar products (also a reduction operator, based on cascading a multiplier and an adder).

6.1.4   Pipelining instructions

So far, we have implicitly considered the same instructions for different data sets and have only used pipelining for data, but it can also be used for instructions. Figure 6.6 illustrates how, generally, an instruction is executed.

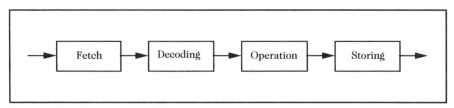

Figure 6.6   Sequence in which an instruction is executed

In pipelining, processing of the first instruction is initialized and, when the first instruction has completed its first stage (fetch), processing of the second instruction begins. Similarly, the third instruction begins when the second instruction enters the second stage and the first instruction begins its third stage – and so on, with all the segments of the pipe active and with each working on a different instruction (Figure 6.7).

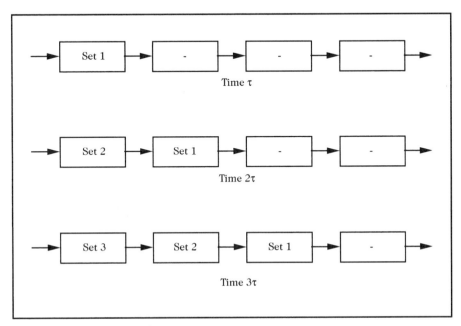

Figure 6.7   Instructions flowing through a pipe

In pipelining instructions, the problem arises as to which instruction is to be executed next. The simplest solution is to anticipate execution of an instruction by loading the instruction that directly follows it in memory. Clearly, if the instruction being worked on is a branch, the program counter, which indicates the location of instructions in memory, will no longer point to the right instruction. The simplest solution is to drain the pipe and reinitialize it, but that entails a significant loss of time when the pipe is reactivated. Below, we look at several methods that have been suggested for overcoming the problem.

Delayed branch is one such method and it provides a simple solution. It works as follows: the job that has been started must be completed, rather than the flow through the pipe being interrupted. The idea here is not to discover whether or not there is a branch instruction, but systematically to execute a (fixed) number of instructions before the branch executes. And that means there is greater control over the microcode.

Another solution is to add special instructions for computations that are executed frequently (for example, computing the minimum of two numbers, which generates a break in the sequence). From this point of view, processing instructions on vectors is of particular interest, as the time taken to execute the instruction is much longer than the time taken to decode it. We shall return to this in Chapter 7.

To conclude this section, we should point out that controlling interrupts poses even greater problems. An interrupt triggers a context switch, which is incompatible with a delayed branch. The only simple solution is to drain the pipe and fill it again.

6.1.5   Hardware design for a pipeline operator

General method

A scalar operator can be changed into a pipelined operator as follows:

- Establish the frequency with which sets of data flow into and results flow out of the pipe. Let τ be the relevant time period.

- Break the scalar operator down into computation stages of approximately time τ. If necessary, the time period should be adjusted to the maximum time of each stage. Where the operator's global time is less than τ there is obviously no point in pipelining it. If the operator cannot be broken down into stages of approaching time τ, find a way of dividing it so that its time is a multiple of τ.

- Insert a register between each stage of the computation, so that all the information passing through it can be stored.

- Synchronize all the registers with a clock time period of τ. The data will be fed into the pipe every τ cycles.

Figure 6.8 illustrates an operator f, which has been broken down into stages A, B and C, all of which take time τ.

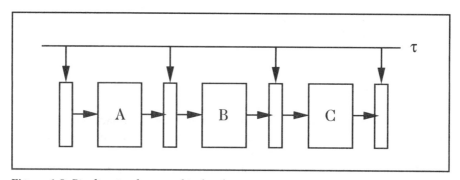

Figure 6.8 Pipeline implemented in hardware

Stages taking different amounts of time

Let's look at an operator g, where one stage of the computation is a multiple of the clock time period. For example, assume that stage B above lasts 2τ. The solution (*see* Figure 6.9) is to duplicate stage B and to alternate activation of its input registers, which, if based on a clock time period of τ, can be very easily implemented in hardware.

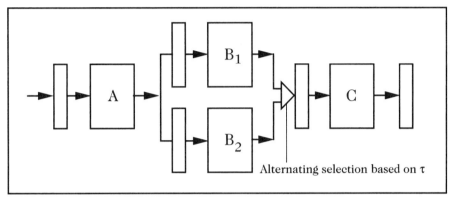

Figure 6.9 Implementation in hardware of the operator g

Multifunction pipeline

The problem here is one of designing an operator that is capable of implementing several functions. Imagine the simple example of two operators, f1 and f2, both of which can be broken down into three stages, all lasting time τ, such that only the middle stages are different. In Figure 6.10, the middle stage, B, implements f1 or f2, according to a given code condition which has been fed into the pipe with the input in order to select f1 or f2.

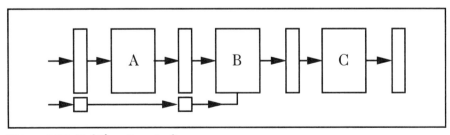

Figure 6.10 Multifunction pipeline

If matters are made a little more complex, by increasing the number of functions that are to be implemented on the one hand and the amount of time taken by each stage on the other, it obviously becomes extremely difficult to implement the operator. A software solution to the problem has to be devised.

6.2   Implementation of pipelining in software

6.2.1   Introduction

The user views pipeline operators differently from the designer. The user has to deal with a permanently fixed set of conditions. Generally, operators are multifunctions and it is difficult to know the 'right' moment to apply a new function to a new data set. Efficient programming (in the absence of optimal programming) of pipelining is the subject of this section.

6.2.2   Allocation tables

Definition

The busy/idle status of various resources needs to be known, so that collisions that may occur when a set of operations is pipelined can be avoided. An *allocation table* is a basic automatic control device used in pipelining. It is a convenient formal device that establishes resources' busy/idle status as a function of clock time periods for a given stage of pipelining. One way of representing this is to use a table (showing resources as a function of clock time periods) and to place an allocation symbol – grey shading, for example – in the cell (i, j) when resource i is needed by time period j.

Examples

Above, we described how a floating-point adder is implemented in hardware. The first stage, called *denorm*, involves comparing exponents and shifting the mantissa. The second stage, which is executed by the ALU, involves adding the mantissas that have been shifted. In the third stage, the result is normalized. Each of the three stages is executed independently of the others. The allocation table for this process is illustrated in Figure 6.11. A shaded cell indicates that a resource is busy at a given moment.

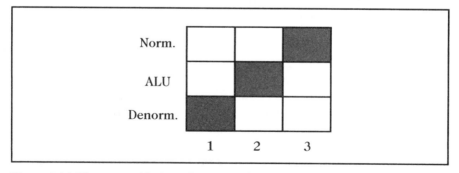

Figure 6.11 Allocation table for a three-stage floating-point adder

To multiply two floating-point numbers, the exponents have to be added, which is performed by the ALU, the mantissas multiplied, which can be executed at the same time as the exponents are added, and the result normalized. Multiplication is normally executed by the ALU in a separate cycle, which generally lasts several clock time periods (three in the example). The allocation table for the above process is shown in Figure 6.12.

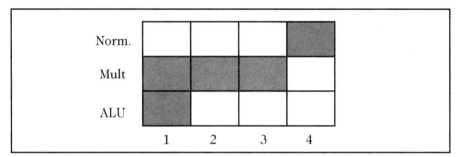

Figure 6.12. Allocation table for a floating-point multiplier

Using an allocation table

Assume that there is a conflict of access to resources, when two different operations that are to be executed in the same pipe are allocated the same stage at the same moment. An adder pipeline is ideal, in that several instances of the addition can be chained without any risk of collision. By contrast, with multipliers, new data sets begin to flow only at a rate of once every three clock time periods, so that conflicts can be avoided when mantissas are multiplied.

In practice, to discover whether a new instance of the operator can be fed at any given moment into the pipe, the base pattern is shifted and overlaid on the allocation table. Let us now look at this using a more complex example.

Consider a single operator that performs a floating-point multiplication followed by an addition. The hardware resources, normalization and the ALU are all shared. The allocation table for the new operator is illustrated in Figure 6.13. We shall see later that this operation acts as a basis for many other operations.

Of course, the constraints imposed by the multiplication of the mantissas remain. Furthermore, as some cycles (norm and ALU) are used several times, a way of ensuring that a conflict will not arise between floating-point multiplication on one data set and floating-point addition on another has to be found. To this end, the basic pattern of the table will be highlighted and overlaid on the time periods. Because the mantissas are being multiplied, a new data set cannot be fed into the pipe until three clock periods have elapsed. What happens when a new data set is released at that moment can be seen clearly from Figure 6.14 – a conflict during the normalization stage.

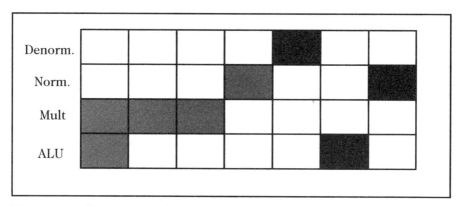

Figure 6.13 Allocation table for a multiplication-addition series

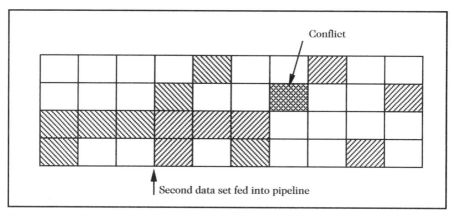

Figure 6.14 Chaining of two instances of multiplication-addition

If the second data set is fed into the pipe one clock period later, no conflict arises. And it can be seen that releasing a new data set four clock periods later does not cause a new conflict (Figure 6.15).

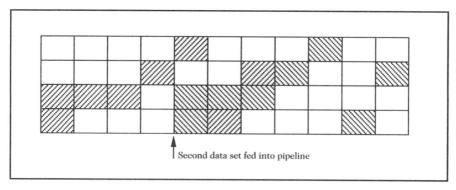

Figure 6.15 Chaining of two instances of multiplication-addition

Pipelining simultaneous addition and multiplication operator

The operator above performed a multiplication followed by an addition (of type a*x+y). The multiplication had to end before the addition could begin. The performance of the pipeline is $k\tau+k'(n-1)\tau$; with k=7, k'=4 this gives $3\tau + 4n\tau$.

Whether this is the best possible result for chaining n multiplication-additions is questionable. The computations can be organized differently if the constraint of only beginning the addition when the multiplication has ended (see Figure 6.16) is removed.

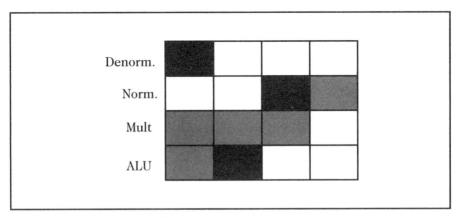

Figure 6.16 Allocation table for a multiplication-addition series

The solution to chaining n multiplication-additions is first to perform a multiplication, then (n–1) parallel multiplication-additions and then the last addition. As Figure 6.17 shows, the resource blocking the process is the mantissa multiplier and the performance $3n\tau$ is reached asymptotically.

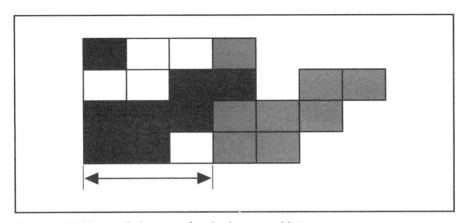

Figure 6.17 'Optimal' chaining of multiplication-additions

6.2.3   Collision vectors

Description

A collision vector can be used to execute automatically the manipulations that were performed manually on allocation tables.

Definition 6.3

The collision vector C that is associated with a pipelined operator is a binary vector whose i^{th} component indicates whether there is a conflict if data is released after i time cycles. Its value is 1 if there is a conflict and 0 if not. Its length is the latency time (the number of stages minus 1).

In other words:

- $C(i) = 1$ if two operations that begin at stages 0 and i result in a collision,
- $C(i) = 0$ if not.

The collision vector is 110 in the example of floating-point multiplication above. A new multiplication can be started after three time cycles, but not after one or two.

Control algorithm

The collision vector is shifted by one bit position from right to left. The leftmost bit that is being controlled is lost and 0 is the new rightmost bit. The way the collision vector works is as follows: if the leftmost bit is 0, that is, if a new data set is fed into the pipe, this state has to be overlaid on the initial collision vector by executing a logical OR.

The collision vector is loaded into a shift register R, one bit position to the left, to indicate whether collisions may occur (*see* Figure 6.18). With each cycle, the shift register is shifted one position to the left and the cell shows whether a collision may occur. The shift function of the register R is written $\Delta(R)$ and 0 replaces the rightmost position.

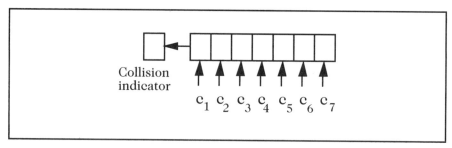

Figure 6.18   Illustration of collision vector in shift register R

For example (*see* Figure 6.19), an attempt is made to discover when to feed data sets into the pipe on the basis of the collision vector 1001011 [Sto87]. Because the first bit is 1, feeding the data in is not allowed in the first phase. The new status is 0010110, and the first bit is 0. Feeding in the new data sets is allowed and the new status is represented by 0101100 or 1001011 = 1101111.

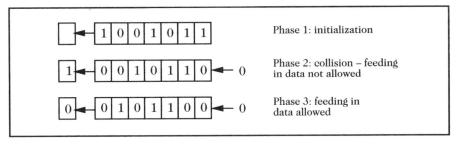

Phase 1: initialization

Phase 2: collision – feeding in data not allowed

Phase 3: feeding in data allowed

Figure 6.19   Controlling collisions

Controlling a simple, general pipeline such as the example used can be described as follows:

```
for t ← 1 to ∞
    if request then
        if R(1) = 0 then request granted
            R ← Δ(R) U C
        if R(1) = 1 then request deferred by one cycle
            R ← Δ(R)
    else R ← Δ(R)
```

It can be seen that the request's maximum latency time is less than or equal to (k–1).

Controlling multifunction pipelines

Consider Stone's example of a floating-point addition and multiplication, whose collision vectors are C_A = 110000 and C_M = 10000000 respectively [Sto87].

The following four situations are possible: addition, followed by an addition or multiplication, and multiplication, followed by an addition or multiplication. Four collision vectors consisting of the following are created:

C_{AA} = 1000000

C_{AM} = 00000000

C_{MA} = 11010000

C_{MM} = 110000

To describe control of the pipeline, two shift registers, RA and RM of size (k–1) are needed, where k is the maximum number of stages for each individual operator (8 in this case). A control algorithm for a multifunction pipeline is obtained by generalizing the control algorithm for a simple pipeline:

```
for t ← 1 to ∞
    if request A then
        if RA(1) = 0 then request granted
            RA ← Δ(RA) U C_AA
            RM ← Δ(RM) U C_AM
        else request deferred by one cycle
            RA ← Δ(RA) and RM ← Δ(RM)
    if request M then
        if RM(1) = 0 then request granted
            RA ← Δ(RA) U C_MA
            RM ← Δ(RM) U C_MM
        else request deferred by one cycle
            RA ← Δ(RA) and RM ← Δ(RM)
    if no request then
        RA ← Δ(RA) and RM ← Δ(RM)
```

6.2.4   Increasing a pipeline's performance

State diagram

The strategy adopted so far has been greedy; in other words, a request is executed as quickly as possible. Of course, this is not necessarily the best strategy.

Take the above example of a collision vector 1001011 and construct a diagram of all the states that are possible, if a new operation begins at any possible moment. A new operation can be fed into the pipe at moments 2, 3 and 5:

$$t=2 \quad R \leftarrow \Delta^2(R) \cup C = 01011 \cup 1001011 = 1101111$$
$$t=3 \quad R \leftarrow \Delta^3(R) \cup C = 1011 \cup 1001011 = 1011011$$
$$t=5 \quad R \leftarrow \Delta^5(R) \cup C = 11 \cup 1001011 = 1101011$$

The process is repeated for each new state that is possible. A graph is then plotted in which the vertices are the states and the arcs the changes to them, labelled with time periods (see Figure 6.20).

The cycles of the state graph have to be considered. The *utilization ratio* (that is, the number of operations that can be initialized per clock period) of each cycle is established:

$$\tau = \frac{\text{number of vertices}}{\text{sum of the weight of the arcs}}$$

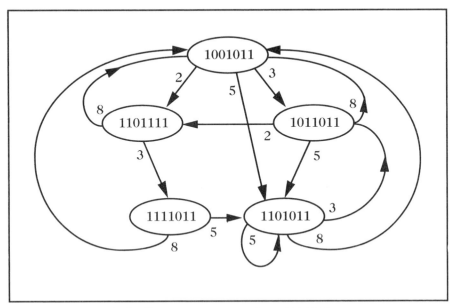

Figure 6.20   Graph of collision states starting from 1001011

The maximum performance is obtained for the cycle with the best utilization ratio. In this case, the best one can obtain is four results every 13 time periods (*see* Figure 6.21) for the cycle 2, (3, 5, 3, 2)$^\infty$.

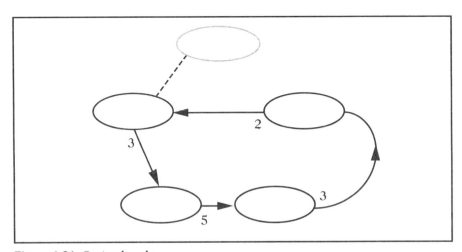

Figure 6.21   Optimal cycle

Deferred release

Note that executing the pipeline used as an example above means that the flow through the pipe is optimal. This is not always the case. It is advisable on some occasions to delay the release of new data sets. Let k be the number of stages in a pipeline and q the greatest number of cells allocated along rows of the allocation table. It is not difficult to see that speed-up is less than or equal to $\frac{k}{q}$ and that the utilization ratio is $\frac{1}{q}$. If $\tau < \frac{1}{q}$ then $\tau' = \frac{1}{q}$ can be obtained by adding a time period (thereby increasing the pipeline's length).

For example, consider the allocation table in Figure 6.22. Its state graph is illustrated in Figure 6.23.

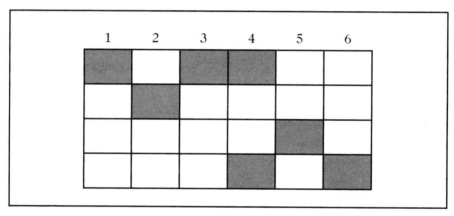

Figure 6.22 Example of an allocation table

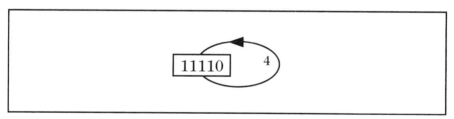

Figure 6.23 State graph

The best ratio is obtained when data sets are released every five cycles. The result can be improved by inserting a delay, referred to as a *bubble*, on the first row between the third and fourth stages. A new table, illustrated in Figure 6.24, is obtained.

To conclude, it should be noted that a solution, which avoids conflicts, is obtained by releasing two consecutive executions every 6 clock cycles – as shown in the state graph in Figure 6.25. The performance can be obtained on the basis of a greedy cycle (data sets released after one, then five cycles) or much more simply, by releasing a new data set every three cycles.

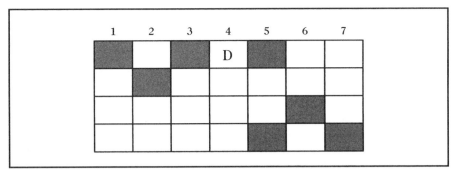

Figure 6.24   New allocation table after delay has been used

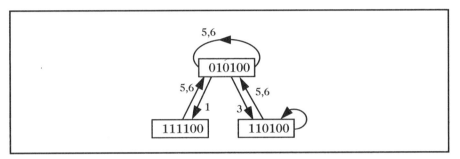

Figure 6.25   State graph after a bubble has been used

6.3   Conclusion

A great deal of research has been conducted on pipeline operators. Further information on the subject can be found in the works of Kogge [Kog81], Herscovici [Her86], Hockney and Jesshope [HoJ81], Hwang and Briggs [HwB84] and Stone [Sto87]. Indeed, pipelines have an importance that extends beyond computer architecture. The principle behind pipelining can be used in all fields where faster repeated processing of data is required.

We have seen that with a pipeline operator consisting of k stages, it can be hoped that speed-up approaching k can be achieved. And, by contrast with parallel architectures, it can be done without duplicating computations. The use of pipeline operators therefore has a special place in studying parallel architectures and algorithms.

Pipeline operators have become very popular in computing and computer science. All modern computing devices use them and the increase in the performance capabilities of microprocessors is due to a large extent to them. A type of computer known as a vector computer has been developed to exploit them to the full. The description of such computers and their implementation is the subject of Chapter 7.

7

Vectorization

In this chapter, we look at the basic principles that govern vector architectures. We demonstrate that they enable a transition to be made from scalar to super-vector modes, resulting in substantially improved performance. A few simple examples are provided to illustrate the principles involved – matrix-vector multiplication, basic linear algebra procedures and, more specifically, matrix multiplication.

7.1   Vector processors

There are several ways pipelining can be implemented to increase the execution speed of operations on regular data items, such as the elements of a vector. About twenty years ago, some manufacturers began to produce vector computers that were capable of processing operations on vectors efficiently.

7.1.1　Vectors

A vector is an ordered set of n elements. Each element is a floating-point number (of 32, 64 or 80 bits), an integer, an element of Boolean algebra or a character. A vector processor processes operations that have vectors as operands. There are several types of vector and transformations of them can be classified as followed:

```
Vector → Vector
    VSIN      B(I) ← sin(A(I))
    VSQR      B(I) ← (A(I))²
Vector → Scalar
    VSUM      S ← A(1) + ... + A(N)
    VMAX      S ← max (A(1), ..., A(N))
Vector/Vector → Vector
    VADD      C(I) ← A(I) + B(I)
    VAND      C(I) ← A(I) and B(I)
Vector/Scalar → Vector
    VSMUL     B(I) ← S*A(I)
```

The following example, drawn from the work of Hwang and Briggs [HwB84], demonstrates the importance of vector instructions. Consider the following iteration:

```
for  i←1 to  n
    A(i) ← B(i) + C(i)
    B(i) ← 2*A(i+1)
```

When executed on a scalar computer, the program is implemented as follows:

```
   initialization  I←1
10 read B(I)
   read C(I)
   add B(I) + C(I)
   store A(I) ← B(I) + C(I)
   read A(I+1)
   multiply  2 * A(I+1)
   store  B(I) ← 2 * A(I+1)
   increment   I ← I + 1
   if I ≤ N goto 10
```

On a vector processor, the code is simply as follows:

```
A(1:n) ← B(1:n) + C(1:n)
T(1:n) ← A(2:n+1)
B(1:n) ← 2*T(1:n)
```

7.1.2   Architectural model

We shall take a general-purpose vector computer as our architectural model (*see* Figure 7.1). This kind of computer is designed to execute vector instructions efficiently. Without going into the details of its internal organization, a vector computer has:

- a pipeline control unit that can decode one arithmetic instruction per cycle;

- an arithmetic unit, with one pipelined floating-point adder and one pipelined floating-point multiplier, consisting of p_+ and p_* stages of a cycle respectively;

- a series of vector registers that enable direct input to each of the pipeline operators. Processing is executed in two stages, which may be called 'memory access' and 'computation'. Vector registers act as an intermediate stage, like buffers. And there are some input and output scalar registers for floating-point operators;

- a shared memory, requiring c read and write cycles, access to which can be pipelined. Figure 7.2 is a diagram of the vector components of the model.

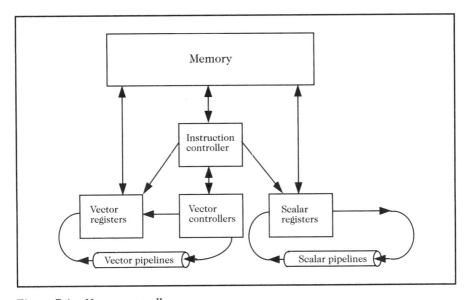

Figure 7.1   Vector controller

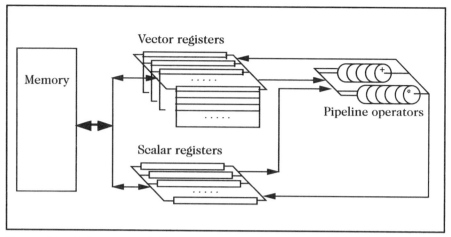

Figure 7.2   Reference model for vector architecture

Each of the devices must perform well enough not to slow down the computer as a whole. In particular, it is essential that memory access is such that operands can be routed and results stored as and when they are used or produced. An architecture with this property is said to be *balanced* and obtaining this property is a matter of priority, if maximum advantage is to be gained from a vector architecture. Balance should be achieved by using pipelining on any unit that could slow down computation speed.

7.2   From scalar to supervector mode

In this section, we look at the time that can be saved by using a vector computer for numerical computations. We demonstrate that optimal implementation of a very simple program can lead to impressive speed-up.

7.2.1   Preliminary example

Let's look at the potential for performing computations on the reference architecture described above. The system's cycle time will be used as the unit of time. Consider how the following instruction is executed in different modes:

```
for  i ← 1  to  n
    X(i) = a*X(i) + Y(i)
```

X and Y are stored vectors of size n.

Scalar mode

Consider first the worst case. The execution time of the scalar instruction $x = \alpha x + y$, where α, x and y are real numbers stored in memory. Reading the operands requires 3c cycles, multiplication p_*, addition p_+ and writing the result c. The total time is therefore:

$$t_s = 3c + p_+ + p_* + c$$

For n of these instructions, the time is n times greater. A function such as this does not use any of the vectorial possibilities of the architecture in question. This is a purely scalar mode and its performance is limited. For example, if we take 10 nanoseconds (ns) as the average cycle time, a memory access time of c=10, p_+=4 and p_*=5, a value of t_s of around 500 ns is obtained, that is, a performance of 4 megaflops for this operation.

Vector mode

Each stage (memory access and arithmetic operations) of the example under consideration can be pipelined. Clearly, when execution of a*X(i) has ended, execution of its addition to Y(i) must begin.

As Figure 7.3 shows, execution can be broken down into as many operations as there are operators, with all the intermediate results being stored in memory. Total execution time is broken down into loading (a scalar and two pipelined vectors), multiplication and addition of the pipelined vectors and storing (pipelining) the vector result. This is equivalent to:

$$t_v = c + 2(c + n{-}1) + (p_* + n - 1) + (p_+ + n - 1) + (c + n {-}1) = 5n + k$$

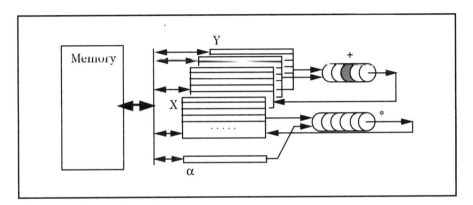

Figure 7.3 Vector mode

As mentioned earlier, the longer the vectors, the better the performance and, asymptotically, a result is obtained every five cycles. Under the same conditions as above, a performance of around 40 megaflops can be obtained. This is called *vector mode*.

Supervector mode

The above performance can be enhanced even more by chaining pipelines in order to process a set of vector instructions. The instructions overlap, that is, reading from, computation of and writing to previous instructions can be executed at the same time. It could be said that this is a kind of pipelining of pipelines. This can only be done if all the chained functions are different. If they are, the time taken is:

$$t_{sv} = 3c + p_* + p_+ + c + n - 1 = n + k'$$

which means that, asymptotically, one result is produced every cycle and that performances of around 200 megaflops can be achieved. This is called supervector mode (*see* Figure 7.4).

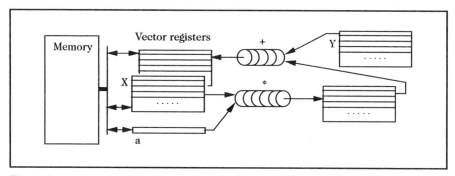

Figure 7.4   Supervector mode

Of course, performance as high as this can only be obtained with particularly optimized programs, as there are many obstacles that need to be overcome.

7.2.2   Obstacles to avoid in vector mode: data dependency

General description

Vector mode (and this is even more true of supervector mode) depends on the computer being able to produce one intermediate result per cycle. There are two main difficulties to be overcome in vector operations.

First, data must be routed quickly enough for it to be fed into arithmetic pipelines. It is therefore best to use vector registers as much as possible and transfer between memory and registers as little as possible. And, where data items are stored in the same memory bank, an additional period of time is required for them to be read. However, they can be ordered in such a way as to minimize access conflicts.

Secondly, chaining arithmetic operations and data transfer between memory and registers leads to programming constraints in the program itself.

Take, for example, vectorizing a simple iteration. There must be no instructions in it that cause control breaks, such as input/output, jumps or calls to subroutines. And vectorizing an iteration will prove difficult if data items are dependent on each other. A distinction is made between *anti-dependency* and *cross-dependency*.

Anti-dependency

Anti-dependency occurs when an iteration uses the result of a previous iteration's computation. The most common examples are recurrences or scalar products:

```
{two examples of anti-dependency}
for  i ← 1  to  n
   X(i) ← a*X(i-1) + c
for  i ← 1  to  n
   S ← S + X(i)*Y(i)
```

Comment

The second iteration is what is called a *reduction*. This kind of operation performs well on some machines.

Cross-dependency

Cross-dependency occurs when an element used by an iteration can be modified by a subsequent iteration:

```
{examples of cross-dependency on vector X}
for  i ←  1  to   n
   X(i) ←   3*Y(i) + 2*B(i)
   B(i) ←  X(i+1) * X(i)
```

We shall see in Section 7.3 that certain kinds of dependency can be removed if the program is restructured. Control breaks are another obstacle – by definition, they make vectorization impossible. However, there is an elegant solution to the problem.

Control breaks

Vector processing is particularly suited to regular computations. A *conditional control break* in a program causes a set of computations to become irregular, because the result of the condition needs to be produced before it is possible to know what the subsequent instruction is. To speed up processing, programs have to be restructured so that control breaks can be replaced by several vector instructions. Masking can be used to restructure programs in certain situations. The following provides an example of this:

```
{example of vectorization with masking}
for   i ← 1  to  n
  if  A(i)>0  then    B(i) ← sqrt(A(i))
  else  B(i) ← 0
```

To vectorize the above iteration, a vector computation of the condition below has to be executed:

```
for   i ← 1  to  n
  cond(i) ← A(i)>0
```

If a vector unit of Boolean algebra is available, both vectors sqrt(A(i)) and 0 can be computed:

```
for   i ← 1  to  n
  R1(i) ← sqrt(A(i))
for   i ← 1  to  n
  R2(i) ← 0
```

Then, all that is needed is the following iteration:

```
for   i ← 1  to  n
  B(i) ← (cond(i) and R1(A(i))) or (not (cond(i)) and R2(i))
```

7.3   A simple example of vectorization – matrix-vector multiplication

Let's look at the above again, in the context of the multiplication of a matrix of n rows and m columns by a vector X of size m – one of the most important computations of linear algebra. We write Y=AX.

7.3.1   Standard rows-columns variant

Matrix-vector multiplication and its algorithm

The most common method of matrix-vector multiplication is to multiply each row of A by column X of the vector. The most natural algorithm to use is as follows:

```
{ij variant}
for  i ← 1  to  n
   Y(i) ← 0.0
   for  j ← 1  to  m
        Y(i) ← Y(i) + A(i, j)*X(j)
```

This is the scalar product of each row i of the matrix A multiplied by the vector X, which yields the ith element of the vector Y (*see* Figure 7.5). Clearly, the partial products A(i, j)X(j) can be pipelined in relation to j. By contrast, *reduction* – accumulation of values in Y(i) – is intrinsically scalar, as anti-dependency occurs. The result of an accumulation of the values of one partial product must have left the addition operator before the subsequent accumulation can be executed.

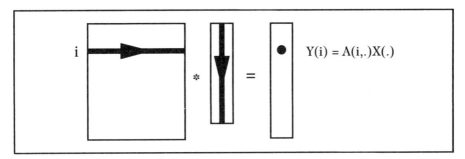

Figure 7.5 ij variant of matrix-vector multiplication, Y=AX

Unrolling iterations

Auto-chaining (or unrolling iterations) can be used to highlight the above problem and to remove the anti-dependency. This generalizes the reduction problem discussed in Section 6.1.3. The procedure involves replacing Y(i) by a number p_+ of variables $B(1),...B(p_+)$, then dividing the iteration from 1 to m into p_+ iterations. B(1) accumulates the values A(i, j)X(j) for j, which, in turn, has a succession of values 1, p_++1, $2p_++1$, and so on.

More generally, the variable B(q) accumulates the values of the indices $q+\lambda p_+$. In reality, each B(q) has the value in the adder's output register. To obtain Y(i), the sum of the B(q) just needs to be calculated. The following pseudocode results:

```
for  i ← 1  to  n
   Y(i) ← 0.0
      for  q ← 1  to  p₊
          B (q) ← 0.0
   for  j ← 1  to  m  in p₊ steps
      for  q ← 1  to  p₊
          B(q) ← B(q) + A(i, j+q-1)*X (j+q-1)
   for  q ← 1  to  p₊
      Y(i) ← Y(i) + B(q)
```

It can be seen that only the fourth iteration poses a problem in terms of vectorization, as it is purely scalar. If m is large compared with p_+ (which, in practice, is the case), one can expect a substantial saving in time.

Comment
The language being used is also relevant here. In Fortran, for example, arrays are stored by column. When elements are accessed by row, two consecutive elements are stored in a number of memory banks that may be different from the size of the column (m in this case). Depending on the value of n and the number of memory banks, memory access conflicts may occur and lead to a serious loss in performance. Specifically, where n is proportional to the number of memory banks, memory access cannot be pipelined and the operating mode is purely scalar. One way of overcoming the problem is to add a fictitious row to the matrix. Stone discusses a number of variations on this theme [Sto87].

7.3.2   'ji' version

A second variant of the multiplication algorithm is obtained by means of a permutation of the iterations' indices i and j. The following is obtained:

```
{ji variant}
for  i ← 1  to  m
   Y(i) ← 0.0
for  j ← 1  to  n
   for  i ← 1  to  m
      Y(i) ← Y(i) + A(i, j)*X(j)
```

In Fortran, the ji algorithm performs better than the other variants. In fact, data is accessed by column in the algorithm. No access conflict arises and access to data can be pipelined. And the basic operation in the third iteration consists of taking a scalar multiple of the vector X and adding it to another vector.

In this variant of the algorithm, each column j of A is multiplied by the scalar X(j), and is part of the partial sum of all the elements of vector Y, as shown in Figure 7.6. It can be seen that the vector Y can be stored in a vector register until the matrix has been multiplied by the vector. A's columns are then loaded one by one into another register, multiplied by a scalar and then accumulated there. All these operations can be pipelined and chained – a supervector operating mode.

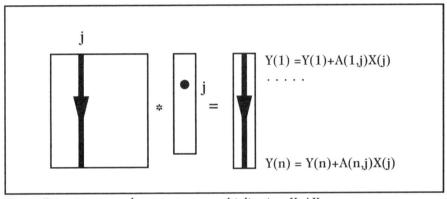

$$Y(1) =Y(1)+A(1,j)X(j)$$
$$\cdots\cdots$$
$$Y(n) = Y(n)+A(n,j)X(j)$$

Figure 7.6   ji variant of matrix-vector multiplication, Y=AX

We shall see in Section 7.3.3 that the operations we have discussed informally, using matrix-vector multiplication, are of fundamental importance in linear algebra.

7.3.3   Dividing iterations into segments

Vector registers can store words of a set length (32, 64 or sometimes 128 bits). When operations have to be carried out on vectors whose size, n, is greater than that of the registers (written vs) – and this is more often than not the case – iterations have to be divided into segments. At a conceptual level, this amounts to replacing the pseudocode:

```
for  i ← 1  to  n
    operation on element i
```

with the pseudocode below, in which the depth of the internal iteration matches the length of the vector registers:

```
for ii ← 1 to n by step vs
    for i ← ii to min(n, ii+vs-1)
        operation on element i
```

The technique can be implemented for both variants of matrix-vector multiplication. Most compilers on vector computers use it to optimize code, without the programmer needing to know anything about the fine structure of the machine. Matrix-vector multiplication is one example of a number of vector computation procedures that are of fundamental importance in linear algebra. We describe it in Section 7.4, using the tools described in this chapter.

7.4   BLAS: Basic linear algebra subroutines

7.4.1   General description of the LINPACK library

Introduction

The main problem the non-specialist programmer faces in computer architecture is striking the right balance between spending a limited amount of time in rewriting, or at least adapting, programs on the one hand and achieving high performance on the other. This explains the development of libraries of modular procedures. The LINPACK project is a good example of the trend in practice [DDD88] [Don88] [DMB79].

LINPACK is a library of numerical procedures, or more specifically, of numerical linear algebra procedures, written in Fortran. There is a specialized variant of the library – EISPACK – for solving problems with eigenvalues. The procedures were designed to be independent of the computer used and to achieve as far as possible maximum efficiency for the majority of computations. Calls to procedures from the LINPACK library are the same as those to other procedures in Fortran.

The names of the procedures are mnemonic and consist of five letters:

- The first letter denotes the type of data in the various matrices – it can be used to distinguish between simple and double-precision real numbers and between simple and double-precision complex numbers.

- The next two letters denote the type of the matrix (general, band, defined, symmetrical, Hermitian, tridiagonal, triangular and so on) or its decomposition (Cholesky, orthogonal, SVD (singular value decomposition) and so on).

- The last two letters denote the type of computation performed on the matrix (with the main types including ordinary factorization with or without condition evaluation, solving linear systems, computing determinants, matrix inversion and decomposition, various matrix-updating methods, matrix transpositions and so on).

For example, SGEFA denotes factorization (FA) of a general matrix (GE) of coefficients with simple-precision real numbers (S). The name of the matrix, the number of rows and columns and any other parameter that is useful to the operation requested are the arguments of the procedure.

Definition of Basic Linear Algebra Subroutines

LINPACK's basic design was heavily influenced by Basic Linear Algebra Subroutines (BLASs), which are basic operating kernels. Anyone who reads the source code of a LINPACK procedure will find it quite easy to locate iterations and clearly delimited logical structures. BLASs contribute to the speed, modularity and clarity of LINPACK subroutines. These are available with BLAS versions (that are written in standard Fortran and that therefore store matrices by column) and provide the user with greater efficiency of execution in many programming environments.

BLASs in the first version of LINPACK relate only to operations on vectors (level 1) and make use of the unrolling iterations technique. This is particularly efficient when used on vector machines. Then, with the advent of parallel machines, BLASs were extended to cover higher levels, BLAS-2 and BLAS-3, which relate to matrix-vector and matrix-matrix multiplication respectively. Let's look at them more closely.

7.4.2   BLAS-1

The example of matrix-vector multiplication above was used to introduce different vector *operating kernels* informally. There are different types of operation for manipulating vectors, depending on the types of data they manipulate and the results they return – multiplication of two vectors yielding a vector, scalar-vector multiplication yielding a vector, vector-vector multiplication yielding a scalar, and so on.

AXPY

The AXPY kernel combines the first two types of result (scalar-vector multiplication yielding a vector and vector-vector multiplication yielding a vector). AXPY stands for AX Plus Y. SAXPY is referred to when single-precision operations are involved and DAXPY for double-precision operations.

```
{AXPY kernel}
  for  i ← 1  to  n
    Z(i) ← a*X(i) + Y(i)
```

This is a level-1 BLAS. If the kernel allows the subprogram to be used in supervector mode, it is referred to as GAXPY.

Dot kernels

The second level-1 BLAS kernel is the sum with accumulation of values, or the dot product. It manipulates vectors and returns a scalar containing the scalar product of the two vectors – in other words, it is a reduction.

```
{dot kernel}
  for  i ← 1  to  n
    s ← s + X(i)*Y(i)
```

7.4.3   Higher-level BLASs

Basic operations with matrices and vectors as arguments are defined in the same way as for BLAS-1: these are BLAS-2, level-2 BLASs. They are broken down into BLAS-1 kernels, as we saw in the example of matrix-vector multiplication.

The main BLAS-2 procedures are as follows:

```
{generalized matrix-vector multiplication}
Y ← α*A*X + β*Y
{row 1 or 2 updated}
A ← α*X.Yᵗ + A
{solution of triangular system}
```

BLAS-3 corresponds to operations such as multiplication of two matrices [DDH90]. It is directly obtained from level 2 by replacing vectors with matrices. It contains matrix multiplication, updating of ranks k and 2k for symmetrical matrices, multiplication of a matrix by a triangular matrix, solutions of triangular systems with several right-hand elements, and so on.

7.4.4   Example of implementing BLASs – matrix multiplication

Let A be an (n, q) matrix and B a (q, m) matrix. Computing the product
C = AB requires the following basic instructions:

$$C(i, j) = C(i, j) + A(i, k) * B(k, j)$$

for i, j, k integers of [1..n], [1..q] and [1..m] respectively.

The same order of the indices i, j and k is generally used on a scalar
computer. In fact, this has little impact on the computation time of the
product, since vector instructions are not used. However, six permutations
of the indices i, j and k of the iterations are possible. The variants described
in the following subsections are obtained. We shall see that, on a vector
computer, the six variants are not equivalent [DGK84].

'Natural' form ijk (and jik variant)

The first of the permutations involves considering the m products of matrix
A multiplied by the columns of vector B (*see* Figure 7.7), which results in
the following:

```
{ijk variant}
for  i ← 1  to  n
   for  j ← 1  to  m
       C(i, j) ← 0.0
       for  k ← 1 to  q
           C(i, j) ← C(i, j) + A(i, k)*B(k, j)
```

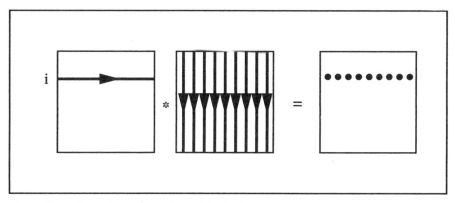

Figure 7.7   ijk variant of matrix multiplication

If BLAS-1 is used, the pseudocode is written as follows:

```
{ijk variant - BLAS 1}
for  i ← 1  to  n
    for  j ← 1  to  m
        C(i, j) ← DOT (row i of A, column j of B)
```

If BLAS-2 is used, the pseudocode is written as follows:

```
{ijk variant - BLAS 2}
for  i ← 1  to  n
    row i of C ← VECT-MAT (row i of A, matrix B)
```

Another possible permutation is to see the product of A and B as successive products of all the rows of A multiplied by a set column of B (*see* Figure 7.8):

```
{jik variant}
for  j ← 1  to  m
    for  i ← 1  to  n
        C(i, j) ← 0.0
        for  k ← 1  to  q
            C(i, j) ← C(i, j) + A(i, k)*B(k, j)
```

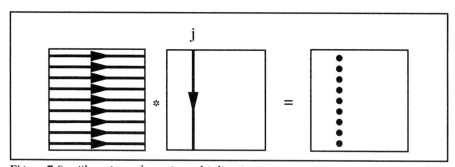

Figure 7.8   jik variant of matrix multiplication

Comment
The ijk and jik variants are both using scalar (dot) products and should not be used on architectures that do not have hard-wired reduction operators.

kij and kji variants

In these two variants, the loop indexed by k becomes the outer loop. The matrix A is searched column by column, so that the outer product of column k of A and row k of B gives a partial sum for the coefficient C_{ij}. In a 'dual' form, easily derived, a row of A is searched by every element of B to contribute to all coefficients of the product matrix.

```
{kij variant}
for i ← 1 to n
    for j ← 1 to m
            C(i, j) ← 0.0
    for k ← 1 to q
        for i ← 1 to n
            for j ← 1 to m
                C(i, j) ← C(i, j) + A(i, k)*B(k, j)
```

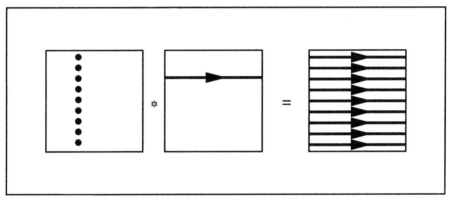

Figure 7.9   kij variant of matrix multiplication

Both variants, kij and kji, use AXPY as their basic kernel. If Fortran is being used, the second variant, kji, should be preferred, as data access is executed by column.

ikj and jki variants

In these last two variants, the loop over k is placed between those over i and j. The two variants, ikj and jki, both use GAXPY as their basic operation – multiples of a set of vectors are accumulated in one vector before it is stored (*see* Figure 7.10). As a result, the jki variant's performance is the best of all six variants. It operates in supervector mode. Furthermore, it should be noted that the matrices are searched in the same direction and that, as a result, they are more efficient than the others, because they require fewer pages.

```
{ikj variant}
for i ← 1 to n
   for j ← 1 to m
      C(i, j) ← 0.0
for i ← 1 to n
   for k ← 1 to q
      for j ← 1 to m
         C(i, j) ← C(i, j) + A(i, k)*B(k, j)
```

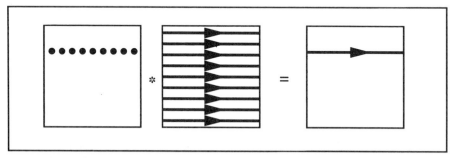

Figure 7.10 ikj variant of matrix multiplication

Where matrices with large dimensions are involved, the columns' lengths may be greater than those of the vector registers, in which case the vectors have to be divided into segments of a length equal to that of the vector registers. The reader is referred to [DGK84] for a detailed description of the procedure.

7.5   Conclusion

Vector computers have played a very important part in the development of parallel computation. The early supercomputers, made in 1975 by Cray and Control Data, were vector computers. Since then, technology has progressed so rapidly that it is now possible for a single circuit to have enough transistors to possess as much power as the early supercomputers, which were huge, with equally huge cooling systems. However, the structure of their architectures has changed little. It is no exaggeration to say that their architectural principles, which are based on intensive use of pipelining and vector computing, had already been developed and were being implemented over 15 years ago.

We have seen that using vector computers efficiently means that algorithms have to be redesigned, in order to reduce dependency between closely related instructions. One very important way of doing this, where a program consists of several nested iterations, is to invert the order of the indices. The technique is based on detailed analysis of the dependencies between instructions and is used in automatic vectorization programs, which are very efficient these days. We described this technique, as applied to matrix multiplication, in detail. However, it should not be inferred too quickly that inverting iterations is always quite so simple. In fact, it may lead to the structure of the program being substantially altered. We shall see this in Chapter 8, where we use it to study and compare several vector variants of Gaussian elimination for solving dense linear systems. The techniques we have just described are the foundations of vectorizing linear algebra algorithms.

Vectorization of linear algebra algorithms

In this chapter, we look at programming linear algebra algorithms on vector architecture – cyclic reduction in computing recurrences, solving tridiagonal linear systems and Gaussian elimination for solving dense systems.

8.1 Review of linear algebra

In this section, we briefly describe Gaussian elimination for solving linear systems with dense matrices.

8.1.1 Gaussian elimination

Gaussian elimination is used to solve non-singular dense linear systems. The initial matrix A is transformed into the product of a lower triangular matrix multiplied by an upper triangular matrix. A solution for the former system is obtained by using back substitution to solve the upper triangular matrix [GoV83]. On many occasions, pivoting is used alongside the above-mentioned technique to ensure stability. But our aim here is to study algorithms for various possible forms of vectorization, rather than to provide a mathematical analysis of their stability. We shall not go into the latter here, but its importance in practice should be underlined.

8.1.2   Description

Assume the system Ax=b, where A is a square n × n matrix and b a vector of size n, is to be solved. The principle is to eliminate the kth unknown x_k of the vector x from all the equations below the kth. This is done by forming suitable linear combinations of the rows of the matrix A, reducing to an upper triangular matrix in n–1 steps.

Gaussian elimination consists of forming a set of matrices $A^{(k)}$ (for k varying from 1 to n–1) as follows. The starting point is the matrix $A^{(1)} = A$. The matrix $A^{(k+1)}$ is obtained from $A^{(k)}$ by using its kth row to reduce to zero the elements on the kth column that lie below the diagonal; in other words, to combine the rows i greater than k with row k. The result of the new elements of row i of step k is written:

$$a^{(k+1)}{}_{ij} = a^{(k)}{}_{ij} - a^{(k)}{}_{ik} * a^{(k)}{}_{kj} / a^{(k)}{}_{kk} \quad \text{for } k<n$$

The term $a^{(k)}{}_{kk}$ therefore has to be non-zero and this condition is true if the determinant of matrix $A^{(k)}$ (which, up to its sign, is equal to the determinant of the initial matrix) is non-zero. Figure 8.1 illustrates one step of the elimination; the shaded area represents those elements that were not modified at step k. Figure 8.2 illustrates step k in progress.

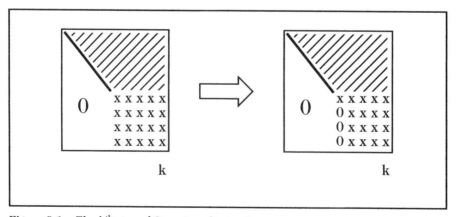

Figure 8.1   The kth step of Gaussian elimination

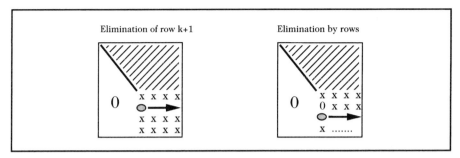

Figure 8.2   Detail of the kth step

The relevant algorithms can be directly deduced from the above:

```
for  k ← 1  to  n-1
   for  i ← k+1  to  n
        coeff ← A(i, k)/A(k, k)
        for  j ← k+1  to  n
             A(i, j) ← A(i, j) - coeff*A(k, j)
```

A variant of this, in which elimination is performed by column, can be easily obtained (*see* Figure 8.3); the iterations of the indices i and j in the algorithm are simply inverted. The pseudocode is as follows:

```
for  k ← 1  to  n-1
   coeff ← 1/A(k, k)
   for  i ← k+1  to  n
        A(i, k) ← coeff*A(i, k)
   for  j ← k+1  to  n
        for  i ← k+1  to  n
             A(i, j) ← A(i, j) - A(i, k)*A(k, j)
```

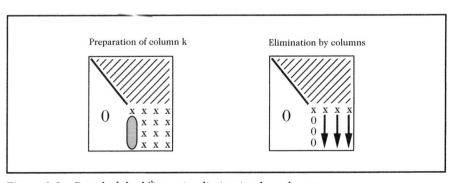

Figure 8.3   Detail of the kth step in elimination by columns

We go into vectorizing Gaussian elimination in detail in Section 8.3. Before that, we describe vector algorithms for two operations that are of fundamental importance in linear algebra – computing linear recurrences and solving tridiagonal systems.

8.2   Cyclic reduction of recurrences

8.2.1   Introductory example

Consider a 3-stage floating-point adder. Suppose that the nth term of the set U_n, defined by recurrence as below (with U_0 and U_1 being given), has to be computed:

$$U_i = U_{i-1} + U_{i-2} \quad \text{for } i = 2, 3, \ldots, n$$

Computation of the value of U_n cannot be pipelined because of the anti-dependency. Let's try to transform the recurrence equation, so that the computation can be pipelined. Thus, if U_{i-1} is replaced by its value, the following is obtained:

$$U_i = 2U_{i-2} + U_{i-3}$$

If U_{i-2} is replaced by its value, the following is obtained:

$$U_i = 3U_{i-3} + 2U_{i-4}$$

The new recurrence equation does not contain any anti-dependencies and so the computation of the value of U_n can be pipelined, as long as there is an operator to multiply by 3 and a shift to multiply by 2. Note that it is easy to generalize this, however many stages p of the floating-point adder there may be. The following may be written:

$$U_i = v_p U_{i-p} + v_{p-1} U_{i-p-1}$$

where v_p is the pth term of this Fibonacci sequence. The ALU's integer adder enables the terms to be computed successively.

8.2.2   Cyclic reduction

General description

Consider a linear recurrence of the order 1:

```
for  i ← 1  to  n
    X(i) ← A(i)*X(i-1) + B(i)
```

Because of the anti-dependency, this cannot be vectorized as it stands. Cyclic reduction involves replacing $X(i-1)$ in the expression for $X(i)$ by its value as a function of $X(i-2)$, then $X(i-2)$ by its value as a function of $X(i-4)$, and so on; repetition of this process leads to indices corresponding to known values, when it is stopped.

Let's describe the procedure in detail, writing the notation in subscripts to ease description. The basic iteration is as follows:

$$X_0 = 0$$
$$X_i = A_i X_{i-1} + B_i \quad \text{for} \quad i > 0$$

We have:

$$X_{i-1} = A_{i-1} X_{i-2} + B_{i-1}$$

and thus

$$X_i = A_i^{(1)} X_{i-2} + B_i^{(1)}$$

with

$$A_i^{(1)} = A_i A_{i-1} \text{ and } B_i^{(1)} = A_i B_{i-1} + B_i$$

Repeating the operation, we get at step k:

$$X_i = A_i^{(k)} X_{i-2^k} + B_i^{(k)} \quad \text{for } k = 0, 1, 2, \ldots, \lceil \log_2(n) \rceil$$

with

$$A_i^{(0)} = A_i \text{ and } B_i^{(0)} = B_i$$

$$A_i^{(k)} = A_i^{(k-1)} A_{i-2^{k-1}}^{(k-1)} \text{ and } B_i^{(k)} = A_i^{(k-1)} B_{i-2^{k-1}}^{(k-1)} + B_i^{(k-1)}$$

Let $m = \lceil \log_2(n) \rceil$. For $k=m$, $X_{i-2^k}=0$ and thus $X_i = B_i^{(k)}$. To compute X_n only $B_n^{(k)}$ has to be computed.

Example of cyclic reduction

To illustrate the technique, take $n=7$, so that $m=3$; the aim is to compute X_7, making the most use of vectorization. By convention, all elements with negative indices are taken to be zero.

$$X_7 = A_7 X_6 + B_7$$
$$= A_7 A_6 X_5 + A_7 B_6 + B_7 = A_7^{(1)} X_5 + B_7^{(1)}$$
$$= A_7^{(1)} A_5^{(1)} X_3 + A_7^{(1)} B_5^{(1)} + B_7^{(1)} = A_7^{(2)} X_3 + B_7^{(2)}$$
$$= A_7^{(2)} A_3^{(2)} X_{-1} + A_7^{(2)} B_3^{(2)} + B_7^{(2)} = A_7^{(3)} X_{-1} + B_7^{(3)}$$

The computation is performed as follows:

First step:

$A_7^{(1)} = A_7 A_6$	$B_7^{(1)} = A_7 B_6 + B_7$
$A_5^{(1)} = A_5 A_4$	$B_5^{(1)} = A_5 B_4 + B_5$
$A_3^{(1)} = A_3 A_2$	$B_3^{(1)} = A_3 B_2 + B_3$
$A_1^{(1)} = A_1 A_0 = 0$	$B_1^{(1)} = A_1 B_0 + B_1 = B_1$

Second step:

$A_7^{(2)} = A_7^{(1)} A_5^{(1)}$	$B_7^{(2)} = A_7^{(1)} B_5^{(1)} + B_7^{(1)}$
$A_3^{(2)} = A_3^{(1)} A_1^{(1)} = 0$	$B_3^{(2)} = A_3^{(1)} B_1^{(1)} + B_3^{(1)}$

Third step:

$A_7^{(3)} = A_7^{(2)} A_3^{(2)} = 0$	$B_7^{(3)} = A_7^{(2)} B_3^{(2)} + B_7^{(2)}$

The computation is performed in three steps, all of which can be vectorized. In the general case, $\lceil \frac{n}{2} \rceil$ products for each term of $A_{2i} A_{2i+1}$ ($i=0, 1,..., \frac{n-1}{2}$) have to be computed in the first step and as many products with accumulation for the $B_{2i+1}^{(1)}$. Clearly, the computations can be vectorized. Similarly, the second step consists of $\lceil \frac{n}{4} \rceil$ operations that can be vectorized, and so on until step m, where the computation is reduced to scalar evaluation.

Organization of computations and benefits of cyclic reduction

The standard program for computing the recurrence relation uses Horner's method:

$$X_n = A_n(A_{n-1}(\dots A_3(A_2X_1 + B_2) + B_3) + \dots + B_{n-1}) + B_n$$

Cyclic reduction corresponds to a more elaborate computation:

$$X_n = A_nA_{n-1}\dots A_3A_2X_1 + A_nA_{n-1}\dots A_3B_2 + \dots\dots + A_nB_{n-1} + B_n$$

The latter computation requires a few more arithmetic operations (3(n–1) compared with 2(n–1) using Horner's method), but is more readily vectorized. As we pointed out for the example above, the $B_i^{(k)}$ can be computed level by level (k by k). The $B_i^{(k)}$ and the $A_i^{(k)}$ just need to be stored in the vectors for fixed k (note that the size of these vectors is divided by a factor of 2 from one level to the next).

Let U and V be the 2m-dimensional vectors of the components of A_i and B_i (which may be completed by 0):

$$U = (A_n, A_{n-1},\dots, A_1, 0,\dots, 0)$$
$$V = (B_n, B_{n-1},\dots, B_1, 0,\dots, 0)$$

The vector obtained by restricting X to the components of 1 to 2^q is written $X_{[1..q]}$. Thus, $U_{[1..2]}$ denotes the vector with four components $(A_n, A_{n-1}, A_{n-2}, A_{n-3})$. The two following vector operations are also defined:

```
{extraction of odd components of X (q is assumed even)}
odd (X[1..q]) ← (X(1), X(3),..., X(2^q–1))
{extraction of even components of X}
even (X[1..q]) ← (X(2), X(4),..., X(2^q))
```

The algorithm for this involves executing the following vector operations on each level (the final result is in $V_{[1..1]}$):

$$U_{[1..q/2]} = \text{odd}(U_{[1..q]}) \otimes \text{even}(U_{[1..q]})$$
$$V_{[1..q/2]} = \text{odd}(U_{[1..q]}) \otimes \text{even}(V_{[1..q]}) + \text{odd}(V_{[1..q]})$$

where $\otimes$ denotes multiplication component by component.

The following pseudocode is obtained:

```
M ← 2ᵐ
for  k ← 1  to m
    U [1..M/2] ← odd(U[1..M]) * even(U[1..M])
    V [1..M/2] ← odd(U[1..M]) * even(V[1..M]) + odd(V[1..M])
    M ← M/2
```

8.2.3   Solving tridiagonal systems

Description

Tridiagonal linear systems are very important in linear algebra. They occur either directly following finite-difference discretization of differential operators or, indirectly, as tools for solving large systems. The aim here is to show how cyclic reduction can be used to solve this kind of problem.

Suppose we have to solve the linear system Ax=v, where A is the tridiagonal matrix:

$$
A = \begin{pmatrix}
b_1 & c_1 & 0 & & & & & \\
a_2 & b_2 & c_2 & & & 0 & & \\
0 & a_3 & b_3 & & & & & \\
0 & 0 & a_4 & & & & & \\
& & 0 & & & & & \\
& & & & & & 0 & \\
& & & & & c_{n-2} & 0 & \\
& 0 & & & & a_{n-1} & b_{n-1} & c_{n-1} \\
& & & & 0 & 0 & a_n & b_n
\end{pmatrix}
$$

This can be be written in the condensed form A = (a, b, c) where:

$$a=(0, a_2,..., a_n), \; b=(b_1, b_2,..., b_n) \text{ and } c=(c_1,..., c_{n-1}, 0)$$

The problem is solved in two steps. First LU factorization is performed on A, where L=(a, e) is the lower bidiagonal triangle and U=(1, w) is the upper bidiagonal triangle with unit diagonal. The e_i and the w_i are computed by the following:

```
E(1) ← B(1)
W(1) ← C(1)/E(1)
for  i ← 2  to  n
   E(i) ← B(i) – A(i)*W(i-1)
   W(i) ← C(i)/E(i)
```

Then, the two bidiagonal systems Ly = v and Ux = y are solved by the following:

```
Y(1) ← V(1)/E(1)
for  i ← 2  to  n
   Y(i) ← (V(i) – A(i)*Y(i-1))/E(i)
X(n) ← Y(n)
for  i ← 2  to  n
   X(i) ← X(i) – W(i)*X(i+1)
```

The first iteration requires 3n floating-point operations, as does the second, while the last requires 2n – a total of 8n on a scalar computer. Moreover, as it is, the algorithm cannot be vectorized, because all three iterations have an anti-dependency.

By contrast, the performance of Gaussian elimination in solving m systems $Ax = v^{(k)}$, k=1,..., m with m being large in relation to n, is high; the E(i) and the W(i) can be computed in 3n floating-point operations. The solution to the system can then be pipelined and chained using vectors of size m. Once an initialization stage of 5n operations has been completed, one result is produced per cycle and the m systems are solved in (8n+m–1) floating-point operations. The price that has to be paid for this is that each of the vector solutions has to be stored in space proportional to m, and the overhead thereby incurred is comparable to solving each system in turn.

Stone's algorithm

This method uses cyclic reduction for all three iterations. Clearly, this can be done quite easily for iterations 2 and 3, but the first iteration is non-linear, $w_i = c_i/(b_i – a_i w_{i-1})$. However, if the variable is changed to z where $w_i = -z_i/z_{i+1}$, a linear relation is obtained:

$$a_i z_{i-1} + b_i z_i + c_i z_{i+1} = 0$$
with $z_1 = 1$ and $z_2 = -b_1/c_1$.

A system with two linear recurrences of the order 1 can be deduced from this: $s_i = Q_i s_{i-1}$.

$$s_i = \begin{pmatrix} z_{i+1} \\ z_i \end{pmatrix} \qquad Q_i = \begin{pmatrix} 0 & 1 \\ \dfrac{-a_i}{c_i} & \dfrac{-b_i}{c_i} \end{pmatrix}$$

The new recurrence can then be reduced cyclically.

Odd-even elimination

In this method, the initial system is reduced cyclically. Three consecutive equations are written:

$$a_{i-1}x_{i-2} + b_{i-1}x_{i-1} + c_{i-1}x_i = v_{i-1}$$
$$a_i x_{i-1} + b_i\, x_i + c_i\, x_{i+1} = v_i$$
$$a_{i+1}\, x_i + b_{i+1}\, x_{i+1} + c_{i+1}\, x_{i+2} = v_{i+1}$$

The x_{i-1} and x_{i+1} in the three equations can then be eliminated. By repeating elimination for the even values i, a tridiagonal system between x_{i-2}, x_i and x_{i+2} is obtained. The problem has thus been changed into one of solving a tridiagonal system of half the size of the original system:

$$a_i^{(1)}\, x_{i-2} + b_i^{(1)}\, x_i + c_i^{(1)}\, x_{i+2} = v_i^{(1)}$$

where

$$a_i^{(1)} = - a_i\, a_{i-1}\, /\, b_{i-1}$$
$$b_i^{(1)} = b_i - a_i\, c_{i-1}\, /\, b_{i-1} - c_{i+1}\, a_{i+1}\, /\, b_{i+1}$$
$$c_i^{(1)} = - c_{i+1}\, c_i\, /\, b_{i+1}$$
$$v_i^{(1)} = v_i - a_i\, v_{i-1}\, /\, b_{i-1} - c_{i+1}\, v_{i+1}\, /\, b_{i+1}$$

By repeating the process, a single equation is obtained after $(\log_2(n))$ steps. Matrix A still has three non-zero coefficients per line, but the two diagonals diverge increasingly, until a diagonal matrix and, with it, the solution to the system, is obtained. The latter equation can be used to compute the value of $X_{n/2}$. By starting the process again, all the unknowns of even rank can be computed. The unknowns of odd rank are obtained using the initial equations.

8.3   Vectorization of Gaussian elimination

Solving dense linear systems is one of the most fundamentally important problems in scientific computing. Gaussian elimination is the most commonly used technique for solving them, and how it functions was described at the beginning of this chapter. The aim of this section is to continue the analysis we began in Chapter 7 and to apply it to Gaussian elimination.

8.3.1   Methods of writing Gaussian elimination

We now describe various versions of the Gaussian method that differ according to how the data are accessed. In a Fortran environment, access by columns is to be preferred, as it was in the case of matrix multiplication, so as to avoid problems with memory paging.

The natural variants kij and kji

If the problem is analysed in the same way as matrix multiplication was in Chapter 7, the following basic program structure is obtained:

```
for  k ← ...
    for  i ← ...
        for  j ← ...
            element A(i, j) updated
```

This is more complicated than the program structure for multiplying matrices, because it is less regular. The algorithm has three nested iterations that are mutually dependent. The indices can be ordered in six different ways.

The 'natural' variant of the algorithm is a search that sweeps across each row in turn at each stage, that is, following the order kij of the iteration indices. The variant was described in Section 8.1.2.

Elimination by columns, following the order kji, is the standard variant of the algorithm for Gaussian elimination. Row k is combined with rows k+1, k+2,..., n at step k to reduce the elements below the diagonal of column k to zero. Here, AXPY is used as the basic operation – the jth column of A, j varying from k+1 to n, is updated by adding a multiple of the kth column to it (see Figure 8.4).

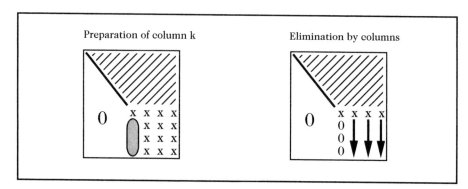

Figure 8.4   The kth step in the elimination by columns variant

The pseudocode is as follows:

```
for  k ← 1  to  n-1
    coeff ← 1/A(k, k)
    for  i ← k+1  to  n
        A(i, k) ← coeff*A(i, k)
    for  j ← k+1  to  n
        for  i ← k+1  to  n
            A(i, j) ← A(i, j) - A(i, k)*A(k, j)
```

jki and ikj variants

Data is also accessed by column in the jki variant. It involves determining which columns are to be eliminated and performing steps on those columns concurrently. The following algorithm is obtained:

```
{jki variant}
for  j ← 1  to  n
    for  k ← 1  to  j-1
        for  i ← k+1  to  n
            A(i, j) ← A(i, j) - A(i, k)*A(k, j)
        for  i ← j+1  to  n
            A(i, j) ← A(i, j)/A(j, j)
```

This algorithm differs from the one above in the way that elimination occurs. Before elements are driven to zero, the elements of the jth column are updated (see Figure 8.5). The jth column is computed once and for all by adding to it, one by one, multiples of the first $j-1$ columns. GAXPY (supervector AXPY) is the basic operation used in this algorithm.

Note that in this algorithm, the jth column is best stored in a vector register while it is being updated.

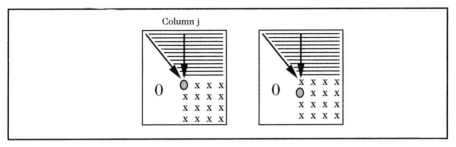

Figure 8.5   Elimination on column j

The ijk and jik variants

We shall describe only the ijk variant in which data are accessed by row; the jik variant follows directly from this. In the ijk variant, the following code is obtained:

```
for  i ← 2  to  n
    for  j ← 1  to  i-1
        A(i, j) ← A(i, j)/A(j, j)
        for  k ← 1  to  j-1
            A(i, j) ← A(i, j) - A(i, k)*A(k, j)
    for  j ← i  to  n
        for  k ← 1  to  i-1
            A(i, j) ← A(i, j) - A(i, k)*A(k, j)
```

In this algorithm, all modifications to row i (with i varying from 1 to n) are made in one step. In the first part of the algorithm (the second and third iterations), elements A(i, j), with j varying from 1 to i–1, are updated, to take account of the fact that all the preceding elements on the ith row have been reduced to zero. In the second part (fourth and fifth iterations), the remaining elements of row i, which were modified as a result of the elements of the first part of the row being reduced to zero, are updated.

In the jik variant, elimination occurs in two stages:

(1) The element a_{ij}, $2 \le j \le i$ is modified by computing a scalar product (DOT operation). Elimination is executed row by row. In this part, the ith row of the lower triangle is constructed: the jth element is obtained by computing the scalar product of the elements that have already been computed and the jth column (*see* Figure 8.6).

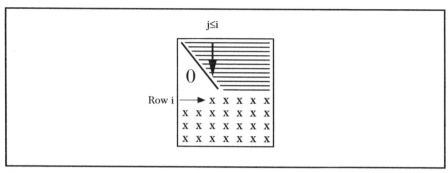

Figure 8.6   First stage of the jik variant

(2) The element a_{ij}, $i \le j \le n$ is modified by computing the scalar product of the small row vector that has just been computed and the elements of the jth column that have already been computed (Figure 8.7).

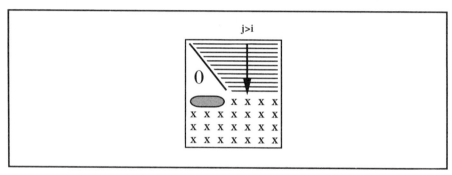

Figure 8.7   Second stage of the jik variant

Comparison of the three variants

How the variants of Gaussian elimination perform depends to a large extent on the machine's underlying architecture. To simplify the comparison, we shall look only at the inner loops. First, we describe a vector code for the three variants:

```
{jik - dot}
for  i ← 1  to  n
    read vector A(i,.) and store it in X
    for  j ← 2  to  i
        read vector A(.,j) and store it in Y
        compute scalar product X.Y
```

Note that, in a Fortran environment, reading vector A(i,.) can lead to conflicts in accessing memory banks. And how the variant performs globally depends very much on the quality of the DOT implementation. But it can produce good results on a machine with an addition pipeline of restricted depth, such as a chained multiplier and adder.

```
{kji - axpy}
for  k ← 1  to  n-1
    read vector A(.,k) and store it in Y
    for  j ← k+1  to  n
        read vector A(.,j) and store it in X
        multiply vector Y(k+1:n) by the scalar X(k)
        add above vector to X(k+1:n) and store it in X
    write X into A(.,j)
```

The variant's performance on a machine that does not allow chaining of arithmetic read and write operations does not seem very good, as it needs to read and write one vector per iteration. By contrast, where the four operations can be chained, the algorithm operates in vector mode.

```
{jki - gaxpy}
for  j ← 1  to  n
    read vector A(.,j) and store it in S
    for  k ← 1  to  j-1
        read vector A(.,k) and store it in Y
        multiply vector Y(k+1:n) by the scalar X(k)
        add above vector to X(k+1:n) and store it in X
    write X into A(.,j)
```

The difference between AXPY and GAXPY is that X is written to $A(., j)$ outside the internal loop. Where operators are chained and instructions can be overlapped, the algorithm can operate in supervector mode.

8.3.2   Higher-level BLASs

The variants that we have just described can be implemented with BLAS-2 kernels in the same way as they were for a matrix multiplied by a matrix.

kji variant

This is the simplest variant. Once a vector operation has been executed to update the pivot column k in step k, a BLAS-2 operation can be called directly to make a rank 1 update of the restriction of matrix A to the last $(n–k)$ rows and columns. This is illustrated in Figure 8.8, where the shaded grey area is the restriction of A and the black dots are the two vectors that are used for updating. The pseudocode is as follows:

```
for  k ← 1  to  n-1
   {column k of A updated}
   A ← A - (column k of A).(row k of A)ᵗ
```

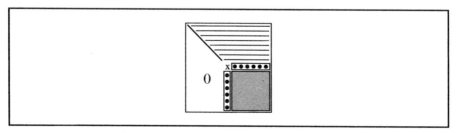

Figure 8.8   Update of rank 1 of the restriction of A to step k

jik variant

Now let's look at the jik variant. First, that part of row j lying to the right of A's main diagonal and, then, the part of column j below the diagonal are directly computed. The two operations are a vector multiplied by a matrix and a matrix multiplied by a vector respectively [DoE84]. They are illustrated in Figures 8.9 and 8.10.

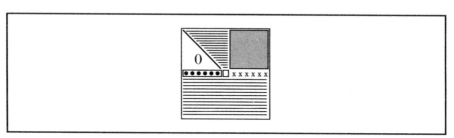

Figure 8.9   Computation of the right-hand part of row j – vector-matrix multiplication

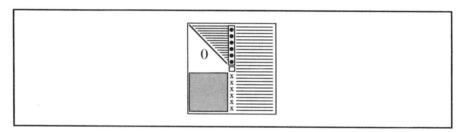

Figure 8.10   Computation of the lower part of column j – matrix-vector multiplication

Its algorithm is as follows:

```
{BLAS2 jik variant}
for  j ← 1 to  n
    {compute right-hand part of row j of A}
    row j of A ← VECT-MAT (beginning of line j of A, top
    right-hand corner of A)
    {update elements below A's diagonal of column j of A}
    column j of A ← MAT-VECT (bottom left-hand corner of A,
    beginning of column j of A)
    {BLAS1 operations: prepare column j and swap rows}
```

8.4   Conclusion

As we have seen, linear algebra algorithms are ideally suited to vectorization, as they are expressed mathematically as vectors. However, there are few algorithms or problems that have not been vectorized. When working on very irregular structures, one simple way of obtaining high performance on a vector computer is to solve at the same time several instances of the same problem that differ only in their parameters or data. It will be seen later (Chapter 16) that the technique is basic to those algorithms on SIMD machines, in which a processor array executes the same operation on an array of data.

The techniques described in Chapters 6, 7 and 8 are now standard and have been incorporated into specialized software packages, vectorizers, that convert standard programs into vector programs. We shall not say any more until automatic vectorization techniques have been discussed. We shall mention only that using them facilitates high performance and that much progress has been made in this area, even if it must be recognized that the techniques are all the more efficient if the structure of the initial program is well formed and avoids irregularities as much as possible.

We saw in Chapter 2 that all microprocessors now have one or more vector units. We shall see in the rest of the book that a computer's power is linked to two combined factors – using vector processors, coupled with an increase in the numbers of arithmetic units used. We have dealt with the former and we now move on to the latter.

9

Parallelizing algorithms

A program is represented by a task graph. In this chapter we deal with the construction of such graphs and also with the design and analysis of parallel programs.

9.1 Introduction

The growth of parallel computers has led to most common algorithms being re-evaluated according to new viability and performance criteria. There are two approaches to dealing with such new concepts; either one can look at how existing methods are best parallelized, or new methods that are specially adapted to parallel machines can be devised. This chapter deals with the first approach, that is, parallelization of an existing method.

9.1.1   Reference model

Parallelization

The first step in parallelizing a problem is to partition it into *tasks*, which consist of instructions or groups of instructions. This can be done either automatically by a program or by hand, case by case: we shall assume the latter, with a view to parallelizing basic methods. Construction of the *task graph* enables the time constraints on the execution of tasks to be specified and the independent tasks found which are amenable to being executed in parallel. The tasks then have to be allocated to processors, while complying with the above constraints and those imposed by the machine's architecture. The most efficient algorithm for the computer being used can then be chosen on the basis of these constraints.

Architectural model

The underlying architecture of our model consists of a set of p identical processors, each with its own local memory and all sharing a central common memory (*see* Figure 9.1). Data is transferred between shared memory and the processors via an interconnection network that is assumed to be non-blocking (it is implicitly assumed that the shared memory is organized into memory banks – *see* Section 3.1). In any one unit of communication time, each processor can receive one data item. In this chapter, we do not make any assumptions as to whether a SIMD or MIMD architecture is being used. All processors can perform elementary operations on their data.

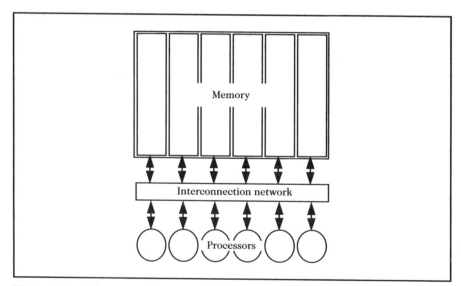

Figure 9.1   Reference architecture

We shall deal with synchronization problems only in so far as they relate to algorithms. More specifically, to ensure that parallel algorithms are executed deterministically and that data integrity is complete, we assume that concurrent reading of data is allowed, whereas concurrent writing by different processors to the same memory address is not (in accordance with the CREW PRAM model described in Section 2.2). These constraints should therefore be taken into account when tasks are scheduled. By contrast, it is assumed that the shared memory is organized in parallel in such a way that contention for memory banks does not occur.

9.1.2   The parallelization process

The same algorithm may have several parallel versions, depending on how data is accessed, how it is partitioned into tasks, how those tasks are allocated to processors and how the processors are synchronized. Some parallel versions of the initial algorithm may be better adapted to the structure of the computer than others – SIMD machines, in particular, are unable to execute asynchronous algorithms. Conversely, problems of synchronizing processors on MIMD machines are related entirely to hardware considerations and do not have any bearing on the algorithm.

Task scheduling

The general problem of allocating tasks to processors in a parallel program, when the tasks can be of any nature and the task graph is not known until run time, is a very difficult one. Here, we look at the simpler problem where the program is known in advance, that is, we know the tasks and their execution times (or at least have estimates for these) and the precedence relations among them. The problem is an old one in terms of task allocation to machines [CoD73], but its application to parallel computation is much more recent. As we shall see, it has stimulated some new ideas.

The general model to which we shall refer is the following. The tasks T_j $\{j=1,\ldots, n\}$ are characterized by their execution times, represented by the function $ex(T_j)$ and may have earliest or latest possible start-times. Preemption – interrupting a task while it is being executed and allocating it to another processor – is not allowed.

All the P_i $\{i=1,\ldots, p\}$ processors are identical. They communicate with each other through a shared memory in a CREW system (processor networks are discussed in Chapter 14).

The precedence constraints on the tasks define a cycle-free directed graph – a *DAG* (*Directed Acyclic Graph*). Finally, the model may have several aims; the most usual is to minimize the function representing the total execution time – the *makespan*.

Practical complexity of parallel algorithms

The aim of analysing the complexity of algorithms is to determine their maximum degree of intrinsic parallelism. The type of parallel architecture underlying the analysis is related to the model we have just described: a shared-memory MIMD system. This is idealized in the sense that in evaluating the speed of a parallel algorithm, we ignore data transfer times, and consider only arithmetical operations.

In our analysis of algorithm complexity on a PRAM in Chapter 5, we did not make any assumptions on the expression of the sequential algorithm that was being used. In this sense, the approach there was purely algorithmic. Here we are dealing with a different problem, as the starting point is a program considered as a set of tasks having a total ordering relation. The constraint related to the granularity of the tasks that is imposed by the program and the constraint of total order form the two main differences between the two approaches.

The main analytical tools to be used in the analysis were described in Chapter 2. As we have already emphasized, algorithm design on a given parallel architecture requires computations to be rearranged, so that the characteristics of the architecture can be best exploited. This means that standard sequential algorithms and, frequently, even the methods used for solving the problems, must be completely rethought, and we therefore need tools specifically adapted to analysing algorithms on these new architectures. Complexity analysis, in the sense of determining the number of elementary operations required for the execution of a parallel algorithm on a system having a number of processors, enables the efficiencies of different algorithms to be measured and compared. With the assumptions given above, an algorithm is said to be *optimal* if its execution time is the least among all possible versions. These may be several different optimal algorithms, differing in the numbers of processors they need.

Review of some basic definitions

Let p be the number of processors. We assume that this is unbounded, although in practice it will be $O(n)$ for a problem of size n: $p = \alpha n$, with $0 < \alpha \leq 1$.

The definition of *speed-up* S_p should be recalled – it is used to measure time saved as a result of parallelization:

$$S_p = \frac{t_1}{t_p}$$

Speed-up has real significance only for shared-memory machines with a fairly small number of processors. *Efficiency* e_p is defined as the ratio of S_p to p:

$$e_p = \frac{S_p}{p}$$

Because it is impossible to achieve a speed-up greater than p for an algorithm executing with p processors, the value of the efficiency must lie between 0 and 1.

The fundamental problem of parallelizing a computation lies in finding the maximum amount of parallelism that it contains. This involves first finding an allocation of tasks to processors, complying with the task graph, that is optimal in the sense that the algorithm executes in minimal time (written t_{opt}) when no bound is placed on the number of processors; and then finding the minimum number of processors needed for the algorithm to execute in time t_{opt}. Further, it must be possible to specify the allocation algorithm and to install it on an existing machine – or at least on a machine that can be simulated, if one is not fortunate enough to have a real machine. This last requirement eliminates procedures that are too complicated, or which require additional operations for preprocessing the data, often difficult to assess. Finally, given a fixed number p of processors, an optional algorithm can be found.

Asymptotic results are obtained when n tends towards infinity. Specifically, asymptotic efficiency $e_{\infty, \alpha}$ is defined as the bound of e_p when n→∞. An algorithm is said to be asymptotically optimal when $e_{\infty, \alpha}$ is at its maximum.

Asymptotic analysis may seem a contradiction in terms when applied to a practical problem, in which the number of processors will be fixed and relatively small. But, as we have already stressed, our intention here is to study the maximum degree of parallelism of a given algorithm with an infinite number of processors on an ideal architecture.

9.2   Task graphs and parallel algorithms

9.2.1   Basic tools

Tasks

The concept of *task systems*, as used by Kumar [Kum82] and Coffman-Denning [CoD73], provides an opportunity for the underlying formal aspects of our analysis of parallel algorithms to be introduced. An algorithm can be segmented into a collection of tasks. From a study of the dependencies among the tasks, taking account of their input/output variables, a precedence system can be constructed that expresses the internal parallelism of the algorithm. In such a system any two tasks are either linked by a precedence relation, in which case they are executed sequentially, or they do not interfere with each other and can be executed in parallel. First, we shall define these intuitive concepts.

Definition 9.1

A *task* is an indivisible unit of processing that is uniquely characterized by its external behaviour: inputs, outputs, instructions and execution time. A task T is therefore characterized by a quadruplet (I(T), O(T), f(T), ex(T)) where:

- I(T) is the set of inputs to T,

- O(T) is the set of outputs of T,

- f(T) is the operator from I(T) to O(T), that is, the set of elementary operations that transforms I(T) into O(T),

- ex(T) is the integer representing the execution time of T.

Generally speaking, the *execution time* (or length) of a task is the sum of two terms – the *computation time* (which relates to the number of transfers performed in the task) and the *communication time* (which relates to the number of transfers between shared memory and the processor executing the task).

Problems of availability and data integrity are not taken into account at this level, as they depend on how tasks are scheduled for execution. Furthermore, problems arising from contention for memory banks – a read conflict from a memory bank, for example – are difficult to incorporate into the model, as they depend on the architecture, storage and transfer mechanisms being used and, of course, on how the algorithm is executed. From here onwards, we assume that the time taken to solve these problems is included in communication time. Finally, pre-emption in task allocation is not allowed. This rule has been adopted for the sake of simplicity and the reader is referred to [CoG72] for a description of the results of scheduling using divisible tasks.

A *sequential algorithm* is a collection of tasks that have a total order relation $A = (T_1,..., T_n, \rightarrow)$. The relation $T_i \rightarrow T_k$ (for $i \neq k$) means that the task T_i must be completed before execution of T_k starts. Even a sequential algorithm can be considered as a single task – (I(A), O(A), f(A), ex(A)). The following relations then exist:

$$I\left(A\right) \subset \bigcup_{i=1}^{n} I\left(T_i\right) \qquad O\left(A\right) \subset \bigcup_{i=1}^{n} O\left(T_i\right)$$

$$f\left(A\right) \bigcup_{i=1}^{n} f\left(T_i\right) \qquad ex\left(A\right) \leq \sum_{i=1}^{n} ex\left(T_i\right)$$

The above definition of a sequential algorithm may seem restrictive. Strictly speaking, it is not, as an algorithm may be considered as a task, which is a rather general concept – all the more general, if execution time is not considered to be determined in advance. In fact, the definition is not complex enough to be used for directly parallelizing algorithms with data dependent stopping criteria or conditional jumps. If there is a conditional jump in an algorithm, the part of the program corresponding to it should be inside the task. The execution time of the tasks then becomes the maximum of all the times of all the possible options. The problem is different for an iterative method because it is linked to the fact that a finite number of tasks, which is known in advance, has been assumed. This formalism could be applied quite easily to the case where the number of tasks is not known.

Granularity

As stated in the introduction to this chapter, decomposing algorithms into tasks can be done either by a program [PKL80] or by hand by the user. The latter case will form the subject of our analysis from here onwards. An algorithm can be decomposed in several different ways. The *granularity* of the algorithm's decomposition is a rough measure of the relation between a task's average execution time and the algorithm's total time [Dun90] [Gon77] [Sar89]. A theoretical definition was given in Section 5.1.3.

As an example, consider the computation of the product C of two $n \times n$ matrices A and B. The execution time of the sequential algorithm is n^3 multiplications and additions. If the following are taken as the task's elementary operations:

```
C(i, j) ← C(i, j) + A(i, k)*B(k, j)
```

the decomposition is fine. If each task is the computation of an element of C:

```
for  k ← 1  to  n
    C(i, j) ← C(i, j) + A(i, k)*B(k, j)
```

the grain size of the decomposition is average. By contrast, if each task is the computation of a row or a column of the product:

```
for  j ← 1  to  n
    for  k ← 1  to  n
        C(i, j) ← C(i, j) + A(i, k)*B(k, j)
```

the decomposition is coarse.

In Chapter 5, we focused on fine-grain decompositions. In the following chapters, it will be seen that this is not realistic, as the communication and memory access costs involved are prohibitively high and, as a result, tasks of average granularity have to be chosen.

The problem of choosing the best decomposition is difficult and is related to the tasks' execution times and the underlying architecture. The main criteria on which tasks are chosen are the number of processors, the relation between unit communication time and unit computation time, memory access and so on. Note that the user needs to use a programming language with which tasks and communication between them can be defined – for example, occam, Fortran90, C* or LESTAP [TrW91]. There are specialized languages, for real time, for example, or high-level languages with special primitives for processing numerical algorithms.

Task systems

Definition 9.2

A *task system* $S = (T_1,..., T_n, <<)$ is a set of tasks with a partial order relation written $<<$. $T_i << T_k$ $(i \neq k)$ means that task T_i must be completed before T_k begins.

A sequential algorithm A is a task system that does not contain tasks that are not ordered by the relation $<<$.

Definition 9.3

Let $S = (T_1,..., T_n, <<)$ be a task system. Two tasks T_i and T_k are *independent* if they do not modify any common variable. The independence relation is as follows:

$$O(T_i) \cap O(T_k) = O(T_i) \cap I(T_k) = I(T_i) \cap O(T_k) = \varnothing$$

The tasks T_i and T_k are *consecutive* if no other task T_j exists, such that:

$$T_i << T_j << T_k \text{ or } T_k << T_j << T_i$$

If two tasks are consecutive, they are either ordered by a total order relation or they are independent. But the alternatives are not mutually exclusive. Two ordered tasks can be independent (which is particularly the case for a sequential algorithm). Some task systems are such that this is not the case.

Definition 9.4

A task system $S = (T_1,..., T_n, <<)$ is a *precedence system* if, for each pair of consecutive tasks (T_i, T_k), one and only one of the three following conditions is satisfied:

1. $T_i << T_k$
2. $T_k << T_i$
3. T_i and T_k are independent.

Therefore, two consecutive tasks are ordered, if and only if they are dependent.

Task graphs

Definition 9.5

The *task graph* G for a precedence system $S = (T_1,..., T_n, <<)$ is defined as follows:

- The set of vertices of G is the set of tasks of S;
- T_i and T_k are linked by an arc, if and only if T_i and T_k are consecutive and ordered by the relation $<<$.

We describe how these concepts are used in the following section and then go on to discuss an example.

9.2.2   Constructing a task graph

The definitions that we have just given may seem rather devoid of interest, but it will be seen that they can be used to construct a simple task graph for a given algorithm, which is an essential step in parallelizing the algorithm.

A task system for a sequential algorithm will be established, independent tasks in the system sought and their precedence system deduced and, finally, consecutive, ordered tasks sought, so that a task graph for them can be obtained.

Lemma 9.1

Let $A = (T_1,..., T_n, \rightarrow)$ be a sequential algorithm. There exists a unique precedence system $S = (T_1,..., T_n, <<)$ such that the relation $<<$ is a sub-order of $\rightarrow$. $<<$ is defined by:

$$T_i << T_k \Leftrightarrow \begin{cases} \exists j \text{ such that } T_i << T_j << T_k \\ \text{or} \\ T_i \rightarrow T_k \text{ and } \left(O(T_i) \cap O(T_k)\right) \cup \left(O(Ti) \cap I(T_k)\right) \cup \left(I(T_i) \cap O(T_k)\right) \neq \varnothing \end{cases}$$

Proof

Clearly, $<<$ is a sub-order of $\rightarrow$. To prove that S is a precedence system we show that if T_i, T_k are any two consecutive tasks of S that are not ordered by $<<$, then they are necessarily independent.

As A is a sequential algorithm, T_i and T_k are ordered by $\rightarrow$ (for example, $T_i \rightarrow T_k$). The following is obtained:

$$O(T_i) \cap O(T_k) = O(T_i) \cap I(T_k) = I(T_i) \cap O(T_k) = \varnothing$$

and T_i and T_k are therefore independent.

The proof of the uniqueness of S is established in the same way.

The above lemma is used to obtain an algorithm for constructing a precedence system $S = (T_1, ..., T_n, <<)$ for a sequential algorithm $A = (T_1, ..., T_n, \rightarrow)$.

Constructing a precedence system

Below is an algorithm for constructing a precedence system. To simplify the description of the algorithm, assume that the order of the tasks in A is the same as that of their indices: $T_i \rightarrow T_k \Leftrightarrow i \leq k$. R(k) denotes the set of nodes i such that $T_i << T_k$.

```
{step 1} A task T1 is considered
R(1) = ∅.
{step k}
for  k ← 2 to n
Tk is considered
    for  i ← 1 to k-1
        if (O(Tᵢ)∩O(Tₖ))∪(O(Tᵢ)∩I(Tₖ))∪(I(Tᵢ)∩O(Tₖ)) ≠∅
        then Tᵢ<<Tₖ and for all indices j belonging to
        R(i), Tⱼ<<Tₖ produces R(k) = {i} U R(i) U R(k)
```

To obtain the task graph G for the precedence system S, we must establish which tasks are ordered consecutively by the relation $<<$. The following algorithm, a variation on the one above, can be used to obtain the task graph directly from A. For each of the vertices k of G, R(k) is the set of indices i, such that $T_i << T_k$ and C(k) is the set of indices i, such that T_i and T_k are consecutively ordered. The pairs (i, k) where $i \in C(k)$ are therefore the arcs of G.

Algorithm for constructing the task graph

```
{step 1} A task T1 is considered
R(1) = ∅ and C(1) = ∅
{step k}
for  k ← 2  to  n
R(k) = ∅ and C(k) = ∅
i ← k-1
while i ≥ 1 do
    if  i ∈ R(k) and (O(T_i)∩O(T_k))∪(O(T_i)∩I(T_k))∪(I(T_i)∩O(T_k)) ≠ ∅
    then R(k) = R(k) ∪ R(i) U {i} and C(k) = C(k) ∪ {i}
    i ←  i-1
```

Example

Let's look at a simple example to illustrate the procedure followed. The example has often been used and is taken from [CoD73]. Consider an algorithm consisting of eight tasks $T_1,\ldots, T_8$ with the following precedence system:

$T_1 << T_3$	$T_1 << T_4$	$T_1 << T_5$	$T_1 << T_6$	$T_1 << T_7$	$T_1 << T_8$
$T_2 << T_3$	$T_2 << T_4$	$T_2 << T_5$	$T_2 << T_6$	$T_2 << T_7$	$T_2 << T_8$
$T_3 << T_7$	$T_3 << T_8$				
$T_4 << T_6$	$T_4 << T_7$	$T_4 << T_8$			
$T_5 << T_7$					
$T_6 << T_8$					

By removing redundant constraints, the following set of relations is obtained. A task graph for the relations is shown in Figure 9.2.

$T_1 << T_3$	$T_1 << T_4$	$T_1 << T_5$
$T_2 << T_3$	$T_2 << T_4$	$T_2 << T_5$
$T_3 << T_7$	$T_3 << T_8$	
$T_4 << T_6$	$T_4 << T_7$	
$T_5 << T_7$		
$T_6 << T_8$		

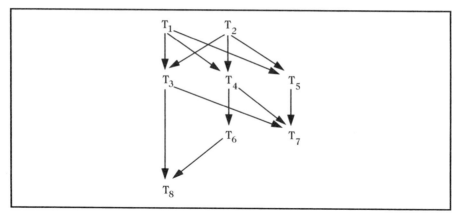

Figure 9.2   Task graph

9.2.3   Task scheduling

Compatible scheduling

When the task graph has been defined, the tasks have to be allocated to available processors, within the constraints of the graph and those relating to execution time. This forms part of the more general problem of scheduling a task system and will be discussed later. This problem is very difficult, as scheduling any given task system is NP-complete [Ull75]. However, the problem can be solved for certain specific precedence systems.

Definition 9.6

A scheduling system that is compatible with a precedence system $S = (T_1,..., T_n, <<)$ is a function Sch from $\{T_1,..., T_n\}$ in $\{1, 2,..., p\} \times IN$, $Sch(T_k) = (prc(T_k), sta(T_k))$, such that:

(i) $T_i \leq\leq T_k \Rightarrow sta(T_i) + ex(T_i) \leq sta(T_k)$.

(ii) $prc(T_i) = prc(T_k) \Rightarrow$
      $(sta(T_i)+ex(T_i) \leq sta(T_k) \text{ or } sta(T_k)+ex(T_k) \leq sta(T_i))$.

$prc(T_k)$ is the processor that executes T_k and $sta(T_k)$ is the start-time for the execution of T_k. Condition (i) simply means that, if T_i and T_k are not independent, T_k will not start until T_i completes. Condition (ii) means that a processor is not allocated to two different tasks at the same time.

Comments

The internal structure of parallel computers was not taken into account in the above definition. Specifically, synchronization mechanisms could entail additional constraints. Generally speaking, scheduling is asynchronous and therefore incompatible with SIMD structures. Using a SIMD computer would mean that the scheduling algorithm was such that the processors had to start executing their tasks at the same time. We shall not elaborate on this in order to keep the description simple.

Example

Consider the graph with eight tasks and assume that p=3. The scheduling algorithm in Figure 9.3 is compatible with its precedence system:

$Sch\ (T_1) = (1, 0)$

$Sch\ (T_2) = (2, 0)$

$Sch\ (T_3) = (1, max(ex(T_1), ex(T_2)))$

$Sch\ (T_4) = (2, max(ex(T_1), ex(T_2)))$

$Sch\ (T_5) = (3, max(ex(T_1), ex(T_2)))$

$Sch\ (T_6) = (2, sta(T_4)+ex(T_4)) = (2, max(ex(T_1), ex(T_2))+ex(T_4))$

$Sch\ (T_7) = (3, max(sta(T_3)+ex(T_3), sta(T_4) +ex(T_4), sta(T_5)+ex(T_5)))$

$\quad = (3, max(max(ex(T_1), ex(T_2))+ex(T_3),$

$\quad\quad\quad max(ex(T_1), ex(T_2))+ex(T_4),$

$\quad\quad\quad max(ex(T_1), ex(T_2))+ex(T_5)))$

$Sch\ (T_8) = (1, max(sta(T_3)+ex(T_3), sta(T_6)+ex(T_6)))$

$\quad = (1, max(max(ex(T_1), ex(T_2))+ex(T_3),$

$\quad\quad\quad max(ex(T_1), ex(T_2))+ex(T_4)+ex(T_6)))$

Figure 9.3   Compatible scheduling algorithm

Fundamental issues relating to parallelization

This chapter's central definition can now be introduced. It renders explicit the concept of parallel algorithms, which so far has been intuitive.

Definition 9.7

A *parallel algorithm* corresponding to a sequential algorithm $A = (T_1,..., T_n, \rightarrow)$ is a pair (S, Sch) consisting of the precedence system S for A and the task-ordering algorithm Sch that is compatible with S.

The parallel algorithm's execution time is the time taken for the last task to be executed to complete:

$t_{par} = max_{k=1, 2,...n}(sta(T_k) + ex(T_k))$

A parallel algorithm corresponding to a sequential algorithm A is *optimal* if no other parallel algorithm for A that has a shorter execution time exists.

The fundamental problem we intend to deal with in the context of algorithm parallelization can then be formulated as follows. Let A be a sequential algorithm, p the number of processors; determine an optimal parallel algorithm for A and compute its execution time.

There is no general solution to this problem. Below we highlight some other problems that are derived from it:

(1) What is the execution time $t_{opt}(p)$ of an optimal parallel algorithm with p processors?

(2) Assuming there is no bound on the number of available processors, what is the time t_{opt} of an optimal parallel algorithm? t_{opt} is defined by:

$$t_{opt} = \min_{p=1, 2,..., n}(t_{opt}(p))$$

(3) What is the minimum number of processors p_{opt} that can be used to design an algorithm that executes in time t_{opt}? p_{opt} is defined by:

$$p_{opt} = \min_{p=1, 2,..., n}(p \text{ such that } t_{opt}(p) = t_{opt})$$

(4) What is the minimum number of processors required to maximize efficiency? This involves finding p, such that maximum $e_{opt}(p)$ is obtained.

9.3   General results

Here, we continue our detailed discussion of scheduling precedence systems and describe results obtained for specific algorithms.

9.3.1   Preliminary remarks

Task graph decomposition

For the sake of simplicity, assume that all tasks have the same execution time, which we shall take (without loss of generality) as being equal to unit time. Tasks are then referred to as *unit execution time* (UET) tasks. It should be recalled that the time taken by a path in a task graph is the sum of the execution times of the tasks it comprises. The longest path in the task graph is the path with the longest execution time.

The *antecedents* of a task T_k are the T_i, such that $T_i << T_k$. T_i is a *predecessor* of T_k and T_k is a *successor* of T_i, if T_i and T_k are consecutive. The sets of the predecessors and successors of T_k are written $Pre(T_k)$ and $Suc(T_k)$.

The *depth* $Dep(G)$ of the task graph is the number of tasks along the longest path.

The set $D(G) = \{N_1, ..., N_{Dep(G)}\}$ is called the *level-decomposition* of the task graph. This is a partitioning of $D(G)$ into subsets (*levels*) as follows:

Level 1 consists of tasks with no predecessors.

Level k comprises tasks with all their predecessors on lower levels and all their successors on higher levels.

Level $Dep(G)$ comprises tasks with no successors. Note that, since $Dep(G)$ is the number of tasks along the longest path, each level is non-empty (it contains one task from each of the longest paths). Note also that one graph can be decomposed into levels in several different ways.

We call *predecessor-oriented decomposition* $PoD(G)$ decomposing the task graph into the following levels: level 1 comprises all tasks that do not have any predecessors; for k varying from 2 to $Dep(G)$, level k comprises tasks with all their predecessors on lower levels and at least one predecessor on level k–1. This form of decomposition is called earliest start-time decomposition, because scheduling by levels means that each task has a minimum start-time.

Similarly, we call *successor-oriented decomposition* $SoD(G)$ decomposing the graph into the following levels: level $Dep(G)$ comprises tasks that have no successors, and for k varying from $Dep(G)$–1 to 1, level k comprises tasks with all their successors on higher levels and at least one successor on level k+1. This is also called latest start-time decomposition, because scheduling by levels means that each task has a maximum start-time.

The maximum of the levels' cardinals is called the *width* of a decomposition $W(D)$:

$$W(D) = \max_{k=1, ..., Dep(G)}(\mid N_k \mid)$$

The widths of predecessor-oriented decomposition and successor-oriented decomposition are written $Wp(G)$ and $Ws(G)$ respectively.

The minimum width of the decompositions of G is called the *width* $W(G)$ of the graph:

$$W(G) = \min_{D(G)}(W(D)) = \min_{D(G)}(\max_{k=1, ..., Dep(G)}(\mid N_k \mid))$$

Example

The depth of the eight-task graph that was used earlier as an example (*see* Figure 9.2) is 4 and its width is 2. It can be decomposed into the following levels:

level(1) = $\{T_1, T_2\}$	level(1) = $\{T_1, T_2\}$
level(2) = $\{T_3, T_4, T_5\}$	level(2) = $\{T_3, T_4\}$
level(3) = $\{T_6, T_7\}$	level(3) = $\{T_5, T_6\}$
level(4) = $\{T_8\}$	level(4) = $\{T_7, T_8\}$
level(1) = $\{T_1, T_2\}$	level(1) = $\{T_1, T_2\}$
level(2) = $\{T_4, T_5\}$	level(2) = $\{T_4\}$
level(3) = $\{T_3, T_6\}$	level(3) = $\{T_3, T_5, T_6\}$
level(4) = $\{T_7, T_8\}$	level(4) = $\{T_7, T_8\}$

The first decomposition is a predecessor-oriented decomposition and the fourth is a successor-oriented decomposition.

9.3.2   UET tasks

In this section, we assume that all tasks have unit execution time and analyse the optimal time and the optimal number of processors for executing a parallel algorithm.

Establishing t_{opt} and p_{opt}

Theorem 9.2

Let $A = (T_1, \ldots, T_n, \rightarrow)$ be a sequential algorithm consisting entirely of UET tasks.

(1) With an unbounded number of processors, the time t_{opt} of an optimal parallel algorithm is equal to the execution time of the task graphs' longest path, that is, Dep(G) (excluding communication time).

(2) The minimum number of processors p_{opt} with which an algorithm that can execute in time t_{opt} can be designed is equal to the width W(G) of the task graph.

Proof (1)

Clearly, t_{opt} is greater than or equal to the time it takes the task graph's longest path to execute, as the tasks on the path are consecutive and must be executed sequentially. Each of the tasks on the path belongs to a different level. As each task is preceded by a task on the level immediately below it, it can be deduced that the graph's longest path takes Dep(G) time to execute.

We now show that there exists a parallel algorithm with p processors that executes in Dep(G), where p is equal to W(D), for each decomposition of the task graph into Dep(G) levels. In order to do this, the application Sch = (prc, sta) is defined by passing along all levels of the decomposition.

If T_k belongs to level 1, $sta(T_k)=0$. If T_k belongs to level j, $sta(T_k)=(j-1)$. Note the following relation:

$$sta(T_k)=\max(sta(T_i)+ex(T_i)) \text{ where } T_i \text{ belongs to } Pre(T_k).$$

In other words, the start-time of T_k is the total amount of completion times of the predecessors of T_k.

Now let's allocate tasks to processors. By assumption, the number of tasks per level is less than or equal to p. By construction, execution of a level only begins after the previous level has been executed. The algorithm is therefore synchronous. At each level, a task is allocated to a different processor (in compliance with whatever rule is being used). Synchronization by levels ensures that one processor will not be allocated to two different tasks at the same time.

Clearly, by construction, the schedule obtained is compatible with the precedence system. To compute the execution time of the parallel algorithm, it is demonstrated by recurrence that the completion time of each of the tasks is equal to the longest path's execution time by linking the tasks to one task on the first level.

The property is proved for the tasks on the first level. Suppose it were proved for levels below j. Let T_k be a task on level j. The paths between T_k and the tasks on the first level are constructed from the paths between the predecessors of T_k and the tasks on the first level by adding the arcs between T_k and its predecessors. By assuming recurrence, $sta(T_i)+ex(T_i)$ is the execution time of the longest path between this task and a task on the first level. By construction, $sta(T_k)=\max(sta(T_i)+ex(T_i))$, where T_i belongs to $Pre(T_k)$, and $sta(T_k)+ex(T_k)$ is the execution time of the longest path between T_k and a task on the first level and that concludes the recurrence.

The execution time of the parallel algorithm is equal to the completion time of the last task to be executed. The latter belongs to the last level. The execution time is therefore Dep(G). The number of processors is equal to the width of the decomposition. Because this is of any given width, the following is obtained:

$$t_{opt} = Dep(G) \text{ and } p_{opt} \geq W(G)$$

Proof (2)

To show that p_{opt} = W(G), we shall prove that an algorithm that executes in t_{opt} with p_{opt} processors exists for scheduling a decomposition into Dep(G) levels. The algorithm is clearly synchronous, as all the tasks have the same execution time. For k from 1 to Dep(G), let level(k) denote the set of tasks that start to execute at time (k–1). If T_i belongs to level(k), its predecessors belong to lower levels and its successors belong to higher levels. A decomposition into levels is obtained and the proof is concluded.

Example

Consider the eight-task graph in Figure 9.2 and assume that all the tasks execute in time 1. The execution time of the longest path (and there are, in fact, two of them: (T_1–T_4–T_6–T_8) and (T_2–T_4–T_6–T_8)) is 4 and, therefore, t_{opt}=4. There is a parallel algorithm for each of these four decompositions into levels.

First decomposition

has a width of 3 and is a predecessor-oriented decomposition (*see* Figure 9.4).

level(1) = {T_1, T_2}	level(3) = {T_6, T_7}
level(2) = {T_3, T_4, T_5}	level(4) = {T_8}

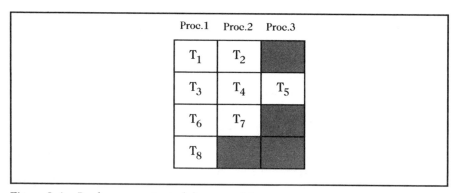

Figure 9.4   Predecessor-oriented decomposition

Second decomposition

has a width of 2 (*see* Figure 9.5).

level(1) = {T_1, T_2}	level(3) = {T_5, T_6}
level(2) = {T_3, T_4}	level(4) = {T_7, T_8}

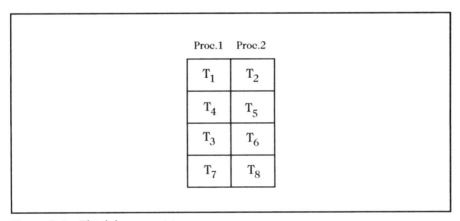

Figure 9.5   Second decomposition

Third decomposition

has a width of 2 (*see* Figure 9.6).

level(1) = {T_1, T_2}   level(3) = {T_3, T_6}
level(2) = {T_4, T_5}   level(4) = {T_7, T_8}

Figure 9.6   Third decomposition

Fourth decomposition

has a width of 3 and is a successor-oriented decomposition (*see* Figure 9.7).

level(1) = {T_1, T_2}   level(3) = {T_3, T_5, T_6}
level(2) = {T_4}   level(4) = {T_7, T_8}

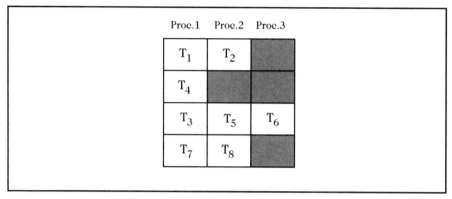

Figure 9.7   Successor-oriented decomposition

Fixed number of processors

Brent's lemma (Lemma 5.1) showed that an algorithm with p processors can be constructed from an algorithm with a greater number of processors. This can be used to link the optimal execution time $t_{opt}(p)$ of an algorithm with p processors to t_{opt} and to the sequential execution time t_{seq} (equal to n) and to obtain bounds for $t_{opt}(p)$.

Theorem 9.3

Let $A = (T_1, ..., T_n, \rightarrow)$ be a sequential algorithm, with tasks that all have the same execution time. Let t_{seq} be A's sequential execution time and p the number of processors.

(1) The optimal execution time of a parallel algorithm for A with p processors satisfies the following inequalities:

$$\frac{t_{seq}}{p} \leq t_{opt}(p) \frac{t_{seq}}{p} + \left(1 - \frac{1}{p}\right) t_{opt}$$

(2) If $t_{opt} = O(\frac{t_{seq}}{p})$ then the parallelization is asymptotically optimal:

$$t_{opt}(p) = \frac{t_{seq}}{p} + O(t_{opt})$$

Proof (1)

The lower bound is obtained by writing that an algorithm using p processors has an execution time which is at best p times shorter than its corresponding sequential algorithm. Now suppose that q_i tasks are executed by the algorithm of time t_{opt} between the moments $(i-1)$ and i. If the algorithm has p processors, this can be subdivided into $\lceil q_i/p \rceil$ steps, as all the tasks have the same execution time. An algorithm with the following execution time is obtained:

$$\sum_{i=1}^{Dep(G)} \left\lceil \frac{q_i}{p} \right\rceil \leq \left(1 - \frac{1}{p}\right) t_{opt} + \sum_{i=1}^{Dep(G)} \frac{q_i}{p} \leq \frac{t_{seq}}{p} + \left(1 - \frac{1}{p}\right) t_{opt}$$

Point (2) follows on directly from (1).

9.3.3 General case

Let us return to the analysis we began in Section 9.3.2 in the case where tasks last for any length of time. Of course, this is a far more difficult problem and the results are much poorer.

Determining t_{opt} and p_{opt}

In the general case where $A = (T_1,..., T_n, \rightarrow)$ is a sequential algorithm with tasks that last any length of time, a fairly approximate result can be obtained by studying the above example again.

Let $S = (T_1,..., T_n, <<)$ be the precedence system for A. If q is the gcd of the $ex(T_k)$, let $n_k = ex(T_k)/q$. A new system, S', is constructed by dividing each task T_k into n_k sub-tasks of time q: $T_{k, 1},..., T_{k, nk}$.

$$S' = (T_{1, 1},..., T_{1, n_1},..., T_{n, 1},..., T_{n, n_n}, \leq \leq)$$

The relation $\leq \leq$ is constructed as follows:

$$T_{k, j} \leq \leq T_{k, j+1} \text{ for } j=1,..., n_k-1$$
$$T_i << T_k \text{ implies } T_{i, n_i} \leq \leq T_{k, 1}$$

Let G^* be the task graph for the new system. Applying Theorem 9.3 means that only general bounds for the optimal number of processors can be obtained.

Theorem 9.4
Let $A = (T_1,..., T_n, \rightarrow)$ be a sequential algorithm, with tasks that take any length of time to execute.

(1) With an unbounded number of processors, the time, t_{opt}, of an optimal parallel algorithm is equal to the execution time of the longest path in the task graph.

(2) The minimum number of processors, p_{opt}, with which an algorithm that executes in time t_{opt} can be written, is such that:

$$W(G) \leq p_{opt} \leq \min (Wp(G^*), Ws(G^*))$$

Proof

We cannot directly apply the previous proof to G^*. Clearly, decomposing G^* into levels constitutes a parallel algorithm for A. By contrast, for this decomposition to constitute a parallel algorithm for A, the same processor has to execute $T_{k,j}$ for fixed k and j varying between 1 and n_k, and $T_{k,j}$ and $T_{k,j+1}$ have to be executed consecutively. Satisfying the first condition is easy, as the scheduling algorithm is such that, on each level, each task has to be allocated to a different processor, but any rule according to which processor tasks are allocated may apply. The second condition is not satisfied by all the decompositions, and that demonstrates the lower bound.

To obtain the upper bound, it just needs to be noted that predecessor- and successor-oriented decomposition satisfy the second condition. Let's take the scheduling algorithm used in the proof and detail how processors are assigned to tasks. The only additional constraint is that the processor that is allocated $T_{k,1}$ will be allocated the tasks $T_{k,j}$ for $j=2,\ldots, n_k$ on all subsequent levels. By grouping all the sub-tasks $T_{k,j}$ into T_k, the following algorithm is obtained:

$$pre(T_k) = pre^*(T_{k,1}) \text{ and } sta(T_k) = sta^*(T_{k,1})$$

where pre^* and sta^* are the scheduling functions for G^*.

Example

Let's take another look at the eight-task graph that was used as an example earlier (*see* Figure 9.2). Suppose that:

$$ex(T_1) = ex(T_4) = ex(T_5) = ex(T_8) = 1$$
$$ex(T_2) = ex(T_3) = ex(T_6) = ex(T_7) = 2$$

The new version of the graph G* is shown in Figure 9.8. The time obtained is t_{opt}=6. The graph's width is 3 and, therefore, $p_{opt} \geq 3$. It can be seen easily that p_{opt}=3.

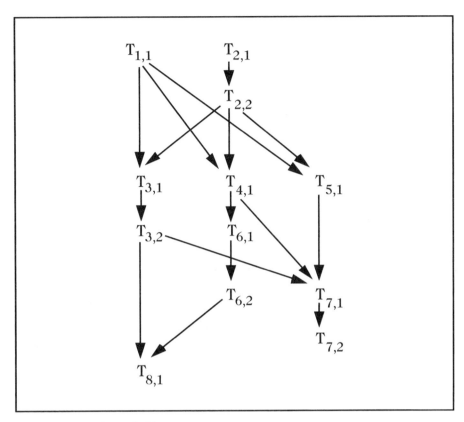

Figure 9.8   Task graph G*

An optimal parallel algorithm can be obtained by means of a predecessor-oriented decomposition of the graph. G* (*see* Figure 9.9) and then G (*see* Figure 9.10) can be scheduled on the basis of the decomposition.

Predecessor-oriented decomposition
    The width of the decomposition is 3.

level(1) = {$T_{1,1}$, $T_{2,1}$}   level(4) = {$T_{3,2}$, $T_{6,1}$}
level(2) = {$T_{2,2}$}   level(5) = {$T_{6,2}$, $T_{7,1}$}
level(3) = {$T_{3,1}$, $T_{4,1}$, $T_{5,1}$}   level(6) = {$T_{7,2}$, $T_{8,1}$}

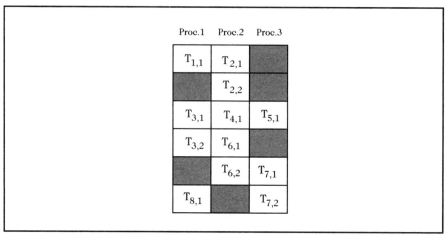

Figure 9.9   First (predecessor-oriented) decomposition of graph G*

From this, the scheduling algorithm for graph G is deduced:

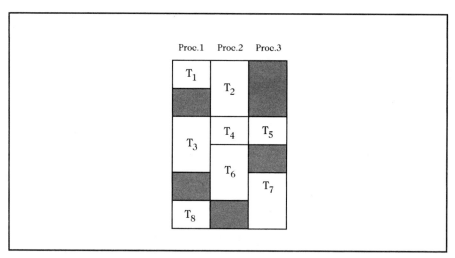

Figure 9.10   Scheduling of graph G

p_{opt} can be strictly greater than $W(G^*)$. Consider the five-task graph G in Figure 9.11 (where $ex(T_1)=1$, $ex(T_2)=ex(T_3)=ex(T_4)=2$ and $ex(T_5)=3$) and the graph G^* that corresponds to it (*see* Figure 9.12).
    The following decomposition has a width of 2:

level(1) = $\{T_{1,1}, T_{5,1}\}$	level(4) = $\{T_{5,2}, T_{4,1}\}$
level(2) = $\{T_{2,1}, T_{3,1}\}$	level(5) = $\{T_{5,3}, T_{4,2}\}$
level(3) = $\{T_{2,2}, T_{3,2}\}$	

However, scheduling for this is not a parallel algorithm, since sub-tasks $T_{5,1}$ and $T_{5,2}$ are not consecutive. p_{opt} is in fact equal to 3.

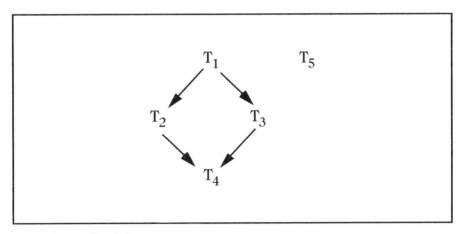

Figure 9.11   Graph G

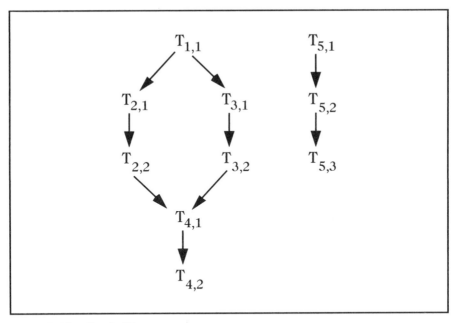

Figure 9.12   Graph G*

The range of the bounds of p_{opt} and $p_{opt}(p)$, where p is known, is described by Hu [Hu61], Ramamoorthy *et al.* [RCG72] and Fernandez and Bussel [FeB73]. Another avenue of research that could be explored is to develop efficient, general scheduling algorithms. This problem is discussed in Chapter 10.

Proc.1	Proc.2
$T_{1,1}$	$T_{5,1}$
$T_{2,1}$	$T_{3,1}$
$T_{2,2}$	$T_{3,2}$
$T_{5,2}$	$T_{4,1}$
$T_{5,3}$	$T_{4,2}$

Figure 9.13   (Unacceptable) optimal decomposition

9.4   Example – two-step graph

The aim of this section is to apply the methods described in the above paragraphs specifically to *Gaussian elimination*.

9.4.1   General description

Gaussian elimination

Gaussian elimination was described in Section 8.3. Triangular decomposition of a matrix A of size n requires $O(n^3)$ arithmetic operations. If the number of processors is restricted to $O(n)$, an execution time of $O(n^2)$ can be expected.

As could be seen from the vector form of Gaussian elimination, one algorithm can be written in several different ways. Clearly, this remains true for parallel algorithms. In this example, one specific variant is considered. The problem will be discussed more comprehensively in Chapter 11.

The algorithm we shall refer to is the kji variant described in Section 8.3.1, the standard column-oriented Gaussian elimination algorithm with pivoting, in which elements are reduced by columns [GoV83]. At stage k, row k is combined with rows k+1, k+2,..., n so that the subdiagonal elements of column k are annihilated. The following algorithm results:

```
{kji variant}
for  k ← 1  to  n-1
    determine the index m corresponding to the maximum element
    in column k swap (A(k, k), A(m, k))
    piv ← 1/A(k, k)
    for  i ← k+1  to  n
        A(i, k) ← A(i, k)*piv
    for  j ← k+1  to  n
        swap (A(k, k), A(m, k))
        for  i ← k+1  to  n
            A(i, j) ← A(i, j) - A(i, k)*A(k, j)
```

Decomposing graphs into elementary tasks

There is a natural form of Gaussian elimination that can be used in order to comply with constraints on the algorithm's granularity (tasks of order $O(n)$):

```
(T_kk) preparation of column k and
(T_kj) modification of column j (for j>k)
```

The detailed algorithm is as follows:

```
T_kk:    determine the index m corresponding to the maximum
         element
         in column k swap (A(k, k), A(m, k))
         piv ← 1/A(k, k)
         for  i ← k+1  to  n
             A(i, k) ← A(i, k)*piv

T_kj:    swap (A(k, k), A(m, k))
         for  i ← k+1  to  n
             A(i, j) ← A(i, j) - A(i, k)*A(k, j)
```

The sequential algorithm is therefore as follows:

```
for  k ← 1  to  n-1
    execute T_kk
    for  j ← k+1  to  n
        execute T_kj
```

This implies that the order relation of the sequential algorithm $A = (T_{kj}, \rightarrow)$ has the following form:

$$T_{kj} \rightarrow T_{k'j'} \Leftrightarrow (j < j' \text{ and } k=k') \text{ or } (k < k')$$

Assume that communication costs can be ignored and only computation costs are taken into account (which is reasonable for the granularity that has been chosen). Then consider that the cost of a multiplication followed by a subtraction is equal to the cost of a multiplication followed by a comparison and that each of these costs is one computation unit; the cost of the various tasks is as follows:

$$ex(T_{kk}) = n - k + 1 \qquad ex(T_{kj}) = n - k$$

Constructing a precedence system

Let $S = (T_{kj}, <<)$ be the precedence system for A. The sets of task inputs and outputs are:

$$I(T_{kk}) = \{A(i, k) \text{ with } k \le i \le n\}$$
$$O(T_{kk}) = \{A(i, k) \text{ with } k+1 \le i \le n\}$$
$$I(T_{kj}) = \{A(i, k) \text{ with } k \le i \le n\} \cup \{A(i, j) \text{ with } k \le i \le n\}$$
$$O(T_{kj}) = \{A(i, j) \text{ with } k+1 \le i \le n\}$$

From this, the following precedence relations can be deduced:

$$T_{kk} << T_{kj} \qquad \text{for } k < j \le n \text{ and } 1 \le k \le n$$
$$T_{kj} << T_{k+1, j} \qquad \text{for } k < j \le n \text{ and } 1 \le k < n$$

A task graph can then be constructed (the pair (k, j) corresponds to the task T_{kj} (*see* Figure 9.14)).

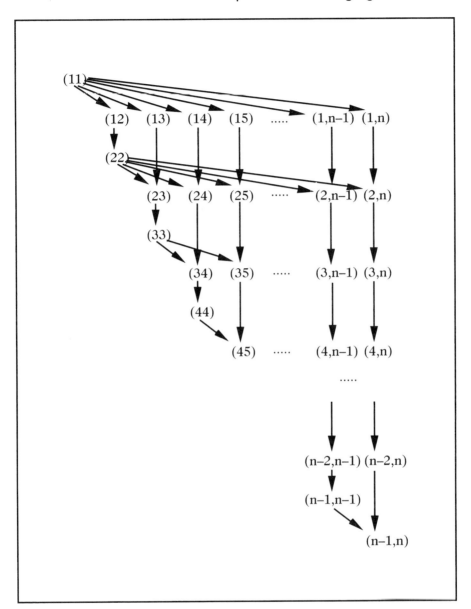

Figure 9.14   Task graph for the kji variant of Gaussian elimination

9.4.2 Scheduling the graph

Now the graph has been constructed, we have to look at how it is scheduled. The first step is to establish bounds on its optimal time and its optimal number of processors.

Theoretical bounds

To establish t_{opt}, the longest path in the graph has to be found. It is not difficult to see that it consists of the following tasks:

$$T_{11} - T_{12} - T_{22} - \ldots - T_{kk} - T_{k,k+1} - T_{k+1,k+1} - \ldots - T_{n-2,n-1} - T_{n-1,n-1} - T_{n-1,n}$$

The following is then obtained:

$$t_{opt} = \sum_{k=1}^{n-1} ex(T_{kk}) + \sum_{k=1}^{n-1} ex(T_{k,k+1}) = n^2 - 1$$

Note that the task graph, as shown in Figure 9.14, is a predecessor-oriented decomposition. All the tasks on the same level have the same execution time. The width of the decomposition is $n-1$. Thus,

$$p_{opt} \leq n-1$$

Predecessor-oriented decomposition is natural in this example. Let's look at successor-oriented decomposition. The task graph's form is illustrated in Figure 9.15. The width of the decomposition is $\frac{n}{2}$. Thus:

$$p_{opt} \leq \left\lceil \frac{n}{2} \right\rceil$$

Computing the lower bound of the theorem is a difficult problem, as all the decompositions of the graph associated with it have to be constructed, and that is impossible in the general case.

A lower bound that is easy to compute is obtained by noting that a parallel algorithm always has an efficiency that is less than 1. Thus:

$$P_{opt} \geq \frac{t_{seq}}{t_{opt}} \geq \frac{\displaystyle\sum_{k=1}^{n-1}\sum_{j=k}^{n} ex\left(T_{kj}\right)}{n^2 - 1} \geq \frac{\dfrac{n^3 + 2n - 3}{3}}{n^2 - 1} \geq \frac{n}{3} + \frac{1}{n+1}$$

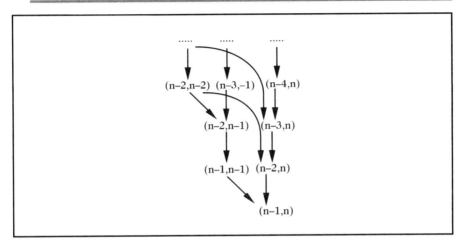

Figure 9.15 Task graph for successor-oriented decomposition

Practical schedule with $\frac{n}{2}$ processors

Let us construct a scheduling of $\lceil \frac{n}{2} \rceil$ processors to improve on the upper bound. It just has to be noted that T_{kk} takes the same time to execute as the $T_{k-1,j}$ for all j. The idea is to execute an entire level, plus the subsequent diagonal task, in two steps. Consider the following decomposition into levels (assume that n is even for the sake of simplicity):

T_{11}							
T_{12}	T_{13}	T_{15}	T_{17}	$\cdots$	$T_{1,n-5}$	$T_{1,n-3}$	$T_{1,n-1}$
T_{22}	T_{14}	T_{16}	T_{18}	$\cdots$	$T_{1,n-4}$	$T_{1,n-2}$	$T_{1,n}$
T_{23}	T_{24}	T_{26}	$\cdots$	$T_{2,n-4}$	$T_{2,n-2}$	$T_{2,n}$	
T_{33}	T_{25}	T_{27}	$\cdots$	$T_{2,n-3}$	$T_{2,n-1}$		
$\cdots\cdots$							
$T_{2k,2k+1}$	$T_{2k,2k+2}$	$T_{2k,2k+4}$	$\cdots$	$T_{2k,n}$			
$T_{2k+1,2k+1}$	$T_{2k,2k+3}$	$T_{2k,2k+5}$	$\cdots$	$T_{2k,n-1}$			
$\cdots\cdots$							
$T_{n-2,n-1}$	$T_{n-2,n}$						
$T_{n-1,n-1}$							
$T_{n-1,n}$							

The tasks' execution time is the same on each level. The decomposition's width is $\frac{n}{2}$. To schedule this, tasks are allocated to processors by levels in any given order – by columns, for example. $\frac{n}{2}$ processors are required to schedule the decomposition.

Constructing lower bounds

Each level will be searched to discover the total number of independent tasks, in order to improve on the upper bound. The set of antecedents of $T_{n-1, n-1}$, written $Ant(T_{n-1, n-1})$, consists of the T_{kj}, such that $1 \leq k, j \leq n-1$. Therefore, when $T_{n-1, n-1}$ completes, the only remaining tasks that cannot be executed are the T_{kn}, for $1 \leq k \leq n-1$. As all these tasks are consecutive, only $T_{n-1, n}$ has not been executed. So p–1 processors are idle during $t_{n-1, n}$ time units.

More generally, $Ant(T_{n-i, n-i})$ consists of the T_{kj}, such that $1 \leq k$, $j \leq n-i$. Therefore, when $T_{n-i, n-i}$ completes, the only tasks remaining that cannot be executed are the T_{kj}, for $1 \leq k \leq n-1$ and $n-i+1 \leq j \leq n$. As T_{kj} and $T_{k+1, j}$ are consecutive, it is deduced that at most i tasks can be executed at the same time. (p–1) processors are therefore idle during $ex(T_{n-i, n-i+1}) + ex(T_{n-i+1, n-i+1})$ time units. Furthermore, T_{11} precedes all the other tasks and p–1 processors are therefore idle during $ex(T_{11})$ time units.

Here, we introduce the concepts of total computational volume and total idle time. We show how a general bound can be obtained using these concepts. The method introduced in this section was put forward by Lord *et al.* [LKK83]. It has become one of the basic tools for using task graphs to study algorithms.

A processor is *busy* when it is executing a task, otherwise it is *idle*.

Definition 9.8
The *computational volume*, written CV(p), is the sum of the actual execution times of each processor; in other words, the total amount of time in which the processors are busy.

The *idle volume*, written IV(p), is the sum of the accumulated periods of time in which the processors are idle.

Theorem 9.5
The following relation exists for an algorithm that executes in optimal time:

$$CV(p) + IV(p) = pt_{opt}(p)$$

Proof
A processor is either busy or idle. The sum of the periods of activity or inactivity is equal to the number of processors multiplied by the computation time of the algorithm, which yields the theorem's formula, where the algorithm executes in optimal time.

Where there is only one processor, the idle volume is zero and the computational volume is equal to the sequential algorithm's time.

If the above is applied to a two-step graph, the following is deduced:

$$IV(p) \geq (p-1)ex(T_{11}) + \sum_{i=2}^{p-1}(p-i)\left(ex(T_{n-i+1,n-i}) + ex(T_{n-i+1,n-i+1})\right) + (p-1)ex(T_{n,n-1})$$

with

$$ex(T_{n-i+1,\ n-i}) = ex(T_{n-i+1,\ n-i+1}) = i.$$

In accordance with Theorem 9.5,

$$CV(p) \leq p(n^2-1) - \left((p-1)n + 2\sum_{i=2}^{p-1}(p-i)i + (p-1)\right)$$

Whatever the number of p, CV(p) must be greater than the sequential algorithm's time and so:

$$\frac{n^3}{3} + \frac{2n}{3} - 1 \leq CV(p) \leq p(n^2-1) - (p-1)(n-1) - \frac{p^3-p}{3}$$

A lower bound for p_{opt} can then be deduced from the above. To do this, let p=αn. The following is obtained:

$$n^2(3\alpha - \alpha^3 - 1) - 3\alpha n + (\alpha + 1) \geq 0$$

It can be deduced from this that $p_{opt} \geq \alpha^* n$ where α^* is the solution of $3\alpha^* - \alpha^{*3} - 1 = 0$. That is, $\alpha^* = 0.34729....$ The following bound is obtained:

$$0.34729\ n \leq p_{opt} \leq 0.5\ n$$

The table below yields the value of p_{opt} obtained using this method for small values of n (with n being even):

$2 \leq n \leq 8$	$P_{opt} = n/2$
$10 \leq n \leq 14$	$P_{opt} = n/2 - 1$
$16 \leq n \leq 22$	$P_{opt} = n/2 - 2$
$24 \leq n \leq 28$	$P_{opt} = n/2 - 3$
$30 \leq n \leq 34$	$P_{opt} = n/2 - 4$

In conclusion, note that we shall show in Chapter 11 how a two-step task graph that reaches this bound is constructed. Clearly, the problem remains open where the graph may be of any kind.

9.5   Conclusion

In this chapter, we showed that a parallel program can be quite easily written as a task graph. Analysing the graph results in a lower bound for the program's execution time, where no bound is placed on the number of processors (an execution scheme is then obtained by allocating tasks by levels to processors). The problem of determining the minimum number of processors in order to attain the optimal time is difficult, as is the problem of determining the optimal execution time with a fixed number of processors. A specific example (a two-step graph) was used to illustrate the problems, which we shall generalize in Chapters 10 and 11.

10

Task scheduling

Task scheduling is central to the study of parallel algorithms. In this chapter, we look at the problem in all its general aspects. First, we discuss the standard problem of schedules that do not take communication between tasks into account, then describe some attempts to extend these solutions by considering communication costs. The last part of the chapter is devoted to the specific example of scheduling nested loops.

10.1   General description

10.1.1   Scheduling – a difficult problem

Definition

Scheduling is a very general problem. It has existed for a long time and occurs in a number of fields, particularly in computing and computer science. There are various forms of scheduling – short-term process scheduling on the same processor, managing process queues and so on [CoD73]. Traditionally, many authors have studied the general problem of resource allocation on a given number of workstations. Since the beginning of the 1980s, this theoretical work has been applied to task allocation in practical parallel computation. There is a great deal of literature on the subject and many papers have been published [Bes92] [CaC88] [Chr92] [DLR82] [ErL90] [GLL79] [Gon77]. The aim of this chapter is not so much to study all the available methods exhaustively, but to describe simply the most important ideas and to concentrate on their practical implications.

Definition of the main scheduling problem:

To schedule in minimum time a set $T = \{T_1, ..., T_n\}$ of n tasks that are subject to fixed precedence constraints (expressed by a partial order relation, written $<<$) on p identical processors.

Throughout this chapter, *makespan* (a schedule's total execution time, which corresponds to the execution time of its parallel algorithm) is denoted by ω.

Basic assumptions

Except where otherwise stated, we make the following assumptions:

Execution is static; that is, all the tasks, their lengths and the way they are structured are fixed once and for all. The assumption is that the task graph is analysed before it is executed. Clearly, there are jobs where allocation is dynamic and the graph cannot be completely known until run time. Readers who are interested in this can refer to [CaK88].

The model adopted is deterministic, as opposed to stochastic (which means that some parameters are known only in terms of probability – for example, only an estimate of the tasks' lengths is known). The reader is referred to [DLR82] or [GLL79] for a more detailed discussion of this.

Finally, tasks are not pre-emptively allocated. In practice, this means that execution of a given task cannot be interrupted to execute another with a higher priority.

Complexity of the scheduling problem

Complete solutions to the general problem of scheduling have been found only for some very simple cases. The problem remains difficult in all its general aspects. In practice, schedules of parallel programs contain a large number of tasks and it is essential that the limits of scheduling problems are defined.

The fundamental parameters of scheduling, as far as task graphs are concerned, include: the number of tasks, n, how long they take, ex(T), and how their precedence constraints are structured. As far as processors are concerned, the essential parameters are: the number of processors, p, and the function that describes the system of communication between processors (which we shall ignore in our description in this chapter and discuss in Chapter 15 instead). Values can be assigned to a task graph's arcs (constraints) in proportion to the amount of communication between tasks.

The general problem of scheduling any given set of tasks is NP-complete [Bra90] [BeS92] [CaC88] [PaS82] [Ull75]. If some parameters are relaxed, the problem can be solved in polynomial time, essentially by considering tasks with unit execution time (UET) and task graphs with their own specific structure. For example, in some numerical problems, the task graph's structure is regular (that is, tasks are grouped together on levels) and relations in the expression of the length of time it takes the tasks to execute are simple. As will be seen in Chapter 11, optimal results can be obtained on the basis of these structures and properties.

Where graphs can be of any kind, the sole fact that tasks take different amounts of time to complete means that the problem is NP-complete (with fixed constraints and number of processors) [Ull75]. Similarly, if the amount of time tasks take to complete is fixed, considered as being UET, the general problem of finding the schedule for any task graph with any number of processors is still NP-complete. Furthermore, the number of machines has no bearing on the complexity of the problem. As Ullman demonstrated [Ull75], the problem of scheduling any graph with tasks that do not have the same execution time is NP-complete, even when only two processors are being used.

10.1.2   State of the art

General results

To deal with the difficulty of the scheduling problem, a great deal of theoretical work has been done on reducing the values of certain characteristic parameters – leading to what is called the relaxation method [BeS92]. Fairly accurate theoretical answers to complexity problems can be found within such constraints, but unfortunately these are of limited interest as scheduling a given precedence system is in general an NP-complete problem. However, as we shall see below, the algorithms we describe for the specific cases mentioned above can provide ideas for scheduling strategies to deal with the general problem and they often prove to be effective in practice. Figure 10.1 summarizes the main theoretical results to date.

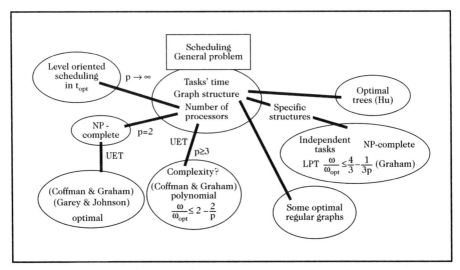

Figure 10.1   State-of-the-art results (excluding communication)

Solving the problem

Finding a general algorithm to solve the problem of task scheduling in a reasonable length of time requires a different kind of approach from the very technical one adopted in finding specific algorithms (as in numerical methods, such as Gaussian elimination, which is discussed in Chapter 11). The aim is to design general scheduling algorithms so that, for example, efficient execution schemes can be used during compilation. In this context, we describe how list-scheduling algorithms operate, and then go on to provide a detailed description of the most well-known and, probably, the most useful strategy for constructing lists – the critical path method.

We consider algorithms as being decomposed into their finest possible grain size; in other words, they have unit execution time (UET). How communication between tasks is taken into account depends on the machine model being used. This chapter essentially deals with analysing architecture-independent complexity. Chapter 14 deals with other techniques that can be used to take communication constraints into account, particularly where processor networks are being used. First, we describe UET scheduling algorithms that ignore communication between tasks, which may constitute an initial approximation of shared-memory machines, then we describe one way of taking communication between tasks into account, which involves considering all data accesses as taking the same time to execute. The model is then said to have unit communication time (UCT).

10.2   Solutions excluding communication between tasks

10.2.1   Introduction – potential tasks

If it is assumed that the number of processors being used is unbounded, there is a simple way of determining scheduling on a graph with a special form (*potential task* graph). The idea is to change any task graph into a potential task graph. But a few concepts ought to be explained before we go on to describe this method.

Earliest/latest possible start-times

As we saw in Chapter 9, a task's earliest start-time is defined as the first possible time when the task can be executed, irrespective of the number of processors being used. Similarly, a task's latest start-time is the last possible time when the task can execute without postponing its final completion time. Start-times are very easy to compute using a level-oriented date stamping algorithm, with a cost that is linear in the number of tasks (for example, Bellman's algorithm [Ber83] [GoM79]). Latest possible start-times can be obtained in the same way, by starting at the end of the algorithm and inverting the direction of the precedence constraints.

A critical task is any task with identical earliest and latest possible start-times. If the number of processors is ignored, the task has to be executed at the relevant start-time, in order to keep the time it takes to execute to a minimum.

Potential tasks and PERT

Given a task graph G with n tasks T_i of arbitrary lengths, there are two fairly close representations which can be used directly with latest start-time date-stamping. They lead, as we shall see later on, to a scheduling that is optimal when the number of processors is unbounded. The two representations are described below.

First, assume that the precedence constraints $T_i \prec\prec T_j$ are expressed as $start(T_j) - start(T_i) \geq ex(T_i)$, which means that task T_j cannot start until T_i completes.

The concept of a potential task graph for G was originated by Roy [Roy70]. It involves adding an imaginary task at the front of all those tasks without predecessors and an imaginary task as the successor to all the graph's final tasks, and then representing the constraints start (T_j) – start$(T_i) \geq$ ex(T_i) as the arcs (T_i, T_j) which are assigned the values of the length of time, ex(T_i), the tasks take to execute.

In PERT, each task is represented by an arc, whose value is the task's execution time. The vertices are constraints. The end of the arc corresponding to a particular task adjoins the beginning of the arc corresponding to any task that precedes it.

These two representations can be used for earliest and latest possible start-time scheduling. Specifically, it can be shown that an earliest possible start-time schedule exists for a potential task graph if, and only if, the graph does not have a strictly positive cycle. In this case, the longest path from the start to the task T_i is the task's earliest possible start-time. The schedule here is of course optimal in terms of minimizing makespan for an unbounded number of processors. Similarly, if the graph does not have an absorbent cycle, an optimal latest possible start-time schedule exists, given the same conditions.

This method is general. The problem of scheduling on parallel machines lies in how an algorithm for a fixed number of processors can be designed, since a choice has to be made in that algorithm on which tasks are to execute at any given time. However, as we shall see later on, criteria for earliest and latest possible start-times can give very good heuristics.

10.2.2   List-scheduling algorithms

How list-scheduling algorithms operate

Traditionally, scheduling has been based on *list-scheduling algorithms*, which create schedules that manage lists of executable tasks. Execution of a task on the list frees its successors, within the precedence constraints that apply. Execution is based on a *greedy* strategy – tasks are executed as soon as possible (if constraints permit), in the order they are listed and without delay. Task lists describe the total order of the set of tasks and define the order of priority of available tasks.

Clearly, there are several ways in which task lists can be constructed, and there is an arbitrary element in how tasks are chosen for execution, particularly as far as tasks with the same priority are concerned. Using the theorem below, Graham [Gra69] showed how the efficiency of list-scheduling algorithms is gauged in relation to optimal efficiency, in the general case of scheduling tasks with arbitrary execution times.

Theorem 10.1 [Gra69]

The worst-case time it takes for a list-schedule to execute on p processors ($p \geq 3$) for any given acyclic graph is:

$$\omega \leq \omega_{opt}\left(2 - \frac{1}{p}\right)$$

where ω_{opt} is the amount of time taken by the best possible schedule.

Proof

The amount of time taken by any given schedule to execute can be broken down into two factors: the total amount of idle time and the total execution time (*see* Section 9.4.2). Thus:

$$\omega = \frac{IV + \sum_{T \in T} ex(T)}{p}$$

Note that total idle time in an optimal schedule is minimal, which means that the following inequality can be easily demonstrated:

$$\omega \leq \omega_{opt} + \frac{IV}{p}$$

Also, the following lower bound (which is valid for all paths of the graph) exists:

$$\sum_{T \in C} ex(T) \leq \omega_{opt}$$

By contrast, the bound on idle time for any task while it is being executed is known (effectively, at most $(p - 1)$ processors are available):

$$IV(T) \leq (p - 1)\, ex(T)$$

The clever part of the proof lies in using the final paths to construct a path C such that:

$$IV \leq (p - 1)\sum_{T \in C} ex(T)$$

(the above is possible because list-schedules that contain no dead time are being considered). It can then be concluded that:

$$\omega \le \omega_{opt} + \frac{IV}{p} \le \omega_{opt} + \frac{(p-1)\sum_{T \in C} ex(T)}{p} \le \omega_{opt}\left(1 + \frac{p-1}{p}\right)$$

List-scheduling algorithm

Let's assume that the tasks in a task graph are arranged in a list, L, that is compatible with the graph's precedence constraints. The list of available tasks is written as L'. The algorithm for creating the list is as follows:

```
L ← ∅
while  L≠T  do
    {priorities established}
    priority (T)
    L ← L ∪ {T}
```

Note that the greatest cost involved in list-scheduling strategies results from creating the list itself. In fact, once the list has been constructed, a greedy execution is polynomial in its number of tasks. As we shall see in greater detail later on, priorities can be established on the basis of the tasks' critical paths, the number of their successors and so on. Of course, a greedy algorithm for executing a list schedules tasks in a compact manner, that is, the schedule's constraints are such that there is no dead time in it.

Below, we describe an algorithm for executing a UET task list (the list L, for which an algorithm was outlined above) on a fixed number of processors, p.

The algorithm starts with tasks being sorted in ascending order of priority. RTL designates the set of tasks that have yet to execute (Remaining Task List). A(k) is the set of tasks on the list that are available at step k. Alloc(T) denotes the processor to which task T is allocated and start(T) the time when task T begins to execute. Succ(T) and pred(T) are the set of successors and predecessors respectively of task T. k represents successive times and i is an index that can be used to control the number of processors.

```
k ← 1 and i ← 1
A(k) ← {T/pred(T) = ∅}
RTL ← L
while RTL≠∅ do
    if ∃ T ∈ A(k) / priority(T) ≥ priority(T') ∀ T'∈ A(k) then
    RTL ← RTL\{T}
    A(k) ← A(k)\{T}
    A(k+1) ← {T'∈ succ(T)/pred(T')∩ RTL) = ∅}
    alloc(T) ← i
    start(T) ← k
    if (i = p) then
        i ← 1 and k ← k+1
        A(k) ← A(k) ∪ A(k-1)
    else i ← i + 1
else
    i ← 1 and k ← k+1
```

10.2.3   Largest Processing Time scheduling

In the special case of a task graph having no constraints (in other words, all its tasks are independent), tasks are not ordered according to random priority criteria. Graham originally proposed *Largest Processing Time* (LPT) scheduling, in which tasks are scheduled in terms of how long they take. It is an interesting result, as it concerns tasks of any length and it can be extended to graphs with any structure by using the principle on which it operates with other scheduling techniques, such as simulated annealing or differentiation/evaluation algorithms [CoL90].

Theorem 10.2
For a graph with no precedence constraints, the length of an LPT schedule on p processors (p ≥ 3) is at worst:

$$\omega \le \omega_{opt}\left(\frac{4}{3} - \frac{1}{3p}\right)$$

Note that the selection criterion can be inverted by scheduling the tasks with the lowest costs (that is, those with the shortest length) first. On average, this is rather less effective than LPT scheduling, as we would intuitively expect.

10.2.4   Critical paths

Definition

Once it has been accepted that a greedy strategy should be adopted to create lists, 'good' criteria have to be found for constructing a good list from all possible lists. One of the most popular ways of creating lists is based on *level-oriented* decomposition, as we originally described it in Chapter 9. One of the most natural strategies (and, as we shall see, one of the most effective) is to construct levels by applying the *critical path* method. A task's critical path is defined as the longest path – understood as the total amount of time remaining tasks take to execute – to be traversed, starting from that task (that is, the distance from the task to the final tasks). It is a natural enough method, as it amounts to the prioritizing tasks with the highest costs, that is, those where the path that remains to be traversed is the longest.

In comparison with Graham's theorem, critical path list-scheduling yields a more accurate result.

Theorem 10.3

For any acyclic graph with UET tasks, the execution time of a list that is scheduled according to the tasks' critical paths (with any given priority on a level) on p processors ($p \geq 3$) is at worst:

$$\omega \leq \omega_{opt}\left(2 - \frac{1}{p-1}\right)$$

Kunde also demonstrated that if the graph is a tree consisting of tasks with lengths that are not necessarily identical, the length of a critical path list-schedule is at worst [Kun81]:

$$\omega \leq \omega_{opt}\left(2 - \frac{2}{p+1}\right)$$

Note also that these worst-case bounds can be attained.

Coffman-Graham list-scheduling algorithm

The algorithm proposed by Coffman and Graham [CoG72] is a fundamental result of list-scheduling using the critical path method. The algorithm, which we shall refer to simply as the CG algorithm, establishes priorities on levels. There are two stages to this. In the first, the task graph is labelled, starting with the last of its precedence constraints. Then tasks are executed in inverse lexicographical order of their labels.

We now describe how the graph is labelled, in other words, how the list is constructed. The first step is to label tasks with no successors. The tasks are ordered randomly. Then, those tasks with immediate successors that have been labelled are considered and the task (or one of the tasks, chosen randomly) with successors that have the smallest labels in terms of lexico-graphical order is chosen.

For example, consider Figure 10.2; T and T' are two tasks that have yet to be labelled, with successors that have been labelled. T is labelled before T' if, and only if, a has a lower priority than b.

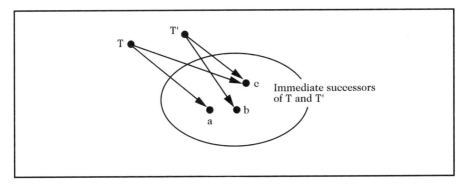

Figure 10.2   CG labelling

The process is complete when all tasks have been labelled.

Theorem 10.4 [CoG72]
    Assuming that p=2, list scheduling with the CG algorithm for any acyclic graph with UET tasks is optimal.

Lam and Sethi [LaS77] also show that for $p \geq 3$, the heuristic quality of the CG algorithm is:

$$\omega \leq \omega_{opt}\left(2 - \frac{2}{p}\right)$$

(this was improved on in [BrT93]).

The complexity of the CG algorithm is in $O(n^2)$, where n is the total number of tasks. However, it should be explained that the task graph's transitive closure is assumed to have been computed (which requires On^3 elementary operations with a usual algorithm [Ber83].) However, Gabow demonstrated a variant of the algorithm that is 'almost linear' in n, without prior computation of the graph's transitive closure [Gab82]. More specifically, its time is $n\alpha(n)$, where α is the inverse of the Ackerman function. Note, however, that Gabow's method is rather difficult to implement.

Garey-Johnson algorithm

Garey and Johnson devised another optimal list-scheduling algorithm [GaJ77] for two processors. The algorithm is constructed by establishing the latest possible start-time $\delta(T)$ for all tasks and ordering them according to those start-times. The final schedule is obtained with a list-scheduling algorithm.

Suppose the algorithm can be executed in t time units; if N tasks share a common predecessor T, T must complete before the start-time $t - \lceil \frac{N}{2} \rceil$ if the N tasks are to complete before t. The GJ algorithm is defined recursively on the basis of this, starting with the maximum elements of the set of tasks (in other words, those with a latest possible start-time of t). The list is constructed as follows:

if T is maximal, then $\delta(T)=t$

$$\delta(T) \min_{T' \in \text{succ}(T)} \left(\delta(T') - \left\lceil \frac{\text{card}\left(\left\{T'' \in \text{succ}(T) / \delta(T'') \leq \delta(T')\right\}\right)}{2} \right\rceil \right)$$

Theorem 10.5 (Garey-Johnson):
Assuming p=2, a GJ schedule for any acyclic task graph with UET tasks is optimal.

Note that prior computation of the graph's transitive closure is required, as in the case of the CG algorithm.

10.2.5   Variations on the critical path method

Generally, list-scheduling algorithms, particularly those that make use of the critical path method, are simple and frequently used. Optimal solutions can be demonstrated for specific graphs for any number of processors. Hu [Hu61] made the additional assumption of a graph with UET tasks and demonstrated that all level-oriented list-scheduling algorithms (that do not necessarily use the critical path method) are optimal for task graphs that are trees. Known as Highest Level First, Hu's algorithm is greedy and orders tasks level by level.

Unfortunately, schedules obtained by applying the critical path method are not optimal in general, as the few simple examples that we describe below demonstrate.

Counter-examples to optimal list-scheduling algorithms

For any given graph with UET tasks, a critical path schedule is not optimal for a number of processors that is strictly greater than 2 (as the example with 12 tasks in Figure 10.3 and the schedules in Figure 10.4 show).

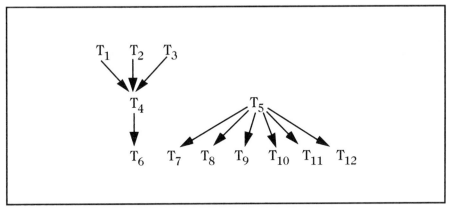

Figure 10.3   Example of a graph with 12 UET tasks

Proc.1	Proc.2	Proc.3
T_1	T_2	T_3
T_4	T_5	
T_6	T_7	T_8
T_9	T_{10}	T_{11}
T_{12}		

Critical path

Proc.1	Proc.2	Proc.3
T_1	T_2	T_5
T_3	T_7	T_8
T_4	T_9	T_{10}
T_6	T_{11}	T_{12}

Optimal

Figure 10.4   Schedules for the graph in Figure 10.3

Similarly, a critical path schedule is not optimal for a graph with tasks of unequal length, even where two processors are used. To illustrate this, consider the eight-task graph in Figure 10.5, where T_1, T_4, T_5, T_6, T_7 and T_8 have a length of one unit and T_2 and T_3 are of length 3.

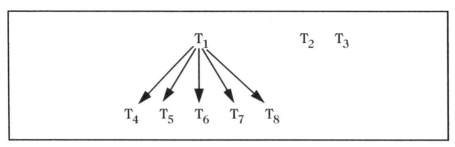

Figure 10.5   Example of a graph with eight, non-UET tasks

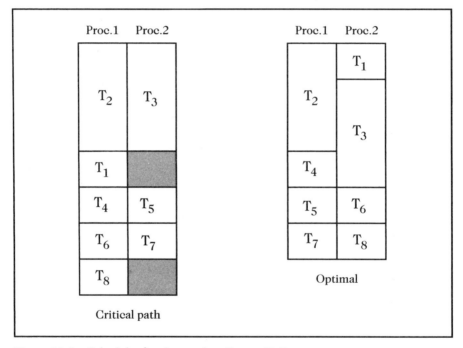

Figure 10.6   Schedules for the graph in Figure 10.5

The allocation in Figure 10.6 shows that the critical path is not optimal. In fact, this coarse-grain heuristic is such that a 'blocking' task (that is, one that frees many other tasks when it is executed) cannot be taken into account.

Other heuristics

The simple variations we have just looked at in terms of their optimality show how difficult the problem is. It should also be pointed out that several possible critical path algorithms exist, if the choice of task to be executed is not specified, in cases where conflicts arise because the critical paths are identical. Generally speaking, the various prioritization criteria are applied together.

Critical path list-schedules can be improved on in some circumstances. For example, the effects of blocking tasks can be taken into account when a list is constructed. This means that the critical path heuristic is modified, in that the number of immediate successors is taken into account, when a choice is made on which tasks are to execute from all those that can execute. This, in turn, means that the schedule can be improved on by considering the possibility of executing the successor of a given task in parallel [ERL90]. In [KaN84], the authors implement a critical path list heuristic (CP/MISF), in which prioritization is also based on the maximum number of immediate successors of tasks that are to execute. Gerasoulis and Nelken [GeN89] used the heuristic in Gaussian elimination. It is also possible to use a critical path variant of the LCA heuristic, based on latest possible start-times; if the same start-times occur, priorities can be based on the number of successors. However, it is easy to find graphs where this modification produces worse results than those where the critical path is used. Anyway, this criterion remains local (only a task's immediate successors are considered); a task that has the greatest total number of successors can also be prioritized.

It should be pointed out that there are two well-known and rather amusing anomalies in list-scheduling algorithms [Gra69]:

- the critical path schedules of some sub-graphs are worse than the schedules of the initial graph;

- in some schedules, increasing the number of processors, or eliminating some constraints, can actually increase the schedule's length.

These 'anomalies', which result from the greedy approach adopted in the list-scheduling algorithm, are related to the apparent paradox, discussed in Chapter 2, which can be seen in some combinatorial optimization algorithms (evaluation/differentiation algorithms) for which speed-up may be super-linear. In fact, executing such algorithms in parallel constitutes scheduling a list.

However, it can be demonstrated that, where the list-schedule is level-oriented and uses the critical path, no anomalies occur regarding the number of processors [BMR90]. Thus: $\forall p$, $\omega_{p+1} \leq \omega_p$.

10.2.6   Other algorithms

The results we have just described yield approximate solutions. Essentially, we used a computational method (list-scheduling) and heuristics that are, for the most part, derived from the critical path method. The quality of these heuristics can be assessed on the basis of the theoretical results of worst-case analysis of their behaviour in special cases, such as UET tasks or regular graph structures.

However, in practice, the results are insufficient for very general cases. But there are other, more general methods (which we elaborate on in Chapter 14) that can be used to compute approximate solutions to the problem of list-scheduling, seen as a problem of combinatorial optimization. A wide variety of solutions have been proposed, but we shall not go into them in detail here. However, it should be emphasized that many algorithms use the heuristics described above.

In subsequent chapters, we elaborate on optimal results obtained for specific task graphs. To conclude this section on list-scheduling algorithms that exclude communication between tasks, the distinction between the length of tasks and the structure of their precedence constraints should be stressed. Optimal results are known only for graphs with UET tasks or for specific regular tasks.

10.3   List-scheduling algorithms that include communication costs

10.3.1   General description

Many authors have attempted to extend the above results by taking communication between tasks into account. The most common model adopted is to take a task graph that has been assigned values, with the cost of its arcs proportional to that of the data transactions between its tasks (written $C(T, T')$). Thus, if the tasks T_i and T_j are such that $T_i << T_j$, the following general relation is yielded:

$$\text{start}(T_j) \geq \text{start}(T_i) + \text{ex}(T_i) \text{ if alloc}(T_i) = \text{alloc}(T_j)$$
$$\text{start}(T_j) \geq \text{start}(T_i) + \text{ex}(T_i) + C(T_i, T_j) \text{ if not}$$

Because this chapter is mainly devoted to shared-memory multiprocessors, the cost of all data transfers from memory to processors will be considered identical; in other words, the function C is constant. It is further assumed that all processors are connected to each other and that communication between them is governed by a routing device. Very few results have been obtained for incomplete interconnection networks. In this context, one could mention the work of Du and Vidal-Naquet [DuV91], who proposed a heuristic for mapping a schedule on an entirely connected, ideal topology to a specific topology.

10.3.2   Extending the above results

Some results for schedules that take communication between tasks into account can be found in [ChP92]. As far as complexity is concerned, one simply has to consider scheduling for an acyclic task graph with tasks that all take the same time to execute (that is, with tasks that are assumed to have UET). Communication between tasks is subject to precedence constraints; the time the tasks spend on execution has no bearing on reducing the problem. Some authors have adapted Coffman and Graham's heuristic, so that communication can be taken into account. They simply showed that there was an additional term in the expression of the worst-case bound [Bra90] [Liu90] [LHC88].

Rayward-Smith proposed a simple list heuristic for any given UET acyclic graph, which included an assumption that communication costs were constant (UCT) [Ray87]. An additional constraint is added to reflect the fact that the immediate predecessors of a given task must be executed at best two units before the task, which yields the following:

Theorem 10.6

The worst-case length of a critical path list-schedule on p processors (p ≥ 3) for any given acyclic graph, which is assumed to have UET and UCT, is:

$$\omega \le \omega_{opt}\left(3 - \frac{2}{p}\right) - \left(1 - \frac{1}{p}\right)$$

where ω_{opt} is the length of the best possible schedule.

10.3.3   Towards distributed memory

Granularity

If we no longer take the time for communication between tasks to be independent of the number of processors, we are approaching a multi-processor system with distributed memory. A model can be used in which communication costs are either a non-zero constant, where two tasks execute on two different processors, or zero, where the two tasks execute on the same processor (which is also the case with shared-memory multiprocessors with a local cache).

The concept of *granularity* has been used intuitively throughout the book. It relates to tasks' sizes; elementary operations are said to be fine-grain. Determining grain size is a difficult problem. The finer the grain size, the greater the potential parallelism, but communication costs are high. By contrast, the coarser the grain size, the less communication takes place and the poorer the parallelism. A compromise between the two has to be found. One promising avenue was explored by Papadimitriou and Ullman [PaU87], Kruatrachue and Lewis [KrL88] and, more recently, Bampis, König and Trystram [BKT91] (a detailed description of this, using a specific example, is provided in Chapter 13). The idea is to start with the greatest potential parallelism (finest grain size), then progressively increase the grain size while reducing communication and attempting to maintain a high quality of parallelism. It should be pointed out that this can result in some tasks having to be duplicated in order to minimize total execution time, as illustrated in Figures 10.7 and 10.8 by the example of the root of a tree and the schedules that correspond to it.

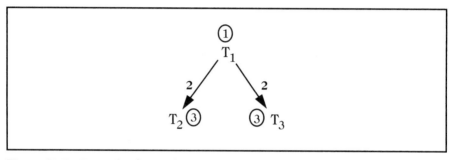

Figure 10.7   Example of a graph including communication (communications are shown in bold on the graph's arcs, task lengths in circles)

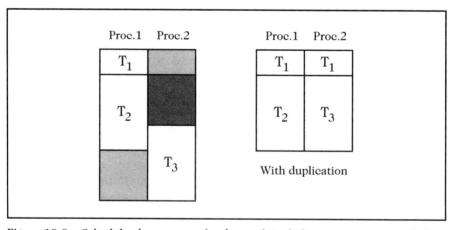

Figure 10.8   Schedules for an example of a graph including communication (light shading represents free periods of time, dark shading represents periods of communication)

Critical graphs

Colin and Chrétienne suggested a similar idea for scheduling with an unbounded number of processors, which is based on the task graph being transformed into a *critical graph* (a tree or a forest) first, then tasks being duplicated, before they are allocated [CoC91]. One processor is allocated to each of the tree's leaves, then all the task sequences are duplicated right down to the root. Let's describe the first stage – constructing a critical graph.

The first step in this stage consists of date stamping earliest possible start-times (taking the costs of the arcs into account, as defined earlier). There are two types of node: forks and joins, illustrated in Figure 10.9.

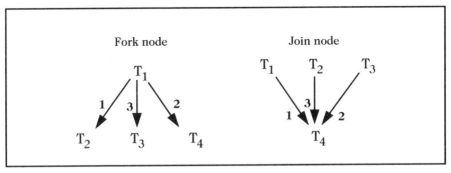

Figure 10.9   Fork and join nodes

With fork nodes, the assumption that tasks are duplicated ensures that a copy of the parent task T_1 can be allocated to the same processor as its children (T_2, T_3 and T_4). Communication between tasks can be simply ignored. The earliest possible start-time is:

$$d(T_i) = d(T_1) + ex(T_1) \quad \text{for } i=2, 3, 4$$

With join nodes, an attempt is made to retain maximum parallelism. Only one of the parent tasks is allocated to the same processor as the child T_4. Of course, the parent task with the highest communication cost, T_2 in this case, is chosen. Thus, if T' is the predecessor task of T with the highest communication cost, the earliest possible start-time is:

$$d(T) = min(max(ex(T') + d(T')), maxpred)$$

where

$$\text{maxpred} = \max_{T'' \in \text{pred}(T) \text{ and } T'' \neq T'}((\text{ex}(T'') + d(T'') + C(T, T'')))$$

The critical graph is determined entirely by date stamping the earliest possible start-times, as we have just done. Intuitively, it means tasks are located in such a way as to minimize the graph's longest paths. It is a natural extension of earliest possible start-time schedules that do not take communication into account. The formula below yields the arcs that are used (whether a tree or a forest is involved can be established quite easily):

let (T, T') be an arc of the initial task graph.
if $d(T') < d(T) + \text{ex}(T) + C(T, T')$ then
the arc (T, T') is an arc of the critical graph.

In Figures 10.10 and 10.11, we provide an example of a task graph with 11 tasks, taken from [Gui91], along with a critical graph for it and a schedule for the critical graph.

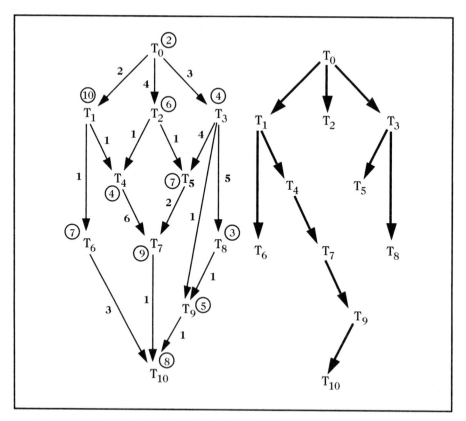

Figure 10.10   Example of a task graph that includes communication and the critical graph for it

The scheduling algorithm designed by Colin and Chrétienne yields an optimal result if an assumption is made about computation and communication times on an infinite number of processors [CoC91]. The assumption is that the computation times of all the tasks T' that immediately precede a task T must be greater than their corresponding communication times (arcs (T, T')). In practice, this is rather disappointing, as it implies a very large number of processors (5 in the example, whereas the task graph's width is 3).

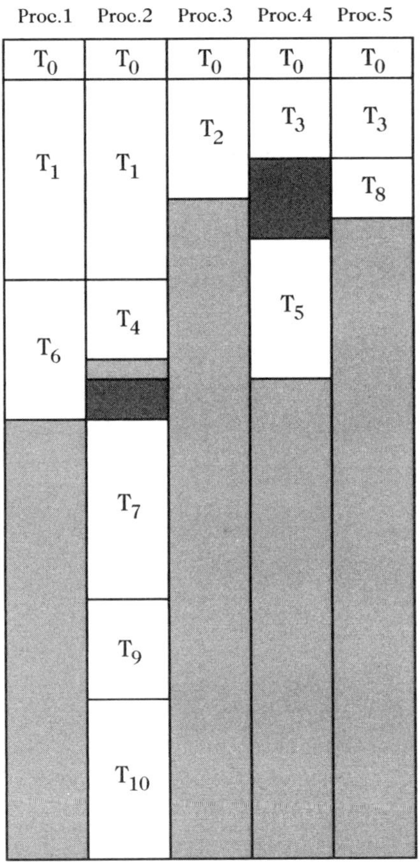

Figure 10.11   Schedule for the critical graph of the example in Figure 10.10

Clustering heuristics

Gerasoulis and Yang [GeY92] and Sarkar [Sar89] proposed an alternative to the solutions described above. Like them, it involves starting with the smallest grain size and clustering tasks with the largest grain size. Here, the various heuristics are characterized according to how tasks are *clustered*.

Generally, this is done in two stages:

• a cluster on the task graph is determined on a complete network with an unbounded number of processors;

• clustered tasks are scheduled on a network with a given topology with a finite (fixed) number of processors.

There are several ways of finding clusters. Most are based on using the critical path method [GeY92]. Figure 10.12 illustrates a 'linear' clustering of tasks, in which sequences are determined by the critical path, with no intermediate communication between tasks within those sequences. The tasks with the highest communication costs are executed on the same processor, so their costs are ignored.

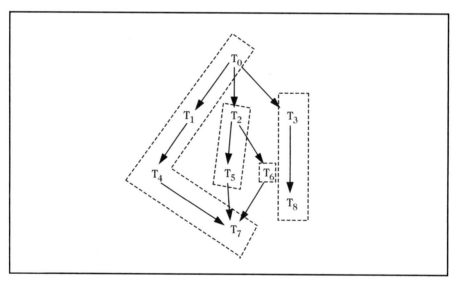

Figure 10.12   Example of linear clustering on a graph

10.4   Introduction to automatic parallelization

10.4.1   How automatic parallelization works

Executing independent tasks is the simplest form of parallelism. A sequential program with independent tasks such as:

```
for  i ← 1  to n
    {task T_i}
```

can be efficiently executed in parallel (to the extent that communication costs are ignored), even if the problem of optimal allocation is in general NP-complete. Parallel code for this form of parallelism could be written as:

```
for  i ← 1  to n do in parallel
    {task T_i}
```

which amounts to assigning tasks in any order, generally in the order of the tasks' indices, to processors that are free.

An even simpler case is where each task consists of the same operation applied to each element in a table, such as:

```
for  i ← 1  to n
    A[i] ← A[i] + C
```

In the above case, any balanced allocation is optimal. *Data parallelism* is very popular, because it can be scaled as the amount of data and the number of processors increase. Of course, it can be found automatically and this is how loop parallelization operates.

Loop parallelization

Loop iterations can be executed in parallel without explicit synchronization if, and only if, there are no dependency relations between instructions belonging to two different iterations.

Things are not quite so simple when tasks have dependency constraints (as defined and described in Chapter 9). Dependencies between instructions in the body of the loop have to be determined. If none of the dependencies affects instructions belonging to different iterations, tasks can be executed in parallel. If they do, the code has to be rewritten to remove the dependencies.

To vectorize a set of nested loops, tasks with no dependencies are placed in the innermost loops. Indeed, synchronization times are small and parallelism may have to be sought among elementary operations. Loops with no dependencies can then be rewritten as vector instructions. We adopted this approach in Chapters 7 and 8. The main projects to use this approach were Parafrase, conducted at the University of Illinois [KKL80] and PFC at Rice University [AlK87].

By contrast, the approach does not result in high performance on MIMD architectures, as synchronization costs are considerably higher, particularly when processors are loosely coupled or memory is distributed. The basic difference between a parallelizer and a vectorizer is that a parallelization system has to find parallelism with greater granularity to compensate for start-up overheads and the costs of synchronizing asynchronous processes. Consequently, the code is rewritten so that loops with no dependency relations are positioned as the outermost loops [ACK87] [CaK88]. Analysis of dependencies between procedures is essential and must be conducted with a great deal of care [CaK87].

10.4.2   Transformations

The purpose of a parallelizer is to construct a parallel program on the basis of an analysis of dependency graphs. Each loop of the corresponding sequential program can be worked on independently. As we have seen, the basic prerequisite for an individual loop to be parallelized is that no dependency arc should exist between two instructions belonging to the iterations of the loop. The initial sequential program has to be transformed for its maximum parallelism to be extracted. Below, we review some techniques for transforming sequential programs. Readers who are interested in the topic are also referred to [Fea92].

Sequence modification

Here, the sequential program is modified by changing the order in which instructions are executed. The first technique is called *loop splitting*. It involves transforming a loop that contains several instructions into several consecutive loops. The following loop:

```
for  i ← 1  to n
    I₁
    I₂
```

becomes:

```
for  i ← 1  to n
    I₁
for  i ← 1  to n
    I₂
```

The precondition for splitting the loop is that no dependency should exist between I_1 and I_2. The first loop should have dependencies and should be able to execute sequentially, while the second should have no dependencies and should be able to execute in parallel, as in the following example:

```
for  i ← 1  to n
  A[i] ← A[i] + C
for  i ← 1  to n
  B[i+1] ← B[i] + C
```

The transformation can be inverted by grouping several loops together into one. The technique is applied when several consecutive loops are parallel. A single parallel loop is thereby obtained, with a body that takes longer to execute, as in the following example:

```
for  i ← 1  to n
  A[i] ← A[i] + C
for  i ← 1  to n
  B[i] ← A[i] + C
```

Note that in the previous example, it is important to observe the order of the instructions within the body of the parallel loop. In the above example, A[i] has to be computed before B[i].

The second sequence modification technique is loop inversion and, in Chapter 11, we shall see that there are some important applications of it. In loop inversion, the order of the loops in a set of nested loops is changed. The code below:

```
for  i ← 1  to n
  for  j ← 1  to m
    T_ij
```

is transformed into:

```
for  j ← 1  to m
  for  i ← 1  to n
    T'_ij
```

This is a rather tricky transformation, in that the task may have to be rewritten. As emphasized in the previous section, the parallel loop should be positioned correctly (in the innermost loop for vectorization and in the outermost loop for parallelization).

Introducing new variables

In sequential code, the same variable can be used to assign different values to the code, but without those values being used at the same time. But optimizing the code sequentially in this manner has a considerably adverse effect on its parallelization. In the following code:

```
for  i ← 1  to n
   C ← B[i]
   A[i] ← A[i] + C
```

using the variable C creates a dependency between two of the loop's consecutive iterations. By introducing new variables (more specifically, by removing C), this artificial dependency can be removed:

```
for  i ← 1  to n
   A[i] ← A[i] + B[i]
```

Semantic transformations

These involve taking the interpretation of the operations that have been executed into account and using some of their properties. A simple example of this is taking association into account in the addition of n numbers. There were several examples of this type of restructuring in Chapter 5. However, note that semantic transformations are difficult to implement automatically.

10.5   Scheduling nested loops

10.5.1   Introduction

One of the most important tasks for parallel compilers is to decompose and parallelize loop nests. That they should be executed efficiently is all the more important for many scientific programs, as the time some loops take to execute constitutes a large part of the total execution time. More often than not, dependency analysis techniques can be implemented and scheduling functions sought, because the structure of loop nests is regular. This section is based to a large extent on the work of Darte and Robert [DaR92], to which readers are referred.

Definition 10.1
A loop nest of depth n is a set of n nested loops, with the following form:

```
for  i₁ ← l₁  to  u₁
    for  i₂ ← l₂  to  u₂
      ...
        for  iₙ ← lₙ  to  uₙ
            T(i₁,..., iₙ)
```

where T is a program with k instructions.

With uniform nested loops, transformations that can be used to determine a parallel scheme that complies with the sequential semantics of the program are known. How their quality can be evaluated is also known. The most common technique is to find a vector of time π to transform the nest into a scheme:

```
for  t ← 0  to  maxtime
    execute the instructions i = (i₁,..., iₙ) in parallel such
    that ⌊π.i⌋ = t
```

This is Lamport's hyperplane method [Lam74]. Below, we describe it, and its variants, in detail.

10.5.2   Dependency analysis of a loop nest

General loop nests cannot be processed using efficient methods. As a result, it is assumed that the indices of internal loops are simple functions of the loops that contain them. For the sake of simplicity, we shall consider only 'perfect nests', that is, nests in which all the instructions are in the innermost loop. The number of nested loops in a nest is described as the nest's *depth*. The notation below is now standard [Ban88] [DaR92]:

```
for i₁ ← l₁ to  u₁
    for i₂ ← l₂(i₁) to  u₂(i₁)
      ...
        for iₙ ← lₙ(i₁, i₂,..., iₙ₋₁) to uₙ(i₁, i₂,......, iₙ₋₁)
            {Instruction I₁}
            {Instruction I₂}
            ...
            {Instruction I_k}
```

where l_1 and u_1 are constants and $l_j(i_1,..., i_{j-1})$ (or $u_j(i_1,..., i_{j-1})$) is the maximum (or minimum) of a finite number of functions that are linear in $i_1,..., i_{j-1}$. For each value of $V = (i_1,..., i_n)$ and for each j, there is an instance of I_j, which we call $I_j(V)$. Parallelizing the loop nest involves determining which values, of all the values of V and j of the instances of I_j, can be executed in parallel. The dependency relations between the instances are computed to that end.

Definition 10.2

A dependency relation between instance V of I_i and instance W of I_j exists, if:

- $I_i(V)$ precedes $I_j(W)$ in the sequential program;

- $I_i(V)$ and $I_j(W)$ can access the same variable and at least one access is a write access;

- the variable has not been written between instances V and W.

$d_{(i, V), (j, W)} = W - V$ is the *dependency vector* between the iterations $I_i(V)$ and $I_j(W)$. The loop nest is *uniform* if the dependency vectors are independent of V and W, in which case they are written $d_{i, j}$.

Dependencies between instructions can be represented by a graph (as discussed earlier in the case of precedence systems) and this is also true of precedence systems. However, the graph is simplified enormously as a result of the uniform nature of the dependencies. In fact, a directed graph with k vertices (instructions), connected by edges corresponding to the dependency vectors, will be used. The characteristics of the loop nest are such that the iteration's domain is equal to the integer coordinate points contained in a convex set $\{x, Ax \leq b\}$, where A can be directly deduced from the expressions of bounds l and u of the iteration intervals.

Consider the following example:

```
for i ← 0 to  r
  for j ← 0 to  s+i
    I₁:  X[i, j] ← Y[i-1, j - 4] + Y[i-2, j-5]
    I₂:  Y[i, j] ← X[i-2, j-3]
```

The iteration domain is a trapezoid:

```
D = {(i, j) | 0 ≤ i ≤ r, 0 ≤ j≤ s+i}
```

$X[i, j]$ is computed by instruction I_1 to instance $V_X=(i, j)$ and used by instruction I_2 for instance $W_X=(i+2, j+3)$, which creates a dependency of I_1 on I_2 of vector $d_X=W_X - V_X=(2, 3)$. $Y[i, j]$ is computed by instruction I_2 to instance $V_Y=(i, j)$ and used by instruction I_1 for instance $W_{Y1}=(i+1, j+4)$ and for instance $W_{Y2}=(i+2, j+5)$, which creates two dependencies, I_2 on I_1 of vectors $d_{Y1}=(1, 4)$ and $d_{Y2}=(2, 5)$. All the above dependencies are uniform.

The matrix whose column vectors are the vectors d is called a dependency matrix. In this case, it is equal to:

$$B = \begin{pmatrix} 2 & 1 & 2 \\ 3 & 4 & 5 \end{pmatrix}$$

The dependency graph corresponding to this is illustrated in Figure 10.13.

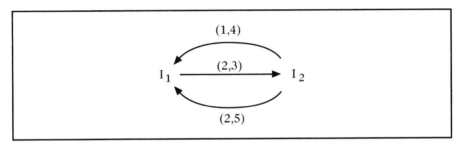

Figure 10.13   Dependency graph for a loop nest

It should not be concluded on the basis of Figure 10.13 that a cycle exists in the task graph. As discussed earlier, this is impossible, because our starting point is a sequential program that is assumed to have deterministic semantics. In fact, the dependency graph of the uniform loop nest is the quotient graph of the task graph, as defined in Chapter 9, by the relation; two tasks are equivalent if they correspond to the same instruction. Interpretation of the graph shows that a dependency exists between X[i, j] and Y[i+2, j+3], between Y[i, j] and X[i+1, j+4] and between Y[i, j] and X[i+2, j+5].

10.5.3   Optimal algorithm

Parallelizing loop nests involves finding a schedule for their dependency graph. The results in Chapter 9 apply, taking into account the fact that each instruction can be considered as having unit execution time, which may entail the body of the loop nest being partially rewritten. If a shared-memory computational model with zero communication costs is adopted, any schedule corresponding to the length of the longest path in the graph will be optimal in time. A greedy algorithm can therefore be used; in other words, each instruction can be computed at its earliest possible start-time. This amounts to executing at time 0 those points of the computational domain that do not have a predecessor, and then, at each time step, executing those points with predecessors that have already been executed.

As discussed earlier, this schedule has a number of disadvantages:

- in general, the number of processors is not optimal;
- the regular structure of the graph and, more specifically, the loop nest's structure, are not complied with;
- the schedule is not always efficient, in cases where communication times are not negligible.

There is another approach, drawn from compiling programs for vectorization, which attempts to maintain the regularity of the initial loop's structure. Nests are transformed at compilation and are such that a new program with explicit parallelism can be obtained from a nest with implicit parallelism. Of course, its efficiency is less than that of the greedy algorithm and depends to a large extent on how the loop is written. Specifically, dependency analysis is based on pessimistic assumptions that may be abandoned on execution – where in doubt, it is always assumed that a dependency exists. However, this can be used for optimization before run time, particularly as far as data allocation to memory and allocation of instructions to processors are concerned.

Parallelization lies in the fact that points in the computational domain that are not connected by dependency vectors can be executed simultaneously. Schematically, the most natural idea is for a vector of time π and a family of linear hyperplanes h(t) to be computed, such that the set of points executed at a time t is equal to the intersection of the domain with the hyperplane h(t). h(t) is transformed into h(t+1) by a translation of vector π. This results in a parallel program, which is expressed in the same way as the one described in Section 10.5.1.

```
for  t ← 0  to maxtime
     execute the instructions i = (i₁,..., iₙ) in
     parallel such that ⌊π.i⌋ = t
```

The outer loop corresponds to an iteration time and $\lfloor \pi.i \rfloor$ is the set of points of h(t). Construction of the vector π is complex.

10.5.4   Lamport's algorithm

Lamport [Lam74] proposes computing a vector π with rational elements, such that, for all dependency vectors d, we have $\pi.d \geq 1$. As the iteration domain is the set of integer points in the convex plane $\{x, Ax \leq b\}$, the set $E(t)$ of the points of the domain computed at iteration t is defined by:

$$E(t) = \{p \,/\, Ap \le b; \lfloor \pi.p \rfloor = t\}$$

Suppose the dependency matrix $B = (d_1,..., d_m)$, of size (n, m), where n is the nest's depth and m the number of dependency vectors, has column vectors that are ordered lexicographically. Note that the first non-zero element of each of the vectors is positive. In the previous example, this amounts to swapping the first two vectors, which yields:

$$B = \begin{pmatrix} 1 & 2 & 2 \\ 4 & 3 & 5 \end{pmatrix}$$

Let j_1 be the index of the first non-zero element of d_1. As $d_{1,k1} \ge 0$, it just has to be written that $\pi_{k1} = 1$ and $\pi_k = 0$ for $k_1 < k \le n$ for the condition to be satisfied. The fact that the columns are ordered lexicographically ensures that whatever the other elements of π may be, we will get $\pi.d_1 > 0$. Now let k_2 be the index of the first non-zero element of d_2. As d_1 is lexicographically smaller than d_2, $k_2 \le k_1$. If $k_2 = k_1$ the vector π is used, if not $\pi_k = 0$ is written for $k_2 < k < k_1$, and the smallest possible positive integer is written for πk_2, such that $\pi.d_2 > 0$. By repeating the process, a time vector is obtained.

10.5.5   Algorithms derived from Lamport's algorithm

Many methods of transforming loops based on Lamport's algorithm have been proposed. In *selective shrinking*, the matrix $B = (d_1,..., d_m)$ of dependency vectors is searched row by row. When a row i whose m elements $d_{i,j}$ are all non-zero is found, the following is used:

$$\pi = \frac{1}{\min d_{ij}} e_i$$

where e_i is the ith base vector.

In *true dependence shrinking*, the number of iterations (in sequential mode) for each dependency vector is calculated, between two dependent instructions being evaluated.

These algorithms go beyond the scope of this book and we shall not go into them in detail. Instead, the reader is referred to [KMW67] [Pol88] and

[PeC89] and to works on designing systolic networks based on uniform recurrent equations [Qui84].

10.6   Conclusion

Throughout this chapter, we looked at scheduling in all its general aspects. We described those methods that can be most readily used in practice for scheduling the tasks of any parallel program on a shared-memory parallel machine. Many satisfactory solutions exist, if communication between tasks is ignored. We described the main solutions that are known for the case where communication costs are taken into account. Finally, we described the simpler problem of scheduling a loop nest and demonstrated the main methods of solving it.

The various heuristics we discussed can be used to develop software whose purpose is to help users obtain greater parallelism on real machines. As yet, there has been little commercial development of these methods, both in terms of automatic parallelization and task allocation to processors. But we believe it will not be long before research and development will lead to high quality tools that can be delivered with real machines.

Parallelization of dense linear systems

In this chapter, we examine programming linear algebra algorithms on a shared-memory architecture.

11.1   Introduction

11.1.1   Algorithms to be parallelized

In this chapter, we apply the methods described in Chapter 9 to parallelizing numerical algorithms for solving dense linear systems. We assume we are seeking to solve the linear system Ax=b in n unknowns.

The most well-known algorithm for solving linear systems is Gaussian elimination [GoV83]. To solve Ax=b, as we recalled in Chapter 8, the pair (A, b) is reduced by successive eliminations to become the pair (U, L^{-1}b), where A=LU, L is a lower triangular matrix and U an upper triangular matrix.

The vector x is then computed by solving the triangular system Ux = $L^{-1}b$, in other words by reducing the pair (U, $L^{-1}b$) to (I_n, $U^{-1}L^{-1}b$), with the second element being the system's solution. Two apparently different operations are carried out in Gaussian elimination: matrix triangularization and inversion of a triangular system. Another way of doing this is to implement these two stages in one, by *diagonalizing* the matrix. Gauss-Jordan elimination [GoV83] is normally used to do this. However, the cost of this ($\frac{n^3}{2}$ multiplications) is higher than that incurred by Gaussian elimination ($\frac{n^3}{3}$).

11.1.2   Review of the machine model

The assumptions we make about the underlying architecture of the model being used are the same as those in Chapter 9 – the model consists of a set of identical processors, all of which have local memory and share common centralized memory. The cost of data transfer operations is negligible in comparison with arithmetic operations, but, initially, we shall adopt the constraint that only column-oriented and row-oriented access to the elements of matrix A are allowed. Transfer of a row or column of A from memory to a processor is, therefore, the only data operation allowed.

A further assumption is that all elementary operations take the same time, and this we take as the unit of time. Duplicating a row or column involves zero communication costs; in other words, we assume that one data item can be transferred simultaneously to several processors, and the processors are not allowed to modify it. A processor can only modify a data item if it is the only processor with a copy of it.

All these assumptions mean that the number of processors is restricted to O(n), where n is the size of the problem. If p is of order n^2, communication time cannot be ignored. Furthermore, it is unrealistic to use a shared-memory architecture with as many processors as this.

11.2   Gauss-Jordan algorithm

11.2.1   Various ways of writing the algorithm

Matrix A is considered of size n by (n+1), resulting from bordering the initial n × n matrix with the right-hand term b.

Sequential Gauss-Jordan elimination works in much the same way as Gaussian elimination – the rows of the matrix are linked by a pivot row and the subdiagonal elements are reduced to zero. However, in Gauss-Jordan elimination, the elements above the diagonal are also reduced to zero (*see* Figure 11.1). The algorithm for this is as follows:

```
for  k ← 1  to  n
   {row k prepared}
   for j← k + 1  to  n + 1
        A(k, j) ← A(k, j)/A(k, k)
   {column k elements reduced to zero}
   for  i ← 1  to  k - 1
        for j← k + 1  to  n + 1
             A(i, j) ← A(i, j)- A(i, k)*A(k, j)
   for  i ← k + 1  to  n
        for j← k + 1  to  n + 1
             A(i, j) ← A(i, j) - A(i, k)*A(k, j)
```

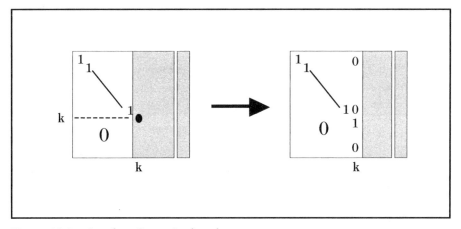

Figure 11.1   Step k in Gauss-Jordan elimination

Depending on how data is accessed, the Gauss-Jordan algorithm can be parallelized either as above, which we call *row-oriented Gauss-Jordan elimination*, or by inverting the nested loops i and j in the above, which we call *column-oriented Gauss-Jordan elimination*. Its algorithm is as follows:

```
{Column-oriented Gauss-Jordan elimination}
for  k ← 1  to  n
   {row k prepared}
   A(k, j) ← A(k, j)/A(k, k)
   {column k elements reduced to zero}
   for j← k + 1 to n + 1
        for  i ← 1  to  k - 1
             A(i, j) ← A(i, j)- A(i, k)*A(k, j)
        for  i ← k + 1  to  n
             A(i, j) ← A(i, j) - A(i, k)*A(k, j)
```

11.2.2   Parallelization of row-oriented elimination

Partitioning the algorithm into elementary tasks

Constraints on accessing elements in the matrix and the assumptions made on the number of processors being used mean that the algorithm is partitioned only once. Tasks are defined as follows:

```
{task JL_kk}
for j ← k + 1  to  n + 1
    A(k, j) ← A(k, j)/A(k, k)
{task JL_ki for i≠k}
for j ← k + 1  to  n + 1
    A(i, j) ← A(i, j)- A(i, k)*A(k, j)
```

This implies that the order relation in the sequential algorithm $A = (JL_{ki}, \rightarrow)$ is as follows:

$$JL_{ki} \rightarrow JL_{mj} \Leftrightarrow (i < j \text{ and } k = m) \text{ or } (k < m)$$

The cost of the various tasks is:

$$ex(JL_{kk}) = n - k + 1$$
$$ex(JL_{ki}) = 2(n - k + 1)$$

Precedence system

We now construct the precedence system $S = (JL_{ki}, <<)$ for this set of tasks. The sets of task inputs and outputs are as follows:

$$I(JL_{kk}) = \{A(k, j) \text{ with } k \le j \le n + 1\}$$
$$O(JL_{kk}) = \{A(k, j) \text{ with } k + 1 \le j \le n + 1\}$$
$$I(JL_{ki}) = \{A(i, j) \text{ with } k \le j \le n+1\} \cup \{A(k, j) \text{ with } k + 1 \le j \le n + 1\}$$
$$O(JL_{ki}) = \{A(i, j) \text{ with } k + 1 \le j \le n + 1\}$$

From this, the following precedence relations are obtained:

$$JL_{kk} << JL_{ki} \quad \text{for } 1 \le k, i \le n$$
$$JL_{ki} << JL_{k+1, i} \quad \text{for } 1 \le k, i \le n$$

The task graph is given in Figure 11.2, where the tasks JL_{ki} are represented by the pair (k, i). It can be seen that this is close to the 2-step graph described in Chapter 9. However, note that here, the number of tasks at each level is the same.

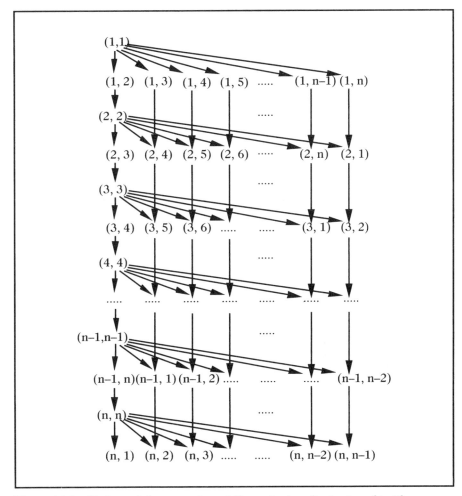

Figure 11.2   Task graph for row-oriented Gauss-Jordan elimination algorithm

Computing t_{opt}

To compute t_{opt}, a longest path along the graph has to be found. It is easy to see that there are n–1 such paths. They differ only in their final tasks, which comprise the following:

$$JL_{11} - JL_{12} - JL_{22} - \ldots - JL_{kk} - JL_{kk+1} - JL_{k+1k+1} - \ldots - JL_{nn} \text{ and } JL_{ni} \text{ for } i=1,\ldots, n-1$$

The following is obtained:

$$t_{opt} = \sum_{k=1}^{n} ex\left(JL_{kk}\right) + \sum_{k=1}^{n} ex\left(JL_{k,\,k+1}\right)$$

$$t_{opt} = \sum_{k=1}^{n} n-k+1 + \sum_{k=1}^{n} 2\left(n-k+1\right) = \frac{3n\left(n+1\right)}{2}$$

The graph of Figure 11.2 is a level-oriented decomposition. All tasks at the same level have the same execution time. The width of the decomposition is n–1 which means:

$$p_{opt} \leq Wp(G^*) = Ws(G^*) \leq n-1$$

A lower bound is obtained by stating that the efficiency of a parallel algorithm is always less than or equal to 1:

$$p_{opt} \geq \frac{t_A}{t_{opt}} \geq \frac{n^3 + \dfrac{n^2}{2} + \dfrac{n}{2}}{\dfrac{3n^2}{2} + \dfrac{3n}{2}} \geq \frac{2n}{3} - \frac{n-1}{3\left(n+1\right)}$$

and therefore, $p_{opt} \geq \lceil \frac{2n}{3} \rceil$.

The bound cannot be appreciably improved on the basis of this technique, which was used in Section 9.4.2 (constructing lower bounds) and is based on using total computation and idle times. $IV(p) \geq (p-1)$ is too low in relation to pt_{opt}.

But n–1 different paths of length t_{opt} do exist and, therefore, all the tasks along these paths cannot be executed with less than n–1 processors (and, similarly, the fact that the paths exist implies that the width of their task graph is greater than or equal to n–1). Therefore, $p_{opt} = n-1$.

The value of p_{opt} is rather disappointing, as n–2 processors are free while the tasks JL_{kk} execute – in other words, for almost a third of the time. The question arises as to whether a small increase in execution time would lead to a substantial reduction in the number of processors.

Before we answer that question, let's try to define it.

Definition 11.1

A parallel algorithm is *asymptotically optimal* (or asymptotically optimal for p processors), if the ratio of its execution time t_{alg} to t_{opt} (or $t_{alg}(p)$ to $t_{opt}(p)$) tends to 1, as the problem size n tends to infinity.

In other words, the difference between the two times is negligible. The question can then be formulated as follows: what is the optimal number of processors for executing row-oriented Gauss-Jordan elimination in an asymptotically optimal period of time?

Scheduling

The following statement is fundamental to answering the above question: the tasks JL_{kk} execute in half the time taken by the tasks $JL_{k-1, i}$, to within a unit. First, divide each of the tasks $JL_{k-1, i}$ into two sub-tasks JL1 and JL2. This results in 2n–2 tasks, whose time can be seen to be t_{kk}. By separating the 2n–1 tasks $JL_{k, k}$, $JL1_{k-1, i}$, and $JL2_{k-1, i}$ into three equal levels (and by repeating the operation for all values of k), the resulting decomposition is such that each level has the same number of tasks – (2n–1)/3 (assume for the moment that 2n–1 is divisible by 3).

Execution time increases by 1 unit for each JL_{kk} – a total of n, which is negligible in relation to t_{opt}. Processors work almost all the time in this decomposition. Unfortunately, the resulting algorithm is incompatible with the initial partitioning of the tasks, since $JL1_{k-1, i}$ and $JL2_{k-1, i}$ are executed on different processors and the decomposition is therefore not valid. However, the underlying principle can be changed slightly so as to give a valid decomposition: the tasks $JL_{k-1, i}$, $JL_{k, k}$, $JL_{k, i}$ and $JL_{k+1, k+1}$ are partitioned into sub-tasks as before, but are all executed on the same processor. Figure 11.3 gives the resulting decomposition.

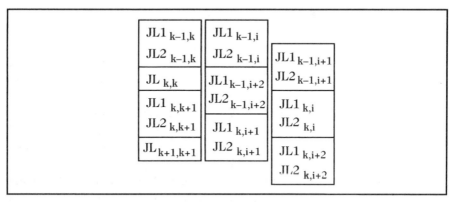

Figure 11.3   Asymptotically optimal schedule

Note that, although the tasks $JL_{k-1, i+1}$ can be executed earlier, $JL_{k, i}$ cannot be brought forward and must wait until $JL_{k, k}$ has completed. While the four tasks along the longest path are executing, two processors execute six tasks.

First, assume that $p=\frac{2n-1}{3}$ is an integer. The algorithm is executed in two stages:

- processor 1 executes the tasks along the longest path;
- each pair of processors executes three of the tasks $JL_{k,\,i}$, following the procedure outlined above.

Rather than describing the algorithm in detail, the schedule obtained where n=11 and p=7 is shown in Figure 11.4.

Proc.1	Proc.2	Proc.3	Proc.4	Proc.5	Proc.6	Proc.7
(1,1)						
(1,2)	(1,3)		(1,6)		(1,9)	
(1,2)	(1,3)	(1,4)	(1,6)	(1,7)	(1,9)	(1,10)
(2,2)	(1,5)	(1,4)	(1,8)	(1,7)	(1,11)	(1,10)
(2,3)	(1,5)	(2,4)	(1,8)	(2,7)	(1,11)	(2,10)
(2,3)	(2,5)	(2,4)	(2,8)	(2,7)	(2,11)	(2,10)
(3,3)	(2,5)	(2,6)	(2,8)	(2,9)	(2,11)	(2,1)
(3,4)	(3,5)	(2,6)	(3,8)	(2,9)	(3,11)	(2,1)
(3,4)	(3,5)	(3,6)	(3,8)	(3,9)	(3,11)	(3,1)
(4,4)	(3,7)	(3,6)	(3,10)	(3,9)	(3,2)	(3,1)
⋯	(3,7)	⋯	(3,10)	⋯	(3,2)	⋯
⋯	⋯	⋯	⋯	⋯	⋯	⋯
⋯	⋯	⋯	⋯	⋯	⋯	⋯
⋯	⋯	⋯	⋯	⋯	⋯	⋯
(10,10)	(9,2)	⋯	(9,5)	⋯	(9,8)	⋯
(10,11)	(9,2)	(10,1)	(9,5)	(10,4)	(9,8)	(10,7)
(10,11)	(10,2)	(10,1)	(10,5)	(10,4)	(10,8)	(10,7)
(11,11)	(10,2)	(10,3)	(10,5)	(10,6)	(10,8)	(10,9)
(11,1)	(11,2)	(10,3)	(11,5)	(10,6)	(11,8)	(10,9)
(11,1)	(11,2)	(11,3)	(11,5)	(11,6)	(11,8)	(11,9)
	(11,4)	(11,3)	(11,7)	(11,6)	(11,10)	(11,9)
	(11,4)		(11,7)		(11,10)	

Figure 11.4 Asymptotically optimal algorithm

To find the algorithm's execution time, note that while JL_{kk} is executing, the other processors execute half of $JL_{k-1,\,i}$ and therefore $ex(JL_{kk})$ has to be extended by one time unit. While the first half of $JL_{k,\,k+1}$ is executing, some processors (half of the remaining processors) execute the second half of $JL_{k-1,\,i}$ and other processors (the other half) execute the first part of $JL_{k,\,i}$. Similarly, as $JL_{k,\,k+1}$ completes, half the remaining processors execute the second part of $JL_{k,\,i}$, while the others execute the first part of $JL_{k,\,i+1}$, with $ex(JL_{kk+1})$ having to be extended by one time unit. Thus:

$$t_{alg} = t_{opt} + 2n$$

and therefore, since $t_{opt} = O(n^2)$, the algorithm is asymptotically optimal.

Where $\frac{2n-1}{3}$ is not an integer, we return to the case above, assume that $p=\lceil \frac{2n-1}{3} \rceil$ and add empty tasks.

The asymptotic efficiency of a parallel algorithm is the bound of its efficiency when n tends towards infinity:

$$e_\infty = \lim_{n \to \infty} \frac{t_{seq}}{p_{alg}t_{alg}}$$

In the above algorithm, this results in:

$$e_\infty = \lim_{n \to \infty} \frac{n^3 + O(n^2)}{\frac{2n}{3}\left(\frac{3n^2}{2} + O(n)\right)} = 1$$

which demonstrates that the value of p is also asymptotically optimal.

Case with a given number of processors

Now let's look at the general case, where the number of processors is given and a minimal execution time is being sought. As in the case above, the following results are optimal and we assume that the number of processors, p, is proportional to n. Without detracting from the general nature of the problem, suppose $p=2q+1$. The algorithm we describe below is an adaptation of the one above.

The first processor executes the tasks along the longest path. The remaining tasks can be partitioned into (n–2) columns, each with n tasks (see

Figure 11.5). Divide them into q blocks, each comprising $r=\lceil\frac{n-2}{q}\rceil$ consecutive columns (apart from the last one, which contains the remaining tasks). Each block is assigned to a pair of processors, with processors 2i and 2i+1 executing the columns (i–1)r+1, (i–1)r+2,…, ir.

While the first processors are executing $JL_{k-1,\,k}$, $JL_{k,\,k}$, $JL_{k,\,k+1}$ and $JL_{k+1,\,k+1}$, processors 2i and 2i+1 execute the two tasks corresponding to the columns (i–1)r+1, (i–1)r+2 and (i–1)r+3 following the procedure outlined above.

If there are no more columns left to be executed (r=3), the process begins again, and exactly the same algorithm as above is obtained with p=(2n–1)/3 processors.

If there are columns that have yet to be executed (r>3), processors 2i and 2i+1 execute the relevant two tasks of the three columns, as the diagram in Figure 11.5 shows, and so on. When all the columns' relevant two tasks have been executed, the process begins afresh for $JL_{k+1,\,k+2}$, $JL_{k+2,\,k+2}$, $JL_{k+2,\,k+3}$ and $JL_{k+3,\,k+3}$.

Proc.1	Proc.2	Proc.3
(1,1)		
(1,2)	(1,3)	
(1,2)	(1,3)	(1,4)
(2,2)	(1,5)	(1,4)
(2,3)	(1,5)	(2,4)
(2,3)	(2,5)	(2,4)
(3,3)	(2,5)	(2,6)
	(1,6)	(2,6)
	(1,6)	(1,7)
	(1,8)	(1,7)
	(1,8)	(2,7)
	(2,8)	(2,7)
	(2,8)	(2,9)
(3,4)	(3,5)	(2,9)
(3,4)	(3,5)	(3,6)
(4,4)	(3,7)	(3,6)
(4,5)	(3,7)	(4,6)
(4,5)	(4,7)	(4,6)
(5,5)	(4,7)	(4,8)
	(3,8)	(4,8)
	(3,8)	(3,9)
	…	(3,9)
…	…	…

Figure 11.5   Initial stages of the algorithm

Asymptotically, processor utilization, except in the case of the first processor, is 1. The algorithm's asymptotic efficiency is therefore 1; in other words, it is asymptotically optimal. Its execution time is r/3 times that of the algorithm with 2n/3 processors. Thus:

$$t_{opt}(p) = \frac{r}{3}t_{alg} + O(n) = \frac{2n}{3p}\frac{3n^2}{2} + O(n) = \frac{n^3}{p} + O(n)$$

Putting all the results together, we can state the following theorem:

Theorem 11.1
For column-oriented Gauss-Jordan elimination, with a number of processors p, proportional to n:

$$t_{opt} = \frac{3n^2}{2} + \frac{3n}{2}$$
$$p_{opt} = \frac{2n}{3} + O(1)$$
$$t_{opt}(p) = \frac{n^3}{p} + O(n)$$

For $p \leq \frac{2n}{3}$, the asymptotic efficiency of the above algorithms is 1.

11.2.3   Parallelization of the column-oriented variant

Matrix diagonalization can also be column-oriented, in which case tasks are defined as follows:

```
{task JC_kj}
for i ← 1  to  n (i ≠ k)
    A(i, j) ← A(i, j) - A(i, k)*A(k, j)
```

The algorithm for this is as follows:

```
for k ← 1  to  n
    for j ← k + 1  to  n + 1
        execute JC_kj
```

The order relation of the sequential algorithm $A = (JC_{k, i}, \rightarrow)$ is as follows:

$$JC_{k, j} \rightarrow JC_{m, i} \Leftrightarrow (j < i \text{ and } k = m) \text{ or } (k < m)$$

The cost of the tasks is: $ex(JC_{k, j}) = 2n-1$.
Its precedence relations are:

$$JC_{k, k+1} << JC_{k+1, j} \quad \text{for} \quad 1 \le k+1 < j$$
$$JC_{k, j} << JC_{k+1, j} \quad \text{for} \quad 1 \le k < j$$

The task graph is shown in Figure 11.6. It is a triangular task graph containing $n-k+1$ tasks to be executed at any given level k. By contrast, all the tasks $JC_{k, j}$ have the same execution time.

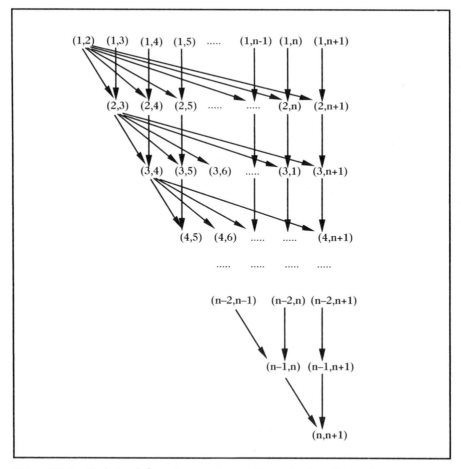

Figure 11.6   Task graph for column-oriented Gauss-Jordan elimination

All the paths between the tasks $JC_{1,j}$ and $JC_{n,n+1}$ are the longest paths in the graph. As there are n of them and they all consist of n tasks of time $2n-1$:

$$t_{opt} = 2n^2 - n$$
$$P_{opt} = n$$

We now try to evaluate t_{opt} for a fixed number p of processors using the following greedy scheduling algorithm G.

Up to level $n-p+1$ there are more than p tasks per level. Scanning the task graph from left to right, divide the set of all these tasks into groups of p tasks; the last of these groups will consist of the tasks remaining at level $n-p+1$. The following groups will consist of the tasks remaining at level $n-p+2,...,n$ of the graph; G assigns each of these to the p processors, and execution of the tasks in group i starts at time $(i-1)(2n-1)$.

Figure 11.7 is a diagrammatic representation of this greedy schedule, where n=5 and p=3.

Proc.1	Proc.2	Proc.3	Time
			0
(1,2)	(1,3)	(1,4)	
			9
(1,5)	(1,6)	(2,3)	
			18
(2,4)	(2,5)	(2,6)	
			27
(3,4)	(3,5)	(3,6)	
			36
(4,5)	(4,6)		
			45
(5,6)			

Figure 11.7   Greedy algorithm

Theorem 11.2
    Using column-oriented Gauss-Jordan elimination:

$$t_{opt} = 2n^2 - n$$
$$P_{opt} = n$$

Using a fixed number of processors p that is less than p_{opt}, the greedy algorithm is:

$$t_{opt}(p) \geq \left\lceil \frac{(n-p)(n+p+1)}{2p} \right\rceil (2n-1)$$

Proof

We need consider only synchronous algorithms, as all tasks have the same execution time. The proof that the greedy algorithm is optimal is in three steps: first, a lower bound is computed for t_{opt}; next, the greedy algorithm is shown to be compatible with the precedence constraints; and finally, the execution time is computed and shown to be equal to the lower bound.

Each of the tasks $JC_{k,j}$ at level k is preceded by $JC_{k-1,j}$. All the tasks at level k cannot therefore be executed until $(2n-1)$ time units have elapsed, following completion of the k−1 previous levels. Because all tasks have the same length, a bound that is lower than the execution time t(k) of the first k levels results from the assumption that the processors are active throughout execution. Thus:

$$t(k) \geq \left\lceil \frac{\sum\limits_{q=1}^{k} n-q+1}{p} \right\rceil (2n-1) \geq \left\lceil \frac{k(2n-k+1)}{2p} \right\rceil (2n-1)$$

Let $k^* = n-p$. The number of tasks at levels that are greater than k^* is less than or equal to p. Their execution time is greater than or equal to that of the longest path between level n−p+1 and n, that is, p(2n−1). Therefore, the execution time of any algorithm will be greater than the sum of the two bounds. Thus:

$$t_{opt}(p) \geq t(k^*) + p(2n-1) \geq \left(\left\lceil \frac{(n-p)(n+p+1)}{2p} \right\rceil + p \right)(2n-1)$$

To show that the greedy algorithm is compatible with the precedence constraints, it suffices to note that the number of tasks between $JC_{k,j}$ and $JC_{k+1,j}$ is greater than or equal to p−1, while k is less than or equal to n−p. Therefore, up to level n−p+1, the groups of tasks that are executed simultaneously do not contain $JC_{k,j}$ and $JC_{k+1,j}$, so the second precedence constraint is satisfied for these levels. It is satisfied for subsequent levels also, since the greedy algorithm executes the tasks level by level. For the first precedence constraint, it suffices to note that no two tasks at the same level can be executed simultaneously and that $JC_{k,k+1}$ is the first task at level k to be executed.

Thus the execution time of the greedy algorithm also is the sum of two terms, each equal to the above two lower bounds. That concludes the proof.

11.3   Gaussian elimination

In Chapter 8, we saw how Gaussian elimination is vectorized and showed that six different variants can be obtained by permuting the loop indices. By using column-oriented elimination, three different forms of the algorithm can be obtained: AXPY (kji variant), GAXPY (jki variant) and DOT (ijk variant).

In this chapter, we look at how the three variants are parallelized. One unit of time corresponds to two arithmetic operations – multiplication followed by addition. The results are all taken from [CMR87].

First, we remind readers of the algorithm's sequential variants, then we describe how they are decomposed into elementary tasks. Finally, we construct a task graph for each of the variants. The resulting graphs can be broken down into four different categories: greedy, two-step, double greedy and double two-step graphs. The schedules for these graphs can be used to obtain complexity results that can be applied to the various algorithms.

11.3.1   Variants on Gaussian elimination

Below, we describe the variants of Gaussian elimination. We give a task graph for each and recall the sequential time.

kji variant – AXPY (Λ)

```
{kji variant - AXPY}
for  k ← 1  to  n − 1
   {task T_kk}
   for  i ← k + 1  to  n
        A(i, k) ← A(i, k)/A(k, k)
   for  j ← k + 1  to  n
        {task T_kj}
        for  i ← k + 1  to  n
            A(i, j) ← A(i, j) − A(i, k)*A(k, j)
```

It is easy to obtain the tasks' costs:

T_{kk} : $(n-k)$ arithmetic operations (for $1 \leq k \leq n-1$)
T_{kj} : $2(n-k)$ arithmetic operations $(k+1 \leq j \leq n, 1 \leq k \leq n-1)$

The total number of arithmetic operations is $\frac{2n^3}{3} + O(n^2)$.
The precedence relations are:

$T_{kk} << T_{kj}$ $k+1 \leq j \leq n, 1 \leq k \leq n-1$
$T_{kj} << T_{k+1, j}$ $k+1 \leq j \leq n, 1 \leq k \leq n-1$

---

which results in the task graph in Figure 11.8 (for n=5).

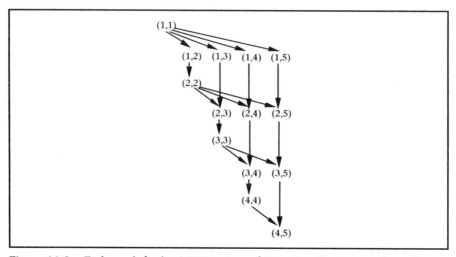

Figure 11.8   Task graph for kji-AXPY variant of Gaussian elimination, for n=5

jki variant – GAXPY (B)

```
{jki variant - GAXPY}
for  j ← 1  to  n
    for  k ← 1  to  j - 1
        {task T_kj}
        for  i ← k + 1  to  n
            A(i, j) ← A(i, j) - A(i, k)*A(k, j)
        {task T_jj}
        for  i ← j + 1  to  n
            A(i, j) ← A(i, j)/A(j, j)
```

Tasks cost:

T_{kj} : $2(n–k)$ arithmetic operations $(1 \le k \le j–1, 1 \le j \le n)$
T_{jj} : $(n–j)$ arithmetic operations $(1 \le j \le n)$

Total number of arithmetic operations: $\frac{2n^3}{3} + O(n^2)$.
Precedence constraints:

$T_{kj} \ll T_{k+1, j}$ $1 \le k \le j–1, 1 \le j \le n$
$T_{jj} \ll T_{jk}$ $j+1 \le k \le n–1, 1 \le j \le n$

The task graph for this variant is the same as for the kji-AXPY variant above. This results from the fact that for any given j, the tasks T_{kj}, $1 \le k \le j$, must be executed sequentially. But, for any given k, the tasks T_{kj}, $k+1 \le j \le n$, can be executed in parallel. And this shows that two different algorithms can have the same parallel implementation.

ijk – DOT variant (C)

```
{ijk variant - DOT}
for  i ← 2  to  n
    for  j ← 2  to  i
        {task T_ij}
        A(i, j-1) ← A(i, j-1)/A(j-1, j-1)
        for  k ← 1  to  j-1
            A(i, j) ← A(i, j) - A(i, k)*A(k, j)
    for  j ← i + 1  to  n
        {task U_ij}
        for  k ← 1  to  i-1
            A(i, j) ← A(i, j) - A(i, k)*A(k, j)
```

Tasks cost:

T_{ij} : $2j–1$ arithmetic operations $(2 \le j \le i, 3 \le i \le n)$
T_{jj} : $2(i–1)$ arithmetic operations $(i+1 \le j \le n, 2 \le i \le n)$

Total number of arithmetic operations: $\frac{2n^3}{3} + O(n^2)$.
Precedence constraints:

$$T_{ij} \ll T_{i,\,j+1} \qquad 2 \leq j \leq i{-}1,\, 3 \leq i \leq n$$
$$T_{ii} \ll U_{ij} \qquad i{+}1 \leq j \leq n,\, 2 \leq i \leq n{-}1$$
$$U_{ij} \ll T_{i+1,\,j} \qquad i{+}2 \leq j \leq n,\, 2 \leq i \leq n{-}2$$
$$U_{i,\,j+1} \ll T_{i,\,j+1} \qquad i \leq j \leq n,\, 2 \leq i \leq n$$

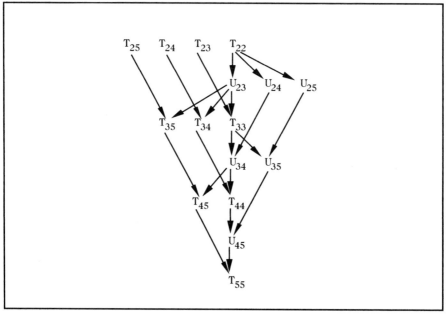

Figure 11.9 Task graph for ijk-DOT variant of Gaussian elimination, for n=5

Modified kji variant (D)

```
{modified kji variant}
for  k ← 1  to  n − 1
   for  j ← k + 1  to n
        {task T_kj}
        coeff ← A(i, k)/A(k, k)
        for  i ← k + 1  to  n
               A(i, j) ← A(i, j) − coeff * A(k, j)
```

Tasks cost:

T_{kj}: $2(n{-}k){+}1$ arithmetic operations (for $1 \leq k \leq n{-}1$)

Total number of arithmetic operations: $\frac{2n^3}{3}+O(n^2)$.
Precedence constraints:

$$T_{k,\,k+1} \ll T_{k+1,\,j} \quad k + 1 < j \leq n,\, 1 \leq k \leq n-1$$
$$T_{kj} \ll T_{k+1,\,j} \quad\ k + 1 < j \leq n,\, 1 \leq k \leq n-1$$

The task graph's triangular structure is identical to those used for parallelizing Gauss-Jordan elimination. In this case, the tasks' time is constant at any given level, but variable from one level to the next.

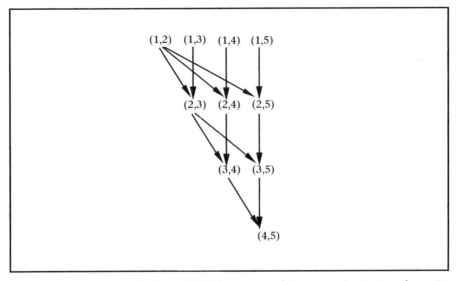

Figure 11.10   Task graph for modified kji variant of Gaussian elimination, for n=5

Doolittle variant (E)

```
{Doolittle variant}
for  k ← 1  to  n
    for  j ← k  to  n
        {task T_kj}
        for  p ← 1  to  k − 1
            A(k, j) ← A(k, j) − A(k, p)*A(p, j)
    for  i ← k + 1  to  n
        {task U_ki}
        for  p ← 1  to  k − 1
            A(i, k) ← A(i, k) − A(i, p)*A(p, k)
            A(i, k) ← A(i, k)/A(k, k)
```

Tasks cost:

T_{kj} :   2(k–1) arithmetic operations (for $k \le j \le n$, $1 \le k \le n$)
U_{ki} :   2(k–1) arithmetic operations (for $k + 1 \le i \le n$, $1 \le k \le n$)

Total number of arithmetic operations: $\frac{2n^3}{3} + O(n^2)$.
Precedence constraints:

$T_{kj} \ll T_{k+1, j}$ $k + 1 \le j \le n, 2 \le k \le n$
$T_{kk} \ll U_{kj}$ $k + 1 \le j \le n, 2 \le k \le n$
$U_{ki} \ll T_{k+1, i}$ $k + 2 \le i \le n, 2 \le k \le n$
$U_{k, k+1} \ll T_{k+1, j}$ $k + 1 \le j \le n, 2 \le k \le n$

The Doolittle task graph is identical to the one used for the ijk-DOT variant.

LDM^t decomposition (F)

```
{LDMᵗ variant}
for  k ← 1  to  n
   {task T_kk}
   for  p ← 1  to  k - 1
         A(k, k) ← A(k, k) - A(k, p)*A(p, p)*A(p, k)
   for  i ← k + 1  to  n
         {task T_ik}
         for  p ← 1  to  k - 1
             A(i, k) ← A(i, k) - A(i, p)*A(p, p)*A(p, k)
         A(i, k) ← A(i, k)/A(k, k)
   for  j ← k + 1  to  n
         {task T_kj}
         for  p ← 1  to  k - 1
             A(k, j) ← A(k, j) - A(k, p)*A(p, p)*A(p, j)
         A(k, j) ← A(k, j)/A(k, k)
```

Tasks cost:

T_{kk} :   3(k–1) arithmetic operations ($1 \le k \le n$)
T_{ik} :   3k–2 arithmetic operations ($k+1 \le i \le n$, $1 \le k \le n$)
T_{kj} :   3k–2 arithmetic operations ($k+1 \le j \le n$, $1 \le k \le n$)

Total number of arithmetic operations: $n^3 + O(n^2)$.
Precedence constraints:

$$T_{kk} \ll T_{kj} \qquad k+1 \leq j \leq n, \, 2 \leq k \leq n$$
$$T_{kk} \ll T_{ik} \qquad k+1 \leq i \leq n, \, 2 \leq k \leq n$$
$$T_{ik} \ll T_{i,\,k+1} \qquad k+1 \leq i \leq n, \, 1 \leq k \leq n-1$$
$$T_{kj} \ll T_{k+1,\,j} \qquad k+1 \leq j \leq n, \, 1 \leq k \leq n-1$$

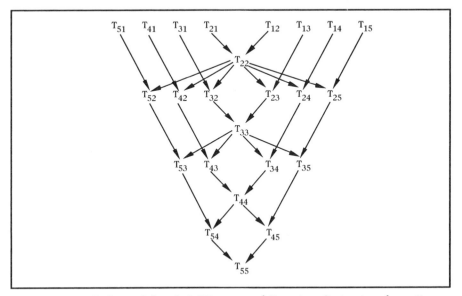

Figure 11.11   Task graph for ijk-DOT variant of Gaussian elimination, for n=5

Optimized LDM^t decomposition (G)

```
{optimized LDMᵗ variant}
for  k ← 1  to  n
   {task T_kk}
   for  p ← 1  to  k - 1
         r(p) ← d(p) * A(p, k)
         w(p) ← A(k, p) * d(p)
         A(k, k) ← A(k, k) - A(k, p) * r(p)
   for  i ← k + 1  to  n
         {task T_ik}
         for  p ← 1  to  k - 1
               A(i, k) ← A(i, k) - A(i, p) * r(p)
         A(i, k) ← A(i, k)/A(k, k)
   for  j ← k + 1  to  n
         {task T_kj}
         for  p ← 1  to  k - 1
               A(k, j) ← A(k, j) - w(p) * A(p, j)
         A(k, j) ← A(k, j)/A(k, k)
```

Tasks cost:

T_{kk} : 4(k–1) arithmetic operations (1 ≤ k ≤ n)
T_{ik} : 2k–1 arithmetic operations (k+1 ≤ i ≤ n, 1 ≤ k ≤ n)
T_{kj} : 2k–1 arithmetic operations (k+1 ≤ j ≤ n, 1 ≤ k ≤ n)

Total number of arithmetic operations: $\frac{2n^3}{3}$+O(n²).

The precedence constraints and the task graph's structure are identical to the one used in the LDM^t variant above, apart from the time it takes for tasks to execute.

LDL^t decomposition (H and J)

```
{LDLᵗ decomposition}
for k ← 1 to n
    {task T_kk}
    for  p ← 1  to  k −1
        A(k, k) ← A(k, k) − A(k, p) * A(p, p) * A(p, k)
    for  i ← k + 1  to  n
        {task T_ik}
        for  p ← 1  to  k −1
            A(i, k) ← A(i, k) − A(i, p) * A(p, p) * A(p, k)
        A(i, k) ← A(i, k)/A(k, k)
```

Tasks cost:

T_{kk} : 3(k–1) arithmetic operations (1 ≤ k ≤ n)
T_{ik} : 3k–2 arithmetic operations (k+1 ≤ i ≤ n, 1 ≤ k ≤ n)

Total number of arithmetic operations: $\frac{n^3}{2}$ + O(n²).
Precedence constraints:

$T_{kk} \ll T_{ik}$ k+1 ≤ i ≤ n, 2 ≤ k ≤ n
$T_{ik} \ll T_{i,\,k+1}$ k+1 ≤ i ≤ n, 2 ≤ k ≤ n

As was the case in non-symmetrical LDM^t, this variant can be optimized. The same results are obtained, with the constraints and the type of graph being the same; only the tasks' lengths and sequential times change.

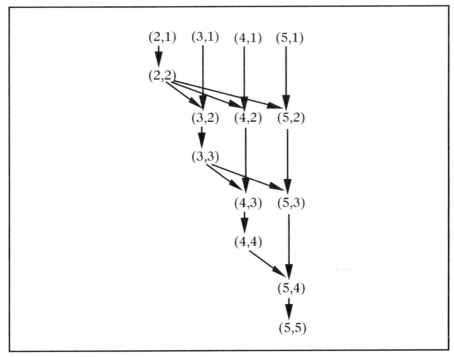

Figure 11.12   Task graph for LDL^t decomposition for n=5

Cholesky decomposition (J)

```
{Cholesky LLᵗ decomposition}
for  k ← 1  to  n
   {task T_kk}
   for  p ← 1  to  k - 1
      A(k, k) ← A(k, k) - A(k, p) * A(p, k)
      A(k, k) ← sqrt(A(k, k))
   for  i ← k + 1  to  n
      {task T_ik}
      for  p ← 1  to  k - 1
         A(i, k) ← A(i, k) - A(i, p) * A(p, k)
      A(i, k) ← A(i, k)/A(k, k)
```

Tasks cost:

T_{kk} : 2k–1 arithmetic operations ($1 \le k \le n$)
T_{ik} : 2k–1 arithmetic operations ($k+1 \le i \le n$, $1 \le k \le n$)

Assuming that obtaining a square root takes one time unit, the total number of arithmetic operations is $\frac{n^3}{3} + O(n^2)$. The precedence constraints and the graph's structure are the same as those in LDL^t decomposition. Tasks in the two decompositions take different amounts of time to execute.

11.4   Task graphs

The ten algorithms described above result in seven different task graphs. They can be grouped into four different classes:

- triangular graphs: for algorithm (D);

- two-step graphs: for algorithms (A), (B), (H), (I) and (J);

- double triangular graphs: for algorithms (C) and (E);

- double two-step graph: for algorithm (F).

Let us first look at the scheduling of the first two, and apply the results to the last two.

11.4.1   Bounds for triangular graphs

The sequential algorithm is as follows:

```
{triangular graph}
for  k ← 1  to  n − 1
    for  j ← k + 1  to  n
        Execute task T_{kj}
```

We examined a similar task graph for column-oriented Gauss-Jordan elimination at the beginning of this chapter. Assume that its execution time $ex(T_{kj})$ is in $O(n)$. All tasks with the same value of k have the same execution time. Its precedence constraints are:

$$T_{k,\,k+1} << T_{k+1,\,j} \qquad k+1 < j \le n,\, 1 \le k \le n-1$$
$$T_{kj} << T_{k+1,\,j} \qquad k+1 < j \le n,\, 1 \le k \le n-1$$

If the same proof as in Theorem 11.2 is used (with the same notation), the following is obtained:

Theorem 11.3

If a triangular graph is such that the costs of executing its tasks are $O(n)$ and are constant for fixed k, then (assuming $ex(T_{kj})=t_k$):

$$t_{opt} = \sum_{k=1}^{n-1} t_k$$

$$p_{opt} = n - 1$$

For a fixed number $p < p_{opt}$ of processors, the greedy algorithm is asymptotically optimal. Its execution time is found as the sum of the times for the first n–k levels that execute with efficiency 1 and that for the sequential execution of the p–1 remaining levels:

$$t_{opt}(p) = \frac{\sum\limits_{k=1}^{n-p}(n-k)t_k}{p} + \sum_{k=n-p+1}^{n-1} t_k + O\left(\frac{n^2}{p}\right)$$

For variant D, $t_k = 2(n-k)$. The following is obtained:

$$t_{opt}(p) = \frac{\sum\limits_{k=1}^{n-p}2(n-k^2)}{p} + \sum_{k=n-p+1}^{n-1} 2(n-k) + O\left(\frac{n^2}{p}\right)$$

with $p = \alpha n$ this reduces to

$$t_{opt}(p) = n^2\left(-3\alpha^2 + 4\alpha - 3 + \frac{2}{\alpha}\right) + O(n)$$

11.4.2   Bounds for two-step graphs

The sequential algorithm is as follows:

```
for  k ← 1  to  n – 1
    Execute task T_kk
    for  j ← k + 1  to  n
        Execute task T_kj
```

For the different versions that lead to parallelization for this type of graph, suppose that task T_{kj} can be executed in at_k+c_1 units and T_{kk} in bt_k+c_2 units, where a, b, c_1 and c_2 are integers, and for all k, either $t_k = k$ or $t_k = n-k$. Suppose also, without any loss of generality, that task T_{11} has been removed: this does not affect the scheduling, because this task must be executed separately at the start.

Tasks in proportion to (n–k) at level k

The following results are for a=b=1 and $c_1=c_2=0$.

The longest path in the graph consists of the 'diagonal' tasks $T_{kk} - T_{k, k+1} - T_{k+1, k+1} - \dots$. The analysis needed for obtaining theoretical bounds for t_{opt} and p_{opt} was given in Theorem 9.5, where we showed that $p_{opt} \geq \alpha_0 n$, where α_0 is the appropriate root of $\alpha^3 - 3\alpha + 1 = 0$. Furthermore, $t_{opt}=n^2-1$.

t_{opt} is computed in the same way as it is in the greedy graph, which results in the following:

$$t_{opt}(p) = n^2\left(\frac{1}{2\alpha} + 3\alpha + \alpha^2\right) + O(n) \text{ for } p \leq \alpha_0 n$$

We now describe an asymptotically optimal scheduling algorithm [RoT89]; we shall not give the proof, which is very technical, but indicate how it works.

First, an informal description of its schedule. The scheduling is based on the longest possible execution time at maximum efficiency. $T_{n-p, n-p}$ is the task after which it is not possible for all the processors to be executing simultaneously, since each of the subsequent levels has fewer than p tasks. Therefore, after this diagonal task, all those remaining have to be executed simultaneously.

Now consider two domains of tasks separated by a path through $T_{n-p, n-p}$ (see Figure 11.13); the aim is to maximize the amount of work for the second of these domains, without increasing the execution time – or, equivalently, to minimize the time lost. It is easy to see that the curve that meets these conditions is the 'equipotential' to $T_{n-p, n-p}$ along the critical path, meaning that all the tasks on the path have the same critical path as $T_{n-p, n-p}$. More precisely, it is defined by the tasks:

$$T_{i(j), j} \text{ where } i(j) = \max \{i/ cp(T_{i, j}) \geq cp(T_{n-p, n-p+1})\}$$

cp meaning the critical path. It is not difficult to prove that the path meets the last column at level $n-p\sqrt{2}$

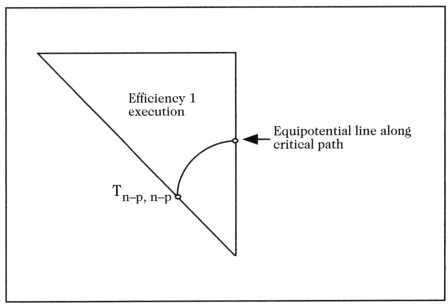

Figure 11.13   Optimal schedule for a two-step graph

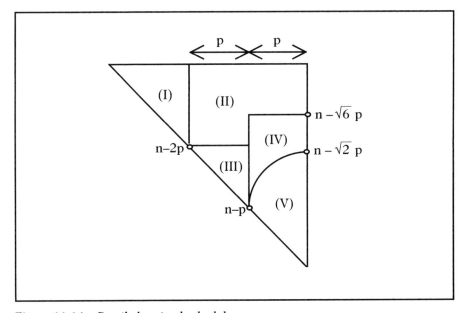

Figure 11.14   Detailed optimal schedule

The problem now is to specify the tasks in the first domain that execute with efficiency 1; for this, we dissect the graph into regions as in Figure 11.14. With $\beta_0 = \frac{1}{\alpha_0}$, the scheduling goes in three successive stages as follows:

(1) Execution of tasks in regions I and II. First,

$$\frac{\left(\beta_0 - 2\right)p}{2}$$

processors are allocated to region I. The others are allocated to region II, where execution is greedy and occurs row by row and from top to bottom. Tasks in region I are executed in blocks of two levels each; at each block, a new processor is released and joins those in region II.

(2) Execution of regions III and IV. For the sake of simplicity, assume the number of processors is odd and number them from 0 to p (so p is even). Processor 0 executes the diagonal tasks of region III. Each processor for the pair (j, p–j+1) for j=1 to p/2, acts on two opposed pairs of columns in regions III and IV as shown in Figure 11.15.

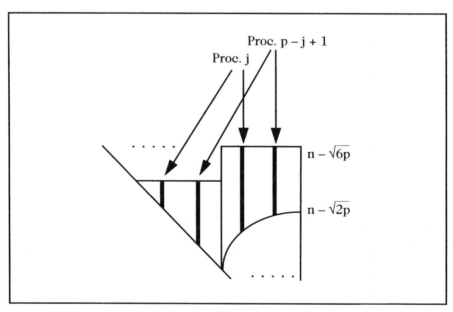

Figure 11.15   Execution of tasks in areas III and IV

Level n–p$\sqrt{6}$ is chosen so that the same amounts of work are done in regions III and IV. The total amount is equal to p times the time needed for sequential execution of all the diagonal tasks between levels n–2p and n–p, and this guarantees an efficiency of 1. The proposed scheme is valid since the sum of the execution times for all the tasks belonging to a group of 4 columns is independent of j.

(3) Execution in region V. Each column is allocated to a given processor, which executes it from top to bottom.

Finally, it can be shown that the execution scheme satisfies the precedence constraints [RoT89].

This result is very interesting, but the scheduling is very difficult to implement in practice. König and Trystram experimented with many values of n and p and found that a simple list schedule based on the critical path, giving priority to tasks on the higher levels, gave results that were very close to optimal, sometimes within less than 0.1% [BKT89]. However, optimality for this has yet to be proved.

Tasks in proportion to k and UET tasks

In LDL^t decomposition (variant H), a=b=3. Assume that $c_1=c_2=0$. It is easy to obtain theoretical results by applying the same principles used in the case above.

Theorem 11.4

For a two-step graph, with task costs of 3k at level k, $t_{opt} = 3n^2 + O(n)$ and $p_{opt} \geq \alpha_0 n$, where $\alpha_0 = 0.206$ is a root of the equation $1-6\alpha+6\alpha^2+2\alpha^3 = 0$.

$$t_{opt}(p) = n^2\left(\frac{1}{2\alpha} + 3\alpha + \alpha^2\right) \text{ for } p \leq \alpha_0 n$$

The proof is left to the reader.

An optimal algorithm has yet to be found for this, but experimentation with critical path list-schedules have yielded results that are very close to being optimal [BKT92].

Similarly, the difficulty in demonstrating optimal results for the critical path schedule lies here in complying with precedence constraints.

By contrast, a formal proof of an optimal algorithm based on the critical path does exist for the schedule for a two-step graph with tasks of a constant length (UET). Note that the graph results from parallelizing Gauss-Seidel's iterative algorithm for solving linear systems [Mis87] [RoT89]. In this case, Coffman and Graham's algorithm, described in Section 10.2.4, does not yield the optimal result. Consider n=7 and p=3; Figure 11.16 illustrates the resulting numbers in Coffman and Graham's algorithm [CoG72].

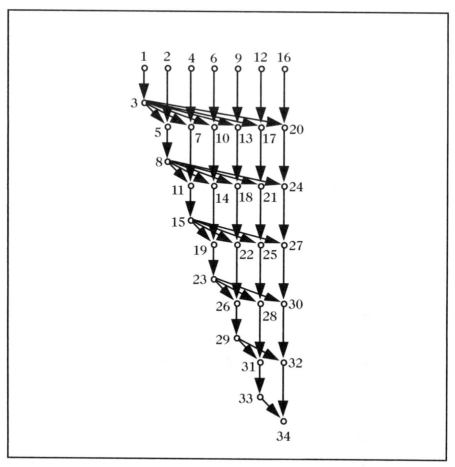

Figure 11.16 Coffman-Graham list-schedule for the two-step UET task graph

Execution proceeds as follows:

1	2	
3	4	
5	6	7
8	9	10
11	12	13
14	15	16
17	18	19
20	21	22
23	24	25
26	27	28
29	30	
31	32	
33		
34		

Execution time is 14, and it is easy to see that $t_{opt} = 13$. The following is an execution in optimal time:

1	2	4
3	6	9
5	12	16
8	7	10
11	13	17
15	14	20
19	18	
23	22	21
26	25	24
29	28	27
31	30	
33	32	
34		

11.4.3 Double graphs

Scheduling for the two double graphs is derived from the results obtained above. The aim of this section is to determine bounds for p_{opt} and to compute $t_{opt}(p)$. The key idea in analysing these graphs is to group the levels in pairs so as to be able to use the known results for simple graphs.

Double triangular graph

The generic form of the algorithm for a double triangular graph is as follows:

```
for k ← 1  to  n
    for j ← k  to  n
        Execute Tkj
    for i ← k + 1  to  n
        Execute Uki
```

We exclude T_{kk} and change the index of the second loop from j to i. One way of approaching the problem is to group the tasks T_{ki} and U_{ki} into a single task R_{ki} (for i<k). The time of the R_{ki} is $(b+c)t_k$, where $t_k = k$ or n–k. The precedence constraints are then as follows:

$$T_{ki} << T_{k+1, i} \text{ and } U_{ki} << U_{k+1, i} \text{ imply } R_{ki} << R_{k+1, i}$$
$$T_{kk} << U_{ki} \text{ and } U_{kk} << T_{k+1, i} \quad \text{ imply } R_{kk} << R_{ki}$$

This results in a 2-step graph, with both diagonal and off-diagonal tasks taking the same amount of time to execute (a=b using the above notation). The required bounds can be found on the basis of the results obtained in Section 11.4.2. However, note that only upper bounds should be taken into account, as the two-step graph is a sub-graph of the double triangular graph:

$$t_{opt}(p) \le (b+c)\left(\frac{\sum_{k=1}^{n-2p}(n-k)t_k}{p} + 2\sum_{k=n-2p}^{n}t_k\right) + O(n)$$

$$p_{opt} \le \frac{n}{2}$$

Another approach is to apply a greedy algorithm directly to the initial graph, as already described. The algorithm executes tasks greedily (as soon as a processor is free, it deals with the next task) from level k=1 to level k=n–p in the following order:

$$T_{11} -... - T_{1n} - U_{11} -... - U_{1n} - T_{22} -... - U_{2n} -... - T_{nn} - U_{nn}$$

which results in:

$$t_{opt}(p) \le (b+c)\left(\frac{\sum_{k=1}^{n-p}(n-k)t_k}{p} + \sum_{k=n-p}^{n}t_k\right) + O(n)$$

It is easy to show that this bound is better than the previous one; for $t_k=k$, it becomes:

$$t_{opt}(p) \le (b+c)\left(\frac{n^3}{6p} + \frac{np}{2} - \frac{p^2}{6}\right) + O(n)$$

and for $t_k=n-k$, it is:

$$t_{opt}(p) \leq (b+c)\left(\frac{n^3}{3p} + \frac{p^2}{6}\right) + O(n)$$

Note that the asymptotic efficiency of the algorithm is 1 from level k=1 to level n–p.

A lower bound is obtained by adding the execution time of the level with the shortest path between n–p and n to that of levels k–1 to n–p:

$$(b+c)\left(\frac{\sum_{k=1}^{n-p}(n-k)t_k}{p} + \min(b,c)\sum_{k=n-p+1}^{n} t_k\right) + O(n) \leq t_{opt}(p)$$

For $t_k = k$:

$$(b+c)\left(\frac{n^3}{6p} - \frac{np}{2} + \frac{p^2}{3}\right) + \min(b,c)\left(np - \frac{p^2}{2}\right) + O(n) \leq t_{opt}(p)$$

All the above results can be summarized in the following theorem:

Theorem 11.5

For a double triangular graph, for which the cost of tasks at level k is proportional to k,

$$t_{opt} = (b+c)\left(\frac{n^2}{2} + \frac{n}{2}\right)$$

$$\frac{n}{3} \leq p_{opt} \leq \frac{n}{2}$$

For a number of processors $p \leq p_{opt}$:

$$(b+c)\left(\frac{n^3}{6p} - \frac{np}{2} + \frac{p^2}{3}\right) + \min(b,c)\left(np - \frac{p^2}{2}\right) + O(n) \leq t_{opt}(p) \leq (b+c)\left(\frac{n^3}{6p} - \frac{np}{2} + \frac{p^2}{3}\right) + O(n)$$

Double two-step graph

The generic form of the algorithm for a double two-step graph is as follows:

```
for k ← 1 to n - 1
    Execute T_kk
    for j ← k + 1 to n
        Execute T_kj
    for i ← k + 1 to n
        Execute T_ik
```

Let the execution time of T_{kk} be at_k units and that of T_{kj} (and T_{ik}) be bt_k units, where a and b are integers and $t_k = k$. Let $s = \lceil \frac{a}{b} \rceil + 1$. For all the integers q, $q^+ = \max(1, q)$.

Recall that the precedence constraints are as follows:

$$
\begin{array}{ll}
T_{kk} << T_{kj} & k+1 \leq j \leq n, \, 2 \leq k \leq n \\
T_{kk} << T_{ik} & k+1 \leq i \leq n, \, 2 \leq k \leq n \\
T_{k, k+1} << T_{k+1, k+1} & 1 \leq k \leq n-1 \\
T_{kj} << T_{k+1, j} & k+2 \leq j \leq n, \, 1 \leq k \leq n-1 \\
T_{k+1, k} << T_{k+1, k+1} & 1 \leq k \leq n-1 \\
T_{ik} << T_{i, k+1} & k+2 \leq i \leq n, \, 1 \leq k \leq n-1
\end{array}
$$

The task graph is identical to that in Figure 11.11, apart from the fact that the indices are modified. As above, it follows directly that:

$$
t_{opt} = (a + b)\left(\frac{n^2}{2} - \frac{n}{2} \right)
$$

$$
\frac{t_{seq}}{t_{opt}} = \frac{2b}{3(a+b)} n \leq p_{opt} \leq 2(n-1)
$$

To determine bounds for $t_{opt}(p)$, we propose a three-stage schedule. Without any loss of generality, assume that p is even.

In the first stage, which is asynchronous, tasks on levels 1 to $(n-sp/2)^+$ are executed. Execution is greedy with an efficiency of 1.

In the second and third stages, which are synchronous, levels $(n-sp/2)^+ + 1$ to $(n-(s-1)p/2)^+$ and $(n-(s-1)p/2)^+ + 1$ to n respectively, are executed. In other words, as soon as a level does not have any more tasks for processors to work on simultaneously, levels are executed one after the other. The difference between stages 1 and 2 arises solely from the expression of the time needed for a given level. Thus:

$$t_1 = \frac{2b \displaystyle\sum_{k=1}^{\left(n-\frac{sp}{2}\right)^+}(n-k)t_k}{p} + O(n)$$

$$t_2 = sb \sum_{k=\left(n-\frac{sp}{2}\right)^+}^{\left(n-\frac{(s-1)p}{2}\right)^+} t_k + O(n)$$

$$t_3 = (a+b) \sum_{k=\left(n-\frac{(s-1)p}{2}\right)^+}^{n} t_k + O(n)$$

$$t_4 = b \sum_{k=\left(n-\frac{sp}{2}\right)^+}^{n} t_k + O(n)$$

Theorem 11.6

For a double two-step graph (D), in which the execution time of T_{kj} and T_{ik} is b_{tk} units and the execution time of T_{kk} is at_k units, where a and b are integers and $t_k = k$:

$$t_{opt} = (a+2b)\left(\frac{n^2}{2} - \frac{n}{2}\right)$$

$$\frac{4b}{3(2b+a)} \le p_{opt} \le 2(n-1)$$

and

$$t_1 + t_4 \le t_{opt}(p) \le t_1 + t_2 + t_3$$

11.4.4   Comparison of optimal algorithms

The performance of optimal algorithms for triangular and two-step graphs can be compared on the basis of the results obtained in the sections above. t_{opt}, a bound for p_{opt} and, wherever possible, $t_{opt}(p)$ were computed for all the variants of Gaussian elimination. These values can be used to rank the variants in order of their relative performance.

Consider the problem of a Gaussian elimination algorithm that can be parallelized in two different ways, with one resulting in a triangular task graph and the other in a two-step graph. Variant (D) results in a triangular graph, with tasks at level k taking $2(n-k)$ to execute, and variants (A) and (B) in two-step graphs, where, at level k, T_{kk} lasts $(n-k)$ and the tasks T_{kj} last $2(n-k)$.

Let's take another look at the results of this:

For variant (D),

$$t_{opt}(p) = n^2 \left(3\alpha^2 + 4\alpha - 3 + \frac{2}{\alpha} \right) + O(n)$$

For variants (A) and (B),

$$t_{opt}(p) = n^2 \left(3\alpha^2 + 4\alpha - 3 + \frac{2}{\alpha} \right) + O(n)$$

The result below is more general: however long their tasks take to execute, schedules for the triangular and two-step tasks can be compared. Consider a triangular graph, with tasks at level k that take bt_k to execute, and a two-step graph, with the task T_{kk} at level k taking bt_k to execute, and the tasks T_{kj} taking at_k.

$t_{opt\text{-}T}(p)$ and $t_{opt\text{-}2P}(p)$ are the values of $t_{opt}(p)$ for both graphs.

Theorem 11.7

For all b, and for p of the order n, we have:

$$t_{opt\text{-}2P}(p) > t_{opt\text{-}T}(p) + O(n)$$

Proof

The precise value of $T_{opt\text{-}T}(p)$ and a lower bound of $t_{opt\text{-}2P}$ are known.

$$t_{opt-T}(p) = \frac{\sum\limits_{k=1}^{n-p}(n-k)bt_k}{p} + \sum\limits_{k=n-p+1}^{n-1}bt_k + O(n)$$

$$t_{opt-2P}(p) = \frac{\sum\limits_{k=1}^{n-p}\left(at_k + (n-k)bt_k\right)}{p} + \sum\limits_{k=n-p+1}^{n-1}(a+b)t_k \leq \frac{\sum\limits_{k=1}^{n-p}(n-k)bt_k}{p}$$

$$+ \sum\limits_{k=n-p+1}^{n-1}bt_k + O(n)$$

11.5   Conclusion

Comprehensive analysis revealed that parallelizing Gaussian elimination is very different from vectorizing it (Chapter 8). The kji and jki variants result in the same task graph and, therefore, in the same parallel implementation, in contrast to vectorization, where it was shown that the performance of the jki-GAXPY variant was higher.

Simple kji (with a greedy schedule) was the best variant in parallel on a shared-memory MIMD machine with n processors.

We made one fundamental assumption throughout the chapter – that the costs of access to memory are negligible compared with the execution times of arithmetic operations. We shall see in Chapter 16 that, on distributed memory architectures, this assumption is not valid, as the time taken by data transfers between processors has to be taken into account. However, the question of the validity of this assumption also applies to shared-memory architectures. In Chapter 13, we raise that question in the context of Gaussian elimination and provide an answer to it.

In Chapter 12, we look at the limits of an approach based on parallelizing sequential programs using Givens factorization. We show that parallel algorithms have to be designed before an optimal algorithm can be found.

Parallelization of the Givens method

This chapter deals with parallelizing QR factorization using the Givens method on a parallel shared-memory computer. We describe the complexity analysis of several algorithms specific to the parallel version of the Givens method.

12.1   The Givens method

12.1.1   Brief review

Description

The problem of linear least squares with no constraints occurs in much scientific computation [Gov83]. It can be formulated as follows: let A be a dense, rectangular m × n matrix, with m ≥ n, and b a vector of size m; find a vector x of size n, such that the norm of the error term ‖Ax–b‖ is minimal, where ‖.‖ is the Euclidian norm. We describe the case where A is of full rank (n).

In Chapter 5, we described how a matrix is orthogonally decomposed to solve linear systems, using the Givens method with plane rotations. The sequential algorithm is well known [Gov83]; the following is a summary.

The rectangular matrix, formed by the square matrix R and completed by (m–n) rows of 0, is written

$$\begin{pmatrix} R \\ 0_{m-n} \end{pmatrix}$$

First stage

- Perform orthogonal decomposition of A,

$$QA = \begin{pmatrix} R \\ 0_{m-n} \end{pmatrix}$$

using plane rotations (Givens factorization) or element reflections (Householder reduction). Q is an orthogonal m × m matrix.

- Compute the vector c with m elements: $Qb = c$.

In the algorithm for orthogonal decomposition using the Givens method, a sequence of plane rotations is constructed. Note that the two rows used for performing the rotations are modified, in contrast to the Gaussian elimination algorithm. The order in which rotations are performed in the Givens method is such that an element that has been previously annihilated is subsequently preserved. Generally, the order means that elements are annihilated from left to right and from the last row upwards. Measured in terms of the number of rotations, the cost of the algorithm is $mn - \frac{n(n+1)}{2}$ computation steps on a single processor architecture, which corresponds to the number of subdiagonal elements in A. Element rotation was described in Chapter 5.

Second stage

- Solve the triangular system $Rx = c$, with the error norm equal to:

$$\|Ax - b\| = \|(c_{n+1}, \ldots, c_m)\|$$

Note also that, if m=n, the problem becomes that of using the QR method to solve a linear system with a dense matrix.

Structure of this chapter

In this chapter, we examine how the first stage of orthogonal decomposition using the Givens method is parallelized. A multiprocessor architecture with shared memory is assumed, with the same assumptions on how this structure functions as in Chapter 9. The results described below are taken from Sameh and Kuck [SaK78], Modi and Clarke [MoC84], Cosnard and Robert [CoR86b], Cosnard, Muller and Robert [CMR86], and, more recently, Cosnard and Daoudi [CoD92].

12.1.2 Parallelization of the Givens method

Assumptions and notation

A is any dense $m \times n$ matrix, with $m \geq n$. The number of processors is denoted p. Orthogonal decomposition of A can be performed using the algorithm for the Givens method with plane rotations. The notation used is the same as in Chapter 5 and R(i, j, k), $i \neq j$, $1 \leq i, j \leq m$ and $1 \leq k \leq n$, denotes the rotation in the plane (i, j) that annihilates element a_{ik}. For example, R(i, j, 1) combines rows i and j, such that a_{i1} is annihilated (*see* Figure 12.1).

$$\begin{bmatrix} c & s \\ -s & c \end{bmatrix} \begin{bmatrix} a_{j1} & a_{j2} & \cdots & a_{jn} \\ a_{i1} & a_{i2} & \cdots & a_{in} \end{bmatrix} = \begin{bmatrix} x & x & x & \cdots & x \\ 0 & x & x & \cdots & x \end{bmatrix}$$

Figure 12.1 Rotation of elements R(i, j, 1)

Parallelization of the Givens method

The basic principle underlying the parallelization is that independent rotations – that is, rotations applied to different rows – are allocated to different processors.

We assume that each processor can read two rows from memory and apply a plane rotation to these so as to introduce a zero element and return the modified rows to memory. This modifying precludes two processors from having a row in common, so the number of processors that can be used is less than $\lfloor \frac{m}{2} \rfloor$. Initially we take $p=\lfloor \frac{m}{2} \rfloor$ implying that p rotations can be performed simultaneously. Execution times are initially measured in terms of numbers of rotations, since it is assumed that a rotation's execution time is independent of the lengths of the vectors it comprises. In general, the assumption is clearly unrealistic, as the vector's size during the algorithm varies from n to 2. However, a comprehensive study of parallelizing QR decomposition using the Givens method can be conducted on the basis of this assumption. Finally, note that parallel algorithms are synchronous in this case, since all the tasks execute in a constant amount of time. Below, the execution time of one arithmetic operation is used as unit time.

Several parallel algorithms are described and the example of m=13 and n=6 is used to illustrate them. In all the algorithms, the subdiagonal elements of A are annihilated from bottom to top and from left to right. An integer r in position (i, k) means that the element a_{ik} has been annihilated in the rth step.

12.2   Some parallel algorithms

12.2.1   Sameh and Kuck's algorithm

Description

Figure 12.2 illustrates the Sameh and Kuck algorithm [SaK78], in which elements are annihilated column by column from bottom to top. The rotations carried out can be notated as being equal to R(i, i − 1, k). The element in position (i, k) is annihilated when rotation R(i − 1, i − 2, k − 1) has completed (the elements in position (i, k − 1) and (i − 1, k − 1) are then zero). In step 2k − 1, the element in position (m, k) is annihilated, followed, in step 2k − 1 + m − i, by the element in position (i, k). The last element to be annihilated is in position (n + 1, n) if m > n and in position (n, n − 1) if m = n. The number of time steps required to execute the algorithm is thus m + n − 2 if m > n, and 2n − 3 if m = n, which for the case of Figure 12.2 gives 17. Note that a zero can be placed on a row by using any row that has the same number of zero elements. For example, in step three, only R(13, 12, 2) can be chosen, whereas rotation R(11, x, 1) could replace R(11, 10, 1), with any x ≤ 10. In this example, the maximum number of simultaneous rotations is six, attained at steps 11 and 12. More generally, the maximum number of simultaneous rotations is $\min(n, \lfloor \frac{m}{2} \rfloor)$ and this is attained in step 2 $\min(n, \lfloor \frac{m}{2} \rfloor) - 1$.

```
        *
     12  *
     11 13  *
     10 12 14  *
      9 11 13 15  *
      8 10 12 14 16  *
      7  9 11 13 15 17
      6  8 10 12 14 16
      5  7  9 11 13 15
      4  6  8 10 12 14
      3  5  7  9 11 13
      2  4  6  8 10 12
      1  3  5  7  9 11
```

Figure 12.2   Sameh and Kuck algorithm (n=6, m=13)

Modified Sameh and Kuck algorithm

One obvious way of modifying the above algorithm is to perform $2\lfloor\log_2(m)\rfloor -1$ rotations in the first step (which is the greatest power of 2 that is less than $\lfloor\frac{m}{2}\rfloor$) and to use the zeros thereby created to annihilate one element in every step (instead of one every two steps) in the first row from column 1 to column $\lfloor\log_2(m)\rfloor - 1$. The total number of steps is then $n+m-\lfloor\log_2(m)\rfloor-1$, if m>n (15 in the case of Figure 12.3) or $2n -\lfloor\log_2(m)\rfloor - 2$, if m = n.

```
        *
      9  *
      8 11  *
      7 10 12  *
      6  9 11 13  *
      5  8 10 12 14  *
      4  7  9 11 13 15
      3  6  8 10 12 14
      2  5  7  9 11 13
      1  4  6  8 10 12
      1  3  5  7  9 11
      1  2  4  6  8 10
      1  2  3  5  7  9
```

Figure 12.3   Modified Sameh and Kuck algorithm

Relevance to precedence

A standard sequential algorithm for the Givens method is as follows:

```
for i ← n-1  to  1
    for j ← n  to  i + 1
        (A_{j-1}, A_j) ← Givens (A_{j-1}, A_j)
```

If T_{ij} is the operation $(A_{j-1}, A_j) \leftarrow$ Givens(A_{j-1}, A_j) executed at step i then the precedence relations for the tasks of this algorithm are as follows:

$$T_{i, j} \ll T_{i, j+1}$$
$$T_{i, j} \ll T_{i+1, j-1}$$

By applying the techniques described in Chapter 9, it is easy to show that the Sameh and Kuck algorithm is optimal for this task graph. Its optimal execution time is m + n − 2 if m > n, and 2n − 3 if m = n. The optimal number of processors is $\lfloor \frac{m}{2} \rfloor$.

We have seen that this execution time can be improved. But this means that the sequential algorithm has to be modified. In the two sections below, we construct parallel algorithms directly, instead of seeking to parallelize sequential algorithms.

12.2.2   Fibonacci algorithms

Modi and Clarke first described Fibonacci algorithms in [MoC84]. A Fibonacci algorithm of order 1 is constructed, as shown in Figure 12.4. The algorithm is constructed in two stages. In the first, the initial column is filled from the top downwards; $u_1=1$ zero is placed in position (2, 1), then $u_2=2$ copies of −1 are placed below that, then $u_3=3$ copies of −2,..., $u_k=u_{k-1}+1$ copies of −(k−1) below that, until the column is completely filled. The second column is obtained by adding 2 to each element in the first column and shifting it one position downwards. Similarly, the third column is obtained from the second column, and so on until the nth column. In the second stage, the elimination algorithm is obtained by adding u+1 to each element in the previous table, with −u being the element in position (m, 1). By contrast with the algorithms above, it is not easy to show that the elements of A can be annihilated in this way. The proof of this property is set out in the section below.

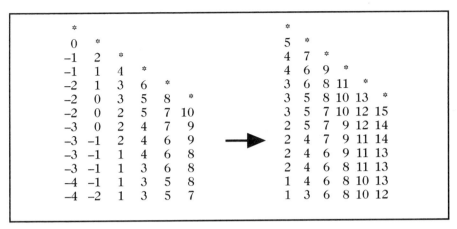

Figure 12.4   Fibonacci algorithm of order 1

Similarly, the Fibonacci algorithm of the order q is obtained by replacing the relation $u_k=u_{k-1}+1$ with $u_k=u_{k-1}+u_{k-2}+\ldots+u_{k-q+1}$ (with $u_0=u_{-1}=\ldots u_{-q+1}=0$) and adding q+1 instead of 2 to the elements in column j, in order to obtain column j+1.

We shall compute the number of steps in Fibonacci algorithms in the next section. Note that 15 steps are required in our example, where n=6 and m=13.

12.2.3   Greedy algorithm

However, the decomposition can be performed in 14 steps simply by using a greedy algorithm [MoC84] [CoR86b]. In this algorithm, the maximum possible number of rotations is performed in each step, with the elements in one column being annihilated from bottom to top and those in each row from left to right. Figure 12.5 is an illustration of the algorithm being used with the example we have chosen. Execution is very fast to start with, as six rotations are performed in steps 1 and 2, five in steps 4 to 8 and four in steps 9 and 10. But it ends slowly with two rotations in steps 11 and 12 and only one rotation in the last two steps.

The choice of which rows are to be used in performing rotations is more complicated in the modified Sameh and Kuck, Fibonacci and greedy algorithms than in the Sameh and Kuck algorithm. But a coherent choice can be made; if r elements are annihilated in column k in the jth step, the r corresponding rows and the r rows just above them are taken and then combined, and one row in each group is chosen. For example, in step 5 of the greedy algorithm, there are two elements to be annihilated in column 3: (9, 3) and (10, 3). Rotations R(9, 7, 3) and R(10, 8, 3) can therefore be executed. Note that this is possible because the elements in position (10, 2), (9, 2), (8, 2) and (7, 2) were annihilated in steps 3 and 4.

```
         *
   4     *
   3  6  *
   3  5  8  *
   2  5  7  10 *
   2  4  7  9  12 *
   2  4  6  8  11 14
   1  3  6  8  10 13
   1  3  5  7  9  12
   1  3  5  7  9  11
   1  2  4  6  8  10
   1  2  4  6  8  10
   1  2  3  5  7  9
```

Figure 12.5   Greedy algorithm

12.3   Standard parallel Givens sequences

12.3.1   General description

In this section, we describe a class of specific parallel algorithms – standard parallel Givens sequences – and show that there exists an optimal algorithm in the class. The number of processors is denoted by p.

Notation

As above, R(i, j, k), $i \neq j$, $1 \leq i, j \leq m$ and $1 \leq k \leq n$, designates the rotation in the plane (i, j) that annihilates the element in position (i, k). Id(i, j) and Perm(i, j) are the rotations in the plane (i, j) corresponding to the identity of rows i and j and their permutation respectively. R(i, j, k) and R(i', j', k') are disjoint if their corresponding rotation planes are disjoint, that is, if $i \neq i'$, $i \neq j'$, $j \neq i'$ and $j \neq j'$.

An algorithm M requiring T steps to perform Givens factorization is written M = (M(1),..., M(T)), where, if $1 \leq t \leq T$, M(t) is a group of r(t) disjoint rotations ($r(t) \leq p$) that can be performed simultaneously at time t. M is used to construct a sequence A(t) such that A(0)=A, if $1 \leq t \leq T$. A(t) is obtained by applying the rotations of M(t) to A(t–1) in parallel. For the sake of simplicity, the notation (M, T, R) represents an algorithm in which R = r(1) +... + r(T). T is the algorithm's execution time.

Given m, n and p, $(M_{opt}, T_{opt}, P_{opt})$ is an optimal algorithm if $T_{opt} \leq T$ for all algorithms (M, T, R). T_{opt} (m, n, p) is the execution time in which a matrix (m, n) with p processors can be factorized using the Givens method. The problem we shall address consists of determining an optimal algorithm and T_{opt}(m, n, p).

Definition 12.1

(M, T, R) is a parallel Givens sequence [MoC84] if elements that have already been annihilated are preserved, that is, for all pairs of separate rotations R(i, j, k) and R(i', j', k') of M, (i, k) ≠ (i', k').

(M, T, R) is a standard parallel Givens sequence (abbreviated below to SPGS), if it is a parallel Givens sequence that reduces matrix A to an upper triangle by annihilating elements from left to right and from bottom to top, that is, if for R(i, j, k) of M(t) and R(i', j', k') of M(t') with t≤t', k<k' or (k=k' and i≥i').

Let (M, T, R) be any algorithm; r(k, t) is the number of zeros introduced into column k in step t and s(k, t) is the total number of zeros introduced into column k following step t.

It follows from the definition of Givens sequences that if (M, T, R) is a Givens sequence, then s(k, t) = r(k, 1)+...+r(k, t).

12.3.2   An initial result

First, we show that an optimal algorithm need be sought only in the class of standard Givens parallel sequences.

Theorem 12.1

Let (M, T, R) be an algorithm that reduces A to an upper triangular matrix. A standard Givens parallel sequence with an execution time of T exists.

Proof

First, an algorithm, (M', T, R) that annihilates the elements in each row from left to right is constructed; then a Givens sequence, M_2, with an execution time of T, that also reduces matrix A to an upper triangle is constructed; and, finally, M_2 is used to construct a standard parallel Givens sequence with the same time.

Stage 1

Let p(i, t) be the number of zero elements in the ith row of A(t). M' and the sequence A'(t) (remember that A'(0) = A and that, if $1 \leq t \leq T$, A'(t) is obtained by applying parallel rotations of M'(t) to A'(t − 1)) are constructed by recurrence on t, such that A'(t) has p'(i, t) zeros in its ith row, where p'(i, t) satisfies the following properties:

$p'(i, t) \geq p(i, t)$ if $i = 1,..., m$

$A'(t) (i, k) = 0$ if $k = 1,..., p'(i, t)$ and $i = 1,..., m$.

For $t = 1$, if $R(i, j, k)$ belongs to $M(1)$, then $R(i, j, 1)$ belongs to $M'(1)$. Clearly, the assumptions of recurrence are satisfied for $A'(1)$. Assume that $M'(t)$ has been constructed such that $A'(t)$ satisfies the above conditions. Because the rotations of $M(t+1)$ are disjoint, each rotation can be considered separately. Let $R(i, j, k)$ be a rotation of $M(t+1)$; a rotation of $M'(t+1)$ that retains the above assumptions of recurrence is constructed. It will do one of three things – introduce another zero, permute the rows i and j or introduce the identity. Which of the three is determined in the various cases below.

A.   The positions of the zeros in rows i and j of $A(t)$ are the same; $A(t)(i, q)=0$ and $A(t)(j, q)=0$ which implies that $p(i, t) = p(j, t)$ and that $R(i, j, k)$ introduces another zero in position (i, k), if $A(t) (i, k) \neq 0$.

A1.   If $A'(t)$ has the same number of zeros as $A(t)$ in rows i and j, that is, if $p'(i, t) = p'(j, t) = p(i, t)$, then we perform the rotation $R(i, j, p'(i, t)+1)$ in $M'(t+1)$. Therefore, $p'(i, t+1) = p'(i, t)+1$ and $p'(j, t+1)=p'(j, t)$.

A2.   If $A'(t)$ has more zeros in row i than $A(t)$: $p'(i, t) > p(i, t)$, then a new zero does not have to be placed in row i of $A'(t)$. The identity $Id(i, j)$ is performed in $M'(t+1)$. Therefore, $p'(i, t+1) = p'(i, t)$ and $p'(j, t+1)=p'(j, t)$.

A3.   If $A'(t)$ has as many zeros in row i as $A(t)$, but more zeros than $A(t)$ in row j: $p'(i, t)=p(i, t)$ and $p'(j, t) > p(j, t)$, then it is enough to perform a permutation of rows i and j for another zero to be introduced in the row i of $A'(t)$. The permutation $Perm(i, j)$ is performed in $M'(t+1)$. Therefore, $p'(i, t+1)=p'(j, t)$ and $p'(j, t+1) = p'(i, t)$.

B.   The positions of the zeros in rows i and j of $A(t)$ are not the same, which implies that $p(j, t+1) \leq p(j, t)$, since introducing a zero in row i may destroy one or more zeros in row j.

B1.   If the number of zeros in row i of $A(t+1)$ is less than or equal to the number in $A(t)$: $p(i, t+1) \leq p(i, t)$, then another zero does not have to be introduced in row i of $A'(t)$. The identity $Id(i, j)$ is performed in $M'(t+1)$. Therefore, $p'(i, t+1)=p'(i, t)$ and $p'(j, t+1) = p'(j, t)$.

B2.   If $A(t+1)$ has one more zero in row i than $A(t)$: $p(i, t+1) = p(i, t)+1$, then the set of zeros in row i in $A(t)$ is strictly included in the set of row j, which implies that $p(j, t+1) = p(i, t) < p(j, t)$.

B2.1   If $p'(i, t) \geq p(i, t)+1$, a new zero does not have to be introduced in row i of $A'(t)$. The identity $Id(i, j)$ is performed in $M'(t+1)$. Therefore, $p'(i, t+1)=p'(i, t)$ and $p'(j, t+1)=p'(j, t)$.

B2.2   If $p'(i, t)=p(i, t)$, the number of zeros in row i of $A'(t)$ can be increased by performing a permutation of rows i and j. Thus, the permutation $Perm(i, j)$ is performed in $M'(t+1)$. Therefore, $p'(i, t+1) = p'(j, t)$ and $p'(j, t+1) = p'(i, t)$.

All the cases have been examined and for each of them the recurrence conditions were satisfied at time t+1. Both M and M' reduce A to an upper triangle.

Stage 2

Construct a Givens sequence M_2, with an execution time of T, that also reduces A to an upper triangle. A rotation is efficient if it strictly increases the number of zeros in the matrix to which the sequence is applied. For M', efficient rotations are those that differ in their identity and permutation of rows i and j. M_2 contains only efficient rotations of M'. Instead of performing a permutation of the rows of A', the indices of the rows are permuted in order to obtain A_2.

Let trans(i, j) be the transposition of (1,..., m) which exchanges the integers i and j. The permutation s of (i,..., m) below is constructed:

- s(0) is the identity;

- $s(t+1)=s(t)$, if $M'(t+1)$ contains no Perm;

- $s(t+1)=s(t)_{\circ}trans(i_1, j_1)_{\circ}trans(i_2, j_2)_{\circ}...$ if $Perm(i_1, j_1)$, $Perm(i_2, j_2)$ and so on, belong to $M'(t+1)$. Note that the way the permutations are formed is commutative in this case, as they operate on disjoint elements;

- s=s(T).

The Givens sequence M_2 is constructed as follows:

$R(i, j, k) \in M'(t)$ functions $\Leftrightarrow R(s^{-1}(s(t))(i), s^{-1}(s(t))(j), k) \in M(t)$ for $1 \leq t \leq T$

Let P(t) be the permutation matrix corresponding to s(t) (or P be that corresponding to s):

$$P(t)=P(i_1, j_1)\ldots P(i_q, j_q) \text{ if } s(t)=trans(i_q, j_q)\circ\ldots\circ trans(i_1, j_1)$$

where $P(i_1, j_1)$ is the permutation matrix corresponding to $trans(i_1, j_1)$.

Let $A_2(0)=P\, A'(0)$ and let us show by recurrence that $A_2(t)=P\, P^{-1}(t)A_1(t)$. Without any loss of generality and to simplify the proof, assume that $A'(t)$ is obtained by applying $R(i, j, k)$ and $Perm(u, v)$ to $A'(t-1)$:

$$A'(t) = R(i, j)\, P(u, v)\, A'(t-1) \text{ and } P(t) = P(u, v)\, P(t-1)$$

Then:

$$A_2(t) = R(s^{-1}(s(t))(i), s^{-1}(s(t))(j))\, A_2(t-1)$$

By recurrence, it follows that:

$$A_2(t) = R(s^{-1}(s(t))(i), s^{-1}(s(t))(j))\, P\, P^{-1}(t-1)\, A'(t-1)$$

Clearly, by defining s and P:

$$R(s^{-1}(s(t))(i), s^{-1}(s(t))(j))\, P\, P{-1}(t) = P\, P^{-1}(t)\, R(i, j)$$
$$= P\, P^{-1}(t-1)\, P^{-1}(u, v)\, R(i, j)$$

Therefore:

$$A_2(t) = P\, P^{-1}(t)\, R(i, j)\, P(u, v)\, A'(t-1) = P\, P^{-1}(t)\, A'(t)$$

It follows that $A_2(T)=P\, P^{-1}\, A'(t) = A'(t)$, that is, that $A_2(T)$ is upper triangular.

Stage 3

The Givens sequence M_2 is used to construct a standard parallel Givens sequence with the same time. Let $r(k, t)$ be the number of zeros that M_2 introduces in column k in step t and $s(k, t)$ be the total number of zeros in column k after step t. An SPGS, M_3, is constructed by recurrence on t.

For t=1, let $R(i_q, j_q, 1)$, $1 \le q \le r(1, 1)$ be the rotations of $M_2(1)$. The rotations $R(m-q+1, m-r(1, 1)-q+1, 1)$ are associated with the rotations $R(i_q, j_q, 1)$. The rotations $R(m-q+1, m-r(1, 1)-q+1, 1)$

annihilate the last r(1, 1) elements of the first column of A, which constitute $M_3(1)$.

For t−1, assume by recurrence that the last s(k, t−1) elements of column k have been annihilated by $M_3(1),\ldots, M_3(t-1)$ if $1 \le k \le n$. Let $R(i_q, j_q, k)$, $1 \le q \le r(k, t)$ be the rotations of $M_2(t)$ in column k. The rotations R(m−s(k, t−1)−q+1, m−s(k, t−1)−r(k, t)−q+1, k) are associated with $R(i_q, j_q, k)$. The former annihilate the subsequent r(k, t) elements of column k of A. As s(k, t)=s(k, t−1)+r(k, t), the last s(k, t) elements of column k of A are zeros. All the rotations, if $1 \le k \le$ n, constitute $M_3(t)$.

Note that the number of rotations at time t in column k remains unchanged. Therefore, if r(k, t) rotations can be performed in parallel by M_2, the same applies to M_3. Because M_2 reduces A to an upper triangular matrix, an SPGS of time t has been constructed. Figure 12.6 illustrates the construction, where m=6 and n=4.

```
    *                    *
1   *                4   *
3   5   *            3   6   *
1   2   4   *        2   5   7   *
4   6   7   8        1   3   6   8
2   3   6   7        1   2   4   7
```

Figure 12.6   Last stage in proof of the theorem

12.3.3   Extension

The complexity of parallel QR decomposition can be studied, if we restrict ourselves to SPGSs. The result below characterizes them.

Lemma 12.2

Let $p \le \lfloor\frac{m}{2}\rfloor$. If M is an SPGS, then:

$$s(0, t) = m \text{ if } t \ge 0$$
$$s(i, 0) = 0 \text{ if } 1 \le i \le m$$
$$s(i, t) \le s(i, t-1) + 1 \left\lfloor \frac{s_+(i-1, t-1) - s(i, t-1)}{2} \right\rfloor \text{ if } i, t \ge 1$$

Conversely, let r(i, t) and s(i, t) be integers that verify the above relations and such that T exists, for which s(i, T)=m–i; there exists an SPGS of time T that annihilates r(i, t) elements in column i at time t.

Proof

If M is an SPGS, elements are zeroed from left to right and from bottom to top. Therefore, at time t–1, the last s(i–1, t–1) elements of column i–1 and the last s(i, t–1) elements of column i are zeros. No more than $\lfloor (s(i-1, t-1)-s(i, t-1))/2 \rfloor$ zeros can be introduced in column i at time t. And the number of zeros introduced at time t in columns 1, 2,..., i is less than or equal to p, since one processor is required to create one zero.

Conversely, making the same assumptions as those in the lemma and using the same argument as above and the same construction as that in the last stage in the proof of Theorem 12.1, an SPGS can be constructed such that A(T) is upper triangular.

12.3.4   Optimality of the greedy algorithm $p=\lfloor \frac{m}{2} \rfloor$

In this section, we assume that $p=\lfloor \frac{m}{2} \rfloor$. We show that the algorithms described in Section 12.2 are in fact SPGSs. Then we show that the greedy algorithm is optimal.

Complexity of the Sameh and Kuck, modified Sameh and Kuck and Fibonacci algorithms

Lemma 12.3

Let $p=\lfloor \frac{m}{2} \rfloor$. The Sameh and Kuck and modified Sameh and Kuck algorithms and the Fibonacci algorithm of order q, for all $q \geq 1$, are SPGSs. Their execution times are, respectively:

- $t_{sk}(m, n, \lfloor \frac{m}{2} \rfloor)=m+n-2$ if m>n and $t_{sk}(m, n, \lfloor \frac{m}{2} \rfloor)=2n-3$ if m=n
- $t_{skm}(m, n, \lfloor \frac{m}{2} \rfloor)=n+m-\lfloor \log_2(m) \rfloor-1$ if m>n
- $t_{skm}(m, n, \lfloor \frac{m}{2} \rfloor)=2n \lfloor \log_2(m) \rfloor-2$ if m=n
- $t_{fib}(m, n, \lfloor \frac{m}{2} \rfloor)=\log_2 \lambda(q)(m)+(q+1)n+o(\log_2(m))$ if q > 1

where $\lambda(q)$ is the largest positive root of $x^q = x^{q-1} +... + x + 1$.

Proof

By construction, this property is easy for the Sameh and Kuck and the modified Sameh and Kuck algorithms. As far as Fibonacci algorithms are concerned, Lemma 12.2 is applied. It is enough to show that the corresponding s(i, t) verify the lemma's assumptions. We set out a proof only for the algorithm of order 1 and refer the reader to [MoC84] for the general case.

As $p =\lfloor \frac{m}{2} \rfloor$, the lemma's condition can be simplified as:

$$r(i,t) \leq \left\lfloor \frac{s(i-1,t-1) - s(i,t-1)}{2} \right\rfloor$$

Note that r(1, 1)=w and r(1, t)=uv−t+1 where v and w are such that it follows from the algorithm's construction that:

r(i, t)=r(1, t−2i+2)−i+1
s(i−1, t−1)= s(i−1, t−3) + r(i−1, t−2) + r(i−1, t−1)
s(i, t−1) = s(i−1, t−3) −1

Therefore, the relation is transformed into:

$$r(i,t) \leq \left\lfloor \frac{r(i-1,t-2) + r(i-1,t-1) + 1}{2} \right\rfloor$$

and, equivalently, into:

$$r(i,t) \leq \left\lfloor \frac{r(i,t) + r(i,t+1) + 1}{2} \right\rfloor$$

which is true, as r(i, t)=r(i, t+1)+1.

The execution times of the Sameh and Kuck and the modified Sameh and Kuck algorithms were computed earlier. The execution time of the Fibonacci algorithm of order q is more difficult to obtain. It follows from its definition that:

$$t_{fib}(m, n, \lfloor \tfrac{m}{2} \rfloor) = t_{fib}(fib(m, 1, \lfloor \tfrac{m}{2} \rfloor) + (q+1)(n-1)$$

Therefore, it is enough to find the value of $t_{fib}(m, 1, \lfloor \tfrac{m}{2} \rfloor)$. First, consider the case where q=1. Thus u_k=k and the sum of the u_k if k=1,..., t is equal to

$$\frac{t(t+1)}{2}$$

which yields the result. If q>1, standard analysis gives $u_k = c(\lambda(q))q$, where $\lambda(q)$ is the largest positive root in the equation $x^q = x^{q-1} + ... + x + 1$. The result is directly obtained from this by deduction.

Greedy algorithm

Now consider the greedy algorithm. We did not provide a very precise definition of this in Section 12.2. In the algorithm, the maximum possible number of rotations is performed, and the elements in a column are annihilated from bottom to top and those in each row from left to right. Lemma 12.2 implies that, if rġ(i, t) and sġ(i, t) are integers associated with the algorithm, the maximum number of rotations is obtained by:

$$sġ(0, t) = m \text{ if } t \geq 0$$
$$sġ(i, 0) = 0 \text{ if } 1 \leq i \leq m$$
$$rġ(i,t) = \left\lfloor \frac{sġ(i-1,t-1) - sġ(i,t-1)}{2} \right\rfloor \text{ if } i, t \geq 1$$

which is equivalent to:

$$sġ(i,t) = sġ(i,t-1) + \left\lfloor \frac{sġ(i-1,t-1) - sġ(i,t-1)}{2} \right\rfloor \text{ if } i, t \geq 1$$

Now we show that the algorithm is optimal.

Theorem 12.4

For all m and n, where m≥n and if $p = \lfloor \frac{m}{2} \rfloor$, the greedy algorithm is optimal.

Proof

From Theorem 12.1, it follows that it is enough to show that the greedy algorithm is optimal among SPGSs. Consider an SPGS and let the numbers associated with it be r(i, t) and s(i, t). The result follows from the inequality below:

$$s(i, t) \leq sġ(i, t) \text{ if } i, t \geq 1$$

This is shown by recurrence on i and t. Where i or t is 0:

$$s(0, 0) = sġ(0, 0) = m, \ s(0, t) = sġ(0, t) = m \text{ if } t \geq 1$$
$$s(i, 0) = sġ(i, 0) = 0 \text{ if } i \geq 1$$

It is assumed that s(j, u) ≤ sġ(j, u), where j and u are such that j<i or (j=i and u<t). From Lemma 12.2, it follows that:

$$s(i,t) \leq \frac{s(i-1,t-1) - s(i,t-1)}{2}$$
$$\leq \frac{sġ(i-1,t-1) - sġ(i,t-1)}{2}$$
$$\leq sġ(i,t)$$

which concludes the proof.

It can be readily shown that the greedy algorithm is optimal among SPGSs. By contrast, we saw in the proof of Theorem 12.1 that it is more difficult to show that an optimal SPGS exists. The difficulty in this analysis derives from the fact that a unique optimal algorithm does not exist and that optimal algorithms that are not SPGSs do exist, as illustrated in Figure 12.7.

```
        *
    3   *
    2   5   *
    2   4   7   *
    1   3   6   8
    1   3   5   7
    1   2   4   6
```

Greedy execution scheme

```
        *
    4   2(4)
    3   1   *   5(7)
    3   5   7   *
    2   4   6   8
    1   3   5   7
    1   2   4   6
```

Execution scheme (M,8,20)

Greedy algorithm   (M,8,20)

	Greedy algorithm			(M,8,20)		
Step 1	R(7,4,1)	R(6,3,1)	R(5,2,1)	R(7,5,1)	R(6,4,1)	R(3,2,2)
Step 2	R(4,2,1)	R(3,1,1)	R(7,6,2)	R(5,4,1)	R(7,6,2)	R(2,1,2)
Step 3	R(2,1,1)	R(6,4,2)	R(5,3,2)	R(4,2,1)	R(3,1,1)	R(6,5,2)
Step 4	R(4,3,2)	R(7,6,3)		R(2,1,1)	R(5,4,2)	R(7,6,3)
Step 5	R(3,2,2)	R(5,6,3)		R(4,2,2)	R(6,5,3)	R(3,2,4)
Step 6	R(5,4,3)	R(7,5,4)		R(5,4,3)	R(7,5,4)	
Step 7	R(4,3,3)	R(6,5,4)		R(4,3,3)	R(6,5,4)	
Step 8	R(5,4,4)			R(5,4,4)		

Figure 12.7   The algorithm (M, 8, 20) has the same execution time as the greedy algorithm. In steps 2 and 5, it annihilates elements that are subsequently destroyed.

12.4   Complexity results

12.4.1   The case where $p=\lfloor\frac{m}{2}\rfloor$

Theoretical analysis of the greedy algorithm

The complexity of QR decomposition using the Givens method is determined by the number of steps required to execute an optimal algorithm. It should be recalled that, in this chapter, a step consists of one plane rotation, irrespective of the length of the vectors that define the rotation. It follows from Theorem 12.1 that the complexity is equal to the number of steps in the greedy algorithm. The following relations result from this:

$$t_{opt}(m, n, \lfloor\tfrac{m}{2}\rfloor)=\min\{t/sg(n, t)=m-n\}\text{ if } m>n$$
$$t_{opt}(m, n, \lfloor\tfrac{m}{2}\rfloor)=\min\{t/sg(n, t)=1\}\text{ if } m=n$$

Theorem 12.5

Let $p=\lfloor\frac{m}{2}\rfloor$. If n is fixed and independent of m, then:

$$t_{opt}(m, n, \lfloor\tfrac{m}{2}\rfloor)=\log_2(m)+(n-1)\log_2\log_2(m)+O(\log_2\log_2(m))$$

If $m=n^2 f(n)$, with:

$$f(n)\geq\frac{1}{n}\,\forall n\geq 1 \text{ and } \lim_{n\to\infty}\left(f\left(n\right)\right)=0$$

then:

$$t_{opt}(m, n, \lfloor\tfrac{m}{2}\rfloor)=2n+O(n)$$

if $m=O(n^k)$ and $m\geq n^2$, with $k\geq 3$, then:

$$2n+O(n)\leq t_{opt}(m, n, \lfloor\tfrac{m}{2}\rfloor)\leq 3n+O(n)$$

Proof

Direct computations obtained from the results above.

Efficiency is one measure of the quality of parallelization of algorithms (*see* Chapter 2). In Corollary 12.6, the asymptotic efficiency, denoted e_∞, of the greedy algorithm for several values of m and n is computed. The fact that efficiency is constant when m is a polynomial in n, whereas it tends towards 0 when n is fixed and m tends towards infinity, is taken into account.

Corollary 12.6
  Let $p=\lfloor\frac{m}{2}\rfloor$.

1. If m=n, then $e_\infty(m, n)=\frac{1}{2}$

2. If m=bn, b≥1, then $e_\infty(m, n)=1-\frac{1}{2b}$

3. If $m=O(n^2)$ and $n=O(m)$, then $e_\infty(m, n)=1$

4. If $m=O(n^k)$ and $m\geq n^2$, with k≥3, then $e_\infty(m, n) \geq \frac{2}{3}$

5. If n is fixed, then $e_\infty(m,n) = \dfrac{2n}{\log_2(m)}$

More practical results

The above sections may appear essentially theoretical, as the greedy algorithm's execution time causes an O to appear. In fact, the greedy algorithm's exact execution time is very close to 2n for reasonable values of n. However, implementation of the greedy algorithm is complicated by the fact that at step k neither the number of elements to be annihilated – as this is the result of a computation – nor which rows are to be used is explicitly known. It may therefore be advantageous on occasions to use another algorithm that has a level of performance close to that of the greedy algorithm, but which is easier to implement. The corollary below can be used to do this. Remember that in this case the algorithm's only parameter is m ($p=\lfloor\frac{m}{2}\rfloor$ and n is a function of m) and that an algorithm is asymptotically optimal if the relation between its execution time and that of an optimal algorithm tends towards 1, when m tends towards infinity.

Corollary 12.7
  Let $p=\lfloor\frac{m}{2}\rfloor$.

1. If m=n, then the Sameh and Kuck algorithm is asymptotically optimal.

2. If m=bn, b≥1, then the Fibonacci algorithm of order 1 is asymptotically optimal.

3. If $m=O(n^2)$, the Fibonacci algorithm of order 1 is asymptotically optimal.

Proof
  The proof follows directly from the results of Theorem 12.5 and Lemma 12.3.

If $m > O(n^2)$, or if m is fixed and independent of n, none of the above algorithms is asymptotically optimal. Whether an asymptotically optimal Fibonacci algorithm of order q exists remains an open question in this case.

12.4.2   Complexity results for any p

In this section, it is assumed that the number of processors available to perform simultaneous rotations is less than $\lfloor \frac{m}{2} \rfloor$. We extend some of the properties described above and then go on to describe briefly the main complexity result.

Greedy algorithms

Theorem 12.1 showed that an optimal SPGS does exist. The characteristics of SPGSs were described in Lemma 12.2. However, the optimal SPGS is substantially different from the case where $p=\lfloor \frac{m}{2} \rfloor$, in that a unique greedy algorithm does not exist. Greedy algorithms can be informally described as follows, executing the maximum number of rotations in each step.

Definition 12.2
Let M be an SPGS. M is a greedy algorithm, if:

$$\sum_{j=1}^{n} r(j,t) = \min\left(p, \sum_{j=1}^{n} \left\lfloor \left| \frac{s(j-1,t-1)-s(j,t-1)}{2} \right| \right\rfloor \right)$$

There are several ways of obtaining the above equality. As examples, we describe two algorithms – the vertical greedy algorithm, which begins by filling the initial columns, and the horizontal greedy algorithm, which begins by filling the last rows.

- Vertical greedy algorithm (*see* Figure 12.8):

$svg(0, t) = M$ if $t \geq 0$
$svg(i, 0) = 0$ if $1 \leq i \leq n$

$$rvg(i,t) = \min\left(p - \sum_{j=1}^{n} rvg(j,t), \left\lfloor \left| \frac{svg(i-1,t-1)-svg(i,t-1)}{2} \right| \right\rfloor \right) \text{ if } i,t \geq 1$$

- Horizontal greedy algorithm (*see* Figure 12.9):

$$\text{shg}(0, t) = m \text{ if } t \geq 0$$
$$\text{shg}(i, 0) = 0 \text{ if } 1 \leq i \leq n$$

$$\text{rgh}(i,t) = \min\left(p - \sum_{j=i+1}^{n} \text{rhg}(j,t), \left\lfloor \frac{\text{shg}(i-1,t-1) - \text{shg}(i,t-1)}{2} \right\rfloor \right) \text{ if } i, t \geq 1$$

Neither of the two algorithms above is optimal, as Figure 12.10 shows. However, it can be shown that an optimal algorithm among all the greedy algorithms always exists.

```
                *
        5   *
        4   8   *
        3   7  11   *
        3   7  10  14   *
        3   6  10  13  16   *
        2   6   9  12  15  18   *
        2   6   9  12  15  17  20   *
        2   5   9  12  14  17  19  22   *
        1   5   8  11  14  16  18  21  23   *
        1   4   8  11  13  16  18  20  22  24   *
        1   4   7  10  13  15  17  19  21  23  25   *
```

Figure 12.8   Vertical greedy algorithm

```
                *
       15   *
       13  16   *
       11  14  17   *
        5  12  15  18   *
        4   7  13  16  19   *
        3   6   9  14  17  20   *
        2   5   8  10  15  18  21   *
        2   4   7   9  11  16  19  22   *
        1   3   6   8  10  12  17  20  23   *
        1   3   5   7   9  11  13  18  21  24   *
        1   2   4   6   8  10  12  14  19  22  25   *
```

Figure 12.9   Horizontal greedy algorithm

```
            *
     7   *
     6  10   *
     5   9  13   *
     4   8  12  15   *
     4   7  11  14  17   *
     2   6  10  13  16  19   *
     2   5   9  12  15  18  20   *
     2   4   8  11  14  17  19  21   *
     1   3   7  10  13  16  18  20  22   *
     1   3   6   9  12  15  17  19  21  23   *
     1   3   5   8  11  14  16  18  20  22  24   *
```

Figure 12.10   Better greedy algorithm

Theorem 12.8

Given m, n and p, an optimal greedy SPGS exists.

Proof

Given an SPGS, a faster SPGS is constructed. This is done by recurrence on t; let $s(i, t)$ and $sg(i, t)$ be the number of zeros associated with it. Assume that $s(i, t) \leq sg(i, t)$ and demonstrate that this is true, for t+1.

Let $d(i, t) = sg(i, t)-s(i, t)$ and $rg1(i, t+1) = r(i, t+1)-d(i, t)$. It follows from the description of the characteristics of SPGSs in Lemma 12.2 that:

$$r(i,t+1) \leq \left\lfloor \frac{s(i-1,t)-s(i,t)}{2} \right\rfloor$$

which implies that:

$$rg(i,t+1) \leq \left\lfloor \frac{s(i-1,t)-s(i,t)}{2} \right\rfloor - sg(i,t) + s(i,t)$$

$$\leq \left\lfloor \frac{s(i-1,t)-s(i,t)}{2} \right\rfloor - sg(i,t)$$

$$\leq \left\lfloor \frac{sg(i-1,t)-sg(i,t)}{2} \right\rfloor - sg(i,t)$$

$$\leq \left\lfloor \frac{sg(i-1,t)-sg(i,t)}{2} \right\rfloor$$

Also:

$$rg1(i,t+1) \le rg1(i,t+1) \le p - \sum_{j=1}^{i-1} r(j,t+1) \le p - \sum_{j=1}^{i-1} rg1(j,t+1)$$

Thus:

$$rg1(i,t+1) < \min\left(p - \sum_{j=1}^{i-1} r(g1(j,t+1), \left\lfloor \frac{sg(i-1,t)-sg(i,t)}{2} \right\rfloor \right)$$

and rg1(i, t+1) satisfies the conditions of Lemma 12.2. A greedy SPGS is then deduced from this by defining rg(i, t+1). If:

$$rg1(i,t+1) < \min\left(p, \sum_{j=1}^{n} \left\lfloor \frac{sg(j-1,t)-sg(j,t)}{2} \right\rfloor \right)$$

then the inequality can be filled with as many zeros as possible, by choosing any greedy algorithm that satisfies rg(i, t+1) ≥ rg1(i, t+1). Thus:

$$s(i, t+1) = s(i, t) + r(i, t+1) = sg(i, t) + rg1(i, t+1)$$
$$\le sg(i, t) + rg(i, t+1) = sg(i, t+1)$$

which concludes the proof.

Complexity of factorization

To obtain a complexity result in the general case, a lower bound has to be constructed. This can be used to find the minimum number of processors p_{opt} for executing the algorithm in optimal time t_{opt} and then to construct algorithms, for a number of processors less than p_{opt}, that execute in the time of the lower bound. This is taken from [CoD92]. It is assumed that the matrix is a square n × n matrix.

In Section 9.4.2, a technique for demonstrating a lower bound was examined. The technique is based on using the computational volume

CV(p) and the idle volume IV(p). It should be recalled that in [LKK83] the computation time of a parallel algorithm with p processors is shown to be:

$$T(p) = \frac{CV(p) + IV(p)}{p}$$

To obtain a lower bound, it is enough to establish a bound on the idle volume. Definition 12.3 is provided to that end.

Definition 12.3

Column i is *active* in step t+1 if at least one element in it can be annihilated, that is, if $s(i-1, t) - s(i, t) \geq 2$, where $s(i, t)$ equals the number of elements annihilated in column i after step t, with $s(i, 0)=0$ and $s(0, t)=n$. The number of active (or idle) columns is written $ac_i(t+1)$ or $id_i(t+1)$ respectively.

Lemma 12.9

If $1 \leq p \leq \lfloor \frac{n}{2} \rfloor$, then

$$B_{inf}(p) = \frac{n(n-1)}{2p} + p - 1 \leq T_{opt}(p)$$

Proof

If we know that m=n, then

$$CV(p) \frac{n(n-1)}{2}$$

from which it follows that:

$$T(p) = \frac{n(n-1)}{2p} + \frac{IV(p)}{p}$$

It therefore suffices to show that $IV(p) \geq p(p-1)$.

Let t_i be the step when the element in position $(i+1, i)$ is annihilated. Because the elements are annihilated from the last row upwards and from left to right, the algorithm's execution time is equal to the time required to annihilate the elements of the first subdiagonal, in position (i+1, i), if i=1,..., n–1. Two rows are required to annihilate these elements, thus at most

$$\min\left(p, \left\lfloor \frac{n-i+1}{2} \right\rfloor\right)$$

elements can be annihilated at the same time as the element in position (i+1, i). From this, it follows that:

$$ac(t_i) \leq \min\left(p, \left\lfloor \frac{n-i+1}{2} \right\rfloor\right) \text{ and } id(t_i) \geq p - \min\left(p, \left\lfloor \frac{n-i+1}{2} \right\rfloor\right)$$

If $i \geq n - 2p + 1$,

$$\min\left(p, \left\lfloor \frac{n-i+1}{2} \right\rfloor\right) = \left\lfloor \frac{n-i+1}{2} \right\rfloor \text{ and } id(t_i) \geq p - \left\lfloor \frac{n-i+1}{2} \right\rfloor$$

Therefore:

$$IV(p) = \sum_{i=n-2p+1}^{n-1} id(t_i) \geq p(p-1)$$

which concludes the proof.

One of the initial consequences of the above result is that the minimum number of processors for executing the algorithm in asymptotically optimal time has the value p as its lower bound, where $B_{inf}(p)=2n - o(n)$, and thus

$$\frac{n}{2 + \sqrt{2}} + o(n) \leq p_{opt}$$

In fact, the bound is attained. To show this, it is enough to construct an algorithm in time 2n–o(n) using

$$\frac{n}{2+\sqrt{2}}$$

processors. A complete family of asymptotically optimal algorithms can then be constructed using this result, whatever the number of processors. The proof of this is long and complicated, and the reader is referred to [CoD92] for a detailed description of it.

Theorem 12.10

For a square matrix of size n and $1 \leq p \leq \dfrac{n}{2+\sqrt{2}} + o(n)$

$$T_{opt}(p) = \frac{n^2}{2p} + p + o(n)$$

The minimum number of processors required to execute the algorithm in asymptotically optimal time is:

$$P_{opt} = \frac{n}{2+\sqrt{2}} + o(n)$$

12.4.3 Fine granularity

Let us continue with the above analysis, taking into account the fact that the length of the rows of A decreases as the algorithm proceeds. Assume that the model being used is a CREW PRAM. To highlight the difference between this and the evaluations above, where the unit of execution time was the time taken to compute a rotation and perform it on two vectors, whatever the dimensions of those vectors, let *flops* be the time required to execute a floating-point arithmetic operation or to compute a square root.

We saw in Chapter 5 that performing a rotation comprises two stages:

- Computing the coefficients c and s, which requires four time units (including the square root):

$$c = \frac{a_{j1}}{\sqrt{a_{j1}^2 + a_{i1}^2}}$$

$$s = \frac{a_{i1}}{\sqrt{a_{j1}^2 + a_{i1}^2}}$$

- Applying the matrix to the vectors, in order to update elements (which requires two time units using a number of processors that is four times the size of the vector):

$$c\, a_{jk} + s\, a_{ik}$$
$$-s\, a_{jk} + c\, a_{ik}$$

It is not difficult to see that if the two stages are executed consecutively, six flops are required to perform the rotation. By contrast, if the two stages are combined, an algorithm can be constructed in four flops. The proof of this is easy and is left to the reader.

Constructing an algorithm on a CREW PRAM basically involves simultaneously performing independent rotations – independent in the sense that they affect different rows.

Theorem 12.11

If there exists an algorithm such that an m × n rectangular matrix can be decomposed using the Givens method in r steps, each of which has r_k independent rotations, then an algorithm executed on a CREW PRAM that solves the problem in 4r flops exists.

We shall not provide a detailed computation of the number of processors, which depends on the size of the vectors used by the rotations. Instead, we shall apply Theorem 12.11, using the Sameh and Kuck and greedy algorithms as the base algorithms.

Corollary 12.12

For the special case of m=n:

1. The Sameh and Kuck algorithm executes on a CREW PRAM consisting of

$$\frac{n(3n-2)}{4}$$

processors in 8n–12 flops.

2. The greedy algorithm executes on a CREW PRAM consisting of n(n–1) processors in 8n–o(n) flops.

Using the algorithms described in this chapter, similar results can be obtained for rectangular matrices.

12.5   Conclusion

In this chapter, we studied the parallelization of the Givens method and showed that the methodology of Chapter 9 is limited because its starting point is a sequential algorithm. Dependency constraints between rotations using the same rows were rendered explicit. It was observed that non-optimal sequential algorithms can result in optimal parallel algorithms and several such algorithms were compared.

Several questions remain open:

- What is the exact complexity of the greedy algorithm?

- What are the optimal times for all values of m and, specifically, how does one get from fixed n to n=m?

- What are the optimal greedy algorithms in the case where $p < \frac{n}{2}$?

- What are the optimal execution times for rectangular matrices when $p < \frac{n}{2}$?

13

Impact of memory access on execution times

The time taken to access large memory may be significant. Its impact on execution times may cause an increase in the grain size of tasks allocated to processors.

13.1 Adaptive Gaussian elimination and Gaussian elimination in blocks

In this chapter, we return to the analysis in Chapter 11 and include in it the algorithmic complexity of data transactions between memory and processors. Although communication costs depend on the structure being considered, they are generally not insignificant in relation to computation costs. Taking the architecture described in Chapter 9 as our model, we study the effect of time taken to access shared memory on the execution time of a specific parallel variant of the Gaussian elimination algorithm.

In this chapter, *communication* time denotes the amount of time taken to access memory. However, this should not be confused with the problem on a shared-memory architecture, where processors communicate with each other. We discuss this in Chapter 15.

13.1.1   Basic assumptions

Review of the architectural model

The underlying parallel architecture consists of a set of p processors, each with a local memory and all sharing a common central memory. Data is exchanged between shared memory and processors through a complete interconnection network, such that p data items can be transferred in one communication time unit. For the sake of simplicity, it is assumed that a processor cannot begin to execute a task until all the data it is using has been stored in its local memory. Similarly, results cannot be transferred to shared memory until the computation has finished.

A unit of computation time is denoted by t_{comp} and of communication time by t_{com}. Without any loss of generality, it is assumed that t_{comp} is constant for each of the four basic arithmetic operations. By contrast, t_{com} depends to a large extent on the architecture under consideration; it is assumed that t_{comp} is an increasing function of the problem's size (n) and of the number of processors (p).

Algorithm to be parallelized

The algorithm that we attempt to parallelize below is the kji variant of Gaussian elimination. It is applied to an n × n matrix. If communication times are taken into account, granularity is also an important parameter in choosing elementary tasks. That explains why we examine the variant in which elements are eliminated in blocks, as well as the simple variant we looked at in Section 11.3.1.

13.1.2   Point-kji variant

The point-kji variant without pivoting is written as follows:

```
{point-kji variant}
  for  k ← 1  to  n-1
    for  j ← k+1  to  n
      {task Tₖⱼ}
      aₖ,ⱼ ← aₖ,ⱼ/aₖ,ₖ
        for  i ← k+1  to  n
          aᵢ,ⱼ ← aᵢ,ⱼ - aᵢ,ₖ*aₖ,ⱼ
```

Analysis including communication costs

Given the same assumptions as above, the computation and communication times of the tasks T_{kj} are $(2(n-k)+1)t_{comp}$ and $(3(n-k)+3)t_{com}$ respectively. The precedence constraints and the task graph were described in Section 11.3.1. Note that taking communication costs into account does not result in modification of the precedence relations between tasks. We obtain a triangular graph for which we have shown that the greedy algorithm is an asymptotically optimal schedule.

However, one assumption made in Theorem 11.3 does not apply here; the tasks' execution time is not in $O(n)$, as t_{com} now depends on n and p. If the proof is looked at again, it is easy to observe that the condition can be replaced and the theorem below is obtained, in which the evaluations of execution times are asymptotic in n.

Theorem 13.1

For a triangular task graph such that the time required for tasks to execute, t_{kj}, is constant for a fixed level k (written t_k) and decreases when k varies from 1 to n:

$$t_{opt} = \sum_{k=1}^{n-1} t_k \qquad p_{opt} = n-1$$

For a fixed number of processors, p, that is less than or equal to p_{opt}, the greedy algorithm is asymptotically optimal and:

$$t_{opt}(p) = \frac{\sum_{k=1}^{n-p}(n-k)t_k}{p} + \sum_{k=n-p+1}^{n-1} t_k$$

If the theorem is applied to the point-kji algorithm, the corollary below is obtained:

Corollary 13.2

If t_{opt} is an increasing function of n and of $p \le n$, then the greedy algorithm is asymptotically optimal for the point-kji algorithm. Asymptotically, its optimal time is:

$$t_{point} = t_{comp}\left[\frac{2n^3}{3p} + \frac{p^2}{3}\right] + t_{com}\left[\frac{n^3}{p} + \frac{p^2}{2}\right]$$

If p = αn (with α≤1), then

$$t_{point} = t_{comp}n^2\left[\frac{2}{3\alpha} + \frac{\alpha^2}{3}\right] + t_{com}n^2\left[\frac{1}{\alpha} + \frac{\alpha^2}{2}\right]$$

Proof

We know that the execution times $t_k = (2(n-k)+1)t_{comp} + (3(n-k)+3)t_{com}$ of the tasks T_{kj} are constant on each level. As t_{comp} is constant and t_{com} is an increasing function of n, they decrease as a function of k. Theorem 13.1 can be applied, which yields the above expressions.

13.1.3   Block-kji variant

Algorithm

To reduce the amount of time taken to access shared memory, the number of computations executed using the same data has to be increased, that is, the tasks' grain size has to be increased. To this end, we consider the kji algorithm using a method in which blocks of elements are eliminated.

Let n=qr. Matrix A is decomposed into q^2 square n × n blocks. The kji variant of the algorithm for Gaussian elimination by blocks is as follows:

```
{block-kji variant}
for  k ← 1  to  q
    for  j ←k+1  to  q
        {task TBkj}
        A(k, j) ← A(k, k)-1*A(k, j)
        for  i ← k+1  to  q
            A(i, j) ← A(i, j) - A(i, k)*A(k, j)
```

Clearly, in the algorithm, A(k, j) represents block (k, j) of matrix A, and the inverses of the block-diagonals A(k, k) are computed by solving r linear systems using the algorithm for Gaussian elimination by points, rather than computing them directly.

A new set of assumptions has to be made in order to determine the computation and communication times of TB_{kj}. Because we wish to conduct an asymptotic analysis and to increase the grain size of TB_{kj}, it is assumed that r and q tend towards infinity with n (rq=n). Processing block algorithms implies that the underlying architecture has to be modified. Specifically, the local memory of all the processors has to be large enough to store matrices. Also, there are fewer processors involved in processing blocks than in processing points. The basic computation time unit t_{comp} remains the same, whereas the communication time unit t_{com}, which depends on the number of processors, is shorter than in processing by points. We shall continue to denote the communication time unit by t_{com}.

Evaluation of time taken by the algorithm

Computing $A(k, j)$ is equivalent to solving $r(r \times r)$ systems of the same matrix. If lower order terms are ignored, it requires

$$\frac{8r^3}{3} t_{comp}$$

units.

Computing $A(i, j)$ involves $(q-k)$ matrix products and additions, representing $2r^3(q-k) t_{comp}$ units. Therefore, processing TB_{kj} costs

$$2r^3 \left[(q - k) + \frac{4}{3} \right] t_{comp}$$

units. All the computations require $A(k, k)$, $A(k, j)$, $A(i, j)$ and $A(i, k)$ for i varying between $k+1$ and q to be known. Therefore, the communication cost is $3r^2[(q-k)+1]t_{com}$.

Let t_{bloc} be the optimal execution time of the block-kji algorithm. As the precedence constraints for the tasks TB_{kj} are the same as those for the point-kji algorithm, Theorem 13.1 applies.

Corollary 13.3

If t_{com} is an increasing function of n, if $n=qr$ with $p \leq q$, and if q and r tend towards infinity with n, the greedy algorithm is asymptotically optimal for the block-kji algorithm. Its execution time is:

$$t_{bloc} = t_{comp} \left[\frac{2n^3}{3p} + \frac{p^2 r^3}{3} \right] + t_{com} \left[\frac{n^3}{pr} + \frac{p^2 r^2}{2} \right]$$

If $p = \alpha q$ (with $\alpha \leq 1$), then:

$$t_{bloc} = t_{comp} n^2 \left[\frac{2r}{3\alpha} + \frac{\alpha^2 r}{3} \right] + t_{com} n^2 \left[\frac{1}{\alpha} + \frac{\alpha^2}{2} \right]$$

The proof is the same as in the above corollary.

13.1.4   Variant combining point-kji and block-kji

Motivation of a combined variant

The efficiencies of block and point algorithms are compared at the end of this chapter. However, it can be observed immediately that the greedy algorithm is of efficiency 1, while there are p tasks per level, that is, until stage n–p of the points algorithm and until stage q–p of the blocks algorithm, which corresponds to stage $(q–p)r=n–pr$ of the points algorithm. Therefore, the greedy algorithm is fully efficient for a shorter amount of time using the block method than when using the points method.

We now describe a different algorithm, with the aim of keeping the advantages of the two above algorithms: maintaining full efficiency for as long as the points method does, while also keeping grain size sufficiently coarse so that communication costs are as low as they are in the block method. This is done by progressively reducing the blocks' size, that is, by adapting it to the number of processors and to the size of the remaining matrix.

How the adaptive algorithm works

Let n and p be fixed. Let $q=p+1$. In the first step, $s_1=n$ and

$$r_1 = \left\lceil \frac{s_1}{q} \right\rceil$$

The first step of the block-kji algorithm is applied to the $s_1 \times s_1$ matrix, which is decomposed into q^2 blocks: $(q–1)^2$ blocks of size r_1, with the rest of size $s_1–(q–1)r_1$. Thus, only one processor works on a smaller task, but this is negligible, as p tends towards infinity with n.

At the kth stage, $s_k=s_{k-1}-r_{k-1}$ and

$$r_k = \left\lceil \frac{s_k}{q} \right\rceil$$

and a stage of the block algorithm is applied to the $s_k \times s_k$ matrix, which is decomposed into q^2 blocks. The process is repeated for as long as the size s_k of the remaining matrix is greater than q. As soon as $s_k < q$, the point-kji algorithm is used.

Figure 13.1. illustrates the various stages.

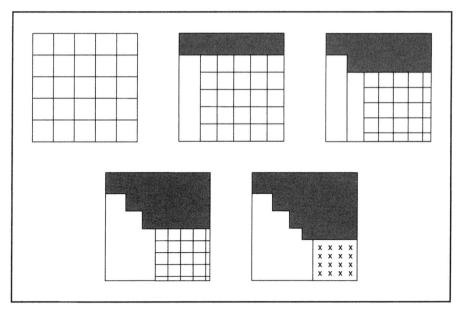

Figure 13.1   How the adaptive algorithm works

The adaptive-kji algorithm below is obtained:

```
{adaptive-kji variant}
s ← n
q ← p+1
r ← ⌈s/q⌉
k ← 1
while s≥q do
    Decompose A into p² (r, r) blocks and the rest into ((s-pr),
    (s-pr)) blocks
    for  j ← 2  to  q
        {task TAkj}
        A(k, j) ← A(k, k)-1*A(k, j)
        for  i ← k+1  to  q
            A(i, j) ← A(i, j) - A(i, k)*A(k, j)
    s ← s-r
    r ← ⌈s/q⌉
    k ← k+1
    Reduce A to an (s, s) matrix by removing the first rows
    and columns
for  k ← n-q-1  to  n-1
    for  j ← k+1  to  n
        {task Tkj}
        aₖ, ⱼ ← aₖ, ⱼ/aₖ, ₖ
        for  i ← k+1  to  n
            aᵢ, ⱼ ← aᵢ, ⱼ - aᵢ, ₖ*aₖ, ⱼ
```

Evaluation of the algorithm's execution time

Computing the execution time for the adaptive-kji algorithm is more difficult than for the two other variants. Note that, if the number of processors
is bounded when n tends towards infinity, the analysis is trivial. But p must
not be too large in relation to n, in order to prevent the blocks' size from
being too small. This motivates the assumptions in the theorem below:

Theorem 13.4

If p and n/p tend towards infinity with n, the execution time of the
adaptive-kji algorithm is asymptotically:

$$t_{adap} = t_{comp} \frac{2n^3}{3p} + t_{com} \frac{3n^2}{2}$$

Proof

In what follows we use the variable q=p+1 instead of p. The assumptions imply that q and n/q tend towards infinity with n. We also have
the following relations:

$$s_1 = n \text{ and } s_k = s_{k-1} - r_{k-1}$$

$$r_k = \left\lceil \frac{s_k}{q} \right\rceil$$

Let k^* be the stage defined by $s_{k^*+1} < q \le s_{k^*}$; the execution times of
the tasks TA_{kj} and T_{kj} are, respectively:

$$2r_k^3 \frac{q+1}{3} t_{comp} + 3r_k^3 t_{com}$$

for k varying between 1 and k^*

$$[2(n-k)+1]t_{comp} + [3(n-k)+3]t_{com}$$

for k varying between n−q−1 and n−1.

Therefore, the execution time of the adaptive-kji algorithm is equal to
the sum:

$$t_{adap} = \sum_{k=1}^{k^*} 2r_{k^3} \frac{q+1}{3} t_{comp} + 3r_{k^2} t_{com} + \sum_{k=n-q-1}^{n-1}\left[2(n-k)+1\right]t_{comp} + \left[3(n-k)+3\right]t_{com}$$
$$= \sum\nolimits_{bloc} + \sum\nolimits_{point}$$

Direct computation can be used to obtain:

$$\sum\nolimits_{point} = q^2\left[t_{comp} + \frac{3t_{com}}{2}\right] + o\left(q^2\left[t_{comp} + t_{com}\right]\right)$$

Computing the first term $\sum_{bloc}$ is more difficult. It is computed in four stages:

1. Find values for s_k, r_k and k^*

$$s_k = s_{k-1} - r_{k-1}$$
$$= s_{k-1} - \left[\frac{s_{k-1}}{q}\right]$$
$$= s_{k-1}\left(1 - \frac{1}{q}\right) - e_{k-1} \text{ for } 0 \le e_{k-1} < 1$$

If $Q = 1 - \frac{1}{q}$, it follows that:

$$Q^{k-1}n - q\left(1 - Q^{k-1}\right) < s_k \le Q^{k-1}n$$

It follows from the definition of r_k that:

$$\frac{Q^{k-1}n}{q} - \left(1 - Q^{k-1}\right) < r_k \le \frac{Q^{k-1}n}{q} + 1$$

which results in:

$$r_k = \frac{Q^{k-1}n}{a} + \rho_k \text{ where } -1 < \rho_{k-1} \leq 1$$

The value of k^* is obtained using the above evaluation of s_k:

$$\left| \frac{\ln\left(\frac{q}{n}\right)}{\ln(Q)} \right| \leq k^* \leq \left| \frac{\ln\left(\frac{q}{n}\right)}{\ln(Q)} + \frac{1}{\ln(Q)} \right|$$

On the basis of the assumptions for q and n/q, the value of k^* may be estimated as follows:

$$k^* = q \ln\left(\frac{n}{q}\right) + o\left(q \ln\left(\frac{n}{q}\right)\right) \geq q \ln\left(\frac{n}{q}\right)$$

A quick calculation shows that Q^{k^*} is negligible in relation to 1.

2. Compute the term in $\sum r_k^2$

$$\sum_{k=1}^{k^*} r_k^2 = \sum_{k=1}^{k^*} \left(\frac{Q^{k-1}n}{q} + \rho_k \right)^2$$

$$= \left(\frac{n}{q}\right)^2 \sum_{k=1}^{k^*} Q^{2(k-1)} + 2\frac{n}{q}\sum_{k=1}^{k^*} Q^{k-1}\rho_k + \sum_{k=1}^{k^*} \rho_k^2$$

Thus, it is clear that:

$$2\frac{n}{q}\sum_{k=1}^{k^*} Q^{k-1}\rho_k + \sum_{k=1}^{k^*} \rho_k^2 \leq \left(2\frac{n}{q}+1\right)k^* = O\left(2n \ln\left(\frac{n}{q}\right)\right)$$

And, taking into account the fact that Q^{k^*} is negligible in relation to 1, we obtain:

$$\left(\frac{n}{q}\right)^2 \sum_{k=1}^{k^*} Q^{2(k-1)} = \left(\frac{n}{q}\right)^2 \frac{1-Q^{2k^*}}{1-Q} = \frac{n^2}{2q} + o\left(\frac{n^2}{q}\right)$$

This is therefore the dominant term, so

$$\sum_{k=1}^{k^*} r_k^2 = \frac{n^2}{2q} + o\left(\frac{n^2}{q}\right)$$

The computation of the $\sum r_k^3$ term is similar, giving:

$$\sum_{k=1}^{k^*} r_k^3 = \frac{n^3}{3q^2} + o\left(\frac{n^3}{q^2}\right)$$

3. Compute $\sum_{\text{bloc}}$

$$\sum_{\text{bloc}} = \frac{2(q+1)}{3} t_{\text{comp}} \sum_{k=1}^{k^*} r_k^3 + 3t_{\text{com}} \sum_{k=1}^{k^*} r_k^2$$

$$= n^2 \left(\frac{2t_{\text{comp}}}{3} \frac{n}{q} + \frac{3t_{\text{com}}}{2} \right)$$

4. Compute t_{adap}

As q=p+1, it follows that the asymptotic value of the execution time of the adaptive-kji algorithm is:

$$t_{\text{adap}} = \sum_{\text{bloc}} + \sum_{\text{point}} = t_{\text{comp}} \left(\frac{2}{3} \frac{n^3}{p} + p^2 \right) + t_{\text{com}} \left(\frac{3}{2} n^2 + \frac{3}{2} p^2 \right)$$

As p can be ignored in relation to n, the formula we provided is obtained.

13.1.5   Comparison of the three variants

In this section, we compare the execution times of the point-kji, block-kji and adaptive-kji algorithms. The following parameters are taken into account: the size of the matrix, n, the number of processors, p, the blocks' size, r, the computation time unit, t_{comp}, and the communication time unit, t_{com}.

Review of results

The execution times of the variants are as follows:

$$t_{point} = t_{comp}\left[\frac{2n^3}{3p} + \frac{p^2}{3}\right] + t_{com}\left[\frac{n^3}{p} + \frac{p^2}{2}\right]$$

$$t_{bloc} = t_{comp}\left[\frac{2n^3}{3p} + \frac{p^2r^3}{3}\right] + t_{com}\left[\frac{n^3}{pr} + \frac{p^2r^2}{2}\right]$$

$$t_{adap} = t_{comp}\frac{2n^3}{3p} + t_{com}\frac{3n^2}{2}$$

Note that the formulae are not completely comparable, as the assumptions made regarding n, p and r are not the same in all three cases. Analysis of the points algorithm is valid, however many p and whatever n (sufficiently large). As far as the block algorithm is concerned, it was assumed that $p \le q$ and that q and r tend towards infinity with n (n=qr). As far as the adaptive algorithm is concerned, it was assumed that p and n/p tend towards infinity with n.

Block algorithm compared with adaptive variant

Let us compare the block algorithm and the adaptive algorithm under the assumptions that p, n/p, q and r tend towards infinity with n. Clearly, the computation cost of the block algorithm is higher than that of the adaptive algorithm. The difference between the two can be easily explained by the fact that, since the blocks' size decreases progressively in the adaptive algorithm, the latter has an efficiency of 1 until a higher level of efficiency than that of the block algorithm is reached.

The communication cost of the block algorithm depends on the blocks' size. It is minimal where pr=n. In this case, the communication costs of the block and adaptive algorithms are equal (asymptotically). It follows from this that the adaptive algorithm is always more efficient than the block algorithm.

Point versus adaptive algorithms

Now let us compare the point and adaptive algorithms. Note that if p is of order n, the above analysis of the adaptive algorithm is not immediately applied. But in this case, the adaptive algorithm executes some steps using small blocks and finishes execution using the points algorithm. By contrast, if p and n/p tend towards infinity with n, the same computation time is obtained asymptotically for both algorithms, but the communication time of the points algorithm is higher. The adaptive algorithm is therefore always more efficient than the points algorithm.

By way of example, let $r=q=p=\sqrt{n}$. We obtain:

$$t_{point} = t_{comp}\left[\frac{2}{3}\sqrt{n^5}\right] + t_{com}\left[\sqrt{n^5}\right]$$

$$t_{bloc} = t_{comp}\left[\sqrt{n^5}\right] + t_{com}\left[\frac{3}{2}n^2\right]$$

$$t_{adap} = t_{comp}\left[\frac{2}{3}\sqrt{n^5}\right] + t_{com}\left[\frac{3}{2}n^2\right]$$

13.1.6   Impact of communications on execution time

In this section, we examine the impact of the architecture being used on the execution time of the above kji Gaussian elimination algorithm. To simplify our description, let $t_{comp}=1$. The value of t_{com} depends to a large extent on the architecture and, more specifically, on the interconnection network that links shared memory to processors. It is therefore reasonable to assume that t_{com} increases as a function of the memory's size and the number of processors. In Chapter 3, we saw that:

- a complete network (crossbar matrix) consists of pb switches, where b is the number of memory banks,

- a Benes network consists of $2\log_2(p)$ stages of p switches (p being the number of switches in this case),

- an Omega network consists of half as many switches.

But we also saw that permutations may require two traversals across the network. If it is assumed that traversing one switch takes a constant amount of time, it follows that t_{com} can have the following values:

$$t_{com} = \lambda \text{ (independent of n and of p)}$$
$$t_{com} = \lambda\sqrt{np}$$
$$t_{com} = \lambda \log_2(n)$$

Consider a constant communication time $t_{com} = \lambda$. The communication cost of the points algorithm

$$\lambda \left[\frac{n^3}{p} + \frac{p^2}{2} \right]$$

is of the same order as its computation cost

$$\left[\frac{2n^3}{3p} + \frac{p^2}{3} \right]$$

By contrast, in the adaptive and block algorithms, the communication costs

$$\lambda \left[\frac{n^3}{pr} + \frac{p^2 r^2}{2} \right] \quad \text{and} \quad \lambda \frac{3n^2}{2} \quad \text{respectively}$$

are negligible compared with their computation costs

$$\left[\frac{2n^3}{3p} + \frac{p^2 r^3}{3} \right] \quad \text{and} \quad \frac{2n^3}{3p}$$

For $r = q = p = \sqrt{n}$, we obtain:

$$t_{point} = \left(\frac{2}{3} + \lambda \right) \sqrt{n^5}$$

$$t_{bloc} = \sqrt{n^5}$$

$$t_{adap} = \frac{2}{3} \sqrt{n^5}$$

For

$$t_{com} = \lambda \sqrt{np} \quad \text{and} \quad t_{com} = \lambda \log_2 (n)$$

the communication cost of the points algorithm outweighs its computation cost. For the same values of t_{com}, we shall examine only the adaptive algorithm, which performs better than the block algorithm.

- If $t_{com} = \lambda\sqrt{np}$, then $t_{adap} = \dfrac{2n^3}{3p} + \dfrac{3\lambda\sqrt{n^5 p}}{2}$ and thus:

  if $p = O(\sqrt[3]{n})$, the communication and computation costs are of the same order;

  if $p > O(\sqrt[3]{n})$, the communication cost outweighs the computation cost;

  if $p < O(\sqrt[3]{n})$, the computation cost outweighs the communication cost.

- If $t_{com} = \lambda\log_2(n)$, then $t_{adap} = \dfrac{2n^3}{3p} + \dfrac{3\lambda}{2}n^2 \log_2(n)$ and thus:

  if $p = O\left(\dfrac{n}{\log_2(n)}\right)$, the communication and computation costs are of the same order;

  if $p > O\left(\dfrac{n}{\log_2(n)}\right)$, the communication cost outweighs the computation cost;

  if $p < O\left(\dfrac{n}{\log_2(n)}\right)$, the computation cost outweighs the communication cost.

In contrast to the case where t_{com} is constant, the execution times of the adaptive and points algorithms do not strictly decrease, as p increases. There exist optimal values of p that can be readily obtained from the above formulae:

	Adaptive	Point	Block
P_{opt}	$\sqrt[3]{\dfrac{64n}{81\lambda^2}}$	$\dfrac{n}{\sqrt[3]{5}}$	——

13.2   Overheads

Above, we described an initial attempt to take communications into account in analysing the complexity of a parallel algorithm. The analysis was modelled on the time taken to traverse multistage interconnection networks and resulted in a new adaptive algorithm. In the second part of this chapter, we return to our examination of memory access and also find values for the processors' idle time. Here again, the problem can be solved by using a model based on task graphs. The results below are taken from [PaY79] [ABR90] [BKT91].

13.2.1   General description

In this section, we describe an alternative solution that can be used to take into account the amount of time that is lost in communications at run time and the idle time imposed on processors by the precedence constraints of the task graph. Reducing communication costs and tasks' potential parallelism are mutually opposed.

A parallel algorithm's execution time can be defined on the basis of the sequential algorithm's execution time, the total amount of time lost in communications between processors and processors' total enforced idle time. The latter two parameters have the greatest impact on a parallel algorithm's execution time:

$$t_{exec} = \frac{t_{seq} + t_c + t_{idle}}{p}$$

The aim of analysing parallel complexity is to find an algorithm that minimizes this time. This amounts to minimizing the overhead, that is, the sum $t_c + t_{idle}$.

For the sake of simplicity, it is assumed below that the tasks' communication time is constant. In this case, the term t_c is equal to the number of tasks in the task graph.

The kji variant of Gaussian elimination is used again as an example, but, of course, the other variants, particularly the kij variant, can be analysed in the same way.

13.2.2   Analysis of the kji variant of Gaussian elimination in terms of overhead

Let us return to our complexity analysis of the kji variant of Gaussian elimination and compute its overhead. As we saw, communication costs can be reduced by grouping tasks together in blocks; ultimately, if all the tasks can be put into a single block, the algorithm does not have any communication costs. Conversely, the smaller the tasks, the shorter the idle time.

Our aims below are twofold: to compute the overhead of the kji variant of Gaussian elimination; and to propose a different way of grouping tasks together, so that the overheads are minimized.

It should be recalled that the kji variant of Gaussian elimination is expressed in the form of a triangular task graph. Its parallel complexity $O(n^2)$ can be obtained with a greedy schedule that orders tasks by levels.

Proposition 13.5

For $p=O(n)$, the overhead of the parallel kji variant of Gaussian elimination is $O(n^3)$.

Proof

Computation of the overhead is easy. The greedy schedule has two stages (separated by the level $(n-p)$ of predecessor-oriented decomposition).

In the first stage, the algorithm has an efficiency of 1 and the overhead results only from communications between tasks (idle time is zero). That is, under our assumption of a constant cost, the overhead results only from the number of tasks:

$$\sum_{k=1}^{n-p} k$$

In the second stage, the overhead is the sum of the communication cost and the idle time:

$$\sum_{k=n-p+1}^{n} k + \sum_{k=1}^{p-1} (n-k)k$$

The total overhead is thus in $O(n^3)$ (due to the idle time in stage 2).

Thus, in the parallelization of the greedy schedule below, the overhead is of the same order as the sequential time. In the next section, another schedule is proposed to minimize the overhead.

13.2.3   Different schedule

UET Gaussian elimination graph

Consider the Gaussian elimination task graph with unit execution time tasks (UET). The tasks are partitioned in such a way that they have the finest possible grain size (a unique variant):

```
{UET variant}
for  k ← 1  to  n-1
    for  j ← k+1  to  n
        a_{k, j} ← a_{k, j}/a_{k, k}     {task (k, j, k)}
        for  i ← k+1  to  n
            a_{i, j} ← a_{i, j} - a_{i, k}*a_{k, j}  {task (k, j, i)}
```

and have the following precedence constraints:

$(k, j, k) << (k, j, i)$ for all i such that $k<i\leq n$
$(k, k+1, i) << (k+1, j, i)$ for all j such that $k+1<j\leq n$
$(k, j, i) << (k+1, j, i)$ for all $i>k+1$ and $j>k+1$

The corresponding task graph is shown in Figure 13.2.

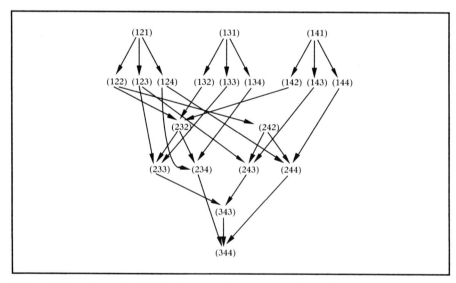

Figure 13.2   Example of UET Gaussian elimination task graph (n=4)

The triangular graph is obtained by grouping the tasks together as shown in Figure 13.3.

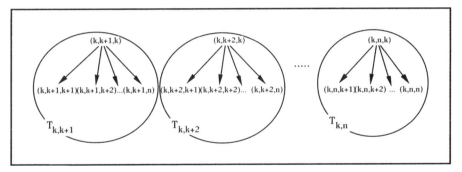

Figure 13.3   Link between the greedy and UET variants of Gaussian elimination

Description of the schedule

The level k is defined as being the set of tasks (k, j, i). It is decomposed into two sub-levels:

k_a, for the (k, j, k)
k_b, for the (k, j, i) where i≠k.

At each level k, each sub-level is executed greedily. Let m be the number of tasks on the sub-level that are to execute. m is divided into p parts which include

$$\left\lfloor \frac{m}{p} \right\rfloor \text{ or } \left\lceil \frac{m}{p} \right\rceil$$

elementary tasks.

At level k_a (for k ≥ n–p+1), tasks of size 1 are considered as the smallest possible tasks, so that idle time is minimized. At level k_b, the tasks' size is

$$\left\lceil \frac{(n-k)^2}{p} \right\rceil$$

and the aim is to minimize communication (that is, under the assumption we made, to minimize the number of tasks).

Note that, in this execution scheme, no processor is idle until level n–√p. This can be used to compute the overhead.

Proposition 13.6

For p=O(n), the overhead for the above parallel algorithm is O(n²).

Proof

The number of tasks is in $O(n^2)$. The $2(n-1)$ sub-levels are both executed with an idle time that is less than p, or $O(np)$. Since the number of processors is in $O(n)$, the idle time is at most $O(n^2)$. The total overhead is the sum of these two values.

Possible extensions

This analysis can be extended to distributed-memory architectures [Bam93]. However, an additional assumption is required, that communication costs are zero for tasks belonging to the same processor. Furthermore, the assumption that a task's communication cost is constant, whatever the size of that task, is easily extended to the case where the cost is proportional to the task's inputs and outputs.

13.3   Conclusion

This chapter serves as an introduction to a more extensive model of the cost of a parallel algorithm on a shared-memory architecture. If a more complex memory hierarchy than the one we adopted is used, this becomes even more necessary. On some parallel computers, the amount of time taken to access memory is greater than computation time.

The problem is fundamental where a distributed-memory architecture is being used, and we shall discuss it in greater detail in Chapter 15.

14

Task mapping

When, in the case of distributed memories, the physical architecture is to be taken into account, the scheduling problem, central to the analysis of parallel complexity, depends also on the way in which the scheduled tasks are mapped on the processors. In this chapter, we address the problem of task allocation on a processor network.

14.1 Introduction to the mapping problem

Throughout this book we have been broadly concerned with the ways in which parallelism can call into question our entire method of programming. Among the new problems that have appeared, apart from that of identifying potential parallelism, which lies at the level of complexity analysis, are those of choice of granularity, in particular, grouping of tasks (partitioning), scheduling and, when the physical architecture is to be taken into account, mapping.

What we might hope to achieve is the creation of automatic tools – or failing these, of aids to efficient programming – that will free the programmer from these difficulties and allow him or her to concentrate solely on the algorithmic aspects of the problem to be solved, without needing to worry about the architecture. Achieving this will also enable programs to be produced that can be ported from one machine to another and help to spread the use of shared-memory multi-processor systems in the industrial environment.

In this chapter we look at the main mapping methods, specifying their scope and, where possible, their limitations. For this we rely greatly on the report [BTV92].

14.1.1   Preliminaries

Program and computer models

As we described in Chapter 9, an algorithm can be represented by a graph made up of a set of basic tasks (the vertices) which are interlinked by precedence constraints (the arcs). Each task is characterized by the time it takes to execute and each arc by the communication cost which represents the amount of information to be exchanged between the various tasks. Figure 14.1 gives an example of such a graph.

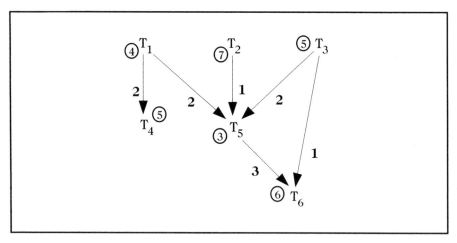

Figure 14.1   An example of a task graph (the time taken for execution is circled, the communication cost is in bold)

There is another way of representing an algorithm by a graph, in which the precedence relations are ignored: an arc represents only a communication, taking no account of its direction. Despite this omission, almost all mapping algorithms are based on this model.

At the same time, a natural representation of a processor network is a graph whose vertices are the processors and whose arcs are the physical links between them, as in Figure 14.2.

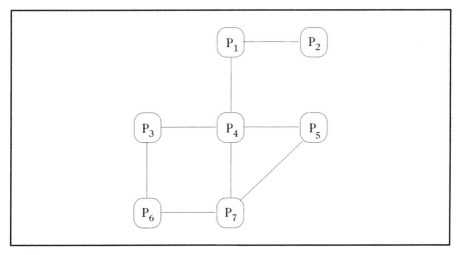

Figure 14.2   An example of a graph representing the architecture of a processor network

Some definitions and the formulation of the problem

Given a task graph and a processor network, whose graph we assume to be homogeneous, meaning that all the processors are identical, let $\mathcal{T}$ be the set of tasks and $\mathcal{P}$ the set of processors.

Definition 14.1

A *mapping* is an application *alloc* which associates a processor q with a task T:

$$\text{alloc: } \mathcal{T} \rightarrow \mathcal{P} \;\; \forall T \in \mathcal{T}, \exists q \in \mathcal{P}, \text{alloc}(T)=q$$

The search for a mapping is performed on the set $\mathcal{PL}$ of all possible mappings. If p is the number of processors and n the number of tasks there are p^n possibilities. The following allocation is a possible mapping of the tasks of Figure 14.1 on the processors of Figure 14.2

$$\begin{array}{lll} \text{alloc } (T_1) = P_1 & \text{alloc } (T_2) = P_3 & \text{alloc } (T_3) = P_5 \\ \text{alloc } (T_4) = P_2 & \text{alloc } (T_5) = P_4 & \text{alloc } (T_6) = P_7 \end{array}$$

Some observations

In the last example, all the neighbouring tasks could be mapped on neighbouring processors. In practice, this is not always the case: some communications therefore need *routing*. This problem is dealt with in Chapter 15.

Certain mapping heuristics consider the case $n \leq p$. In the opposite case (in practice, the more common of the two) a solution involves implementing a preliminary clustering phase and so working with $n'=p$ (where n' is a group of tasks). Similarly, the previous example does not require task duplication.

In mapping, the problem is one of optimizing a cost function (which may, for example, be the total time taken for execution as in the case of scheduling) under certain criteria (such as balancing the computation load, communications, and so on).

We are primarily interested in *static mappings*, that is, those carried out before the execution of the parallel program. There are some studies which deal with task or data migration at run time and we shall mention this at the end of the chapter.

Moreover, the processor network can be *configurable* (the processors are linked by a programmable, not fixed, interconnecting network). In this case, we have to deal with the problem of determining the best possible configuration of the architecture for a given problem. We shall consider this case at the end of the chapter.

Mapping criteria

As before, let $ex(T)$ be the duration of task T and $C(T, T')$ that of the communication from task T to task T', proportional to the volume of data transferred.

A feature of a mapping is the cost function, which allows us to measure its quality. This appears explicitly in all mapping algorithms that are based on optimization techniques. In contrast, it is implicit in most of the heuristic algorithms. There are a number of choices for this cost function; here we look in detail at the one which seems the most relevant.

The most objective of the costs is the total program execution time which, on a parallel machine, corresponds to the execution time of the processor that ends the program. Computing the execution time of a processor depends on the chosen architecture model. In particular, some processors have the possibility of either computing or not computing while communicating; in the first case we speak of *overlapping* computation and communication. Also, a single processor may or may not be able to make several communications simultaneously. As a first approach we consider a homogeneous model (all the processors are identical) with no overlapping and no simultaneous communication. The execution cost of a task T for the mapping alloc is:

$$ex(T) + \sum_{T'/alloc(T') \neq alloc(T)} C(T, T')$$

This expresses the fact that the total execution time for the task T, mapped on the processor alloc(T), is the sum of its own execution time and the time it uses in communicating with other tasks T' mapped on other processors – clearly, there are no costs for communication between tasks on the same processor. The cumulative cost for a given processor q is the sum of the individual costs for all the tasks allocated to that processor:

$$t_{alloc}(q) = \sum_{T/alloc(T)=q} \left[ex(T) + \sum_{T'/alloc(T') \neq alloc(T)} C(T, T') \right]$$

The cost of the complete mapping alloc is the highest execution cost of all the processors, that is:

$$C_{alloc} = max_{q \in P}(t_{alloc}(q))$$

and therefore the cost C^* of the best mapping is

$$C^* = min_{alloc \in PL}(C_{alloc})$$

We can easily modify this function if we wish to take into account, for example, overlapping of computation and communication (in which case, in the expression for $t_{alloc}(q)$, the sum is replaced by the computation of the maximum) or simultaneous communication (when all we need do is weight the communication term with the average degree of the task graph). Again, it may be possible to distinguish processors from one another, as in a heterogeneous network, and so on.

There are many other possible cost functions and criteria; one example, opposite to load-balancing, is minimization of the total inter-processor communication cost. However, using this alone leads to the trivial solution of mapping all the tasks on the same processor; it should therefore be used in conjunction with some other constraint, such as limiting the memory size or imposing a *task interference cost* that increasingly penalizes the mapping of successive tasks on the same processor.

Criteria that bear exclusively on the graph structure can also be envisaged. One [Bok81] involves maximizing the *cardinality*, that is, the number of arcs when the tasks are 'well mapped', meaning that neighbouring tasks are mapped on neighbouring processors. Formally, the function to be minimized is:

$$\sum_{i=1}^{n} \sum_{j>i} \text{mat}_{i,j} \ \text{arc}_{\text{alloc}(i),\text{alloc}(j)}$$

where *mat* and *arc* are the *adjacency* matrices for the graph and the processor network respectively, as are generally used to express the edges of a graph. The element $\text{mat}_{i,j}$ represents the cost of communication between task i and task j (0 if they are not linked directly). Similarly, the physical architecture of the processor network is represented by a binary network of the same type, here called *arc*, in which a non-zero element corresponds to a physical link between two processors.

Considering constraints

We have seen that it may be necessary to constrain a problem so as to avoid useless trivial solutions such as mapping all the tasks on a single processor. Generally, there is the constraint of the limited size of a processor's memory; for another, we can require the computational load to be balanced over the processors.

If the mapping is constructed without routing, a pair of communicating tasks must be mapped either on the same processor or on physically neighbouring processors. In general, there will be only a single physical communication channel between any pair of processors, but it is increasingly common for processors to be provided with *virtual channels* that enable several communications to be sent over the same physical channel – by interleaving messages, for example.

Routing by software penalizes the processors that support the communicating tasks, in proportion to their distance apart. Here also constraints can be imposed: for example, we can require that a specified task is mapped on a specified processor (in the interests of its input/outputs, say), or that two specified tasks are mapped on the same processor or on two different processors – or anything between these two extremes.

14.1.2   Relation to scheduling

Review of scheduling

A natural way to express a program is by means of a task graph; however, most existing mapping software takes no account of precedence relations –

in contrast to the case for scheduling. Generally speaking, the scheduling problems that have been solved are very much idealized: as we showed in Chapter 10, concrete results have been obtained only for very restricted cases, far from practical reality – an optimal algorithm is known only for the case of a UET task graph for two processors and without communication.

In the ideal situation of having an unlimited number of processors available we can, for example, execute every task as soon as it is ready (soonest-start scheduling); we are then certain of achieving the minimal execution time, but this scheduling provides no information about the physical allocation of tasks to processors. In practice, only a limited number of processors will be free at any given moment and the problem will be to choose from among the tasks that are ready those that *must* be executed. This problem has been studied for many years, for the case of task graphs fully known in advance (from a static study, as in Chapter 11) with certain assumptions concerning the durations of the tasks' executions, the structure of the graph or the number of processors. But the general problem is NP-hard and the only hope is to find heuristics that will give approximate solutions.

We shall assume a MIMD model made up of a set of identical processors, each with its own memory, executing different programs asynchronously and linked by a communication network; the processors can perform all the standard arithmetical operations. Knowledge of the relation between the computing and communication speeds enables us to decide the appropriate granularity for the tasks to be executed. The mapping problem can be regarded as that of scheduling with additional physical constraints – the assignment of a task to a processor depends on its location in the network. The solution can be sought by using scheduling heuristics adapted to these new constraints, but in general this is not the approach taken.

A program can be regarded more simply as a set of communicating processes, and as such can be modelled by a non-directed graph which has to be embedded in the physical processor network. The heuristics employed in this situation are often simpler, and with few exceptions are not applicable to task graphs.

Communications and mapping

In most existing machines, communication times between tasks running on different processors are of the same order as the computation times – they can be much longer if the processors have local fast computing units, as is the case with vector co-processors. The effect of taking these times into account is to add new constraints to the scheduling problem, thus increasing its complexity. In practice, communication times between processors depend on their distance apart in the network, even when communication in machines having special routing hardware can be considered as independent of the inter-processor distance.

The communication network is a fundamental feature of these machines. A rough classification distinguishes between static networks (fully-connected, hypercube, mesh and so on) and reconfigurable networks (usually of fixed degree). The functional features can be different, and usually the machine will have capabilities for routing or for global communication. It is this great variety of possibilities that is the main obstacle to generalizing the programming model for machines of this type.

Just as we should like to have efficient scheduling tools that can be used with any task graph (or failing that, with certain classes of graph), solving the problem of task mapping should form an integral part of the analysis of parallel systems and should not lead to solutions that are too costly in terms of time. Some results – heuristics that are more or less capable of being evaluated – are known for distributed systems with static topology; but the general problem of an arbitrary processor network, as in reconfigurable machines, is still unsolved.

Various solutions

Numerous task mapping strategies have been proposed in [AnP89] [Bok81] [CaK88] [CHL80] [Tal92]. Several possible solutions can be considered.

Casavant and Kuhl proposed a very full classification of task-allocation methods for parallel architectures with distributed memory [CaK88]. These can be viewed as describing the interaction between resources, consumers and the policy for assigning resources to consumers. The principal goals are efficiency and performance; the first means satisfying the consumers while using as few resources as possible, and these in a balanced manner; the second, maximizing the total satisfaction. Clearly, these requirements are contradictory.

The proposed classification distinguishes five main features:

- Strategies that are or are not static according to whether the allocation is fixed at the start or can be modified during execution (dynamic adaptation of certain parameters).

- Balancing the load. This is fairly natural; it works well in the case of large programs but clearly can entail excessive communication costs.

- Probabilistics. Since the space to be searched is very large, a small number of solutions are generated by random choices, and compared among themselves.

- Fixed or revisable policy. An allocation may turn out to be a bad choice, and we might like to query it; revisable policies can prove useful, especially if the parameter values are not very reliable.

- Adjudication. Power of decision is given to the consumers, who exercise this by inviting bids and waiting for the replies before deciding.

Static policies can be used when the majority of the parameter values are known before execution. In this context, methods can be classified hierarchically, as in Figure 14.3, distinguishing between methods that give an optimal solution (exhaustive methods, such as by listing of cases) and approximate or heuristic methods.

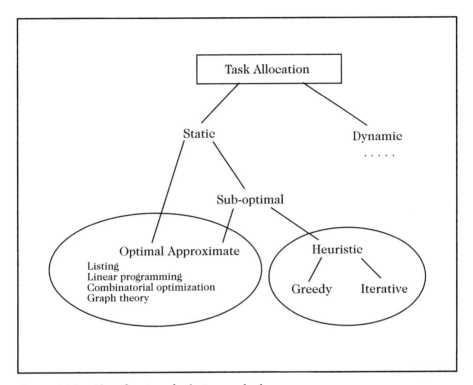

Figure 14.3   Classification of solution methods

More precisely, the distinction is between:

- *exact algorithms* based on an exploration of all possible solutions. In theory this will give the optimal solution, but in practice it can be very costly and unusable for large problems;

- *heuristics*, leading to approximate solutions, and themselves in two categories. On the one hand are *greedy algorithms* which enable a solution to be built up step by step, starting from a solution to a simplified problem and successively removing the simplifications. On the other, *iterative algorithms*, which start with an approximate solution to the complete problem and make successive improvements by applying elementary transformations.

We now look at these methods in more detail.

14.2   Exact algorithms

Exact algorithms are based on an exploration (and comparison) of all possible solutions; they will give an optimal solution to the mapping problem, but in the worst cases can be of exponential complexity. This, however, can be considerably reduced by using appropriate strategies.

There are many possibilities. We can use the classical methods of graph theory – maximum flow, coupling, minimal cuts and so on [GoM79], or the techniques of mathematical programming – linear programming, dynamic programming, combinatorial optimization and so on [Had89], [PaS82]. Or we can consider solving the problem by a method of the Branch&Bound type. Many studies have been based on the A* algorithm, with a best-first strategy [Sin87], [ShT85], depth-first, breadth-first, ε-approximation and so on. Further, in the case of the best-first approach, different choices of the cost function and of the heuristic function lead to different mapping strategies which we discuss in more detail in the next section. [MLT82] gives a Branch&Bound algorithm that takes into account constraints such as memory capacity, allocation preferences and mutually exclusive tasks.

14.2.1   Branch&Bound

The method in general

This is based on an algorithm for searching by enumeration, suggested by the well-known A* algorithm of Artificial Intelligence [Pea90]. It involves mapping the tasks progressively on the processors, by scanning a search tree that gives all possible combinations. In practice, we do not go so far as as an exhaustive search, but try to find good estimates for the quality of a given configuration by pruning from the tree branches that lead to poor solutions.

A task is chosen and mapped on each of the p processors in turn, each mapping giving a 'partial' solution. For each of these a set of less restricted partial solutions is constructed similarly by mapping a second task, and so on until all the tasks have been mapped. The process is illustrated in Figure 14.4; the depth of the tree is given by the number of tasks.

More details

At each node N of the search tree the cost $g(N)$ of the partial mapping is computed, to which is added an estimate $h(N)$ of the cost of the best mapping of the remaining tasks; the sum $f(N) = g(N) + h(N)$ is a sub-estimate of the cost of any mapping that starts with this partial mapping as far as node N. All the nodes of the tree are developed simultaneously, starting with those for which $f(N)$ is smallest. When all the tasks have been assigned (that is, the leaves of the tree are reached) all those branches can be pruned for which which the sub-estimate is greater than the cost of the best complete mapping obtained. The estimating function h(N) is called the *heuristic function*; the efficiency of the method depends critically on the sharpness of this function.

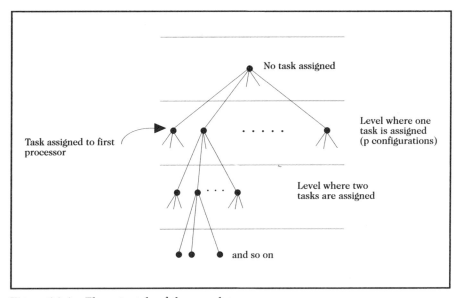

Figure 14.4   The principle of the search tree

Choosing the sub-estimating heuristic

A good heuristic must be able to give a sub-estimate that is as close as possible to the cost function, and also must be simple to calculate. In most cases these objectives are incompatible, which is why the choice of a heuristic can seem very difficult. The heuristic must, first of all, be matched to the problem that is being tackled. It must take into account the interaction between the constraints on the mapping and the cost function. Another possibility for defining the heuristic is to start with the original problem and remove certain constraints; this method – relaxation of constraints – enables a number of heuristics to be constructed systematically, among which one has only to make a choice.

An example of a heuristic is LPT – Largest Processing Time (first), proposed in [BTV92] as an efficient method for scheduling independent tasks (*see* Section 10.2.3); we now describe the strategy.

LPT is a heuristic for load balancing. In the present case it operates in two phases: first, the tasks are sorted into order of decreasing execution time; then, after each node of the search tree has been evaluated, a conceptual mapping is made for the remaining tasks, putting the longest-running task on the least-loaded processor, and so on until all the tasks have been mapped; communication costs are not taken into account in this. The cost function f(N) can then be evaluated. The efficiency of the method is rather disappointing, since, when only a few tasks remain to be mapped, the part h(N) often does not distinguish between different mappings, with the result that little benefit is gained from traversing the densest part of the tree. Also, the cost of an LPT computation is high. The combinatorial explosion can be controlled by the algorithm's pruning of unnecessary nodes. This is done with the aid of a two-dimensional table of frequencies of developed nodes, classified by the number of tasks already mapped and by the value of the cost function; the pruning limits the frequency to some previously-chosen value. It will be clear that the method does not guarantee an optimal mapping.

Another heuristic was given by [ShT85]: after task i has been mapped, an estimate is made of the overhead arising from the mapping of task i+1: this is computed as the minimum of the costs of computing (i+1) and of communication between (i) and (i+1), and corresponds to choosing to put (i+1) either on the same processor as (i) or on some other. If (i) is on the most heavily-loaded processor (that is, the processor that determines the cost of the objective function) then h(N) is taken as this sub-estimate, otherwise it is zero.

14.2.2   Methods from graph theory

Stone [Sto77] gives an interesting treatment of the task-allocation problem, based on the idea of a minimal cut in a bipartite graph, which enables an optimal solution to be found for the problem of mapping tasks optimally on a set of two processors. Using a recursive cut algorithm, the idea was further developed to deal with an arbitrary number of processors [ERS90], [Lo84]. In this second reference Lo also gives an algorithm based on maximum coupling (and hence polynomial cost) and minimizing the inter-task communication cost, with the constraints that the number of tasks is less than twice the number of processors and at most two tasks are mapped on any processor. Under these conditions this algorithm gives an optimal mapping when all the tasks have the same duration.

Here is the principle of modelling by minimal cut in a bipartite graph for the two-processor problem. Figure 14.5 is the graph for the tasks we wish to map on two processors P_1, P_2. Let $G = (\mathcal{T}, \mathcal{E})$ be the graph for n tasks, in which the values attached to the arcs correspond to the communication costs. Thus $c_{i, j}$ is the cost of communication between T_i and T_j; in our previous notation, $c_{i, j} = C(T_i, T_j)$.

Consider now the extended graph GP of Figure 14.6, derived from G by adding vertices corresponding to the processors and arcs joining these to all the task nodes:

GP = (T∪P, E) where E = E∪{arcs(P$_i$, T) i=1, 2 and ∀T ∈ T}

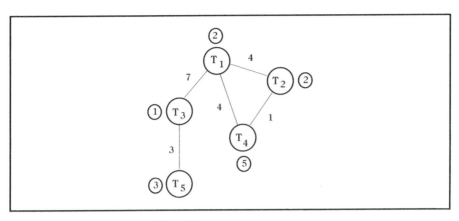

Figure 14.5   An example of a graph

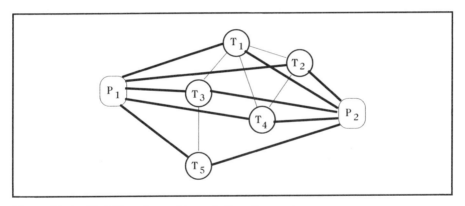

Figure 14.6   Modelling the problem of allocation on two processors

The new arcs are valued in such a way that the cost of a cut is exactly equal to the sum of the computing and communication costs. If the processors are identical, the cost of the arc joining task T$_1$ and processor P$_q$ is simply the execution time ex(T$_i$). However, the same approach enables the more general case of non-identical processors to be dealt with. In that case, if x$_{i, r}$ is the cost of executing task T$_i$ on processor P$_r$, then the cost w$_{i, q}$ of the arc joining task T$_i$ to processor P$_q$ is given by:

$$w_{i,q} = \left[\frac{1}{p-1} \sum_{r \neq q} x_{i,r} - \frac{p-2}{p-1} x_{i,q} \right]$$

14.3 Approximate methods

14.3.1 Greedy algorithms

The exact algorithms just described are very costly in computing time, but, provided one has that time available, will give good solutions. Opposed to these are methods that enable a rough mapping to be found quickly; this is the case for *greedy algorithms*.

Underlying principle

With a greedy algorithm the mapping is constructed by making a succession of approximations to the problem that is to be solved, without ever questioning a choice already made. Thus the allocation of the ith task is made according to some criterion that depends on the partial mapping made for the first (i–1) tasks. This is often a structural criterion and may or may not make explicit use of a cost function.

We can distinguish two categories of such algorithms: those based on purely empirical strategies, and those that are adaptations of standard algorithms from graph theory and combinatorial optimization, which are optimal in certain limited cases.

The first category includes algorithms such as LPT described above, for which a theoretical bound is known in the worst case [Lee91] and which we have already used in A*; the sole criterion here is balancing the load. The same criterion can be used when communication times are negligible, and it can be modified to take account of their becoming significant. Here are some solutions that are characteristic of the category.

Some examples

Modulo mapping, the first to be considered, is a straightforward solution: a greedy algorithm which distributes the tasks equitably among the processors. The algorithm, the simplest imaginable, is incorporated into many of the software packages and operating systems on the market; it involves numbering the tasks and the processors in any way whatever and assigning tasks to processors modulo their numbers. The first task is mapped on the first processor that has sufficient memory; the ith task T_i is mapped on processor $(\text{alloc}(T_{i-1}) + 1)$ modulo p provided that this has sufficient memory, otherwise on $(\text{alloc}(T_{i-1}) + j)$ modulo p where this is the next subsequent processor with sufficient memory for T_i.

This can clearly be improved without greatly increasing the time needed for solution. This underlies the greedy algorithm based on LPT, which attempts to distribute the computing load equitably while taking memory constraints into account. It gives an acceptable mapping for many applications of the 'compute bound' type, for which communication time is negligible in comparison with computation time. The first task, again, is mapped on the first processor with memory enough; the first $(i-1)$ tasks having been distributed, the ith task is mapped on the most lightly loaded processor that has sufficient memory.

Our next example is based on a preliminary classification of the tasks according to a structural criterion, their numbers of input/output channels. The greedy algorithm distributes tasks among processors by choosing for each task the processor carrying the smallest overall load – meaning the sum of the computing costs for all the tasks already assigned to that processor, plus the costs for communication with the other processors. The first task, chosen from among those having the greatest number of I/O channels, is mapped on the first processor with memory enough; and after $(i-1)$ have been distributed, the ith is mapped on the most lightly loaded processor, in this overall sense, that has sufficient memory. Communication costs are taken into account only in mapping tasks that are involved in communication.

A third method, given in [AnP88], also uses a structural criterion. The idea behind this *friendly greedy algorithm* is to choose for the next task to be mapped the one needing minimum routing. Starting with an arbitrarily chosen task, at each step the task chosen is the one that communicates most with those already mapped: in the case of equality one might choose, for example, the task having the minimum communication costs. Having chosen the task, the processor is chosen so as to minimize some function of the cost of the partial mapping at that stage.

In contrast to these, there are greedy algorithms which classify tasks according to quantitative criteria. They may, for example, use one of the cost functions that we have discussed, such as the global cost for each task, as just defined; in that case, when the tasks are distributed among the processors the cost of any communications internal to a processor will be taken as zero. A two-fold criterion, structural and quantitative, can be used: for example, tasks which are not differentiated by their numbers of links with the outside world can be distinguished by using their global costs. Afterwards, the proper allocation is done, as described in the two previous algorithms.

Quality of the solution

These greedy algorithms are mostly not costly to use, but they are not very powerful. Clearly, the results they give depend on the choice of the first task, made arbitrarily: this choice conditions the whole process, for there is no questioning of any intermediate solution. Further, towards the end the choices for mapping become fewer and fewer, and this can wreck performance. They are used mostly to get a rough solution quickly, which can then be improved iteratively.

14.3.2   Iterative algorithms

All iterative algorithms start with a complete solution – not necessarily very good, possibly found by means of a greedy algorithm – that is to be improved by some iterative process. They are based on the principle of optimizing some cost function, and in most existing cases the procedure is one of making successive permutations of tasks and keeping only those that improve this function. From time to time random permutations have to be made in order to find better solutions.

This approach has led to some rather exotic methods such as those based on neural networks, or on genetics [KrM88]; here we consider only two methods which seem to us to be representative.

Simulated annealing

This is quite an old technique; there are many published papers reporting results given by it, and comparisons with other algorithms [BoM88], [HaB88], [Had89]. The idea underlying idea, suggested by observations of physical phenomena, is based on an analogy with statistical physics. When a sample of metal is required to have the most regular structure possible, this is produced by what is called *annealing*: the metal is heated and then cooled very slowly so that it is in thermal equilibrium throughout the cooling; when the temperature is low enough it remains in an equilibrium state corresponding to minimum energy. When the temperature is high there is a great deal of thermal agitation, which can increase the internal energy in local regions and the probability of this occurring falls with the temperature; mathematically, this corresponds to allowing a jump from a local minimum of a function that is to be optimized.

The approach is often presented in an intuitive manner; it is difficult to support theoretically by a simple analogy, and especially to find a meaning for physical parameters such as temperature. We decided to give an interpretation that is closer to the problem to be solved.

Mapping can be regarded as the problem of optimizing a certain cost function. Starting with an initial mapping, we attempt to improve this by applying some local operation and criterion, such as interchanging a pair of tasks and accepting this interchange if it improves the mapping. On occasion, and with a probability that decreases as the process continues, we will accept a change that gives a worse mapping, to take the solution away from a local minimum of the 'energy' – here, of the cost function to be minimized. Figure 14.7 gives a schematic picture of the principle.

The algorithm for the general process is given below. At each temperature, equilibrium is reached when either an exchange has been made or all the tasks T' have been considered.

```
(start with an initial mapping and an initial temperature)
while final temperature not reached do
    repeat for all tasks T
        find neighbouring task T'
        evaluate gain from exchanging T, T'
        if gain ≥ 0 then exchange T, T'
        else
            choose random number ran
            if ran < prob(temperature) then exchange T, T'
    until equilibrium
    increase temperature
end
```

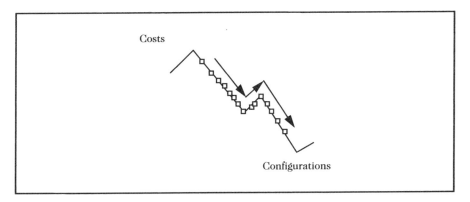

Figure 14.7   A scheme of the simulated annealing principle

This method can give very good results in polynomial time, but it has its disadvantages; among the greatest of these are the high computing costs when the numbers of tasks and processors are large, and especially the difficulty of modifying the parameters that depend on the mapping to be made. Further, the random aspect of these modifications makes the behaviour of the algorithm unpredictable, and can give poor results.

Bokhari

This very well-known algorithm applies to the case where the number of tasks is equal to the number of processors. Its criterion is to maximize the *cardinality*, here meaning the number of well-mapped links; the following is an implementation.

```
while this gives an improvement do
    for all processors containing task T
        find another processor containing T'
        evaluate gain from exchanging T, T'
        if gain ≥ 0 then exchange T, T'
if cardinality of resulting mapping > preceding cardinality then
    permute tasks randomly and evaluate mapping
    restart algorithm
```

In this iterative algorithm, improvements to intermediate solutions result from random permutations of pairs of tasks; the process is stopped when there has been no change after some chosen number of iterations. As before, random permutations can be made from time to time to restart the process.

The basic paper on the process [Bok81] shows good results, especially when the task graph closely resembles the graph for the architecture. The method can be adapted to different circumstances by extending the definition of cardinality, to take account, for example, of the distance between processors or to put special emphasis on certain arcs, such as the most costly. The more usual case of there being many more tasks than processors can be dealt with by making a preliminary grouping of the tasks.

There are other possibilities for iterative algorithms. Instead of cardinality we could use any of the cost functions we have described. Lee and Aggarwal [LeA87] consider novel cost functions suggested by image-processing, that take account of actual distances over the network rather than nominal distances.

14.3.3   Mixed solutions

The methods we have given are complementary in that they relate to different circumstances; there is clearly a case for putting together a battery of algorithms, containing one or more of each type: greedy, iterative, exact. There is also a case for mixed algorithms, intermediate between greedy and exact: thus a rough mapping provided by a greedy algorithm could provide a good initial cost estimate for the A* algorithm and the latter could then reject all those nodes N for which f(N) exceeded this. The mixed approach could be viewed as a heuristic algorithm in which some choices could be questioned, so that some mappings would be systematically reconsidered. Alternatively, it could be viewed as Branch&Bound with the number of combinations rigorously limited by a strategy for choosing the branches to be visited – in the end, a greedy algorithm is a simple path through the search tree.

This approach seems very promising. Allowing some choices to be reconsidered makes it possible to avoid the pathological situations that inevitably arise with algorithms in which arbitrary decisions are made. The limitation of the combinatorial explosion gives such an algorithm a solution time that is acceptable in comparison with that for any simple Branch&Bound algorithm. Regrettably, so far as we are aware no serious study has been made of algorithms of this type.

14.3.4   A new approach

We end this discussion of static mapping strategies with a practical mixed solution proposed by Bouvry, Trystram and Vincent [BVT92], an outline of which is given in the flow diagram of Figure 14.8.

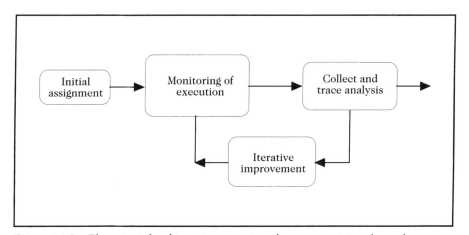

Figure 14.8   The principle of iterative mapping after summarizing the paths

It starts with a rough solution given by a greedy algorithm, in response to values such as task execution times and communication costs, or estimates of these, supplied by the user. The parallel program operates on this, listing the important parameters such as the load on each communication channel and the CPU time needed by each processor. Analysis of these gives information that will be of great value to the process of improving the solution: for example, it will enable the most heavily loaded processor to be identified and hence tasks to be moved from this to other processors on which there are tasks that communicate with those transferred, or an attempt made to exchange one of its tasks with a task from another processor. If after such changes – always improving the mapping – another processor becomes the most heavily loaded, the process is continued with this one. It is stopped when some chosen number of transformations has ceased to give any local improvement.

These local transformations can lead to a local minimum, and there is no guarantee that this will be the global minimum sought; recourse is therefore made to what is done in simulated annealing, and a randomly-chosen transfer of tasks made from time to time.

This method can give very good results in practice, especially when there are only very rough estimates for the initial data – or none. However, we have here the problem of the non-deterministic execution of a parallel program on a MIMD machine, which makes some of the parameter values uncertain; this makes statistical analysis necessary, but that adds a great burden.

The method, in involving reviews of information during execution, forms a natural transition towards dynamic allocation.

14.3.5   Dynamic partitioning

Casavant and Kuhl's classification [CaK88], described in Section 14.1.2, also considers dynamic allocation. The corresponding strategies are very costly and difficult to implement, and consequently are restricted to special applications such as parallel implementation of functional languages or of formal algebra systems. Figure 14.9 outlines the classification.

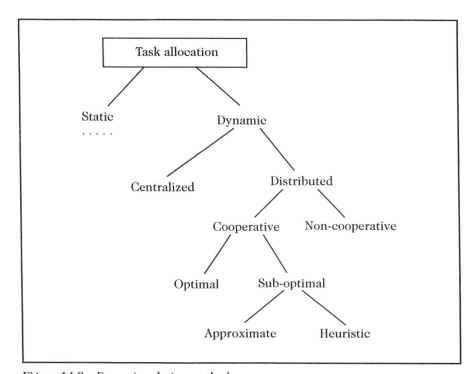

Figure 14.9   Dynamic solution methods

The first level in dynamic allocation is the distinction between centralized and distributed decision-making, whether this done by a single processor or shared among several. In the latter case, a decision may be made one of the processors alone or as a collective effort by several.

Dynamic methods can prove valuable for certain irregular problems, or for problems where precise values for the parameters are not known. In general they are costly, and are based mainly on some form of load-balancing criterion.

14.4   Conclusion

In this chapter we addressed the problem of physically allocating tasks to processors. In contrast to Chapter 10, we modelled the parallel program by a non-directed graph, meaning that our treatment did not take precedence relations into account. From the point of view of parallelism this model is less rich than that for task graphs and scheduling, but it enables efficient heuristics for task mapping to be incorporated into a parallel programming environment in a practical manner. Communication times between processors depend on their relative locations in the network, but most present-day machines have special hardware for routing, which makes it possible for communication to be taken as independent of distance.

As a final comment, heuristics are both useful and necessary in all parallel programs here. For problems with a regular structure, such as the majority of the numerical algorithms we shall study in Chapters 16 and 17, mapping is guided by the structure and in general is made by the programmer in performing such operations as partitioning matrices into rows, columns or blocks.

15

Communications in processor networks

In this chapter, we study the different models of communication in networks. We describe in detail the most important schemes in these different models, for several topologies.

15.1 Modelling

15.1.1 Introduction

Communications form the weak point of distributed memory architectures. Nonetheless, different communication models do exist according to the architecture under consideration. The main processor network topologies were discussed in Chapter 4. The aim of this chapter is to study those communication schemes which are most widely known and most useful for these different models. The interested reader can study these concepts in more depth in [Rum92].

Parallel architectures with shared memories are very attractive because of the relative simplicity of implementing algorithms on them. They enable us to achieve good performance with less effort, but in practice they are limited to a small number of processors – ten at the most. Use of distributed memory broadens horizons but brings new and difficult problems. If a processor needs a data item that is in another processor, that item will have to traverse the interconnection network. Communication is the key element in architectures of this type. There are many who hold that a good distributed programming environment must contain, beside the phase of extraction of parallelism (similar to that for shared-memory computers), a tool for allocating processes and data to processors and a library of general communications procedures, or at least software that enables shared memory to be simulated: that is, virtual shared memory.

Inter-processor communication is usually structured – hypercube, ring, toric grid, binary or non-binary tree, De Bruijn network, perfect shuffle and so on. This chapter aims, on the one hand, to to present and discuss the different communication models and on the other to present the main results known concerning global communication procedures – broadcasting, total exchange, distribution, clustering, permutation and so on. Throughout, we assume a physical network of p processors, each with its own local memory. The problems arising from combining communication and computation are addressed in Chapter 16.

15.1.2   Which model for communication?

Introduction

The model for our distributed memory architecture is such that each processor ensures communication with its neighbours; it also performs as an arithmetical-logical unit and controls the program – this is the case, for example, for the Transputer and for most present-day microprocessors. The local memory barely exceeds a few megabytes and therefore is quick to access. If the number of processors is large, communication between them is costly and in most real applications predominates over the computation itself.

We take the costs of memory management for messages within a single processor to be negligible: this is quite realistic, in view of the fact that it is often done by dedicated circuits such as DMA – Direct Memory Access. We distinguish between two models for the communication time between neighbouring processors, and several transmission modes.

Basic time model

The most general model for the communication cost for L elementary data items between two directly-neighbouring processors is the linear relation,

$\beta + L\tau$, where β is the initialization or *start-up* time and τ is the transmission rate, the inverse of the link's *bandwidth*. β can be of the same order of magnitude as τ, and therefore negligible if L is large, or predominant, as in the case of high-speed machines such as vector multi-processors, or of machines in which communication is managed by software.

On certain machines, such as most massively parallel synchronous machines, the basic communication phases concern direct neighbours and a message of given length is transferred in a constant time [FrL91]. For multi-processors with *routing* hardware, communication time can be taken as constant, independent of the distance between the processors, whether neighbours or not: this time is therefore very important. We shall return to this point at the end of the chapter.

Types of link

The general communication model allows for parallel dispatches (and/or receptions) by the same processor (*see* Figure 15.1); it is then said to be *link-bound*. However, there are machines that do not allow simultaneous use of all the processor's links, for which the model is *processor-bound*. In general, communication is bi-directional, when we say that the links are *full duplex*; but they may be uni-directional, or *half duplex*.

Except where otherwise stated, we shall assume parallel bi-directional links between processors and the general linear cost relation: this is the most usual state of affairs with existing processor networks.

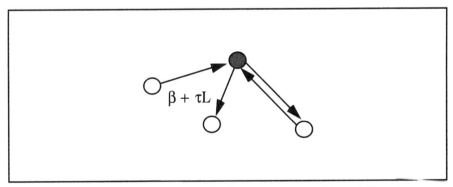

Figure 15.1   The communication model for a processor and its neighbouring processors

15.1.3   The different communication modes

Messages can be transmitted from one processor to another in different ways. We describe the commonest communication modes below.

Message switching

This is the oldest mode [SaS89], also known as *store and forward*. Messages arriving at a processor in the network are stored before continuing their journey; if there is no link available, the message waits. As we shall see later, if a path between two processors can be found, time can be saved by subdividing the message and pipelining the dispatches.

A message generally consists of of a *header* which gives the path to the destination processor, followed by the message itself (Figure 15.2).

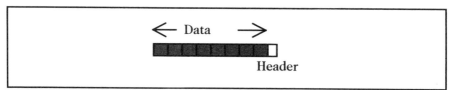

Figure 15.2   A basic message

In simple message switching mode the complete message is transmitted step by step, from one processor to the next (Figure 15.3); we are assuming that no conflicts arise in this.

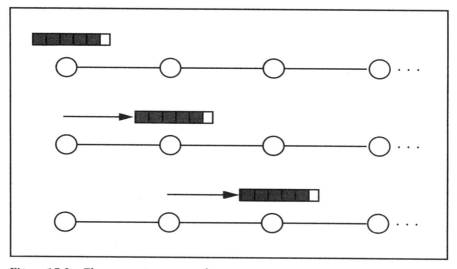

Figure 15.3   The successive stages of a transmission in message switching mode

Circuit switching

In contrast to message switching, we can seek to establish a complete path and send the whole message as a unit. Again assuming no conflict, the path is set up according to the information in the header and, when confirmation that it is free is received, the whole message is sent along it (Figure 15.4). This is *circuit switching*. The path is reserved for the whole of the duration of the transmission and is released when the complete message has reached its destination.

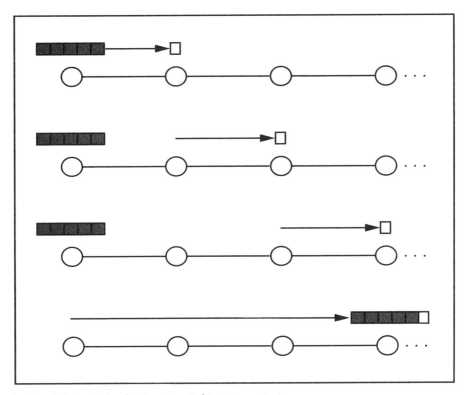

Figure 15.4   A simple circuit switching transmission

A possible improvement on this involves starting the transmission before the complete path is established. If it is not fully available, intermediate packets are stored on intermediate processors; as before, the path is released when the whole message has been received. This, which could be called *dynamic circuit switching*, became very popular in the early 1990s for constructing routing hardware [DaS87]. Messages are split up into packets of fixed size (*flits*), 32 bytes. We shall see in Section 15.2 that this mode differs slightly from *pipelined message switching*, where packet size is calculated so as to minimize the total transmission time.

A variant of dynamic circuit switching is *wormhole* [DaS87], in which the path is released in stages as the transmission proceeds rather than in full at the end (Figure 15.5).

If conflicts arise on a link, the messages are stored on all those intermediate nodes of the path that have already been traversed. In a variant of this, called *virtual cut through*, all the intermediate packets are sent to the processor that has detected the conflict [KeK79]: this clearly requires each processor to have a large storage capacity.

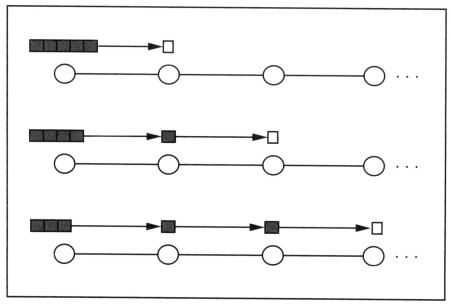

Figure 15.5   A dynamic circuit switching transmission

15.1.4   An overview of the different types of communication

Every distributed programming environment must possess an efficient library of general communications. There are different procedures for structured communication which are commonly encountered and must therefore be implemented very efficiently. Chapter 16 is devoted to some examples of the implementation of communication schemes in applications. Amongst the most important are:

- any communication from one processor to another (not necessarily immediate neighbours);
- the broadcasting of a message from one processor to all the others;
- personalized broadcasting, which involves a processor sending different parts of a message to all the others, so that each processor receives a different sub-message;
- multibroadcasting, where a processor sends a message to a fixed group of processors;
- the total exchange of messages from all processors to all the others;

- personalized total exchange, where different parts of one message are sent from each processor to all the others;
- the gathering of messages sent by all the processors in a single processor;
- reduction, which is a gathering process, with combinations by means of intermediate operations, of all the small messages;
- other regular schemes such as permutations, transpositions of data from spreadsheets, histograms, and so on.

15.2   Communication between two processors

Transferring a message from one processor to another (one-to-one, OTO) is in general fairly simple. For message switching mode the best technique involves splitting the message into packets and pipelining these. We shall assume the general linear cost model with parallel links, and in general try to use several links simultaneously so as to provide as many paths as possible between the two processors. Thus the problem is that of finding paths of equal length, if such exist.

Contention can arise if several OTO dispatches are to be made at the same moment: that is, if two communications need the simultaneous use of at least the same two links. This will be dealt with by a *routing algorithm*; we go into this in detail at the end of the chapter, where we give general routing algorithms for all communication modes on all common network topologies.

15.2.1   Some general results for message switching mode

We want to send a message of length L from processor i to processor j, separated by $h(i, j)$ links. The first idea that comes to mind is to send the complete message, one link after another, over one of the paths of length $h(i, j)$ between the processors. The duration of this transfer will be

$$h(i, j)(\beta + L\tau)$$

Pipelining the message

This simple (and naïve) solution can be improved by splitting the message into q packets of equal size; as Figure 15.6 shows, the idea is to fill up all the links in the path more quickly by pipelining the dispatches.

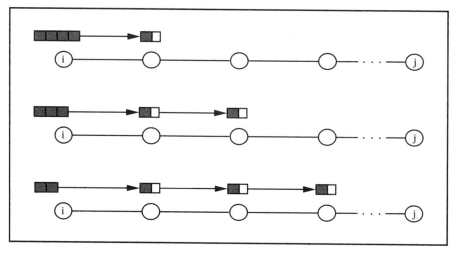

Figure 15.6   The principle of pipelined communication (the first stages)

We now have:

Proposition 15.1

The minimum transmission time in pipelined mode for a message of length L between two processors h apart is:

$$\left(\sqrt{(h-1)\beta} + \sqrt{L\tau} \right)^2$$

Proof

The time for an elementary step is $\beta + \frac{L}{q}\tau$. Since the distance between the processors is h steps, there are a total of h+q−1 steps to be traversed sequentially, so the time for the whole message to arrive at its destination is:

$$(h+q-1)\left(\beta + \frac{L\tau}{q} \right) = (h-1)\beta + L\tau + q\beta + \frac{L(h-1)}{q}\tau$$

It is easily seen that this is minimized if q is given by:

$$\beta - \frac{L(h-1)}{q^2}\tau = 0$$

giving

$$q = q_{opt} = \sqrt{\left\{ \frac{L(h-1)\tau}{\beta} \right\}}$$

from which the result follows.

This shows that for long messages the duration is asymptotically $L\tau$, meaning that the length of the message has to some extent hidden the influence of the distance between the processors.

Influence of parallelism of the links

We assume that the processor network is regular, meaning that in the processor graph all the nodes are of the same degree Δ, and that there are Δ disjoint paths between any pair. The communications model then allows a processor to communicate with Δ neighbours simultaneously.

Pipelining message packets allows us to ignore, asymptotically, the distance between processors. It can be combined with parallel dispatches over the links by first dividing the message into lengths L/Δ and pipelining these simultaneously over the Δ links. This gives the following:

Proposition 15.2
The minimum transmission time for a message of length L between two processors h apart, using Δ disjoint paths, is:

$$\left(\sqrt{(h-1)\beta} + \sqrt{\frac{L}{\Delta}\tau} \right)^2$$

Proof
This follows directly from the previous result, with the message length L/Δ.

Example: toric grid

We consider a network in the form of a 2-dimensional toric grid (*see* Chapter 4), with the processors referenced by their cartesian coordinates (i, j) and (i', j').

If the two processors are on the same horizontal or vertical grid line there is a single path of minimum length joining them. To compute the communication time we apply Proposition 15.1 along this path, getting:

$$\left(\sqrt{(h-1)\beta} + \sqrt{L\tau}\right)^2 \dots \text{where } h = \max\left(\left|i'-i\right|, \left|j'-i\right|\right)$$

If they are not on the same grid line there are two disjoint paths of minimum length, along each of which we can send a message of length L/2, pipelining these as before: see Figure 15.7. Applying Proposition 15.2 we have for the time:

$$\left(\sqrt{(h-1)\beta} + \sqrt{\frac{L}{2}\tau}\right)^2 \dots \text{where } h = \max\left(\left|i'-i\right|, \left|j'-j\right|\right)$$

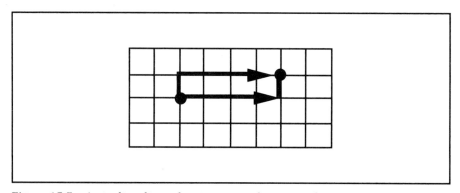

Figure 15.7   A pipeline dispatch using two paths on a grid

However, we can construct four disjoint paths of length h+2 (Figure 15.8) along each of which we can pipeline a quarter of the message, giving the still shorter time:

$$\left(\sqrt{(h-1)\beta} + \sqrt{\frac{L}{4}\tau}\right)^2$$

Clearly we cannot improve on this, because the degree of each processor is 4.

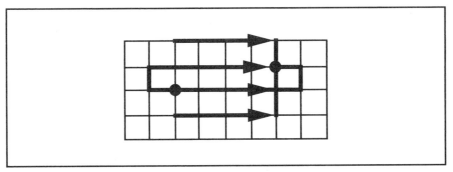

Figure 15.8   A dispatch using four paths whose lengths are h+2

Hypercube geometry

Suppose we want to send a message of length L over a d-cube network from one processor, which without loss of generality we can label 0, to some other at a distance h, where $1 \le h \le d$. A first solution would be to pipeline the message on one of the paths of length h, getting as before:

$$\left(\sqrt{(h-1)\beta} + \sqrt{L\tau} \right)^2$$

This can be improved by recalling the property of the hypercube that says there are h distinct paths of length h joining any pair of nodes a distance h apart. We can use this parallelism by pipelining h messages of length L/h along all these paths simultaneously, getting a time:

$$\left(\sqrt{(h-1)\beta} + \sqrt{\frac{L}{h}\tau} \right)^2$$

There is however another strategy that will send a message as quickly as possible from processor 0 to any other processor at a distance h, in which we restrict ourselves to a hypercube of degree h and send messages of different sizes over h stages. In this hypercube, let C_k be the set of processors at distance k from the sending processor (*see* Section 4.1.2); the principle for the algorithm is as follows:

```
at each stage k for k ← 0 to h-1
    each node of Cₖ (level k) divides its data into (h-k) equal
    packets and sends in parallel 1 packet to each of its (h-k)
    neighbours in Cₖ₊₁
```

Figure 15.9 illustrates this for the case of a dispatch to a processor at a distance of 3.

It is rather more difficult to determine the time for this algorithm than for the previous cases. There are h successive stages, for each of which we have to find the size of the packets sent.

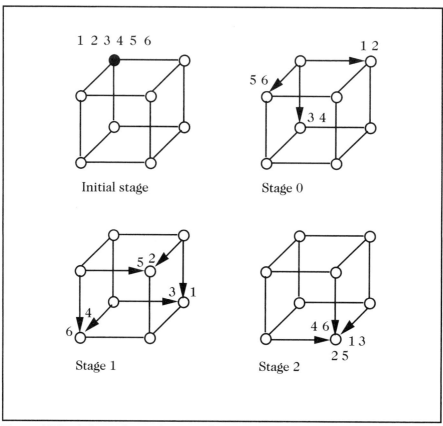

Figure 15.9   A dispatch at a distance of 3 in a hypercube

At stage k the number of processors in C_k is $C(_h^k)$ and each sends a message of the same size to its (h–k) successors; this size is therefore:

$$\frac{L}{(h-k)C\left(_h^k\right)}$$

and the cost of stage k is therefore:

$$\beta + \frac{L}{(h-k)\binom{h}{k}} \tau$$

Since

$$(h-k)\binom{k}{h} = h\binom{h-1}{k}$$

the total cost is:

$$\sum_{k=0}^{h-1} \beta + \frac{L}{(h-k)\binom{h}{k}} \tau = h\beta + \left(\sum_{k=0}^{h-1} \frac{1}{\binom{h-1}{k}}\right) \frac{L}{h} \tau$$

For an order-of-magnitude result,

$$\sum_{k=0}^{h-1} \frac{1}{h-1} \approx 2 + \frac{2}{h-1}$$

giving a time of

$$h\beta + \left\{ \frac{2L}{(h-1)} \right\} \tau$$

This algorithm is difficult to implement because of the need to regroup the fragments of message at each stage, an operation that entails non-negligible overheads.

15.2.2   Circuit switching

Here, we are still considering a linear communication time between neighbouring processors.

General points

The expression for the duration of the transmission in circuit switching mode of an L-sized message between two processors, h apart, differs from that obtained in message switching. Emission always requires an initialization time plus a time for establishing the link (proportional to the distance) plus the transmission of the message itself, whose expression is identical to that of message switching. This leads to the following proposition.

Proposition 15.3

Transmission time for an L-sized message in circuit switching mode between two processors, h apart, is equal to $\beta + \alpha h + L\tau$.

Comparing this mode with message switching makes little sense. Here, the setting-up is managed by hardware, so the parameter α is small, and the initialization time β is near enough the same in the two modes. The new generation of distributed memory machines prefers to use circuit switching mode as it enables message routing across the network to be managed by hardware.

An application to a toric grid

Let's continue the previous calculation on a toric grid in circuit switching mode for a transmission between two processors (i, j) and (i', j') which do not belong to the same line (either horizontally or vertically). If we use dispatches on the four disjoint links, h+2 in length, we obtain:

$$\beta + \alpha h + \frac{L}{4}\tau \text{ where } h = |i' - i| + |j' - j|$$

In general, for simple transmissions from one processor to another, the results always show a better performance than in message switching mode, even when using the pipelining technique (and asymptotically, are of the same order of size for large messages). However, in contrast to what happens in message switching mode, intermediate processors do not recognize intermediate messages. We should note in conclusion that simple message switching is a special case of circuit switching, solely concerned with dispatches along a distance of 1.

15.3   Broadcasting

The problem with broadcasting lies in finding an algorithm which enables us to send information to all the processors. Simple broadcasting (or OTA for One-To-All), where a single processor must send its message to all the others, is distinguished from personalized broadcasting (when we tend to refer to *distribution*), where the source processor must ensure that different messages reach each of the processors. The latter situation will be dealt with in Section 15.5.

15.3.1   Some preliminary results

Consider a processor network of diameter D and maximum degree Δ over which we want to send a message of length L; we continue to assume a linear transmission model with parallel bi-directional interprocessor links. [Rum92] deals with an analysis of the broadcasting problem.

Theoretical limits

Proposition 15.4
A lower bound for the broadcast time for a message of length L in a linear model on a network $G(D, \Delta)$ with parallel bidirectional links in message switching mode is:

$$D\beta + \left(\frac{L}{\Delta} + D - 1 \right)\tau$$

Proof
The broadcast time for a message of length L is greater than or equal to the sum of D stages of communicating the smallest possible elementary messages (that is, size 1), plus the time taken by the rest of the message (which gives L–Δ) which arrives via all the links at the same time (assuming ideally that this is possible). We thus obtain:

$$D(\beta + \tau) + \frac{L - \Delta}{\Delta}\tau$$

With the assumption that the duration of a transmission between neighbouring processors is constant, whatever the message's size, it is easy to broadcast a message in optimal time (equal to the graph's diameter) under the previously stated hypothetical conditions, by means of the following greedy algorithm: as soon as one processor has received the message, it broadcasts it in turn to all its neighbouring processors.

Proposition 15.5

A lower bound for the broadcast time for a message of length L in a linear model on a network G(D, Δ) in circuit switching mode with parallel bidirectional links is:

$$\log_{\Delta+1}(p)(\beta+\tau)+D\alpha$$

Proof

In contrast to what happens in message switching mode, only one message can travel along one path. In order to contact all the processors, at least $\log_{\Delta+1}(p)$ stages are necessary when dealing with elementary sized messages. Moreover, the minimum distance to cross in order to reach all the network's nodes is equal to the graph's diameter.

We now look at the known results for the main topologies in detail. In general terms, the best algorithms in linear models and in message switching mode use a pipeline strategy on several spanning trees. If we consider a transmission where messages are stored on intermediate processors, broadcasting is the same as in the previous instance, with the diameter as its distance.

15.3.2   Broadcasting on a ring

Message switching

Consider a ring of p processors (whose diameter is equal to $\lfloor \frac{p}{2} \rfloor$). The algorithm which performs pipelined dispatches where the message is split into packets of an equal and optimal size can be used in a ring which uses both directions simultaneously (Figure 15.10).

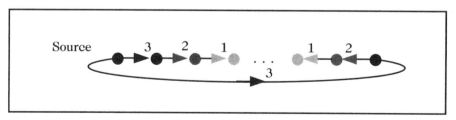

Figure 15.10   The first stages of pipeline communication on a ring

The broadcast's duration is calculated from Proposition 15.1, which gives:

$$\left(\sqrt{\left(\left\lfloor\frac{p}{2}\right\rfloor-1\right)\beta+\sqrt{L\tau}}\right)^2$$

with the number of packets equal to:

$$\sqrt{\frac{L\left(\left\lfloor\frac{p}{2}\right\rfloor-1\right)\tau}{\beta}}$$

The extension which corresponds to the bidirectional link model results in a pipeline algorithm of p stages, with two disjoint paths, each occupied with a message of size $\frac{L}{2}$ (which we assume to be an integer). The two paths are shown in Figure 15.11.

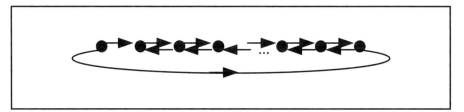

Figure 15.11   Bi-directional broadcasting on a ring

The broadcast's duration then becomes:

$$\left(\sqrt{(p-1)\beta}+\sqrt{\frac{L}{2}\tau}\right)^2$$

This running time is best for large messages.

Broadcasting in circuit switching mode

For simplicity, let us assume that the number of processors p is a power of 3. The principle of broadcasting is as follows.

At the first stage, the root contacts the two processors which are at a distance of p/3. Then each of the three processors in turn contacts two processors. The ring is thus split into nine equal regions, and so on, until all the processors have been contacted, that is, after $\log_3(p)$ stages. Figure 15.12 is a diagram of a broadcast on a ring of 27 processors.

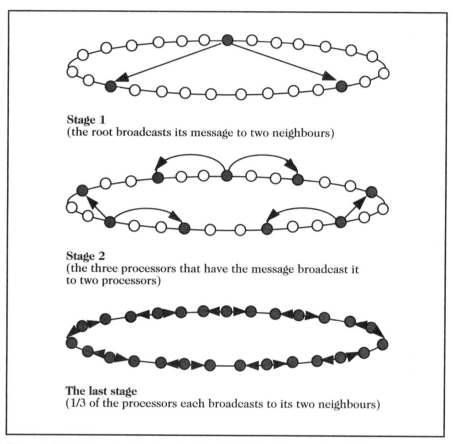

Stage 1
(the root broadcasts its message to two neighbours)

Stage 2
(the three processors that have the message broadcast it
to two processors)

The last stage
(1/3 of the processors each broadcasts to its two neighbours)

Figure 15.12   Broadcasting in circuit switching mode on a ring of 27 processors

That this broadcasting algorithm can be performed is easily proved (all the processors are reached without there being any conflicting conditions). Let us evaluate its running time. The broadcast is performed in $\log_3(p)$ stages. One stage costs $\beta+d_i\alpha+L\tau$ where d_i is the dispatching distance to stage i, which gives, $d_i=\frac{p}{3^i}$.

The broadcast's duration is thus:

$$\log_3(p)(\beta+L\tau) + \sum_{i=1}^{\log_3(p)} \frac{p}{3^i}\alpha = \log_3(p)(\beta+L\tau) + \left\lfloor \frac{p}{2} \right\rfloor \alpha$$

15.3.3   Broadcasting on a toric grid

For simplicity, let us consider a square toric grid of $\sqrt{p}$ by $\sqrt{p}$ processors, where $\sqrt{p}$ is assumed to be an integer (the results can easily be extended in the common instance of a grid of any dimension).

Pipeline on the two dimensions in message switching mode

One method involves broadcasting the message first vertically, then horizontally, as shown in Figures 15.13 and 15.14 in the case of a 7×7 grid (the source is at the centre).

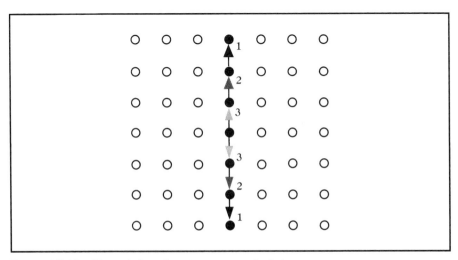

Figure 15.13   Phase 1: broadcasting on a vertical ring

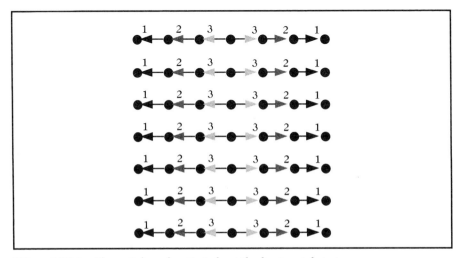

Figure 15.14   Phase 2: broadcasting along the horizontal rings

There are two phases, both of which correspond to the pipeline broadcasting time of the whole message on a ring of $\sqrt{p}$ processors. According to Proposition 15.1, the total time taken is:

$$2\left(\sqrt{\left(\left\lceil\frac{\sqrt{p}}{2}\right\rceil-1\right)\beta}+\sqrt{L\tau}\right)^2$$

The preceding solution can be improved by pipelining the two phases by means of a simultaneous dispatch on the two dimensions. This principle is given in Figure 15.15.

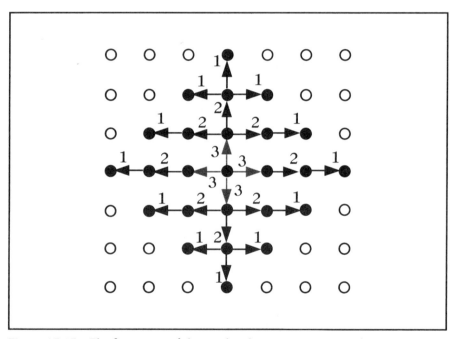

Figure 15.15   The first stages of the pipelined communication on the two dimensions in message switching mode

The algorithm contains one phase. The pipeline still carries the whole message, but the number of stages has doubled. The running time becomes:

$$\left(\sqrt{\left(2\left\lceil\frac{\sqrt{p}}{2}\right\rceil-1\beta\right)}+\sqrt{L\tau}\right)^2$$

This result can be interpreted with the help of a spanning tree whose depth is equal to the diameter of the square grid. The reader will note that only half the links are occupied (and mainly in only one direction).

An optimal algorithm

Michallon, Trystram and Villard constructed a family of four spanning trees with disjoint arcs equal in depth to $(D+1)$ where D is the diameter [MTV92]. These trees are discussed in Chapter 4. The algorithm produced is the best known algorithm under the previous assumptions of linear time and parallel bidirectional links. The principle is to broadcast a quarter of the initial message on each of the trees. The running time is deduced from Proposition 15.2:

$$\left(\sqrt{2\left\lfloor \frac{\sqrt{p}}{2} \right\rfloor} \beta + \sqrt{\frac{L}{4}} \tau \right)^2$$

Broadcasting in circuit switching mode on a toric grid

Let us consider the same hypothetical conditions as were stated earlier in circuit switching mode. One broadcasting algorithm on a square toric grid of p processors can be obtained by recursively dividing the network into four equal regions (or thereabouts, when the number of processors by dimension is not in the form of $4K+1$) as shown in Figure 15.16 (the processors that have received their message are shown in black). At each stage, the message is transmitted to the centre of each region. In the example 9×9 processors, the last stage is doubled and irregular. This stage can be acquired in each quadrant from regular schemes produced by rotating $\pi/2$ in relation to the dimensions. It is left to the reader to prove the adaptation of this algorithm, if the dimensions are not in the form of $(4K+1)(4K+1)$, where K is an integer.

Computing the broadcasting time is performed in the same way as for the ring. Firstly the number of stages is noted as being equal to $k+4$ with $[4.2^k+1, 4.2^{k+1}+1]$ in between. It is deduced that there are $\lfloor \log_2(\sqrt{p}-3) \rfloor + 2$ stages; stage i corresponds to the dispatch of a message at a distance of $d_i = \lfloor \frac{D}{2^i} \rfloor$ where D is the diameter of the toric grid. The cost of one stage is $\beta + d_i \alpha + L\tau$, with the last stage equal to $2(\beta + \alpha + L\tau)$. Thus we obtain $O(\log_4(p)L\tau)$.

We should note that in the previous strategy, a source processor at one stage only emits once. Starting with this observation, Peters and Syska [Sys92] proposed a better scheme where all the processors that have an item of data at any one instance broadcast it. The complexity analysis is identical to the previous case, replacing factor $\beta + L\tau$ with $\log_5(p)$. This gives a broadcast in two stages instead of the three in the 5×5 toric grid (Figure 15.17).

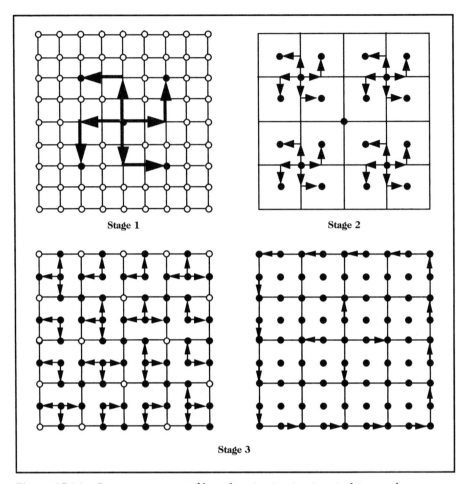

Figure 15.16   Successive stages of broadcasting in circuit switching mode

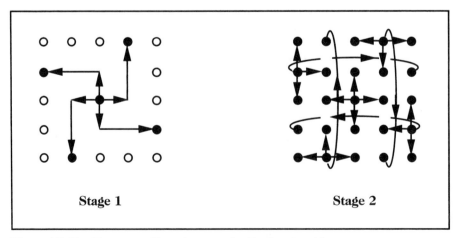

Figure 15.17   The optimal broadcast on the 5 × 5 toric grid

15.3.4   Broadcasting on a hypercube in message switching mode

An initial algorithm

The first broadcasting algorithm on a hypercube of the order d involves sending a message in pipeline mode along a spanning tree (such as the balanced example presented in Section 4.3.1). Following the same principle as before, computing the best process for splitting messages into packets of equal size is easy. Figure 15.18 demonstrates this principle in detail on a 3-cube.

The first packet arrives at the last processor in d stages; the (q–1) remaining packets arrive at a new rate at each stage. Since the network is d in diameter, the broadcasting time is equal to:

$$\left(\sqrt{(d-1)\beta} + \sqrt{L\tau} \right)^2$$

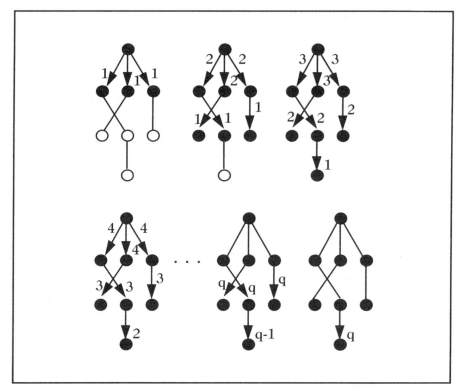

Figure 15.18   The principle of simple pipeline broadcasting on a 3-cube

A second algorithm

There is another algorithm which is based on the simultaneous use of d binomial spanning trees (presented in Chapter 4) and a preliminary split into d packets. Simultaneously using communications on d links in parallel results in the masking of the network's d degree. The feasibility of this algorithm hinges on the fact that the same arc is never used by several trees at the same stage. A study of Figure 15.19 will show that this is indeed the case. Each tree is occupied by a given L/d sized packet, which is pivoted circularly at each stage in successive directions, while progressing along the same tree.

The running time of this rotative broadcast is easy to calculate. There are d stages which are concerned with L/d sized packets, which gives $d\beta+L\tau$.

Note that asymptotically for large sized messages, these two broadcasting algorithms have the same performance. Evidently in the latter type of communication, at any given time, all the processors are engaged in sending data along all their links and thus pipelining is not possible as it stands, since these trees possess communal arcs (which are used at different times).

A better algorithm

Performance can be improved by parallel-pipeline broadcasting, using edge disjoint spanning trees, as described in Chapter 4. Figure 15.20 shows the principle of the broadcasting algorithm in detail on a 3-cube.

The running time corresponds to a pipeline broadcast in (d+1) stages of the messages split optimally on each tree with messages sized $\frac{L}{d}$, which gives, according to Proposition 15.2:

$$\left(\sqrt{d\beta} + \sqrt{\frac{L}{d}\tau} \right)^2$$

The latter strategy is possible only under the assumption of a processor network whose links are bidirectional. However, with unidirectional links, it is easy to perform a communication on two links, one in each direction, in order to avoid conflicts on the links if used in both directions (the time is simply multiplied by two).

The latter method enables us to accumulate the improvements which are due to the pipelining and the parallelism of the links. However, there is one last possible improvement: Stout and Wagar [StW90] showed how to reduce the number of stages to a minimum, that is, to d. The principle is as follows. The initial message is divided into $\frac{L}{d}$ packets. The number of messages corresponding to the pipelined dispatching of the sub-messages

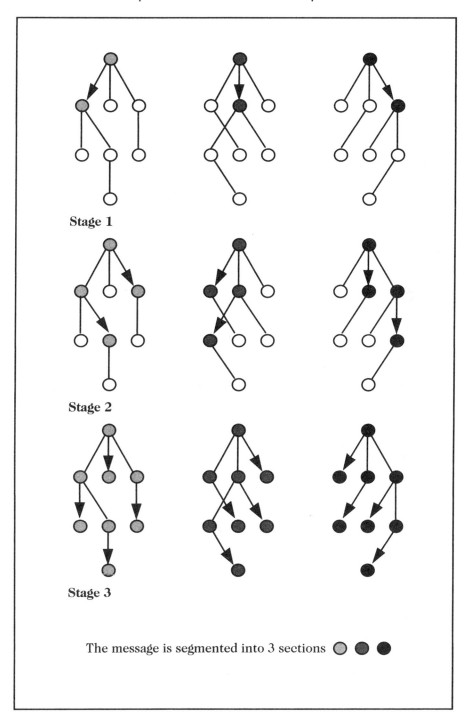

Stage 1

Stage 2

Stage 3

The message is segmented into 3 sections

Figure 15.19   The principle of rotative broadcasting on a 3-cube

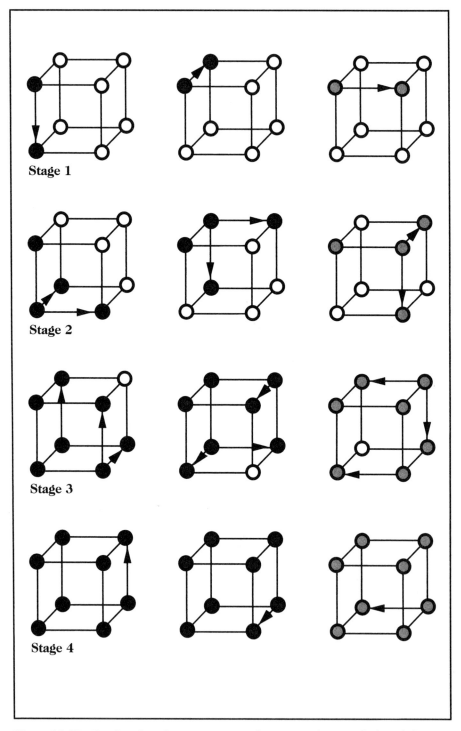

Figure 15.20   Pipeline broadcasting on several trees simultaneously (3-cube)

along each of the d trees with disjoint arcs and (d+1) in depth is easy to determine: there are

$$q_{opt}\left(\frac{L}{d}\right) = \sqrt{\frac{(d-1)L\tau}{d\beta}}$$

stages covering messages

$$\sqrt{\frac{L\beta}{d(d-1)\tau}}$$

in length. The basic idea behind this is to send, as in the previous case, the first

$$q_{opt}\left(\frac{L}{d}\right) - 1$$

packets, immediately followed by a second wave of the last packet of each of the sub-messages sent along the adjusted trees. This allows us to obtain a time equal to

$$\left(\sqrt{(d-1)\beta} + \sqrt{\frac{L}{d}\tau}\right)^2$$

15.4   Total exchange

15.4.1   Theoretical analysis

The lower bound

We can study, as we did earlier, *total exchange*, a communication scheme where each processor on a network of p processors must communicate its own L-sized message to all the others (each having, thus, p messages). To an extent, all the processors are broadcasting.

Property 15.6

For any network of p processors, diameter D and maximum degree Δ, a lower bound for the full-exchange time in message-switching mode, under the assumptions of linear time and bi-directional parallel links, is:

$$\max\left(\beta D, \tau L\left\lceil\frac{p-1}{\Delta}\right\rceil\right)$$

Proof

The lower bound to the communication time for total exchange is obtained by noting that each node must necessarily receive $(p-1)L$ messages. The minimum propagation time per processor assuming an ideal situation where all the links can be used in parallel, is therefore:

$$\tau L\left\lceil\frac{p-1}{\Delta}\right\rceil$$

Moreover, at least D stages are necessary to perform the total exchange. From this we can deduce the previous lower bound.

The reader will note that for any scheme it is not generally possible to hold the two arguments concurrently and thus to obtain a lower bound equal to the sum (an example of this is given in [Rum92]). However, without being able to prove this, we assume that the lower bound of total exchange for a regular network is equal to:

$$\beta D + \tau L\left\lceil\frac{p-1}{\Delta}\right\rceil$$

In the case of total exchange, all the processors must send their own message and receive $(p-1)$ messages.

Let us quickly examine total exchange in circuit switching mode: it is possible to simulate message switching mode with circuit switching mode for exchanges at a distance of 1. Since pipelining is impossible for total exchange, any algorithm in message switching mode can be directly transposed into circuit switching mode.

A general principle

We will be using a similar general principle in all the total exchange algorithms: all the processors do the same thing at each stage. This allows us, in part, to consider the algorithm in a single processor (sending and receiving), making sure, of course, that there are no conflicting conditions.

We now examine total exchange on the main networks in message switching mode.

15.4.2   Total exchange on a ring

Let us consider a ring of p processors in message switching mode (we assume, in addition, that p is an odd number and the processors are indexed from $-\lfloor\frac{p}{2}\rfloor$ to $+\lfloor\frac{p}{2}\rfloor$). The communication algorithm is the same as for a simple broadcast. However, here we cannot split the message up and pipeline the dispatches (in fact, it is necessary that at any given communication stage, there are no conflicting conditions on the links).

Following the principle above, we present the algorithm executed by processor 0; the other processors execute equivalent algorithms. The algorithm involves sending to the two neighbouring processors the most recently received message in the same direction (and thus, as a corollary, to receive a message from each of the two neighbours). Figure 15.21 schematizes the successive communication stages (the numbers associated with each processor correspond to the message sent and received).
The algorithm is as follows:

```
for all the processors
        send its message to two neighbours
        receive the message from the right-hand neighbour and
        from the left-hand neighbour
        for i ← 2 until ⌊p/2⌋ do in parallel
                send the message received at stage (i-1)
                from the left to the right-hand neighbour
                send the message received at stage (i-1)
                from the right to the left-hand neighbour
                receive the messages from the right- and
                left-hand neighbours
```

Proposition 15.6
    With the previous assumptions, the total exchange scheme is optimal. Its running time is:

$$\beta \left\lfloor \frac{p}{2} \right\rfloor + \tau L \left\lceil \frac{p-1}{2} \right\rceil$$

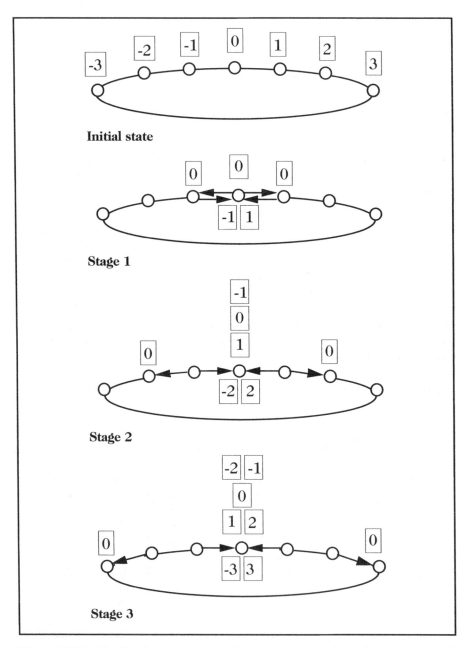

Figure 15.21   Total exchange on a ring of seven processors (seen from processor 0)

Proof

It is easy to show that the lower bound on a ring, a 2-degree regular network, is the predicted value. The running time of the previous algorithm corresponds to $\lfloor\frac{p}{2}\rfloor$ elementary stages of the complete L-sized message, which gives $\lfloor\frac{p}{2}\rfloor(\beta+L\tau)$, which is equal to the proposition's formula.

15.4.3   Total exchange on a toric grid

An initial method

We present an initial method which is a generalization of total exchange on a ring. It involves two successive phases of total exchange on rings. Once again, we are applying the principle that all the processors are doing the same thing at each stage. For simplicity, let us consider a square toric grid ($\sqrt{p}$, $\sqrt{p}$) where $\sqrt{p}$ is an integer.

The first phase involves completely exchanging half of the message on the horizontal ring and the other half on the vertical ring simultaneously. At the close of this stage, each processor knows all the messages in the column (or row) to which it belongs. So that each one receives the others' messages, it is then sufficient to exchange completely all the messages in its row, which gives $\sqrt{p}L/2$ (or all the messages in its column). Figure 15.22 illustrates this algorithm, starting from the processor in the centre of the toric grid; all the other processors do likewise. The movements concerning the two halves of the messages are represented in black and grey.

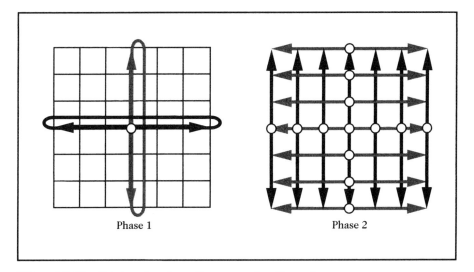

Phase 1   Phase 2

Figure 15.22   Total exchange on the successive dimensions

Proposition 15.7

The execution time of the previous total exchange algorithm on a toric grid is equal to

$$
2 \left\lfloor \frac{\sqrt{p}}{2} \right\rfloor \beta + \left\lfloor \frac{\sqrt{p}}{2} \right\rfloor \frac{\left(\left(\sqrt{p} + 1 \right) \right)}{2} L\tau
$$

Proof

This running time is the sum of how long each of the two phases lasts:

(1) the total exchange of L/2 messages on the vertical and horizontal rings sized $\sqrt{p}$ gives:

$$
\left\lfloor \frac{\sqrt{p}}{2} \right\rfloor \left(\beta + \frac{L}{2}\tau \right)
$$

(2) the total exchange of $\sqrt{p}L/2$ messages on the $\sqrt{p}$ horizontal and vertical rings sized $\sqrt{p}$ gives:

$$
\left\lfloor \frac{\sqrt{p}}{2} \right\rfloor \left(\beta + \sqrt{p}\frac{L}{2}\tau \right)
$$

In total, we obtain the forecast running time:

$$
\left\lfloor \frac{\sqrt{p}}{2} \right\rfloor \left(2\beta + (\sqrt{p} + 1)\frac{L}{2}\tau \right)
$$

The reader will note that implementing this algorithm is fairly complicated, requiring a substantial storage facility. There is another very simple solution which does not require any intermediate storage and which is equivalent for large messages, but it involves a longer initialization period [PIT92].

Another solution for large messages

This total exchange algorithm is based on a family of spanning trees with disjoint arcs, such that superposition of these trees on all the nodes at a given instant will cause no conflicts on the links. This condition is very restrictive and requires the use of p octopuses (Hamiltonian paths in each sub-domain) whose superposition must formally be without conflicting conditions (Section 4.3.2).

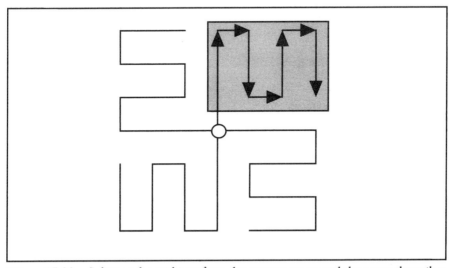

Figure 15.23   Splitting the grid into four elementary zones and the route through a zone

At each stage, each processor sends its whole message in all four directions and receives four messages (Figure 15.23). The only thing that needs to be known is how to describe the paths in each of the four zones of

$$\left\lceil \frac{p-1}{4} \right\rceil$$

processors (identical, close to a rotation), by means of a Hamiltonian path. The execution time is easy to calculate. There are

$$\left\lceil \frac{p-1}{4} \right\rceil$$

stages for L-sized messages. Thus, in total:

$$\left\lceil \frac{p-1}{4} \right\rceil (\beta + L\tau)$$

15.4.4   Total exchange on a hypercube

A simple initial solution

Consider a d-degree hypercube of p processors. As Figure 15.24 shows, a simple algorithm is based on a two-by-two exchange of the whole message known at a given moment, successively in each direction. The running time is easy to calculate: there are d stages and stage i is concerned with 2^{i-1} L-sized messages, which gives:

$$d\beta + \sum_{i=1}^{d} 2^{i-1}L\tau = d\beta + (p-1)L\tau$$

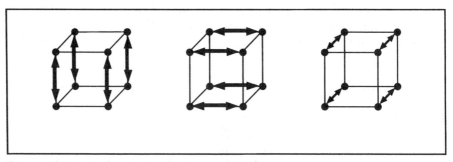

Figure 15.24   Exchanges two by two on a 3-cube

A better algorithm

This result can be improved when we consider splitting all the messages into d packets and using all the directions simultaneously. The reader will note that this algorithm requires extensive buffering and that implementing it locally is a delicate operation.

The running time then becomes:

$$d\beta + \sum_{i=1}^{d} 2^{i-1}\frac{L}{d}\tau = d\beta + \frac{(p-1)L}{d}\tau$$

This algorithm has the minimum number of stages (equal to the diameter of the hypercube) and a minimum transmission rate (p–1 processors must receive an L-sized message via d links, at best). As all the links are working all the time, the problem of optimality arises.

15.5   Distribution

Recall the problem of distribution. A processor has a message composed of (p–1) packets and wishes to send a different packet to each processor. All the packets are assumed to be of an identical size. Let us explain the known solutions for all the main topologies. They all follow the general principle of first sending the messages destined for the most remote processors. The model here is still a network of p processors linked by parallel bidirectional links, with a linear communication time between neighbouring processors.

15.5.1   Distribution on a ring

There is an optimality theorem for distribution on a ring in message switching mode which is fairly difficult to demonstrate [FMR90]. The algorithm that produces the minimum running time is the most 'natural'; it is described in Figure 15.25.

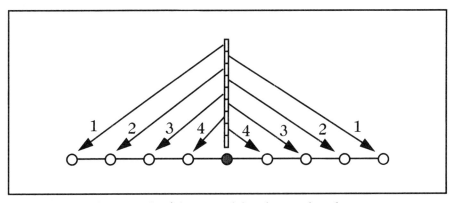

Figure 15.25   The principle of the optimal distribution algorithm on a ring

Let us assume that the data items are located on processor P_0. The processors are located by means of their index i using $-(p-1)/2 \leq i \leq (p+1)/2$ (where p is an odd number for simplicity's sake). The message to be sent to processor P_i is denoted as x_i; it is sized L. The program for processor P_i is given below for i>0. The program is similar for processors negatively indexed.

```
for k ← (p-1)/2 to i+1 by steps of -1
        receive (xk) on the left-hand link and send (xk)
        on the right-hand link
receive (xi) on the left-hand link and store on
the processor
```

Note that all the processors receive the message destined for them at the same time. Computing the algorithm's running time is done immediately. The algorithm corresponds to $(p-1)/2$ stages of communicating L-sized data items. This gives:

$$\left\lfloor \frac{p}{2} \right\rfloor (\beta + L\tau)$$

15.5.2   Distribution on a toric grid

We now consider distribution on a square toric grid of p processors. We assume, without loss of generality, that the source processor is in the centre. As the previous algorithm showed, there is a great similarity between distribution and total exchange. The algorithm illustrated in Figures 15.26 and 15.27 is inspired to a great extent by the results of total exchange on a toric grid. The concept is of a distribution in two phases using rings. In Figures 15.26 and 15.27, the numbers on the arcs indicate the stages.

Proposition 15.8
  The execution time of a distribution algorithm on a toric grid is equal to:

$$2 \left\lfloor \frac{\sqrt{p}}{2} \right\rfloor \beta + \left\lfloor \frac{\sqrt{p}}{2} \right\rfloor (\sqrt{p} + 1) L\tau$$

Proof
  This running time is the sum of the two phases:

(1) the distribution of $\sqrt{p}$ L-sized messages on the vertical and horizontal rings of size $\sqrt{p}$, which, according to Section 15.5.1, gives:

$$\left\lfloor \frac{\sqrt{p}}{2} \right\rfloor (\beta + \sqrt{p}L\tau)$$

(2) the distribution of L-sized messages on $(\sqrt{p}-1)$ horizontal and vertical rings of size $\sqrt{p}$, which gives:

$$\left\lfloor \frac{\sqrt{p}}{2} \right\rfloor (\beta + L\tau)$$

In total, we obtain the forecast time:

$$2\left\lfloor \frac{\sqrt{p}}{2} \right\rfloor \beta + \left\lfloor \frac{\sqrt{p}}{2} \right\rfloor (\sqrt{p} + 1)L\tau$$

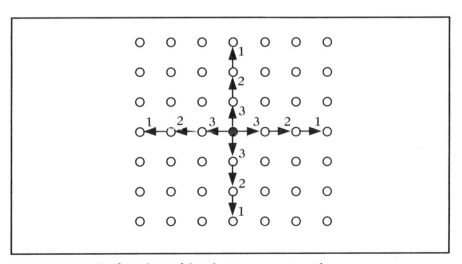

Figure 15.26   The first phase of distribution on a toric grid

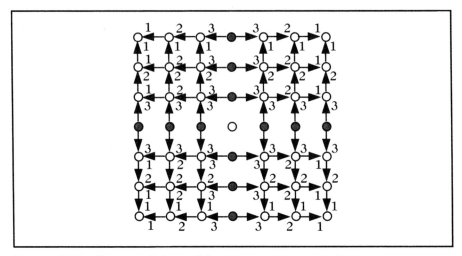

Figure 15.27   The second phase of distribution on a toric grid

15.5.3   Distribution on a hypercube

Like total exchange, the distribution algorithm on a hypercube can be easily described using all the dimensions successively [FrL91]. We suggest another strategy based on the balanced spanning trees introduced in Section 4.3.1. The algorithm involves sending along each branch the messages destined for the most remote processor first [HoJ89]. Here, the whole problem is to sort out the messages in dispatch order beforehand (C_d^{i-1}/d L-sized messages are sent at stage i in each of the d sub-trees).

There are d stages and the running time is easily calculated:

$$d\beta + \sum_{i=1}^{d} \frac{C_d^{i-1}}{d} L\tau = d\beta + \frac{p-1}{d} L\tau$$

We should mention that Stout and Wagar suggested an improvement to this algorithm [StW90]. The basic idea is to send the message destined for a particular processor by means of the strategy proposed in Section 15.2, considering the smallest sub-cube which contains this vertex and the source processor. We do not describe this fairly technical strategy here, which allows us to obtain the following result:

$$\frac{d}{\log_2(d)}\beta + \frac{p-1}{d}L\tau$$

This result demonstrates that the lower bound of a communication scheme is difficult to calculate and, in part, that superposing the two criteria, namely the minimum initialization time and the maximum bandwidth, is not enough to decide upon a lower bound in the case of distribution. For total exchange, this limit is doubtless reached, but, as yet, no one has demonstrated it!

15.5.4   Variations on distribution

Multi-distribution

The problem of multi-distribution corresponds to a distribution of messages from all the processors. This scheme can be viewed as a personalized total exchange. In the case of a hypercube in message switching mode, still within a model of linear time and parallel bidirectional links, Ho and Johnsson show how to use rotative binomial trees (such as those presented in Section 4.3.1) in order to carry out simultaneous distributions without the messages colliding [HoJ89]. On a hypercube of degree n, their algorithm takes n stages (the minimum possible) with a transmission rate in $2^{n-1}L\tau$.

Another elegant solution was suggested by Edelman [Ede91], still within the context of a hypercube with a model of communication between neighbouring processors proportional to the message length (thus, where the initialization parameter β is ignored). The contrast is based on relations between bits in the coding of the vertices. The advantage of this method is that the algorithm is obtained without buffering; the running time is $2^{n-1}L\tau$.

Clustering or merging

Clustering is the opposite of distribution. We begin with messages distributed across the network and want to bring them onto one processor. The algorithms which we have developed can be directly transposed in this instance. Note, however, that clustering is frequently used with intermediate computations on each message, for example in the case of computing the sum or the maximum of the components of a distributed vector. This more specific problem, which combines communications with computation, will be addressed in Chapters 16 and 17.

15.6   Routing permutations

15.6.1   Preliminaries

Description of the general context

In this last section, we tackle the problems of more general data exchanges than those we have just described. We are still in a static context, where the movement of data is known in advance (the *off-line hypothesis*). To be more precise, the problem we are dealing with here is that of permutations on a processor network. Data permutations are the basis of many algorithms and their high performance is a factor in efficiency.

Some useful permutations

Let us assume that the data items are distributed equally in the ratio of one per processor (a basic data item or a group of data items). The processors are indexed from 0 to p–1 (we are assuming that the number of processors is a power of 2, and binary code is used $(k_0, k_1, \ldots k_{q-2}, k_{q-1})$ where $k_i \in \{0, 1\}$). The permutation π of p data items is considered (that is, a bijection on $\{0, 1, \ldots, p-2, p-1\}$). Amongst the most useful and well-known permutations are:

- circular shift: $\pi(k) = k+1$ modulo q,

- exchange: $\pi(k) = (k_0, k_1, \ldots, k_i, \ldots, k_{q-1})$,

- transposition: $\pi(k) = \left(k\frac{q}{2} - 1, k\frac{q}{2} - 2, \ldots k_0, k_{q-1}, \ldots, k\frac{q}{2}\right)$,

- inverse binary: $\pi(k) = (k_{q-1}, k_{q-2}, \ldots k_1, k_0)$,

- butterfly permutation: $\pi(k) = (k_{q-1}, k_1, \ldots k_{q-1}, k_0)$,

- perfect shuffle: $\pi(k) = (k_1, k_2, \ldots k_{q-1}, k_0)$.

The communication network is represented by the graph $G = (R, C)$ where the set of vertices R represents the routers and the set of arcs C represents the communication channels between the routers (which can be divided more precisely into input and output channels). Each communication channel possesses a few local registers for storing messages. Implementation is mostly based on a routing function [Sys92] defined in the following manner:

$r: R \times C \rightarrow R$ such that $r(c, d) = c'$

It associates a destination channel with each pair, where the pair is composed of a routing device (channel c) and a route to take (destination d).

The dependence graph associated with the routing function r is defined as a graph $D_{G,\,r}$ whose vertices are the channels of the communication network G and whose set of arcs is defined by:

$$\{(c,\,c') \in C \times C \,/\, \exists v \in R,\, c' = r(c,\,v)\}$$

Deadlock and virtual channels

As we have seen, we basically distinguish between routing modes in message switching and circuit switching modes. In the first mode, messages are transferred from one processor to another, and the exclusive use of each arc on the network must be guaranteed in order to transmit a message without conflicting conditions. The routing of permutations is *a priori* more complicated in the second mode. An arc is not available until the whole route on which it lies is released.

In these two cases, the system can become blocked when waiting for a resource (either a register or a communication channel), in which case we say there is *deadlock*. The problem is fundamental and several general solutions have been proposed to get around it. We can distinguish between methods that have a preventive approach and those that have a curative approach. In this chapter, we only consider static preventive methods. One of the most interesting solutions for avoiding deadlock in circuit switching mode involves using virtual channels [BeS92] [DaS87] [Dua91] [Lei91]. This method is based on the observation that deadlock occurs when there is a cyclic dependency in the registers of certain channels. To be more precise, there is the following theorem [DaS87]:

Theorem 15.1
> The routing function r associated with network G is non-blocking if and only if the dependence graph $D_{G,\,r}$ is cycle-free.

Introducing *virtual channels* enables the deadlock to be lifted. The key idea involves dividing the communication network's physical links into several virtual channels, so as to allocate supplementary resources. In the case of the grid, for example, where it is easy to notice that there might be deadlock, it is sufficient to replace each link with two virtual channels and label the channels according to their dimensions.

We will describe a general solution to the problem of routing permutations in the two communication modes (message switching and circuit switching) on two particular topologies (the grid and the hypercube). For all the algorithms, we assume that the messages to be routed are the same size on all the processors.

15.6.2   Permutations on a grid in message switching mode

The principle

Before describing the algorithm on a grid, let us consider routing on a linear network for which there is a simple optimality result.

Theorem 15.2
> Every permutation can be performed on a linear network of n processors in n stages without buffering (that is, with only one message per processor).

Consider a rectangular grid of l rows and c columns. The first thing that comes to mind for extending the result of the linear network to grids (which are the Cartesian products of linear networks) is to use first one dimension (for example, along the columns), and then the other (along the rows). It is easily seen that this algorithm can lead to deadlock, as Figure 15.28 shows.

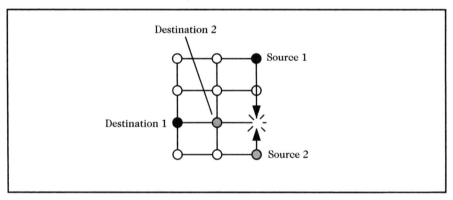

Figure 15.28   An example of deadlock for a routing algorithm by dimensions (columns/rows)

However, there is a possible solution, which avoids deadlock; it proceeds in three phases, adding a preliminary phase of positioning the messages. These results are taken from [BaA91] [Del92] [Lei91]. To illustrate this algorithm, consider the routing permutation in Figure 15.29 where the processors are indexed by their Cartesian coordinates. The destination (i, j) is indicated on each processor.

Phase 1
> The messages are permuted along the columns (or, equivalently, along the rows) so that each message on a given row is destined for a different column.
>
> This phase is the most delicate. Good permutations are sought in order that the other two phases can be performed without deadlock. It hinges on the clever numbering of the arcs, so that two arcs incident to two similar vertices are assigned two different numbers. Routing

can then take place without conflicting conditions on each of the two dimensions. The condition is in fact a perfect coupling condition [Lei91] (Figure 15.30).

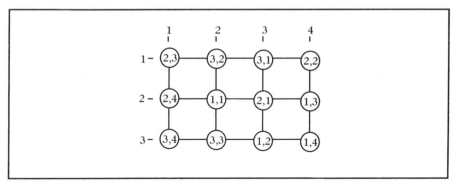

Figure 15.29 Permutations to be performed on a 3×4 grid

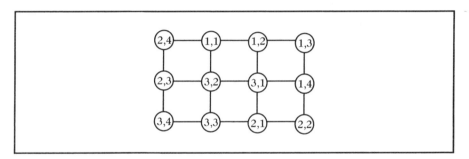

Figure 15.30 The positioning of the columns after the first phase

Phase 2

Routing is performed in parallel on the rows for each of the messages that have just been positioned so that they can be conveyed to their destination columns (Figure 15.31).

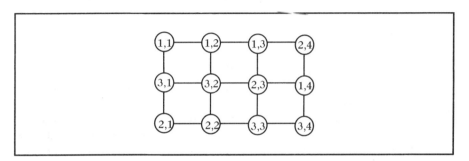

Figure 15.31 Permutations along the rows after the second phase

Phase 3

Finally, the routing of each message on the columns is performed to convey it to its destination row (Figure 15.32).

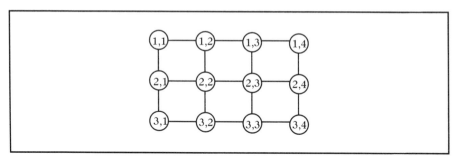

Figure 15.32   Permutations along the columns after the third phase

Evaluation of the running time

Given Theorem 15.2, the number of elementary exchange stages is equal to 1 for stages 1 and 3 and to c for phase 2. Thus, in the case of a square grid of p processors, a total of $3\sqrt{p}$ stages is produced. Note that this algorithm extends to cases of toric grids with execution times of

$$\frac{3}{2}\sqrt{p}$$

(any permutation of n/2 can be routed on a ring of processors).

We should note that this result was improved by Krizanc [Kri91]. He suggests modifying it by sub-dividing the grid into two equal parts and routing in each part by means of the previous algorithm. It allows the routing of any permutation of

$$\frac{5}{2}\sqrt{p}$$

elementary exchange stages on a square toric grid of p processors with two intermediate data items per processor at most.

15.6.3   Permutations on a hypercube

Szymanski [Szy89] conceived of a very efficient heuristic in the case of circuit switching mode. However, it does not allow all permutations to be carried out along the shortest routes (as a counter-example on a 5-degree hypercube given by Lubiw [Lub90] shows).

Permutations can be classified into different sets. In particular, *complemented linear permutations* represent most of the permutations found in numerical computations (different storage strategies for matrices, fast Fourier transforms, and so on). This class is characterized by the following property: the bits that contain the address of the message's destination processor are a combination of the bits referring to the addresses of the source processors. The messages contain a header with the address of the destination processor, followed by the message itself. They are all the same length.

The routing algorithm which we describe below roughly involves successively changing the dimensions of the hypercube in a fixed order. It avoids deadlock and performs an optimal routing (which requires at most n stages on an n-degree hypercube) [BoR90].

Before giving the algorithm in detail, we must state a property on which its validity depends. That is that the hypercube can only be in two states: (A) in which all the processors only have one message to route; (B) in which half have two messages and the other half have none. The number of messages in any given processor can vary during the routing process. This property ensures that only states (A) and (B) can occur during the running of the algorithm.

```
for q ← 1 to n
    if the hypercube is in state (A) then
            each processor routes its message in order to
            correct the weak bit in the header not yet
            corrected at the earlier stages
    if the hypercube is in state (B) then
            the processors that possess two messages
            compare the headers and route the one that
            differs from the processor's address by
            more than one bit; the weak bit is used
            for routing
```

We should note that this routing algorithm does not use the parallelism feature on the links. Moreover, the 'by dimensions' algorithm functions in message switching mode, where each pair of adjacent processors communicate once and only once. Each message moves towards its destination dimension by dimension and is stored at each stage. This principle can easily be extended to circuit switching mode. It is sufficient to note that the algorithm never reuses a dimension that has already been used (and therefore a link). A complete route can therefore be constructed without conflicting conditions, a route which is comprised of only different dimensions.

15.6.4   The special problem of transposition

General discussion

Consider a matrix A of dimensions (n, n) partitioned into equal square blocks of dimensions ($\frac{n}{\sqrt{p}}$, $\frac{n}{\sqrt{p}}$), each associated with a particular processor.

The problem of transposition is defined as follows: the processor initially loaded with element $A_{i,j}$ (alloc(i, j) according to the notation in Chapter 14) must receive element $A_{j,i}$. If dividing the elements in the matrix into rows and columns is considered, this communication scheme corresponds to a personalized total exchange (or multi-distribution) which we have just studied in Figure 15.5. As we will see, partitioning into blocks enables us to obtain distinctly shorter running times. Here, we are studying transposition on grid and hypercube networks in message switching with parallel links communication mode. The interested reader may refer to [CaT93] for more details, in particular for transposition on De Bruijn networks.

Transposition on a toric grid

Let us first consider a grid network and an allocation function that maps the blocks from the matrix onto the most natural processors, that is, the function that corresponds to the Cartesian coordinates. The principle of transposition is illustrated in Figure 15.33: the blocks to be exchanged circulate horizontally, then vertically along one of the shortest paths that connect processors alloc(i, j) to alloc(j, i) (and similarly, symmetrically for those that connect processors alloc(j, i) to alloc(i, j)).

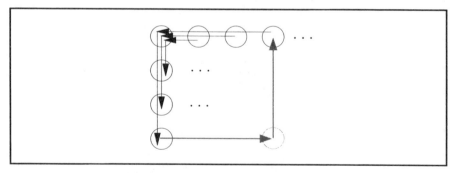

Figure 15.33   The principle of transposition on a grid

Note, first of all, that the diagonal blocks are in place. At every other stage, a new wave of blocks arrive at their destination. Figures 15.34, 15.35, 15.36 and 15.37 show the first stages on a 6 × 6 grid in detail (the processors receiving their blocks are shown in grey).

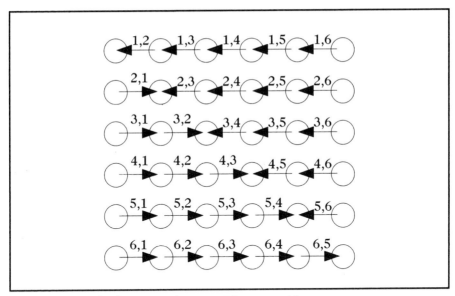

Figure 15.34   The first stage of transposition on a grid

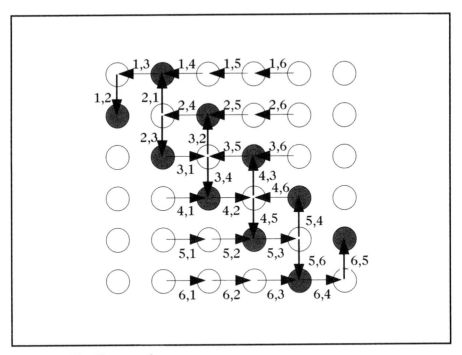

Figure 15.35   The second stage

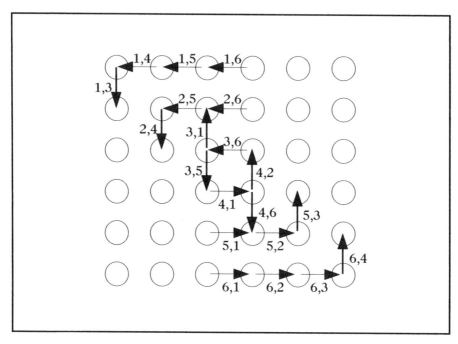

Figure 15.36   The third stage

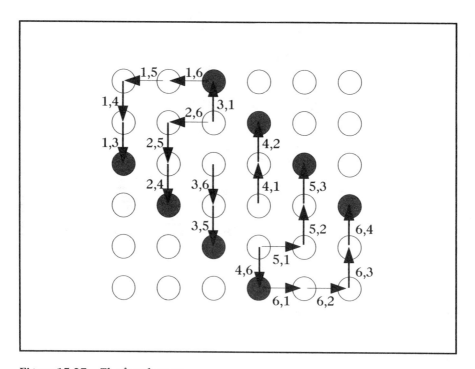

Figure 15.37   The fourth stage

Let us now evaluate this algorithm's running time. One stage corresponds to dispatching a block to a neighbouring processor, which gives

$$\left(\beta + \frac{n^2}{p}\tau\right)$$

Moreover, the algorithm requires a number of stages equal to the diameter of the square grid, which gives $2(\sqrt{p}-1)$. Thus, we obtain in total:

$$2(\sqrt{p}-1)\left(\beta + \frac{n^2}{p}\tau\right)$$

Adaptation to a toric grid is a little trickier. The same idea of dispatching along the shortest routes is used. The principle is described in Figure 15.38, where we can distinguish two zones for dispatching block (i, j) on processor alloc(j, i) for i≤j (in the opposite instance, the symmetrical path, which is represented in the diagram, is taken).

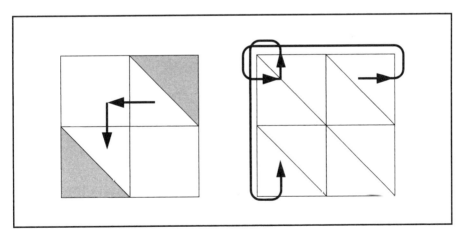

Figure 15.38   The principle of transposition on a toric grid

Transposition on a hypercube

In this section, we assume that p is an even power of 2 and write $q=\log_2(p)$, so q is even. We consider a network whose topology is a hypercube of degree q. The principle of transposition we are considering here is recursive

[JoH91]. From a matrix point of view, first, all the elementary sub-matrices are transposed, then the diagonal blocks of the sub-matrices, and so on, as shown in Figure 15.38.

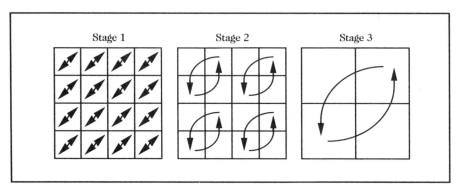

Figure 15.38a   The recursive transposition of an 8 × 8 matrix

The journey on a hypercube network is simple. Let us assume that the directions are written as d_i for i=0,..., q–1. We saw in Chapter 4 that the toric grid, whose dimensions are a power of 2, is a partial graph of the hypercube. Thus, the (natural) mapping of the blocks being considered is alloc(i, j) = $(i–1)_2|(j–1)_2$ (the chaining of the binary codes of the row and column indices). It is illustrated in Figure 15.39 where the diagonal blocks are shown in bold.

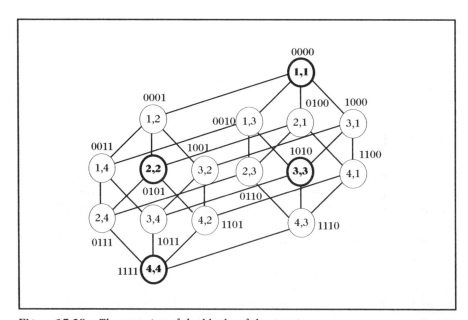

Figure 15.39   The mapping of the blocks of the matrix

The first stage of the recursive transposition amounts to associating as follows, for all the odd indices in row i:

$$alloc(i, j) \rightarrow alloc(i+1, j-1) \; \forall j \text{ even}$$

---

that is:

$$(i_0 i_1 \ldots i_{\frac{q}{2}-2} \, 0) | (j_0 j_1 \ldots j_{\frac{q}{2}-2} \, 1)$$
$$\downarrow +1 \qquad\qquad\qquad \downarrow -1$$
$$(i_0 i_1 \ldots i_{\frac{q}{2}-2} \, 1) | (j_0 j_1 \ldots j_{\frac{q}{2}-2} \, 0)$$

This transformation affects only the last bits in the coding of i and j, so the communication is made in the directions with indices $q/2-1$ and $q-1$. It is easily proved that this holds analogously for the successive stages: stage k in which $alloc(i, j)$ is sent to $alloc(i+2^{k-1}, j-2^{k-1})$ corresponds to communication in the directions $q/2-k$ and $q-k$.

The running time of this algorithm is easy to calculate. There are $\log_2(\sqrt{p})$ stages and each stage requires two elementary communications (dispatching blocks between neighbouring processors), which gives in total:

$$\log_2(p)\left(\beta + \frac{n^2}{p}\tau\right)$$

15.7   Conclusion

In this chapter we have given the basic algorithms for communication and routing on processor networks. This has enabled us to suggest a simple methodology for designing a parallel algorithm in which an algorithm is a synchronous sequence of computing phases, each followed by a communication phase. The communication can be local or global and use either message switching or circuit switching mode.

For such algorithms, reducing the volume of communications is an important factor in achieving good performance. For certain classes of algorithm the possibility could arise of simultaneous computation and communication: this is only a recent possibility, because it is only since the early 1990s that parallel computers have appeared that are equipped with communications hardware that takes this load off the processor. This simultaneous execution of the two phases is referred to as overlapping computation and communication, and is transparent to the user. We study parallelization of algorithms in Chapters 16 and 17, where we compare computing and communication.

16

Basic procedures on processor networks

In this chapter, we analyse some parallelizations of fundamental procedures on processor networks: distributed computation on vectors, matrix-vector multiplication and matrix multiplication. We end by analysing sorting procedures (odd-even sorting on a ring and bitonic sorting on a hypercube).

16.1 Designing algorithms on processor networks

In this chapter, we examine parallelization of certain basic algorithms (simple manipulations of vectors, matrix-vector multiplication, matrix multiplication and sorting processes) on processor networks that use message passing. The approach that we have adopted here takes into account the fact that data

435

transfers between processors are not negligible compared with computation time. The unit of time is taken as being equal to the time required to read the data, transform it and write the new values. Our aim is not to conduct a quantitative analysis on the results of several algorithms on particular machines, but rather to show the qualitative influence that the architecture, especially interprocessor connections, has on the complexity of parallel algorithms. It is only rarely that complexity results can be obtained, and in general, only for simplified models.

16.1.1   A brief reminder of the motivation for processor networks

From shared-memory computers...

In the parallel machine models developed in the 1980s, the basic architecture consists of a large main memory shared by several processors. Its architectural problems essentially arise from problems in accessing this memory. In order to improve the flow of data from memory to processors, a number of solutions have been proposed: sharing several memory banks, establishing a memory hierarchy by introducing caches, greater use of 'pipeline' operators, designing high-performance interconnection networks, and so on. There are several supercomputers that use all of these solutions to some extent. Software tools aim to enable an optimal, or at least an efficient, management of parallelism, guaranteeing the integrity of data in main memory. Since processors are identical, the method for designing parallel algorithms is essentially based on the scheduling techniques we examined in Chapter 10.

...to processor networks

The problems of accessing a shared memory limit the number of processors. Beyond a few tens of processors, interconnection network performances deteriorate. In order to obtain massively parallel machines, we have to turn to architectures where memory is decentralized and connections limited; each processor has a local rapid access memory and is connected to only a certain number of neighbouring processors. The basic principles behind this kind of architecture are not new [HwB84]. Numerous prototypes have been produced and systolic networks are directly based on them. By contrast, it was not until the early 1990s that the first supercomputers based on this principle appeared. Programming on them is still difficult and, except for systolic algorithms (and even then, only in simple cases [QuR89]), there is no systematic methodology for designing parallel algorithms.

In shared-memory architectures, processors work by sharing the data stored in main memory. Each processor reads the data that it needs from memory, processes it and then writes the results to memory. In processor networks, processors work by exchanging messages. Each processor reads the data that it needs from other processors on one or more communication channels, processes it and then transfers the results to the processors that require them. The time taken to execute by a series of tasks does not just depend on the execution time of each task, but also on the position within the network of the processor executing the task. Just as a sequential algorithm leads to several parallel variants on a shared-memory architecture, there are several possible parallel variants of the same algorithm on a processor network.

16.1.2   The systolic model

The systolic model originated with Kung and Leiserson [KuL78] in 1978. In view of the significant development of integrated circuits at the time, they proposed a new type of massively parallel architecture, with distributed control and local communications and functioning synchronously. The term *systolic* stems from an analogy with the human heart. The systole is the phase in which blood is pumped around the body. In a systolic network, the data is sent across the network at a regular rate. Systolic algorithms are referred to in relation to a given network.

Note that this model leads to applications that can actually be used [QuR89]. But it fell out of favour in the late 1980s. However, theories on the design of systolic algorithms can be of great use with massively parallel SIMD machines.

16.1.3   Designing parallel numerical algorithms

Some general principles

Parallelism that involves the decomposition of a program according to its data is often natural in numerical analysis and more especially in linear algebra, with the manipulation of vectors and matrices. Thus, in order to parallelize a numerical problem, the most standard procedure is first to identify a decomposition of the data (which means computations are performed locally), then to distribute these data items to the network's processors and, finally, to implement communications between the different computation stages (in general, if data is assigned fairly regularly, data transfers will be structured and similar to those we examined in Chapter 15).

The processor network model

The processor network model that we assume below is of the type referred to in Chapter 4, where p processors are interconnected by a given topology (ring, mesh, hypercube, De Bruijn network, and so on). The network is connected to a host computer by a particular processor on which all the input/output operations are performed (*see* Figure 16.1). The communications between neighbouring processors are parallel and bidirectional: they are based on the linear time model described in Section 15.1.2.

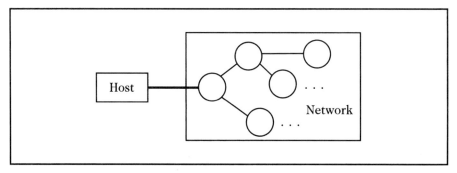

Figure 16.1   A general model of a processor network

16.1.4   Data scattering

Motivation

One of the most basic questions that arises in the context of distributed machines is how data is to be mapped.

Here, we are concerned with structured data, and particularly with n×n square matrices which are most naturally assigned using two methods: row-oriented (or, similarly, column-oriented) assignment and block assignment. In both cases, dividing data in a balanced fashion means that each processor contains in the order of $\frac{n^2}{p}$ data items, that is $\frac{n}{p}$ rows (or columns), of length n or blocks of $\frac{n^2}{p}$ data items in total. To simplify this description, we will assume that n is divisible by $\sqrt{p}$.

Assume that the processors are indexed from 0 to p–1. As in Chapter 14, data assignment corresponds to the *alloc* application, which assigns an element (a block, row or column) to a processor. Below, we describe the main allocations [MiT90].

Division by points or by blocks

There are several ways of dividing a matrix into blocks. The simplest way is to divide it into p blocks of $\frac{n^2}{p}$ data items, which yields small matrices of dimension

$$\left(\frac{n}{\sqrt{p}}, \frac{n}{\sqrt{p}} \right)$$

if square blocks are considered (which is by no means obligatory). Figure 16.2 represents the case where n=12 and p=4.

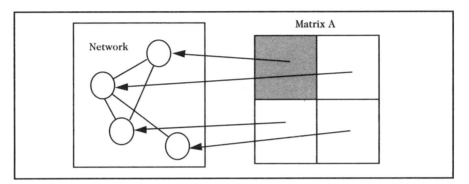

Figure 16.2   Balanced application with the matrix divided into p square blocks

More precisely, several allocation functions are given in the literature, each corresponding to the scanning of the blocks in a particular order. Firstly, as Figure 16.3 illustrates, the elements can be allocated according to the order in which the rows appear (or of course, the order in which the columns appear). The numbers represent the processors' indices. Thus:

$$\text{alloc}(i, j) = (i{-}1)\, \sqrt{p} + j - 1 \quad \text{or} \quad (j{-}1)\, \sqrt{p} + i - 1$$

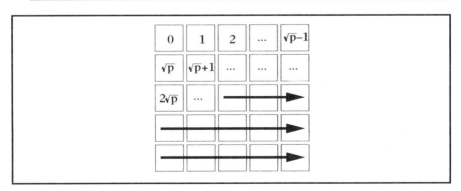

Figure 16.3   Division into consecutive rows

Allocating elements in the order in which they appear can be cyclic (*see* Figure 16.4):

$$\text{alloc}(i, j) = (i-1)\sqrt{p} + j-1 \text{ if i odd}$$
$$= i\sqrt{p} - j \text{ if i even}$$

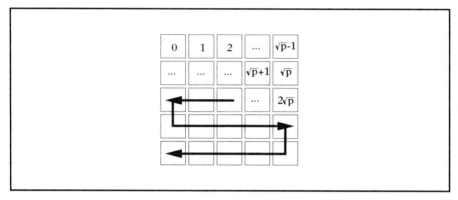

Figure 16.4   Snake configuration division

Recursive allocation is another way of dividing the blocks. At each stage, allocation can be consecutive, in a snake configuration (*see* Figure 16.5), or by proximity (*see* Figure 16.6).

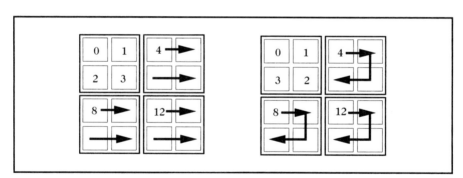

Figure 16.5   Recursive division (consecutive and in snake configuration)

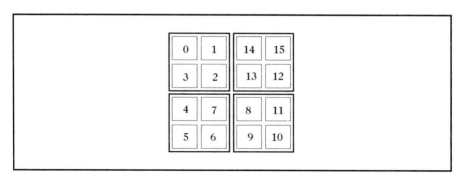

Figure 16.6   Recursive division by proximity

Division by rows or columns

The most natural allocation entails distributing the rows (or columns) as consecutive packets. This allocation, which is shown in Figure 16.7, is such that processor 0 contains rows 1 to $\frac{n}{p}$, processor 1 those from $(\frac{n}{p}+1)$ to $2\frac{n}{p}$, and so on. The allocation function is as follows:

$$\text{alloc(i)} = \left\lfloor \frac{i}{r} \right\rfloor, \text{ where } r = \frac{n}{p}$$

A more sophisticated allocation, illustrated in Figure 16.8, is where each processor has $\frac{n}{p}$ rows, selected at intervals of p; thus, processor 0 has rows 1, 1+p, 1+2p,..., 1+(n–p), processor 1 has rows 2, 2+p, 2+2p, and so on (*see* Figure 16.8). The allocation function is:

$$\text{alloc(i)} = \text{i modulo p} - 1$$

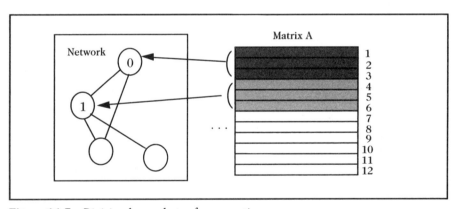

Figure 16.7   Division by packets of consecutive rows

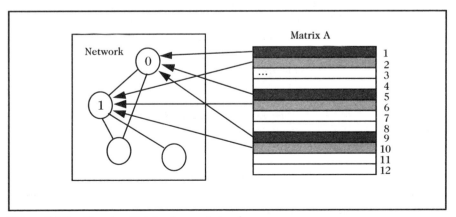

Figure 16.8   Circular division by packets of rows

Note here that division by blocks in one sense constitutes an intermediate solution between consecutive and circular divisions by rows or columns, which are limits if rectangular blocks are considered.

16.2   Distributed computation on vectors

In Chapter 15, we described global communication procedures. Most parallel algorithms require the computation and the communication stages, which can be either distinct or overlapping, to be alternated. In this section, we describe regular manipulations of vectors which combine computation and communications. As we will see later, these procedures are basic to many, more complex algorithms.

16.2.1   Reduction

Definition

The problem of reduction involves computing the scalar variable

$$S = \bigoplus_{i=0}^{n} x_i$$

where the operation $\oplus$ is an addition, a computation of the maximum, a multiplication followed by an addition, a logic operation, and so on. The data is initially either located on a single processor (for example P_0), or distributed in balanced fashion on all the processors (each processor then possesses $\lfloor \frac{n}{p} \rfloor$ or $\lceil \frac{n}{p} \rceil$ components of vector x). The result must be read on a predetermined processor, or broadcast to all the processors.

Implementation on a hypercube

Assume that the complete vector x is on one processor; if this is not the case, the algorithm's first stage becomes redundant. The result is sent to a predetermined processor; if all the processors are required to know it, we need only add a broadcasting stage at the end. The algorithm is as follows:

```
{reduction of vector x - the stages marked  * are optional}
* distribute the components of vector x on the hypercube
for all the processors P_q do in parallel
      for all x[k] on processor P_q do
            sq ← sq⊕x[k]
      combine the partial results sq
* broadcast the result produced
```

Now let's look at the reduction operation in detail. On a hypercube of p processors, it requires $\log_2(p)$ stages, as shown in Figures 16.9 and 16.10. The numbers correspond to the stages of communication between neighbouring processors and, therefore, also to instances of the elementary computation of operation ⊕.

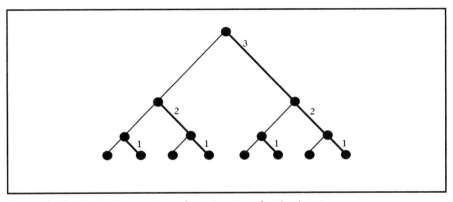

Figure 16.9   Logical execution of a reduction of eight data items

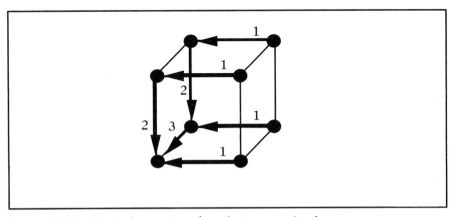

Figure 16.10   Physical execution of a reduction on a 3-cube

16.2.2   Computing partial sums on a hypercube

Computing prefixes on PRAM was presented in Section 5.2.3. Adapting the computation to a HypercubeRAM was studied in Section 5.5.2. In this section, we look at this problem again in detail and focus on communications in the hypercube.

It is assumed that each processor contains data item x_i to begin with. By the end, each processor P_q (the processors are assumed to be indexed from 0 to p–1) is required to know the value:

$$S[q] = \bigoplus_{i=0}^{q} x_i$$

where $\oplus$ is an associative operation.

This computation is useful, for example, for obtaining the elements of a linear recursion of the first order. Assume that the data items have already been allocated in order of their reflected Gray codes. Implementing this algorithm directly on a hypercube is impossible. For some stages there are no physical links. The trick is to use the relations of transitivity to establish impossible links. Figure 16.11 shows how this is done for the initial values of s.

The algorithm which we have just presented consists of $\log_2(p)$ stages (computation layers). Each stage is implemented on each of the hypercube's dimensions in turn. Each processor q uses two data items (the partial sum s[q] and the total sum at this stage $\sigma[q]$). The algorithm [NaS81] is as follows:

```
{Algorithm for computing prefixes: processor Pq}
for d ←  0  to  log(n-1)  do
{d travels across all the dimensions of the hypercube}
    if qd = 1 then   s[q] ← s[q] * σ[q⊕d]
    σ[q] ← σ[q] * σ[q⊕d]
```

Figure 16.12 summarizes the different stages on a 3-cube (the numbers represent the stages).

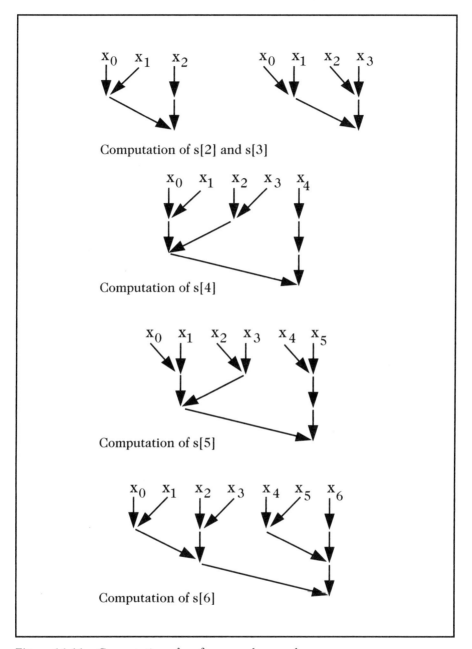

Computation of s[2] and s[3]

Computation of s[4]

Computation of s[5]

Computation of s[6]

Figure 16.11   Computation of prefixes on a hypercube

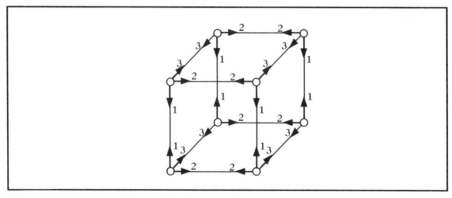

Figure 16.12   Computation of partial sums on a 3-cube

16.2.3   General computation and communication schemes

Dynamic switching between topologies

Here, we address more general schemes of algorithms that combine computation with communication. Generally speaking, different classes of algorithm can be defined according to their execution schemes (for example, reduction can be viewed as a binary tree, standard matrix multiplication as a toric grid). To illustrate this point, let us look at the class of algorithms that can be executed naturally on a hypercube in consecutive stages of elementary computations and message exchanges ('ascend-descend' algorithms, to use the terminology in [Lei91]).

Emulating a hypercube on a ring

Consider an algorithm whose logical structure is a hypercube. Each step taken by the algorithm on the successive dimensions is simulated on a ring. As Figure 16.13 shows, emulating the hypercube is such that the first dimension corresponds to processors that are immediate neighbours on the ring, the second to processors at a distance of 2, the third to those at a distance of 4, and so on.

Readers will realize that the method naturally extends to toric grids. The communication cost on a ring of an algorithm being executed dimension by dimension on a hypercube is:

$$\sum_{i=0}^{\log_2(p)} 2^i = p$$

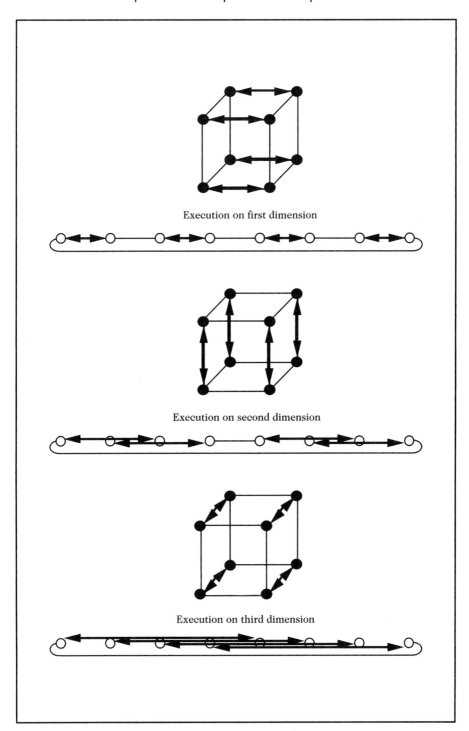

Execution on first dimension

Execution on second dimension

Execution on third dimension

Figure 16.13   Emulation of a hypercube on a ring of processors

16.3   Matrix-vector multiplication

16.3.1   Analysis of the problem

Definition

Let A be a square n×n matrix and x a vector of R^n. The problem that we propose parallelizing in this section is that of computing the product of a matrix by a vector, v=Ax, on different types of parallel machine. A_{ij} refers to the element of matrix A in row i and column j. Recall that the most natural form in which to write the sequential algorithm is as follows:

$$\forall i \in \{1,2,...,n\} v_i = \sum_{j=1}^{n} A_{ij}x_j$$

or, in algorithmic form:

```
for i ← 1 to n
    v(i) ← 0
    for j ← 1 to n
        v(i) ← v(i) + A(i, j)*x(j)
```

Note that there is an additional constraint when the algorithm is parallelized. Matrix-vector multiplication is one of the most frequently used numerical procedures. For example, as we will see in Chapter 17, it is the basis for all the iterative methods of solving linear systems, in which the matrix-vector products have to be chained (still with the same matrix) and then the result vector v allocated on the network in the same way as the vector x.

Dependency between computations

The processor network we are considering consists of p processors. The granularity of such a machine means that each processor has a number of data items of the order $O(n)$. No matter what order the computations are performed in, for every index i, element A_{ij} must encounter X_j. We also want to chain successive matrix-vector products (components with the same indices of x and v must therefore encounter one another).

The two natural allocations of A are the row- and column-oriented allocation (the algorithms for these are examined in Chapter 7 on vectorization).

As in Section 16.1.4, it is assumed that the allocation is balanced, which means that each processor contains $\frac{n}{p}$ rows (or columns) assuming, to simplify description, that n is divisible by p. Now let us examine parallelization of algorithms for the circular allocation of rows (or columns) as packets.

16.3.2   Row-oriented allocation

If A is stored in rows, the way the computations are organized stipulates that the ith component of the result vector v is on the same processor as the ith row of A. And, in this case, the initial allocation of vector x follows that of v. There is a single communication stage which consists of an 'all-to-all exchange' (a scheme studied in Chapter 14 and denoted as ATA, where each processor sends the same message to all the other processors, with the result that all the processors know the whole of vector x, since it has to encounter all the components of the ith row of A) (see Figure 16.14).

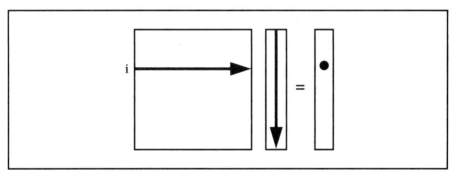

Figure 16.14   Allocating a matrix-vector product by rows

The algorithm is written:

```
ATA on the n/p local components of vector x
for all processors q from 0 to p-1 do in parallel
    for all k ← 1 to n/p do
        v(q+(k-1)p+1) ← scalar product of
        row q+(k-1)p+1 of A and vector x
```

The computational cost is exactly $\frac{n}{p}$ computations of scalar products, each requiring 2n–1 arithmetic operations (counting additions and multiplications as equal). This gives, in total, (2n–1) $\frac{n}{p}\tau_a$ (where τ_a is the basic unit of computation). The cost in terms of communications is that of an all-to-all exchange and depends on the network's topology.

16.3.3   Column-oriented allocation

For the variant in which columns are allocated circularly, the computation stipulates that the jth column of A encounters the jth component of vector x. Each processor, therefore, produces a complete result vector whose components are partial sums (*see* Figure. 16.15). This amounts to performing the following computations on each of the processors:

$$\forall i \in \{1, 2, \ldots, n\} v_i = \sum_{j=1}^{\frac{n}{p}} A_{i,(j-1)p+q+1} x_{(j-1)p+q+1}$$

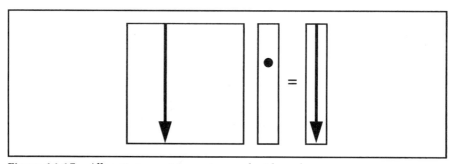

Figure 16.15   Allocating a matrix-vector product by columns

This algorithm uses only one communication stage which consists of a 'total personalized exchange with accumulation', that is, each processor sends a personalized message (of $\frac{n}{p}$ components) to each of the other processors, with all the messages sent to any given processor being added together. The algorithm reduces to:

```
for all processors q ← 0 to p - 1 do in parallel
        for all k ← 1 to n/p do
            v-temporary ← multiplication of column q+(k-1)p of A
            by the component q+(k-1)p +1 of vector x
        personalized-ATA with accumulation of the temporary
        vectors v
```

The computational cost is exactly $\frac{n}{p}$ computations of n multiplications for each component; the cost of adding the partial sums of the whole of vector v has to be added to this, that is, p sums for each of the $\frac{n}{p}$ local components of vector v. Note that the latter cost may, or may not, be added to the communications cost. The communications cost is of the same order as a simple all-to-all exchange on all regular topologies [DTW90].

16.3.4   Allocation by blocks

General presentation

We have just seen how row- and column-oriented assignment of matrix A have approximately the same computational complexity. They also use two communication schemes which have similar costs. We now present an intermediate solution (by blocks) which can be used to reduce the communication cost.

Once again, it is assumed that data is divided equally into blocks, with each processor having only some of the rows and some of the columns (described in Section 16.1.4). Assume, to simplify description, that n is divisible by $\sqrt{p}$. In this variant, there are two types of encounter between data: on the one hand, the components of vector x are partially distributed, so that all the processors have the part that they need (that is, the part corresponding to the sections of the rows that they have); and on the other hand, the computation by each processor of the section of the partial result vector (that corresponds to the sections of the columns of $\frac{n}{p}$ components that it has).

The algorithm is as follows:

```
(Partial) ATA of vector x
for all processors q ← 0 to p - 1 do in parallel
        partial vector v ← matrix-vector product of the block
        by the partial vector x that has just been received
personalized ATA with (partial) accumulation of the
partial vectors v
```

The computational cost of this algorithm corresponds to a matrix-vector product on blocks of $\frac{n}{\sqrt{p}}$ rows by $\frac{n}{\sqrt{p}}$ columns. Local computations thus require

$$\frac{n}{\sqrt{p}}\left(\frac{2n}{\sqrt{p}} - 1\right)$$

arithmetic operations. This is as many computations as in previous cases (obviously, when efficiency is still at 1). By contrast, there are two communication stages. From a logical point of view, this corresponds to a partial ATA exchange and a partial personalized ATA exchange on those parts of the vectors that are of size $\frac{n}{p}$. These two schemes are far less costly than their equivalent global scheme. In order to illustrate the different possible variants for computing the product of a matrix and a vector in parallel, let us look again at the complexity computations of a square toric grid of p processors.

Application to a toric grid

All the variants that we have presented have the same computational complexity; they differ only in terms of communications. Let us discuss the computation in detail.

The first variant (row-oriented allocation) uses an ATA exchange on messages of size $\frac{n}{p}$ for which it is known that the best algorithm on a toric grid is:

$$2\left\lfloor\frac{\sqrt{p}}{2}\right\rfloor\left[\beta+\frac{n}{p}\left\lceil\frac{p-1}{4}\right\rceil\right]\tau = O(n)$$

The second variant (column-oriented allocation) concerns complete vectors with partial values; each processor must know $\frac{n}{p}$ individual components. This variant is of the order $O(n)$, the same as the previous variant.

The third allocation corresponds to the 'by blocks' variant. The partitioning is into p blocks, all of the same dimensions; these are distributed one per processor, following the natural order for mapping on the mesh. The vector itself is also divided into p sections, one per processor (see Figure 16.16).

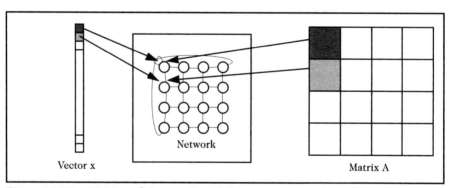

Figure 16.16   Division of the matrix and the vector on a toric grid

There are two communication stages: an ATA exchange, covering vectors of size $\frac{n}{p}$ on the columns, which form a ring of $\sqrt{p}$ processors and thus require a time of

$$\left\lfloor\frac{\sqrt{p}}{2}\right\rfloor\left[\beta+\frac{n}{p}\left\lfloor\frac{\sqrt{p}}{2}\right\rfloor\right]\tau$$

and a personalized ATA exchange with accumulation on the rows for partial vectors of size $\frac{n}{p}$. As each exchange sends one part to $(\sqrt{p}-1)$ others, this corresponds to a length of:

$$\left\lfloor \frac{\sqrt{p}}{2} \right\rfloor \beta + \frac{n}{\sqrt{p}\sqrt{p}} \left\lfloor \frac{\sqrt{p}}{2} \right\rfloor \tau$$

In other words, a total of only $O(\frac{n}{\sqrt{p}})$ compared with $O(n)$ for the other two variants.

This result is general for all processor graphs written as the Cartesian sum of graphs, each of these sub-graphs being assigned to structured subsets of the matrix.

16.3.5   Pipelined allocation

Consider now an asynchronous improvement to the row-oriented variant, based on pipelined exchanges, on a network of p processors connected in a ring and assuming that communication and computation can go on simultaneously. The concept is fairly natural: rather than waiting for the all-to-all exchange to finish, the local computations can be started. Partial scalar products with $\frac{n}{p}$ data items, which each processor has to begin with, are calculated in parallel and their $\frac{n}{p}$ components are communicated to the processor's neighbours. For example, for processor 0, the following is performed:

$$A_{11}x_1 + A_{1,\,p+1}x_{p+1} + A_{1,\,2p+1}x_{2p+1} + \cdots$$
$$A_{p+1,\,1}x_1 + A_{p+1,\,p+1}x_{p+1} + A_{p+1,\,2p+1}x_{2p+1} + \cdots$$

Figures 16.17, 16.18 and 16.19 illustrate the first stages of this algorithm for an 8×8 matrix on a ring with four processors.

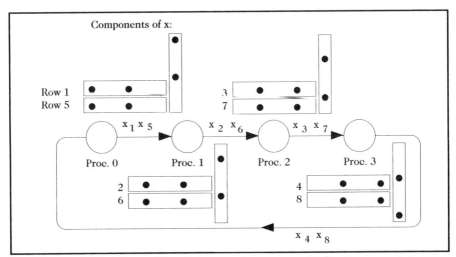

Figure 16.17   First stage of pipelining matrix-vector multiplication on a ring

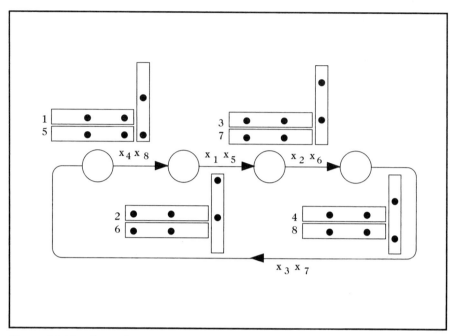

Figure 16.18   Second stage

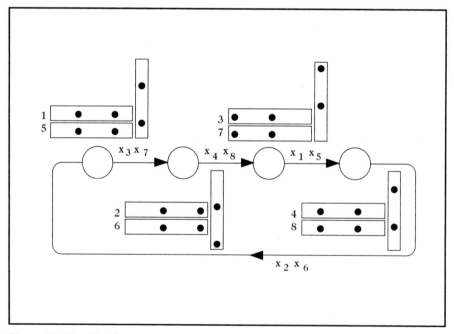

Figure 16.19   Third stage

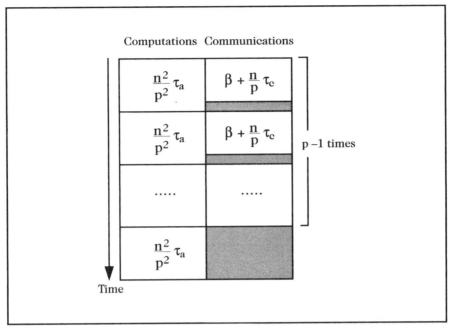

Computations Communications

$\frac{n^2}{p^2} \tau_a$ $\beta + \frac{n}{p} \tau_c$

$\frac{n^2}{p^2} \tau_a$ $\beta + \frac{n}{p} \tau_c$ $p - 1$ times

....

$\frac{n^2}{p^2} \tau_a$

Time

Figure 16.20 Execution scheme for matrix-vector multiplication

At the beginning, each processor performs $\frac{n^2}{p^2}$ elementary computations in parallel ($\frac{n}{p}$ partial scalar products of size $\frac{n}{p}$) and simultaneously passes a message relating to $\frac{n}{p}$ components. If the communication is not very costly, the computation time is dominant and a second series of local computations can be chained without delay, while the data the processor has just received is transmitted to a neighbour. By assuming that store-and-forward message passing applies, using the same notation as above, we obtain the execution scheme described in Figure 16.20. In this solution the communication is completely hidden. The case in which the communication time dominates is rather more tricky to analyse, but the same principle applies.

16.4 Parallel matrix multiplication

16.4.1 Description of the problem

The same processor network as in the above section is considered. The problem we propose to parallelize here involves computing the product C of the two matrices A and B of size nxn; the matrices are square to simplify description. The algorithm can be written as follows (the computations are illustrated in Figure 16.21):

```
for i ← 1 to n
    for j ← 1 to n
        C(i, j) ← 0
        for k ← 1 to n
            C(i, j) ← C(i, j) + A(i, k)*B(k, j)
```

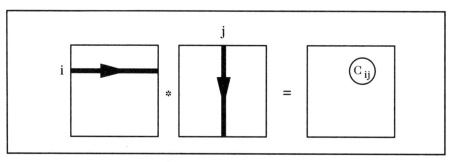

Figure 16.21   Computation of an element of the product A∗B

16.4.2   Parallelization on a toric grid

Method

Assume that the network is a square toric grid of p processors (or a hypercube containing a toric grid). If the dimensions of the matrix are greater than the number of processors on the network, several elements are allocated to each processor (for example, a square $\frac{n}{\sqrt{p}}$ by $\frac{n}{\sqrt{p}}$ block, as above). This is illustrated in Figure 16.22.

A_{11}	A_{12}	...	$A_{1\sqrt{p}}$
A_{21}	A_{22}	...	$A_{2\sqrt{p}}$
		...	
		...	
$A_{\sqrt{p}1}$	$A_{\sqrt{p}2}$	...	$A_{\sqrt{p}\sqrt{p}}$

Figure 16.22   Division of matrix A into p square blocks

In matrix multiplication, the small block C_{ij} in the matrix to be calculated is naturally associated with the processor corresponding to the Cartesian coordinates i and j on the toric grid, which we denote [i, j] below. It is assumed here that the processors are indexed from 1 (and not from 0 as previously). At any given moment, if elements A_{ik} and B_{kj} for any index k are in processor [i, j], the processor only has to add their product to its partial result C_{ij}. The basic idea behind the parallel algorithm is therefore to circulate the elements of the two matrices A and B so that blocks A_{ik} and B_{kj}, for k varying from 1 to $\sqrt{p}$, encounter one another in processor [i, j].

In an example of matrices containing nine blocks, the elements of product C that have to be computed are as follows:

$$C_{11} = \mathbf{A_{11}}^*\mathbf{B_{11}} + A_{12}^*B_{21} + A_{13}^*B_{31}$$
$$C_{12} = A_{11}^*B_{12} + \mathbf{A_{12}}^*\mathbf{B_{22}} + A_{13}^*B_{32}$$
$$C_{13} = A_{11}^*B_{13} + A_{12}^*B_{23} + \mathbf{A_{13}}^*\mathbf{B_{33}}$$
$$C_{21} = A_{21}^*B_{11} + \mathbf{A_{22}}^*\mathbf{B_{21}} + A_{23}^*B_{31}$$
$$C_{22} = A_{21}^*B_{12} + A_{22}^*B_{22} + \mathbf{A_{23}}^*\mathbf{B_{32}}$$
$$C_{23} = \mathbf{A_{21}}^*\mathbf{B_{13}} + A_{22}^*B_{23} + A_{23}^*B_{33}$$
. . . . .

Assume that initially elements A_{11} and B_{11} are already on processor [1, 1]; computing the first partial product of C_{11} can therefore be performed. As A_{11} is being used for the computation in processor [1, 1], it cannot be used to compute C_{12} at the same time. On the other hand, A_{12} is available and will encounter B_{22} (which will have to have been transferred beforehand). When A_{11} is released for the second stage and is on a neighbouring processor on the mesh, it can be sent from [1, 1] to [1, 2]. In the expression of the elements C_{ij} above, the computations carried out in the first stage are shown in bold.

Therefore, the elements of A and B must be put into position before computation starts. This can be done by projecting the diagonals from A onto the columns of the toric grid of processors, and those from B onto the rows, as Figure 16.23 shows.

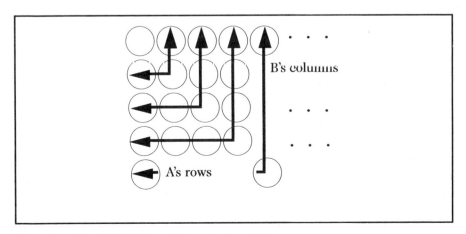

Figure 16.23   Initial shifts of elements A and B

Generalization

Block A_{ik} (or B_{kj}) must travel through all the processors on row i (or column j) and only through these. As duplicating the matrices' elements is not allowed by definition, the elements of matrix A (or B) must therefore circulate horizontally (or vertically) and travel through all processors with the same row (or column) index.

The parallel algorithm therefore has to contain a loop on k. Moreover, as we suggested for the previous 3×3 matrix, it is essential that the elements of the matrix move from one processor to another at each stage, from neighbour to neighbour, so that the communication scheme is local and regular.

So that blocks A_{ik} and B_{kj} encounter one another in processor [i, j] with the previous assumptions, it is necessary to take (i+j−1) modulo $\sqrt{p}$ as the initial value of k and to increment it at each stage (obviously still modulo $\sqrt{p}$). Let us return to the 3×3 matrix in order to allow the algorithm to progress to its conclusion: Figures 16.24, 16.25 and 16.26 show its execution in detail.

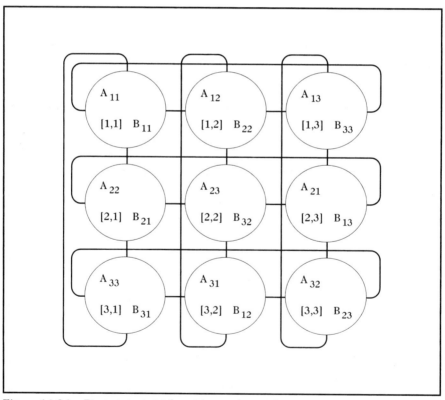

Figure 16.24   First stage: initial position and partial computation

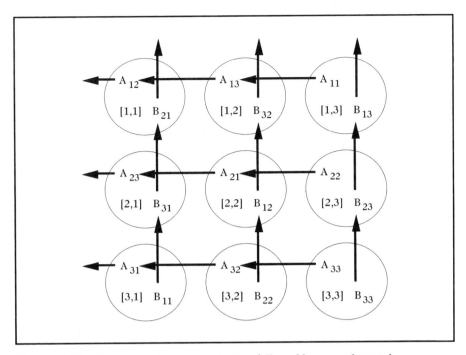

Figure 16.25   Second stage: communication followed by second partial computation

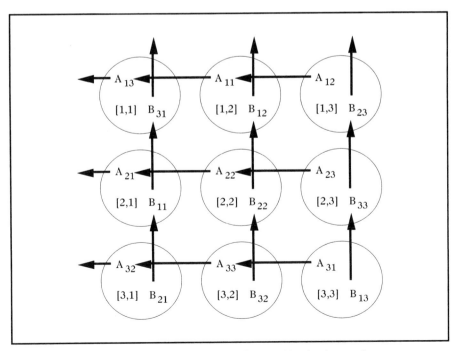

Figure 16.26   Third stage: communication followed by final partial computation

The full algorithm can be written as follows:

```
{initial positioning}
do in parallel
    A sent from processor [i, j] to processor [i, (i-j) modulo √p]
    B sent from processor [i, j] to processor [(j-i) modulo √p, j]
for  k ← 1  to   √p
    for all processors [i, j] do in parallel
        C(i, j) ← C(i, j) + A(i, k)*B(k, j)
        shift A towards its neighbour on the left
        shift B towards its neighbour above
```

We can compute the cost of this parallelization assuming communication in linear time. It is the sum of the following two terms:

- a preliminary communication stage, in which blocks of $\frac{n^2}{p}$ data items are sent simultaneously on each of the dimensions, whose most distant processors are at a distance of $\sqrt{p}$, with the processors being able to send pipelined messages (*see* Chapter 15):

$$\left(\sqrt{\beta\left(\sqrt{p}-1\right)} + \sqrt{\tau\frac{n^2}{p}} \right)^2$$

- then, $\sqrt{p}$ elementary computation stages of multiplications on the blocks (that is $\left(\frac{n}{\sqrt{p}}\right)^3$ multiplications and additions) with, at each stage, a block communicated between immediately neighbouring processors $\beta+\tau\frac{n^2}{p}$. In total this yields:

$$\sqrt{p}\left(\left(\frac{n}{\sqrt{p}}\right)^3 \tau_a + \beta + \tau\frac{n^2}{p} \right)$$

that is, in $O(\frac{n^3}{p})$ operations.

The link with systolic algorithms

In this simple example, control is distributed to each cell, all the communications are local and synchronization is ensured by data flow. The algorithm we have just described is actually a simple adaptation of the systolic algorithm. Consider the network (*see* Figure 16.28) where each elementary processor performs a multiplication followed by an addition as soon as the data is input. To obtain the previous algorithm, it is necessary only to send out the data at the beginning, at the rate of one data item (or one small block) per processor.

Assume that there are n^2 elementary processors (denoted [i, j] as above, with i and j varying from 1 to n), each of which has a local memory whose size is significantly smaller than n. If the computation of element C_{ij} is allocated to processor [i, j], then all the coefficients A_{ik} and B_{kj} have to be received by [i, j] for the partial storing $C_{ij} \leftarrow C_{ij} + A_{ik} * B_{kj}$ to be computed.

The systolic model solves this problem by allowing a number of computations to be performed with each memory access, as Figures 16.28 and 16.29 show. For example, a variable B_{kj}, which is required for computing element C_{1j}, is used by processor [1, j] to compute $C_{1j} \leftarrow C_{1j}+A_{1k} * B_{1j}$ and then sent to the neighbouring processor [2, j], which requires it for computing $C_{2j} \leftarrow C_{2j}+A_{2k} * B_{kj}$; after computing $C_{2j} \leftarrow C_{2j}+A_{2k} * B_{kj}$, processor [2, j] sends B_{kj} to [3, j], and so on.

So it can be seen that the basic operation of each processor entails multiplying two input values, and adding the result to an internal register. The communication channels of the elementary processor are shown in Figure 16.27.

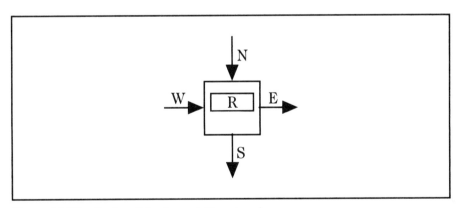

Figure 16.27   Basic cell in the systolic network

The operations performed by each cell are as follows:

- read an operand on channel N: $op_1 \leftarrow N$

- read an operand on channel W: $op_2 \leftarrow W$

- execute the internal operation: $R \leftarrow R + op_1 * op_2$

- transmit an operand on channel S: $S \leftarrow op_1$

- transmit an operand on channel E: $E \leftarrow op_2$

In order to describe the network completely, it only remains to explain the input order of matrices A and B. Contrary to the previous algorithm, the rows of A circulate from left to right and the columns of B from top to bottom. Figure 16.28 illustrates the arrangement of data for 3×3 matrices.

Note that, in Figure 16.28, the last element is C_{33}, computed by processor [3, 3]. As $2n-1$ clock beats (units of time) are needed to input elements A_{n1} and B_{1n} to processor [n, n], executing the algorithm requires $3n-1$ beats. At this point the results are inside the processors. For these results to become known, the network has to be emptied, which requires $n-1$ additional beats.

This can be improved upon, saving time during the start-up and emptying stages. The improvement is simple: it is sufficient for the computations on the processor to start as soon as possible. In the first unit of time, all the more distant cells can perform a computation, provided that the right data is in place. For this to occur, certain elements of A and B are duplicated on input, as Figure 16.29 shows.

At the first beat, only processor [1, 1] is working and it computes $A_{11}*B_{11}$. At the second beat, four processors are working: [1, 1] computes $A_{12}*B_{21}$ and accumulates the result in C_{11}, and [1, 2], [2, 1] and [2, 2] respectively compute $A_{11}*B_{12}$, $A_{21}*B_{11}$, and $A_{23}*B_{32}$ respectively.

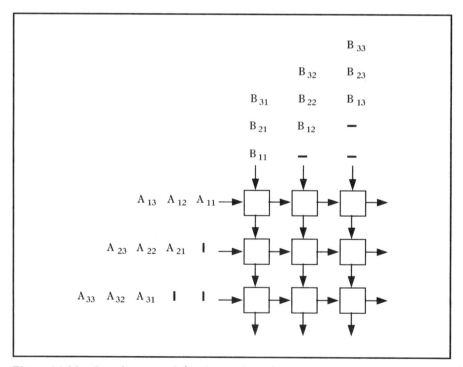

Figure 16.28   Systolic network for the product of square matrices

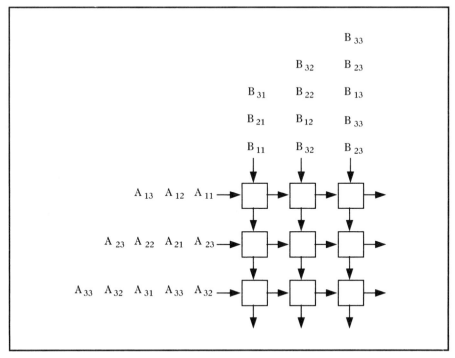

Figure 16.29   Adaptation of the computation network for the product of two matrices

The time complexity of this solution is easily evaluated: 3n–1 beats are required to compute the product, including emptying the network. However, it is true that this solution requires some redundant data.

Finally, another network has been proposed in the literature [KuL80]. It comprises n rows of 2n–1 cells identical to those above (that is, almost twice as many). The result is not calculated in one go, but is produced as each row progresses.

16.4.3   Algorithm with consecutive broadcasts

This is closely linked to the systolic algorithm. After data is allocated during a preliminary stage, the algorithm requires only local communications. The parallel computation of the matrices' products can be envisaged differently, while the initial data allocation is maintained. Consider a toric grid of p processors. The n×n matrices are divided into square $(\frac{n}{\sqrt{p}}, \frac{n}{\sqrt{p}})$ blocks, which enables us to consider $\sqrt{p}$, $\sqrt{p}$ matrices. Block C_{ij} is on processor [i, j]. For every row i and column j $(1 \le i, j \le \sqrt{p})$, C_{ij} computes the contribution $A_{ik}*B_{kj}$ at stage (i–k+1) modulo $\sqrt{p}$. At each stage (i–k+1) modulo $\sqrt{p}$, the A_{ik} for all rows i have to be broadcast and, of course, the B_{kj} that are on the neighbouring processors have to be transferred, as in the variant above. The algorithm's initial stages are shown in detail in Figures 16.30 and 16.31.

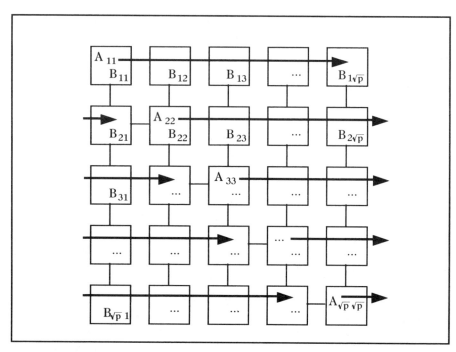

Figure 16.30   Stage 1: broadcasting A_{ii} followed by local computations $A_{ii}*B_{ij}$

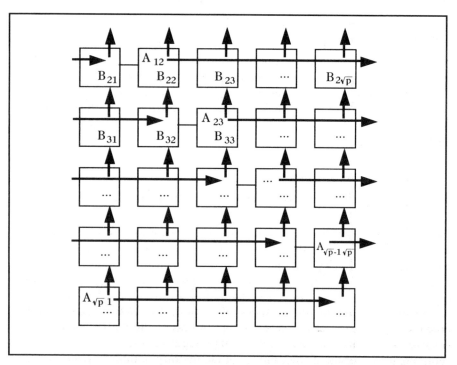

Figure 16.31   Stage 2: broadcasting $A_{i,\,i+1}$ on the rows, followed by elements $B_{i+1,\,j}$ moving locally to the processors [i, j] on the columns, then local computations $A_{i,\,i+1}*B_{i+1,\,j}$

The total cost is $\sqrt{p}$ broadcasts on rings of dimension $\sqrt{p}$ and local multiplications (followed by additions) on the $(\frac{n}{\sqrt{p}}, \frac{n}{\sqrt{p}})$ matrix blocks, which yields $O(\frac{n^3}{p})$. Once again, computation outweighs communication. Note that the latter algorithm can be easily adapted to other network topologies, provided that an efficient broadcast is used, and that the topology naturally contains a toric grid.

16.4.4   Fast parallel multiplication

Description of the algorithm

As we have just observed, many studies on parallel matrix multiplication have been conducted. In this section, we describe and discuss the parallelization of a rapid sequential algorithm on a ring. The results in this section are mainly based on [DRT92].

In 1969, Strassen proposed a new method of matrix multiplication that was faster than the standard algorithm [Str69]. It is based on replacing multiplication by less costly additions in classic formulae. This cleverly enables the number of elementary multiplications to be reduced from n^3 to only $n^{\log(7)} \approx n^{2.81}$. Many other studies have been motivated by this result and, at present, the best known method uses only $n^{2.37}$ multiplications [CoW87].

Below, we describe Strassen's algorithm for a square, n×n matrix factorized into four $(\frac{n}{2}, \frac{n}{2})$ blocks. It is based on the following formulae:

$$C = \begin{bmatrix} A_{11} A_{12} \\ A_{21} A_{22} \end{bmatrix} \begin{bmatrix} B_{11} B_{12} \\ B_{21} B_{22} \end{bmatrix} = \begin{bmatrix} M_0 + M_1 + M_2 - M_3 & M_3 + M_5 \\ M_2 + M_4 & M_0 - M_4 + M_5 + M_6 \end{bmatrix}$$

where

$$M_0 = (A_{11} + A_{22})(B_{11} + B_{22})$$
$$M_1 = (A_{12} - A_{22})(B_{21} + B_{22})$$
$$M_2 = A_{22}(B_{21} - B_{11})$$
$$M_3 = (A_{11} + A_{12})B_{22}$$
$$M_4 = (A_{21} + A_{22})B_{11}$$
$$M_5 = A_{11}(B_{12} - B_{22})$$
$$M_6 = (A_{21} - A_{11})(B_{11} + B_{12})$$

In order to obtain the complete algorithm, this factorization is applied recursively on each of the seven sub-problems of the matrix multiplication of size $(\frac{n}{2}, \frac{n}{2})$, with each sub-block being refactorized. It is easy to deduce its complexity in terms of the number of elementary additions t_+ and multiplications t_*:

$$t_+(n) = 7t_+\left(\frac{n}{2}\right) + 18\frac{n^2}{4}$$

$$t_*(n) = 7t_*\left(\frac{n}{2}\right)$$

Taking the initial conditions $t_*(1) = 1$ and $t_+(1) = 0$ into account, we obtain in total:

$$t_+(n) = 6n^{\log_2(7)} - 6n^2$$

$$t_*(n) = n^{\log_2(7)} \approx n^{2.81}$$

The task graph

On the basis of the above formulae, the following tasks are defined for one stage of Strassen's algorithm:

task $T_1 = A_{11} + A_{22}$
task $T_2 = B_{11} + B_{22}$
task $T_3 = A_{12} - A_{22}$
task $T_4 = B_{21} + B_{22}$
task $T_5 = B_{21} - B_{11}$
task $T_6 = A_{11} + A_{12}$
task $T_7 = A_{21} + A_{22}$
task $T_8 = B_{12} - B_{22}$
task $T_9 = A_{21} - A_{11}$
task $T_{10} = B_{11} + A_{12}$
task $M_0 = T_1 \cdot T_2$
task $M_1 = T_3 \cdot T_4$
task $M_2 = A_{22} \cdot T_5$
task $M_3 = T_6 \cdot B_{22}$
task $M_4 = T_7 \cdot B_{11}$
task $M_5 = A_{11} \cdot T_8$
task $M_6 = T_9 \cdot T_{10}$
task $T_{11} = M_0 + M_1$
task $T_{12} = M_2 - M_3$
task $T_{13} = M_5 - M_4$
task $T_{14} = M_0 + M_6$
task $T_{15} = T_{11} + T_{12}$
task $T_{16} = M_2 + M_4$
task $T_{17} = M_3 + M_5$
task $T_{18} = T_{13} + T_{14}$

The graph in Figure 16.32 shows the associated precedence relations.

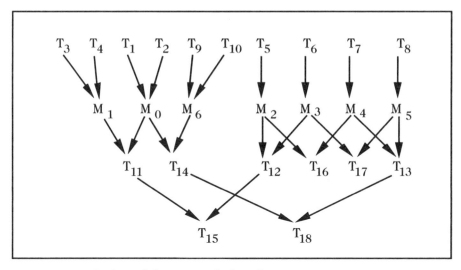

Figure 16.32   Task graph for Strassen's algorithm

Implementation on a ring of processors

We have just constructed a task graph for an elementary stage in Strassen's algorithm. The tasks have to be scheduled and the problem of how they are allocated physically – for example by taking a ring of p processors (indexed from 0 to p–1) as the target network – has to be solved. The choice of allocation is guided by the constraint of executing the seven most costly tasks (multiplications) in parallel on the seven processors. An execution in optimal time, which is equal to the longest path, is fairly easily obtained from the initial allocation described in Figure 16.33. The successive execution stages are illustrated in Figure 16.34.

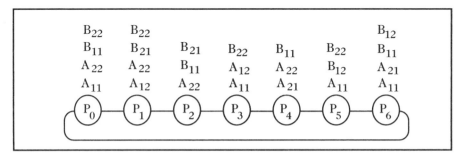

Figure 16.33   Initial allocation of matrix blocks to processors

Finally, note that the above result can be extended to a toric grid of processors by executing each of the seven $(\frac{n}{2}, \frac{n}{2})$ multiplications in parallel on rings of seven processors, while the amount of data to be stored is reduced to two sub-matrices per processor [DRT92]. Data storage constituted a constraint which until now limited the use of this method.

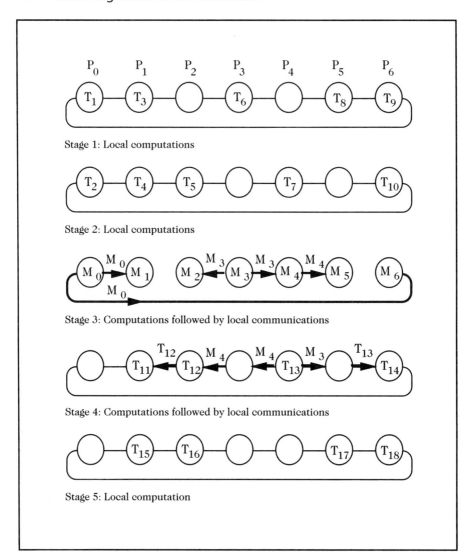

Figure 16.34   Execution scheme for Strassen's algorithm on a ring of seven processors

16.5   Sorting problems

In this section, we examine the complexity of parallel sorting on processor networks and provide two examples: on a ring and on a hypercube. We have already described sorting algorithms for the PRAM model and examined how they relate to the sorting networks in Chapter 5. We have also described algorithms for the HypercubeRAM model, which are adapted to rings and hypercubes, and they are the algorithms we will study in greater depth.

16.5.1   Granularity of sorting algorithms

It is assumed that the elements to be sorted are integers on a one-dimensional array Key [1..n]. We are interested only in algorithms based on comparisons. In the case of a fine-grain model, the basic operation is therefore *compare-exchange*, in which two elements of Key are compared and then exchanged, if necessary. This operation was described in Chapter 5 as follows:

```
compare-exchange (Key, i, j)
Key[min(i, j)] ← min (Key[i], Key[j])
Key[max(i, j)] ← max (Key[i], Key[j])
```

To construct a coarse-grain algorithm, it is sufficient to replace the comparison with a merge operation and the exchange operation with a dichotomy operation (dividing a sorted list into two equally-sized sub-lists). We obtain the following result.

Lemma 16.1

If A is a fine-grain algorithm that consists of only compare-exchange operations and executes on a given network topology in time T(n), then there exists a coarse-grain algorithm that executes on a network with the same topology with p processors in time $\frac{n}{p}T(p)$.

Proof

Let us consider the algorithm A with p data items on p processors and construct an algorithm A' with n data items on p processors. We will assume, to simplify description, that n is divisible by p. The array Key is partitioned into p sub-arrays S_i, each containing $\frac{n}{p}$ elements. To construct A', any compare-exchange operation on (Key[i], Key[j]) is replaced by a merge-dichotomy operation on (S_i, S_j).

Thus, we will only describe the following algorithms for fine-grain networks. We assume that the n items of data to be sorted are on a ring of n processors, with each processor having only one data item.

16.5.2   Odd-even sorting algorithms on a ring

The algorithm consists of n *compare-exchange* stages of adjacent elements. The program for processor P_i is described below for an even value of i ($0 \leq i \leq n-1$) and illustrated by an example in Figure 16.35. Alternatively, the elements are compared and exchanged between the processors with the indices i–1 ($1 \leq i$) and i, and between the processors with the indices i and i+1 (i<p).

```
{program for processor Pi}
for stage ← 1  to n
    if even stage then
        compare-exchange(Key[i-1], Key[i])
    else
        compare-exchange(Key[i], Key[i+1])
```

This sorting algorithm is not very good sequentially, since it requires n stages, each costing at worst n/2 compare-exchanges, which yields $O(n^2)$ compare-exchanges. However, it becomes very efficient in parallel because of the localization of the operations. It is natural to consider the hardware performance of this network on a linear processor network. In fact, this algorithm is optimal on such a network. Its execution time is $O(n)$, which cannot be improved since there are instances where a data item must be transferred from processor 0 to processor n−1.

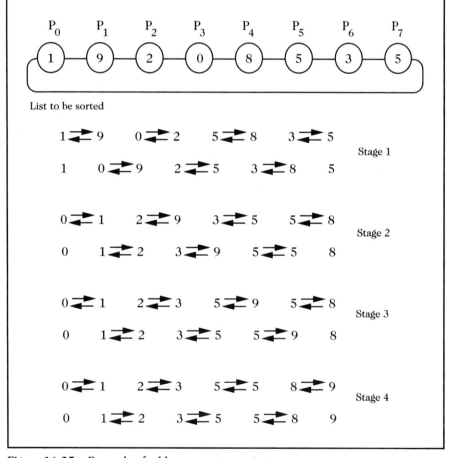

Figure 16.35   Example of odd-even sort on a ring

16.5.3   A bitonic sorting algorithm on a hypercube

In Chapter 5, we saw two sorting networks that can be used to obtain a
parallel algorithm whose execution time is $O(\log^2 n)$. Both these networks
are based on parallel merging, which is used to merge two sorted lists into a
single list. In this section, we look again at the second network, which is
based on bitonic merging. A series is said to be *bitonic* if, to within a circular
permutation, it is a chaining of two sorted sequences, the first in increasing
order and the second in decreasing order. Bitonic merging transforms a
bitonic sequence into a sorted sequence. It is based on the following result,
which reveals an important relation between compare-exchange operations
and bitonic sequences. To simplify description, it is assumed in this section
that n is a power of 2.

Lemma 16.2
> Let $S = \{s_i\}$ be a bitonic sequence of size n. Consider the two sequences
> of size n/2, $L = \{l_i\}$ and $R = \{r_i\}$ such that

$$l_i = \min\{s_i , s_{i+n/2}\}; r_i = \max\{s_i , s_{i+n/2}\}$$

L and R are thus also bitonic sequences and all the elements in L are less
than those in R.

Note that in calculating l_i and r_i, a compare-exchange stage is applied to
the two halves of S. Lemma 16.2 provides the key to bitonic merging: it is
sufficient to apply the lemma recursively to the sequences L and R, until
they contain only one element. S is then sorted. Let the first half of S be
called beginning(S) and the second half end(S). The bitonic merge is
described in the following manner:

```
Bitonic merge (S, n)
    if n = 1 then end
    else
        (L, R) ← compare-exchange (beginning(S), end(S))
        bitonic merge (L, n/2)
        bitonic merge (R, n/2)
```

On a hypercube, the operation (L, R) ← compare-exchange (begin-
ning(S), end(S)) corresponds to a communication along one dimension of
the hypercube. The same transformation is then applied to the two sub-
cubes that are obtained by partitioning the hypercube along that dimension.
Expressing the algorithm recursively results in the following program, which
is comparable to the algorithm for calculating partial sums (Section 2.2) or
prefixes (Chapter 5):

```
for all the dimensions k of the hypercube do
    for all pairs (q, q') of processors in correspondence to k do
        compare-exchange (S[q], S[q'])
```

where $S[q]$ represents the element stored by processor q. Thus, we obtain Lemma 16.3.

Lemma 16.3

Let S be a bitonic sequence of size n. Bitonic merging is executed in $O(\log n)$ steps on a hypercube of n processors.

To sort any sequence, it is enough to change it into a bitonic sequence. For this, we only have to observe that if two sequences of size k are sorted, one in ascending and the other in descending order, then bitonic merging produces a sorted sequence. Let us begin with k = 1 and sort the sequences of size 2 in ascending and descending order alternately. This can then be repeated until a sequence of size n is achieved. We thus obtain a sorting algorithm called bitonic or Batcher's sorting.

```
Bitonic sort (S, n)
    for k = 1 to log n do
        in parallel for i = 0 to n-1-k steps k do
            S[i, i+k-1] ← bitonic merge (S[i, i+k/2-1],
                S[i+k/2, i+k-1])
            k ← 2k
```

At stage k, the bitonic merges can be executed in parallel on sub-cubes of size 2^k in a time of k. The total execution time of the algorithm is thus $O(\log^2 n)$. Theorem 16.4 is thus obtained.

Theorem 16.4

Let S be a sequence of size n. Bitonic sorting is performed in $O(\log^2 n)$ steps on a hypercube of n processors.

16.6   Conclusion

In this chapter, we described the use of basic algorithm procedures on distributed-memory architectures. We concentrated on reduction, matrix multiplication and sorting. There are other operations, such as searching for closely related components or for minimum spanning trees for graph theory problems, for convex envelopes for problems of algorithmic geometry or for common sub-series for problems of character strings.

These procedures will be used in Chapter 17 for constructing parallel algorithms with the aim of solving more complex problems.

17

Solving linear systems in parallel

In this chapter, we describe parallelization of solvers for linear systems on processor networks. We look first at Gaussian elimination and solving linear systems, then at the Gauss-Seidel iterative and conjugate gradient methods. At the end of the chapter, we describe finding the roots of polynomials.

17.1 Solving linear systems in parallel

17.1.1 Statement of the problem

In this chapter, we consider parallelization on processor networks of solvers for the linear system Ax=b, where A is a regular, square n×n matrix with real coefficients. We assume that the matrix has all the necessary numerical properties [GoV83].

There are two ways of solving such systems: *direct* methods, where the exact solution is obtained (to within rounding errors, which can be considerable if n is large) in a finite number of operations; and *iterative* methods, where a series of vectors which converge on the system's solution vector is constructed [LGT89] [GoV83].

We first describe the parallelization of various algorithms used to solve triangular systems and then, in Section 17.2, go on to address parallelization of direct Gaussian elimination. We discuss parallelization of these algorithms on various types of architecture, ranging from systolic networks to ring and hypercube networks, taking into account data loading, or not, as required. In Section 17.3, we review the general principle of iterative methods, looking at the Gauss-Seidel and the conjugate gradient methods in detail, and then discuss their parallelization. We show how to take the particular structure of the matrix into account so as to achieve an efficient parallelization.

17.1.2   Parallelizing algorithms for solving triangular systems

Review of sequential algorithms

Solving triangular systems is of fundamental importance in linear algebra: it is at the heart of many methods (such as solving linear systems). Consider the solution of the system Ux=b, where U is an upper triangular n×n matrix which is assumed to be invertible. In the solver, the solution vector is built up component by component, updating at each step the set of unknowns already computed. As an example, we look at parallelizing this procedure on a hypercube with p processors and describe variations on the Li and Coleman algorithm [LiC86].

Column-oriented parallelization

If we write the algorithm so as to operate on the columns of the matrix, we obtain the scheme shown in Figure 17.1, where we assume that vector x contains vector b initially:

```
{column-oriented solution of upper triangular system Ux=b}
for  j ← n  to 1
    x(j) ← x(j)/U(j, j)
    for  i ← 1 to j-1
        x(i) ← x(i) - U(i, j)*x(j)
```

There are two ways of breaking this into tasks. With a granularity of the order of a column of U, a totally sequential task graph is obtained:

```
{sequential algorithm}
  for j ← n  to 1
    execute T_j
```

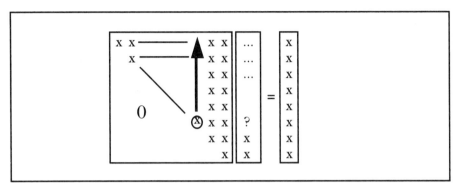

Figure 17.1   Column-oriented back substitution

An associated 'parallel' algorithm would entail assigning each task to a different processor. This would not work, since the total execution time would remain the same as that of the sequential algorithm. With the convention that communication with a (fictitious) processor indexed 0 or n+1 is not performed, the code for processor P_j is:

```
{processor Pj}
receive information from P_{j+1}
execute T_j
send information to P_{j-1}
```

Obviously, no parallelism can be obtained from such a structure; a finer grain size, of the order of one or more arithmetic operations, is needed. This results in:

```
{sequential algorithm}
  for j ← n  to 1
    execute T_{jj}
      for i ← 1  to  j-1
        execute T_{ij}
```

with the following constraints:

$$T_{jj} \ll T_{ij} \quad \text{and} \quad T_{ij} \ll T_{ij+1} (1 \le j \le n \quad \text{and} \quad 1 \le i \le n-1)$$

The task graph for this is illustrated in Figure 17.2. It has similarities with the two-step graph in Chapters 9 and 11.

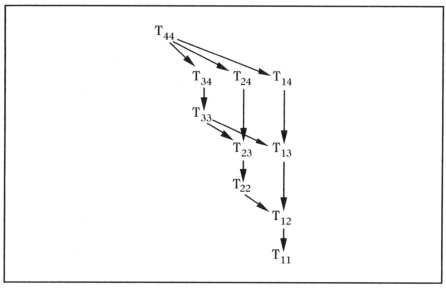

Figure 17.2   The task graph of the column-oriented parallelization for a 4×4 matrix

An initial parallelization closely follows the task graph shown. Suppose we have n processors and assign one to each column of the graph. At stage j, the jth processor computes the final value of x_j and sends it to the processors that continue the computation: one way to do this is to use a broadcasting procedure, as given in Chapter 15. At the same stage, the processors with an index lower than j receive x_j and update their variable. The following program is then obtained:

```
{processor Pj}
for  i ← n  to  j+1
    receive x_i from P_i
    execute T_ji
execute T_jj
broadcast x_j to P_i (i<j)
```

This algorithm presents several important characteristics. First of all, its structure is based on computation stages that are separated by global communication (broadcasting). It is therefore synchronous by construction. And it could easily be altered so that it can be executed on a SIMD computer. This structure crops up frequently in problems of scientific computation, particularly in linear algebra. Furthermore, analysing this algorithm is simplified by its structure, since computation and communication do not overlap. The execution time t_{alg} is therefore the sum of the computation time t_{comp} and the communication time t_{com}:

$$t_{alg} = t_{comp} + t_{com}$$

The computation time is equal to the critical path on the task graph. For this parameter, the algorithm is optimal. The communication time is the sum of n–1 broadcasts (to processors whose indices are lower than the source processor's).

It still remains for us to apply this algorithm in the case where the number of processors is less than n, that is, to divide up the different computations among the p processors. We have already studied a similar problem in Sections 16.3 and 16.4 in the case of matrix-vector and matrix-matrix multiplication. Here, the computational load on the processors has to be balanced as well as possible. In the algorithm below, we propose distributing the graph's columns, with column k assigned to the processor indexed (k – 1 modulo p)+1 (a circular allocation):

```
{processor Pj}
for  i ← n  to  j+1
   q ← (i-1) mod p + 1
   if q≠j then
      receive x_i from P_q
      execute T_ji
   else
      execute T_ii
      broadcast x_j
   for  k ← 1  to  (i/p-1)
      execute T_j+kp, i
```

In this case also, the overhead due to parallelism is related to the communication operations. Using broadcasts is questionable as they incur high costs. But the cost can be reduced without the computation time being increased significantly, as suggested by the algorithm below, in which the broadcast is executed on a ring of processors. The parallelization of this graph is based on the previous algorithm, which is not in parallel. In fact,

the information that allows the subsequent processor to begin its computation is transmitted before the columns update is completed. To simplify
procedures, we present an algorithm for n processors.

```
{processor Pj}
for  i ← n  to  j+1
    receive x_i from P_{j+1}
    send x_i to P_{j-1}
    execute T_{ji}
execute T_{jj}
send x_j to P_{j-1}
```

In order to construct the algorithm with p processors, we refer to the
method used in the first variant of the algorithm.

```
{processor Pj}
for i ← n  to j+1
    q ← (i-1) mod p + 1
    if q≠j then
        receive x_i from P_{j+1}
        send x_i to P_{j-1}
        execute T_{ji}
    else
        execute T_{ii}
        send x_j to P_{j-1}
    for k ← 1  to (i/p-1)
        execute T_{j+kp, i}
```

We will not go into the complexity analysis of this algorithm in detail, as
it requires assumptions to be made about the target machine. However, we
will observe that this algorithm is asynchronous and that, where communications are suitably implemented, computation and communication can be
overlapped, which ensures high efficiency.

Row-oriented parallelization

Solving the triangular system is shown in Figure 17.3; the algorithm is as
follows:

```
{row-oriented solution of the upper triangular system Ux=b}
    for  i ← n  to 1
        for  j ← n  to i+1
            x(i) ← x(i) - U(i, j)*x(j)
        x(i) ← x(i)/U(i, i)
```

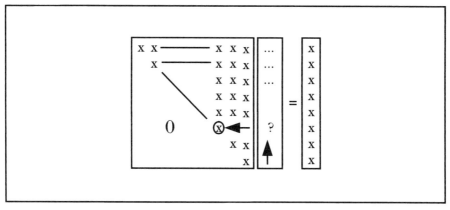

Figure 17.3   Row-oriented back substitution

Analysing this algorithm leads to decomposition into tasks of a finer granularity and the revision of the previous algorithm in the form of:

```
for  i ← n  to  1
    for  j ← n  to  i+1
        execute T_ij
    execute T_ii
```

There is a dependency relationship between tasks T_{ij} since the variable $x(i)$ has to be updated. The algorithm thus obtained does not contain parallelism. The j-loop forms the scalar product of vector X and the ith row of U. To extract the parallelism from this loop, the scalar product has to be parallelized. We will not look at this analysis in detail and refer the reader to Section 16.2.1, where the parallelization of reduction operations is discussed.

17.2   Solving linear systems using Gaussian elimination

17.2.1   Parallelization of Gaussian elimination

Review of the kji variant of Gaussian elimination and its parallelization on a shared-memory machine

The Gaussian elimination algorithm was first discussed in Chapters 8 and 11. Below, we review the variant in which columns are scanned in a series of stages, that is, in the order kji of the loop indices. At stage k, row k (referred to as the *pivot row*) is combined with rows i for i>k so that the sub-diagonal elements of column k are annihilated.

Measured in terms of the number of eliminations, the cost of the algorithm is $\frac{n(n+1)}{2}$ units (which corresponds to the number of sub-diagonal elements of A). Below, we recall the sequential algorithm.

```
for  k ← 1  to  n-1
   {task Tkk}
   coeff ← 1/A(k, k)
   for  i ← k+1  to n    A(i, k) ← coeff*A(i, k)
   for  j ← k+1  to  n
      {task Tkj}
      for i ← k+1  to  n
         A(i, j) ← A(i, j) - A(i, k)*A(k, j)
```

At a given stage, a single row can be used in several eliminations. The basic idea for parallelizing this algorithm is to assign independent eliminations, that is, eliminations on different rows, to different processors by duplicating the pivot row. The reader is referred to [LKK83] [CMR87] and to Chapter 11 for the results of the complexity analysis of this algorithm on a shared-memory architecture.

In this context, we will consider the implementation in detail. Assume that the underlying architecture is a MIMD machine with p processors, each of which can be a vector processor. The processors communicate by means of data sharing, using a shared memory which they access via an interconnection network. We should recall that, for simplicity, the time unit (denoted ε) corresponds to the execution of the following operations: reading from two rows of the matrix, computing the coefficients of the elimination operator, applying the operator and writing the new rows to shared memory. In practice, the execution time of all these operations depends on the length of the rows, but, in order to make the procedure simpler, we will not take this parameter into account here. Let p=n−1 and consider the following *GaussMP* algorithm:

```
for  k ← 1  to  n-1
   for all processors q ← k+1  to  n
      read pivot row (k)
      read row q
      eliminate A(q, k) {update row q}
      store row q
```

This algorithm is described in Figure 17.4 for n=8. The integer t is placed in position (i, j) of the matrix if the corresponding element was annihilated at time t.

```
        *
    1   *
    1   2   *
    1   2   3   *
    1   2   3   4   *
    1   2   3   4   5   *
    1   2   3   4   5   6   *
    1   2   3   4   5   6   7
```

Figure 17.4 Scheduling of eliminations on a shared-memory architecture

Theorem 17.1

On a shared-memory architecture under the previous assumptions, the GaussMP algorithm is optimal. Its execution time is $(n-1)\varepsilon$. The minimum number of processors required to execute an algorithm in optimal time is $n-1$.

Parallelization on a distributed-memory machine

Saad has investigated the potential for communication of several architectures with a large number of processors in relation to the size, n, of the problem, taking the Gaussian method as the test algorithm [Saa85]. His main result shows that linear execution times cannot be achieved if communications have to be taken into account, since communication time is $O(n^2)$, however many processors there are.

In [Saa86], he studies the implementation of the Gaussian algorithm on a hypercube network. He shows that ring and two-dimensional mesh sub-networks enable the problem to be solved efficiently, by duplicating the rows of the matrix (the mesh) and pipelining them (the ring). It is the latter principle that we are using to obtain optimal algorithms.

17.2.2   Systolic Gaussian elimination

The Gentleman and Kung network

First, we describe a systolic network for executing Gaussian elimination. It was proposed by Gentleman and Kung [GeK81]. The network in Figure 17.6

globally schematizes Gaussian elimination on an orthogonal systolic network. The network consists of cells of different types:

- A round cell inverts the first element it receives and stores the inverse (this is the pivot of the Gaussian algorithm); then, each of the following elements is multiplied by this pivot (an element of the Gaussian transformation is obtained) and the result is sent to the processor on the right.

- The first element to arrive at a square cell is stored. It comes from the cell above; more precisely, A_{kj} is stored in the cells whose Cartesian coordinates are (k, j). Then the cell receives, from the cell on the left, element $A_{k+1,\,k}/A_{k,\,k}$ from the Gaussian transformation that is being applied and receives, from the cell above, element $A_{k+1,\,j}$ of the column that is being transformed; the cell computes the Gaussian modification of the element:

$$A_{k+1,\,j} \leftarrow A_{k+1,\,j} - A_{k+1,\,k}{}^{*}A_{kj}/A_{kk}$$

and then sends the modified element downwards and transmits the element of the Gaussian transformation that has not undergone any modification to the right. These transformations are illustrated in Figure 17.6. The operation is repeated for all the subsequent steps on all the rows.

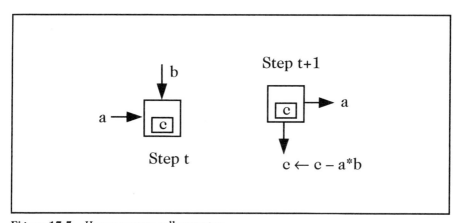

Figure 17.5   How a square cell operates

The reader will notice that the upper triangular matrix is stored in the network, and that the elements of the lower triangular matrix are output to the right of the network. The elements of column i exit via the cell on the network's last column. Moreover, the transformed vector b is stored in the network's last column.

The execution time for the algorithm is 3n for an n×n matrix on a network of n(n+1)/2 elementary cells. We will not present any other systolic networks and we refer the reader to the book by Quinton and Robert [QuR89].

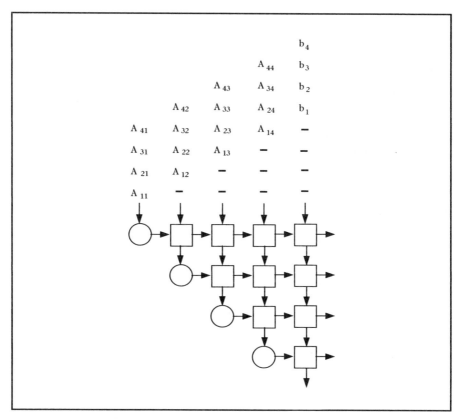

Figure 17.6   Systolic Gaussian elimination

17.2.3   Parallel algorithms on a linear network

Description of the architecture

Broadly speaking, the shared-memory architecture considered in Section 17.2.1 can be viewed as a complete processor network. A network of this kind with p processors consists of px(p–1) communication channels and from this point of view, it has the maximum potential for communication. Consequently, an algorithm for a particular processor network can be executed on a shared-memory architecture. Of course, the opposite is not true! The processor network with the minimum potential for communication is a linear network. In this section, we study the implementation of the methods above on such a network.

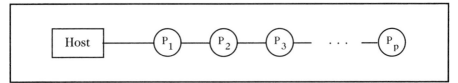

Figure 17.7   Linear processor network

The architecture under consideration is shown in Figure 17.7 (each link is bidirectional). The host computer communicates with processor P_1 via a read and write channel. Each processor P_i ($2 \le i \le p-1$) also communicates with P_{i-1} and P_{i+1} via intermediate read and write channels. P_i ($1 \le i \le p$) has a local memory which can contain two rows of A. At the beginning of the algorithm, the host computer contains the complete matrix A. At the end, it contains the required result.

The link with systolic algorithms

If the Gentleman and Kung systolic algorithm is considered and the processors are arranged as in Figure 17.8 (by projecting the columns on the same processor), an algorithm on a linear network is obtained. Note that the major disadvantage with any systolic algorithm lies in storing and loading data. Very fine-grain computations are pipelined.

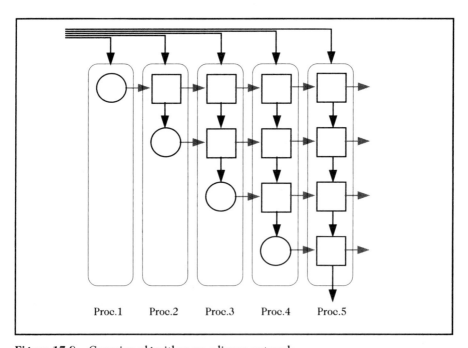

Figure 17.8   Gaussian algorithm on a linear network

Implementation

Consider a linear network with $p=\lfloor\frac{n}{2}\rfloor$ processors. The algorithm is implemented in two stages. The rows are introduced into the network one after another, from row n to row 1 from left to right. At the start, from t=1 to t=n, the rows are pipelined into the network, with each row staying two units of time in P_{i-1} before being transferred into P_i. At each moment, P_i reads a row from P_{i-1} and performs the corresponding elimination. From t=n+1 to t=2n, the direction of the communication is reversed: P_i reads a row from P_{i+1} and performs the corresponding elimination. During this phase, processor P_i delivers at each time unit a new row from the triangular matrix. Note that this mechanism does not require global control, since the direction of communications is changed when processor P_i reads row (2i–1). The execution of the algorithm is described in Figure 17.9 by a Gantt diagram; the initial values in a column of processors correspond to the number of rows available and E(i, i', j) eliminates element (i, j) with the element in row i'. The execution time of this algorithm is 2nε where, by an analogy with the shared-memory algorithm, ε represents the unit time it takes to read two rows in local memory, perform the elimination and send a row to a neighbouring processor's memory.

	P_1		P_2		P_3		P_4	
t =1	8							
2	7,8	E(8,7,1)						
3	6,7	E(7,6,1)	8					
4	5,6	E(6,5,1)	7,8	E(8,7,2)				
5	4,5	E(5,4,1)	6,7	E(7,6,2)	8			
6	3,4	E(4,3,1)	5,6	E(6,5,2)	7,8	E(8,7,3)		
7	2,3	E(3,2,1)	4,5	E(5,4,2)	6,7	E(7,6,3)	8	
8	1,2	E(2,1,1)	3,4	E(4,3,2)	5,6	E(6,5,3)	7,8	E(8,7,4)
9	2,3	E(3,2,2)	4,5	E(5,4,3)	6,7	E(7,6,4)	8	
10	3,4	E(4,3,3)	5,6	E(6,5,4)	7,8	E(8,7,5)		
11	4,5	E(5,4,4)	6,7	E(7,6,5)	8			
12	5,6	E(6,5,5)	7,8	E(8,7,6)				
13	6,7	E(7,6,6)	8					
14	7,8	E(8,7,7)						
15	8							

Figure 17.9   The GaussLN1 algorithm on an 8×8 matrix

There is a subtle variation on the above algorithm – GaussLN2. In this two-stage algorithm, rows are sent consecutively in the inverse order to that used above (from row 1 to row n). Thus, from t=1 to t=n, P_i reads a row from P_{i-1} and eliminates the corresponding element. When row i arrives at P_i, in the time (2i–1)ε, it is stored there. From t=n+1 to t=2n-1, the communication direction is reversed: P_i reads a row from P_{i+1} and eliminates the corresponding element. During this phase, processor P_i issues a new row from the triangular matrix at each unit of time. The execution time of the algorithm is also $2n\varepsilon$.

Figure 17.10 shows the order in which the elements of matrix A are annihilated in the two algorithms.

```
*                                    *

8    *                               2    *

7    9    *                          3    4    *

6    8    10   *                     4    5    6    *

5    7    9    11   *                5    6    7    8    *

4    6    8    10   12   *           6    7    8    9    10   *

3    5    7    9    11   13   *      7    8    9    10   11   12   *

2    4    6    8    10   12   14   * 8    9    10   11   12   13   14   *
```

Figure 17.10   Order in which elements in the GaussLN1 and LN2 algorithms are annihilated

Theorem 17.2

On a linear network, the GaussLN1 and GaussLN2 algorithms are optimal for performing the Gaussian elimination of a square matrix. Their execution time is $2n\varepsilon$.

The optimal number of processors for executing an algorithm in optimal time is $\lfloor \frac{n}{2} \rfloor$.

17.2.4   Implementation on a ring

Description

A processor ring has greater communication properties than a linear network. The architecture under consideration is shown in Figure 17.11. The host computer communicates with processor P_1 via a bidirectional channel. Each processor P_i also communicates with its neighbouring processors P_{i-1} and P_{i+1} (modulo p) via a bidirectional channel and has a local memory which can contain two rows of A. It is assumed that in one unit of time P_i is capable of reading a row, performing an elimination and sending the results, regardless of the position occupied by the element to be annihilated. As above, we denote this time as ε. As in Section 17.2.3, at the beginning of the algorithm the host contains matrix A; at the end, it contains the required result.

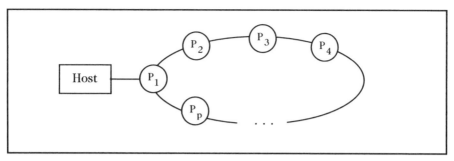

Figure 17.11   A processor ring

The linear network is a sub-network of the ring. As a result the algorithms in the previous section are applied to this type of architecture. It is easy to demonstrate that Theorem 17.2 can be extended to a ring.

Theorem 17.3

On a ring, the GaussLN1 and GaussLN2 algorithms are optimal for executing Gaussian elimination of a square matrix. Their execution time is $2n\varepsilon$.

The optimal number of processors for executing an algorithm in optimal time is $\lceil \frac{n}{2} \rceil$.

The impact of the network on performance

We have studied Gaussian elimination on several different topologies, taking into account the loading of the matrix rows onto the network: the complete network (global memory with data sharing), the linear network and the ring (local memory with message exchange). In the complete network, processors have parallel access to the host computer (here, shared memory) whereas, in the other two cases, access is sequential. We have shown that communications between processors and the host are far more important than communications between processors.

17.2.5   Data in place

Now let's look at the case where the matrix is already on the network. The network is still considered to have p processors communicating by message exchange. It is assumed that a very general model with linear communication time between processors with parallel and bidirectional links is being used (*see* Chapter 15). Data-loading from the host computer is not considered.

The case where data is assumed to have been pre-distributed on the network is realistic in the common situation where matrices are generated *in situ* by a parallel program, or where several linear systems are solved for the same matrix.

The problem of data allocation

A good allocation function must achieve the best compromise between balancing computational load and a short communication time (therefore, local computation). There are several ways of distributing the matrix so that Gaussian elimination can be performed. However, it can easily be seen that the matrix can be efficiently partitioned by column: all the elements of the same column have to communicate with each other at each new stage [Saa86] [GeH85]; this is clearly the case in the task graph in Figure 17.12.

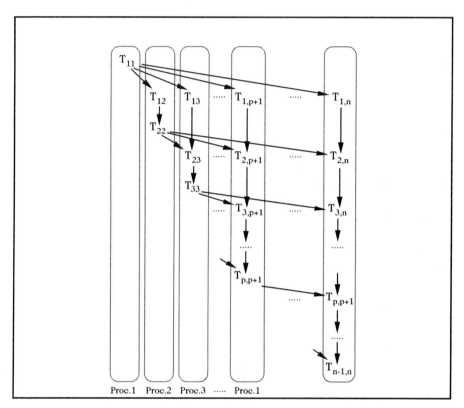

Proc.1   Proc.2   Proc.3   ·····   Proc.1

Figure 17.12   Column-oriented distribution

As in Section 16.1.4, the first allocation that comes to mind is to divide the matrix into consecutive blocks of r columns, where r= $\frac{n}{p}$ (which is assumed to be an integer in order to keep computations simple). This division is shown in Figure 17.13. The corresponding allocation function is:

$$\text{alloc}(j) = \left\lceil \frac{j}{r} \right\rceil$$

where, using the previous notation, alloc(j) represents the index of the processor that contains column j.

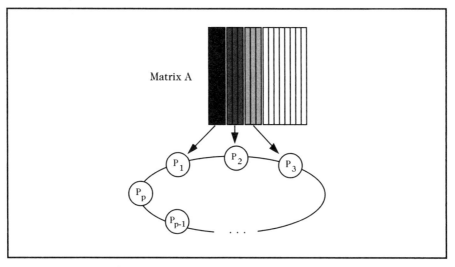

Figure 17.13   Distribution in consecutive blocks

The solution above has one major disadvantage: after $\frac{n}{p}$ stages, the first processor does not have any work to do, the second is free after $2\frac{n}{p}$ stages, and so on. Allocation by columns, described in Figure 17.14, is more balanced. The allocation function is:

alloc(j)=j modulo p

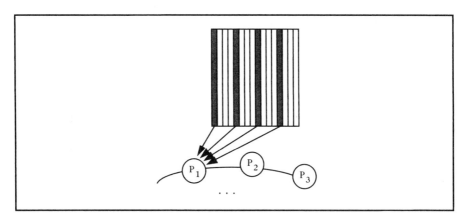

Figure 17.14   Circular distribution

The Gaussian algorithm with broadcasting

In this section, we describe a centralized algorithm. The processor using the pivot column, at a given stage, sends it to all the others. They can then carry out eliminations on the columns they already have. The code for processor P_i is presented below. There is no pivoting in this variant, but it can be easily adapted so that there is [Saa86] [Rob90].

```
{broadcast Gaussian elimination}
for k ← 1  to  n-1
   if alloc(k) = i then
      execute task T_kk
      broadcast column k
   else
      receive column k
   {eliminations}
   execute tasks T_kj for all the columns j≥k+1 such that alloc(j)=i
```

The complexity of this variant can be computed on any network topology. The execution time for an elementary operation (multiplication or addition) is written as τ_a. Consider the case of circular distribution by columns on a hypercube of p processors. As far as computation is concerned, each processor must compute $\frac{n}{p}$ pivots (operations on vectors of size $(n-k)$ at stage k) and perform the eliminations in parallel on the columns it has. Since the distribution is balanced, the eliminations can be executed with no overhead.

$$t_{comp} = \left(\frac{2n^3}{3p} + \frac{n^2}{2} \right) \tau_a + O\left(\frac{n^2}{p} \tau_a \right)$$

For communication, the best algorithm known so far for broadcasting a message of length L on a hypercube of p processors under the same assumptions as above (message switching and parallel and bidirectional links) gives a time for each stage of:

$$\left(\sqrt{\log_2(p)\beta_c} + \sqrt{\frac{L}{\log_2(p)} \tau_c} \right)^2$$

Here, the size of the messages sent is $(n-k)$ at stage k. Thus, the total communication time is:

$$t_{com} = \sum_{k=1}^{n-1} \left(\sqrt{\log_2(p)\beta_c} + \sqrt{\frac{n-k}{\log_2(p)}}\tau_c \right)^2$$

$$t_{com} = O\left(n\log_2(p)\beta_c + \frac{n^2}{2\log_2(p)}\tau_c \right)$$

17.2.6   Pipeline ring

The network's topology is a ring and the data items are still assumed to have been distributed across the network. The solution that we look at now is such that the processors can begin to work (execute eliminations on the columns they have) before they have all received the pivot column. More specifically: assume that, at a given stage, processor P_i has the pivot; it sends it to processor P_{i+1} which can begin its eliminations and, in turn, send the pivot to P_{i+2}. The data is still initially divided into circular blocks.

The code for processor P_i is set out below:

```
{Gaussian elimination on pipeline ring: processor P_i}
for  k ← 1  to  n-1
    if alloc(k) = i then
        execute task T_kk
        send column k to processor P_i+1
    else
        receive column k from processor P_i-1
        if (i modulo p) ≠ alloc(k) then
            send column k to P_i+1
        execute tasks T_kj for all the columns j≥k+1 such
        that alloc(j)=i
```

Additional assumptions have to be made in order to evaluate the computational time. The execution scheme in Figure 17.15 illustrates the initial stages of the algorithm.

The implementation that we have just described is based on a directed ring, with one direction. Its granularity can be reduced even further and elements sent as the algorithm progresses, before complete rows are updated. This new variant can be compared with the systolic algorithm, where the columns are cleverly assigned to processors. Its execution time is set out in detail below.

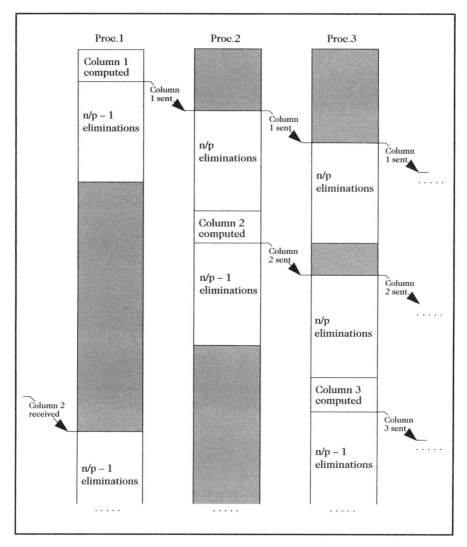

Figure 17.15   Initial stages of the execution scheme for Gaussian elimination of a matrix on a ring of processors

First of all, there is a start-up stage in which processor 1 prepares column 1 and sends it to its neighbour (namely, processor 2). Processor 2 executes eliminations on the columns it has, then updates column 2 and transmits it, in turn, to its neighbour, and so on, until processor p transmits column 2 to processor 1 which will then be able to execute eliminations on and update column $n/p+1$. From this point, the algorithm uses the critical path sequences defined by the following: preparing the pivot column, sending the column and local eliminations. The total execution time is as follows:

$$\sum_{i=1}^{n-1} \left\lceil \frac{n-i}{p} \right\rceil (n-i)\tau_a + \beta_c + (n-i)\tau_c = O\left(\frac{2n^3}{3p}\tau_a\right) + (n-1)\beta_c + \frac{n(n-1)}{2}\tau_c$$

17.2.7   Chaining

Once the matrix has been factorized into an upper triangular matrix, the solution of the triangular system must be chained. This can present difficulties in so far as the data items may not be allocated to the right processors at the start of the solution of the triangular system. So the data has to be distributed. This can be done efficiently, as we saw at the end of Chapter 15.

17.3   Parallelizing iterative methods

17.3.1   Solving linear systems with iterative methods

This involves constructing a set of vectors which converge on the solution. We assume A to be symmetrical and positive definite – the latter condition is not necessary, but it simplifies the analysis and guarantees convergence. Iterative methods can also be expressed as follows.

Consider partitioning matrix A of the system into M − N, where M is a regular $n \times n$ matrix, with a simple structure (diagonal, upper triangular, and so on). The series of vectors is constructed from the iteration below:

x^0 given
for $k \leftarrow 0$ **to** convergence
    $Mx^{k+1} = Nx^k + b$

Convergence is ensured when, for example, $\| x^{k+1} - x^k \| \leq \varepsilon$, where ε is a fixed precision. Note that sequential variants of these methods are very commonly used when the system's matrix is sparse. Direct methods are based on factorizing matrices, but the computations involved in these methods observe the matrices' structure.

Depending on the values of M and N, elimination can be executed using the Jacobi method (in which M is A's diagonal), or the Gauss-Seidel method (in which M is A's upper triangle). Parallelizing the former basically involves

parallelizing the product of a matrix multiplied by a vector. The parallelization of the latter is set out below.

17.3.2   Gauss-Seidel elimination

Review

In Gauss-Seidel elimination, the matrix M is A's upper triangle. The solver is
as follows:

```
for k ← 0 to convergence
    {computation of matrix-vector product} v ← Nx
    {addition of vectors} v ← v+b
    {solution of the triangular system} Mx = v
    {evaluation of the convergence}
```

Computing the matrix-vector product and solving the triangular system
incurs the highest cost (they are both of order $O(n^2)$); adding the vectors or
evaluating the convergence is of the order $O(n)$.

The sequential Gauss-Seidel elimination above is matrix-oriented. If the
computations are decomposed, it is written as follows:

```
for   k ← 0 to   convergence
    for   i ← 1 to   n   do
```

$$x_i^{k+1} = \frac{1}{a_{ii}} \left(b_i - \sum_{i<j} a_{ij} x_j^{k+1} - \sum_{i>j} a_{ij} x_j^k \right)$$

Linear systems can be directly parallelized in two ways: either by using
the results obtained in Section 16.3 for the product of a matrix and a vector
[BIT90], or by using those obtained in Section 17.1 for solving upper
triangular systems, in which case computations are parallelized during each
iteration. Both methods can be parallelized by dividing the matrices into
rows and columns; the data movements are then compatible, and can be
chained. Vector additions, however, can be computed at a purely local level
and performance is much the same as for solving triangular systems. Later
we demonstrate how the specific structure of the matrix can be taken into
consideration, so that parallelization can be improved.

Complexity analysis

Using a shared-memory architecture, Missirlis [Mis87] and Robert and
Trystram [RoT89] provided an optimal algorithm for this problem. First,

note that the basic iteration can be decomposed into two stages: computing the right-hand element $b + Nx^k$ and solving the triangular system in M with it. Expressing this as a task graph results in two sets of tasks J_1 and J_2 which, respectively, correspond to the two stages. To be more precise:

$$J_1 = \{T_{ij} \text{ for } 1 \le i < j \le n\}$$
$$J_2 = \{T_{ij} \text{ for } 1 \le j < i \le n\}$$

The tasks are defined by:

$$\text{for } i < j \; T_{ij}: x_i^{k+1} \leftarrow x_i^{k+1} - a_{ij} x_j^k$$
$$\text{for } i > j \; T_{ij}: x_i^{k+1} \leftarrow x_i^{k+1} - a_{ij} x_j^{k+1}$$

$$T_{ii}: x_i^{k+1} \leftarrow \frac{x_i^{k+1}}{a_{ii}}$$

The graph for J_2 is a two-step graph with UET tasks for which an optimal execution is known [KoT89]; the graph for J_1 is shown in Figure 17.16. It can be easily optimized, as Figure 17.17 shows.

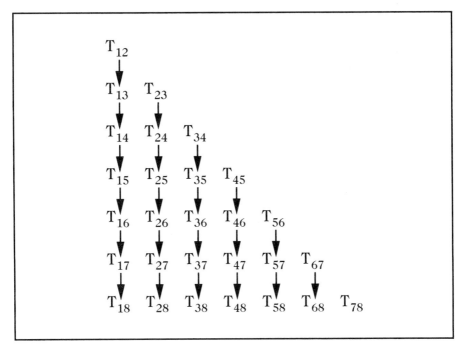

Figure 17.16   Task graph of the set J_1

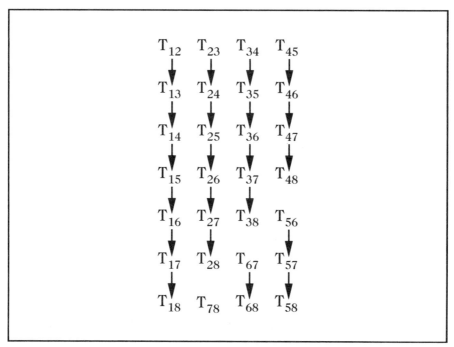

Figure 17.17   Optimized task graph

'Red-black ordering' in discretization of the Laplace operator

We have just seen that the Gauss-Seidel method is not very efficient, mainly because of the solution of the upper triangular system. For some individual problems, cleverly ordering the variables can result in an efficient execution [Sto73a]. Let us take as an example discretization of the Laplace operator:

$$\begin{cases} \Delta f(x,y) = g(x,y) \text{ on } \Omega \\ f(x,y) = 0 \text{ on the boundary} \end{cases}$$

where Ω is the square $[0, 1]^2$.

Consider discretizing the domain into N^2 points, shown in Figure 17.18. Let $h = \frac{1}{N}$. The discretization of this operator is the well-known five-point scheme:

$$\text{for all } 0 < i, j < N - 1 \quad g_{i,j} = N^2(f_{i+1,j} + f_{i-1,j} + f_{i,j+1} + f_{i,j-1} - 4f_{i,j})$$

$$g_{i,j} = 0 \text{ on the boundary}$$

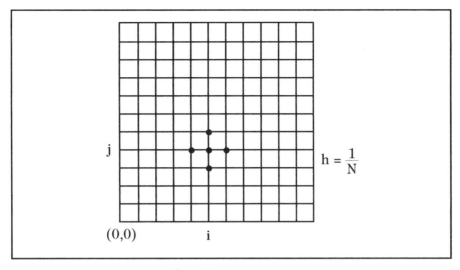

Figure 17.18 Discretization of the domain

To solve this system, $(N-1)^2$ unknowns $f_{i,j}$ have to be determined in the domain. The Gauss-Seidel iteration is:

$$
\begin{aligned}
&\textbf{for} \quad i \leftarrow 1 \ \textbf{to} \ \ N{-}1 \\
&\quad \textbf{for} \quad j \leftarrow 1 \ \textbf{to} \ \ N{-}1 \\
&\quad f_{i,j}^{k+1} = -\frac{1}{4N^2}\, g_{i,j} + \frac{1}{4}\left(f_{i,j-1}^{k} + f_{i-1,j}^{k} + f_{i,j+1}^{k+1} + f_{i+1,j}^{k+1} \right)
\end{aligned}
$$

Consider alternating colours in the domain, as shown in Figure 17.19.

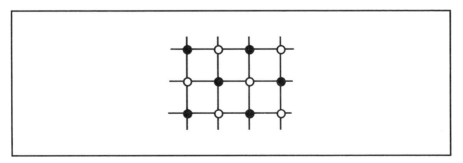

Figure 17.19 The principle of black and white colouring of the domain

The method of solving the system is derived from the observation that the alternate use of black and white in the graph is such that only black variables need to be known for the white variables to be determined, and vice versa. Consequently, all the unknowns of a given iteration can be computed in only two stages. Complete efficiency can be obtained if one further observation is noted: initially, one white and one black variable can be distributed to each processor.

17.3.3   Parallelization of the conjugate gradient method

Gradient methods

'Gradient' methods for solving linear systems are a little different. They are iterative methods based on optimization methods. If the matrix is symmetrical and positive definite, it can easily be demonstrated that solving the linear system Ax=b is equivalent to the following minimization:

$$\min\left(\Phi(x)\right) \text{ where } \Phi(x) = \frac{1}{2}x^t . Ax - x^t . b$$

This optimization problem is solved by a descent method [GoV83] in which one direction is chosen for descent (for example, that of the gradient g^k which is equal to $Ax^k - b$) and the new vector is iteratively computed along this direction as follows:

$$x^{k+1} = x^k - \lambda_k d^k$$

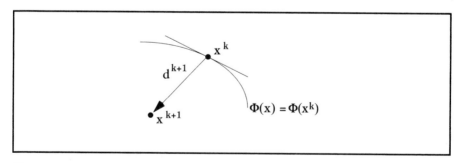

Figure 17.20   Descent method

Figure 17.20 illustrates a descent on a plane along the direction d^k. The scalar parameter λ_k is calculated at each stage as the best for this direction. Computing its expression is straightforward:

$$\lambda_k = \frac{\left(g^k\right)^t \cdot g^k}{\left(Ad^k\right)^t \cdot d^k}$$

We should note that there are some descent methods (referred to as constant step methods) where the parameter λ is fixed for each iteration. In terms of algorithms, the gradient vector is not explicitly computed using matrix-vector multiplication, but iteratively by a simple vector update. The device does not alter the numeric behaviour of the method too much.

Preconditioning

In general, iterative methods, such as we have just presented, are quite slow. The speed of convergence depends on the spectral condition of the matrix (more precisely, on the distribution of the eigenvalues in the spectrum and the ratio of the largest to the smallest). In order to accelerate convergence, a variable in the matrix can be changed before iterations are performed. Thus, the new system $M^{-1}Ax=M^{-1}b$ is solved (intuitively, if M is an 'approximation' of A, solution x will be obtained in only a few iterations).

Preconditioning using M translates in the algorithm into solving the linear system in M at each iteration. The number of iterations can be reduced considerably by doing this, but it results in iterations with higher overheads. However, this method may not have the same efficiency in parallel.

Conjugate gradient algorithms

In practice, it is better to use conjugate gradient methods than simple methods. The former entail iterating a series of vectors from conjugate directions to conjugate directions (that is, orthogonal directions, in terms of the scalar product defined by matrix A) and the result is faster convergence, which can be proved to be obtainable in less than n iterations for a system of order n. The basic formulae are the following:

$$\lambda_k = \frac{\left(g^k\right)^t \cdot g^k}{\left(Ad^k\right)^t \cdot d^k}$$

$$x^{k+1} = x^k - \lambda_k d^k$$

$$g^{k+1} = g^k - \lambda_k Ad^k$$

$$\beta_{k+1} = \frac{\left(g^{k+1}\right)^t \cdot g^{k+1}}{\left(g^k\right)^t \cdot g^k}$$

$$d^{k+1} = g^k - \beta_{k+1} d^k$$

The effect of preconditioning the matrix is that the scalar product is changed. Thus, vector g is replaced by a vector z in the above formulae. The standard sequential algorithm for a preconditioned conjugate gradient is given below:

```
for k ← 0, 1,... to convergence
v ← Ad                          {1. computation of the product
                                    of a matrix by a vector}
computation of the scalar λ     {2. scalar product}
x←x - λd and r←r - λv           {3. vector operations of the
                                    type AXPY}
Mz = r                          {4. solution of the triangular
                                    system}
computation of the scalar β     {5. scalar product}
d←z - βd                        {6. addition of vectors}
```

The cost is mainly the result of multiplying matrices by vectors and solving the system that has been preconditioned in M. Note that two scalar products are computed at each iteration, which correspond to the evaluations of the scalar parameters.

The problem, once again, is basically one of finding the parallel solution of the system in M. In practice, the majority of preconditioning matrices are either diagonal, simple band or triangular, or the product of triangular matrices [GoV83].

Standard parallelization

Most studies on parallelizing the conjugate gradient algorithm relate to partitioning the whole of the matrix into blocks on coarse-grain machines.

As in most iterative methods, the inner loops are parallelized. Broadly speaking, two ways of doing this have been reported:

- The matrix is equitably distributed among the processors and parallelization uses elementary computation and communication procedures.

- The matrix is decomposed into sub-domains. Here, the matrix is decomposed into blocks and preconditioning is such that a local solution results. This variant is very well adapted to problems of finite elements, for example, where preconditioning can be done by using elementary matrices [LGT88].

Below, we provide an example of how to parallelize conjugate gradient algorithms using the first method. Consider partitioning the matrix into blocks of $\frac{n}{p}$ rows (for simplicity, we take n to be a multiple of p, so that this is integral). The vectors' components are partitioned similarly. The method does not take into account the possibility of the matrix being sparse, but it can be adapted to do so. Consider a preconditioning by an upper triangular matrix, calculated in advance. The evaluation of the parallelization of the conjugate gradient on a square toric grid of p processors is set out in detail. τ_a and τ_c are units of time for computations and communications respectively.

1. We saw in Chapter 16 that matrix-vector multiplication requires an all-to-all exchange of the $\frac{n}{p}$ components of vector d, followed by $\frac{n}{p}$ scalar products of the vectors of magnitude n, which yields:

---

communications: $\quad 2\left[\dfrac{\sqrt{p}}{2}\right]\beta_c + \dfrac{n}{p}\left[\dfrac{p-1}{4}\right]\tau_c$

computations: $\quad n\dfrac{n}{p}\tau_a$

---

2. Evaluating the scalar λ requires computing scalar products of vectors that are distributed over the whole network. There are two ways of doing this:

   - parallel computation of the local scalar products of vectors of dimension $\frac{n}{p}$, then combining them on a specific processor and broadcasting the scalar thereby obtained to all processors (note that pipelining cannot be used here, since the message is too small);

- or, as above, computing the scalar products locally, followed by execution of an all-to-all exchange of data items of order 1 and computation of a scalar product on the p components processors have received.

Let us use the first solution. We obtain:

---

computations: $\dfrac{n}{p}\tau_a$

communications (combination): $2\left\lceil\dfrac{\sqrt{p}}{2}\right\rceil(\beta_c+\tau_c)$

communications (broadcast): $2\left\lceil\dfrac{\sqrt{p}}{2}\right\rceil(\beta_c+\tau_c)$

---

3. Local updates of vectors ($\frac{n}{p}$ components without communication):

---

computations: $\frac{n}{p}\tau_a$

---

4. This stage depends on the kind of preconditioning. If the data is stored in a way that is compatible with that of the previous stage, a method similar to the one in Section 17.1.2 for triangular matrices can be adopted.

5. The scalar β is evaluated as in 2:

---

computations: $\dfrac{n}{p}\tau_a$

communications: $4\left\lceil\dfrac{\sqrt{p}}{2}\right\rceil(\beta_c+\tau_c)$

---

6. The same stage as in 3, that is:

---

computations: $\frac{n}{p}\tau_a$

Note that the convergence test is evaluated completely at stage 2 for example. Since all the processors have the value of the criterion for ending the computation, the algorithm can terminate itself. The method can be improved in the case of structured sparse matrices; this requires a more careful mapping of the elements, to favour local communications.

Some other solutions

Note that there are other solutions based on different methods. Saad [Saa83] suggested a cleverer approach based on the following observation: scalar product computations are expensive because they require global communication. The two scalar products of an iteration are replaced by three scalar products computed simultaneously. Note that these algebraic transformations, although quite valid in theory, are not very stable numerically.

Preconditioning is useful in speeding up convergence, but, generally, it results in a parallelization that is not very efficient. Some researchers have sought a solution to this problem by proposing that parallel preconditioning be used. In particular, polynomials can be preconditioned, an idea based on the notion of approximating matrix A's inverse by means of a polynomial in A, of a low degree. A sum of the first few powers of A has to be computed, noting that if product Ad has already been computed, the computation A^2d = A(Ad) does not incur high costs, and so on.

Some authors have suggested modifying the basic iteration in the conjugate gradient method. For example, Delesalle, Desbat and Trystram studied a method where the two parameters λ and β are computed only once, and remain constant throughout the iterations [DDT93]. Each iteration then becomes very parallel, since it is reduced to a matrix-vector multiplication. They show that this new method has the same properties, asymptotically, as the conjugate gradient method and is only another way of viewing Richardson's second-order extrapolation method. This method becomes especially efficient for individual matrices such as those resulting from Laplace operator discretization, discussed in Section 17 3.2.

17.4   Parallel computation of the roots of a polynomial

In this section, we study the specific problem of designing and analysing parallel algorithms for finding all the roots of a polynomial. We have two aims. The first is to give a numerical application from outside the field of linear algebra. The second is to describe a new class of algorithms: asynchronous parallel algorithms. We will see that these algorithms are natural solutions to the problem [CoF90].

17.4.1   Introduction

Finding all the roots $\omega_1,\ldots,\omega_n$ of a complex polynomial P of degree n:

$$P(z) = \sum_{i=0}^{n} a_i z^{n-i} \quad \text{with } a_1 = 1, a_n \neq 0 \text{ and } a_i \text{ in } C$$

is a well-known problem in pure mathematics and in applied mathematics, with many applications in the engineering sciences. Normally, this problem is solved by Newton's method for each root, with the polynomial being divided by the factors found at each stage. There are also simultaneous methods which can be used to find all the roots at the same time. Many of them construct a series:

$$Z^{(k)} = H\left(Z^{(k-1)}\right)$$

in C^n, from any initial vector $Z^{(0)}$, where H is an operator in C^n constructed such that the $Z_i(k)$ tend towards ω_i, $i = 1,\ldots,n$. The Durand-Kerner method [Dur60] is based on the use of the Weierstrass operator:

$$H_i(Z) = z_i - \frac{P(z_i)}{\displaystyle\prod_{j=1, j\neq i}^{n}(z_i - z_j)}; \; i = 1,\ldots,n$$

This iteration is the Newton method applied, within C^n, to symmetrical functions of the roots (the Viete system). It follows that the method converges locally. The convergence is quadratic when the Jacobian is not singular (that is, when the roots ω_i are simple). It is assigned by groups of zeros, and in the case of multiple zeros it is only linear. If the multiplicity of ω_i is υ_i then there are υ_i components of Z which tend towards ω_i.

One method with cubic convergence (in the case of simple roots) was introduced by Ehrlich [Ehr67] and described by Aberth [Abe73]:

$$H_i(Z) = z_i - \frac{1}{\dfrac{P'(z_i)}{P(z_i)} - \displaystyle\sum_{k=1, k\neq i}^{n} \dfrac{1}{z_i - z_k}}; \; i = 1,\ldots,n$$

Each component i is an iteration of the Newton method applied to the ith correction in the Durand-Kerner method. Convergence is slow in the instance of multiple zeros. As in the Durand-Kerner method, if the multiplicity of ω_i is υ_i then there are υ_i components of Z that tend towards ω_i.

Our aim here is to implement these methods (denoted as method DK and method EA respectively) on a distributed-memory MIMD machine. It appears that the communication cost greatly influences the total execution time: in fact, an all-to-all data exchange is obligatory at each stage. Therefore, as Bertsekas and Tsitsiklis [BeT89] suggest, we propose modifying the communication strategy so that at each iteration a processor need not wait at specific points in the program, such as the end of the all-to-all exchange. The advantage that we hope to gain is to reduce the higher costs incurred by the synchronous algorithm and to increase speed in comparison with it. In [CoF92], Cosnard and Fraigniaud demonstrated that, under certain standard conditions, the asynchronous algorithms always converge locally, even if the order of the convergence is reduced. We also analyse the behaviour of asynchronous algorithms according to the time they take (measurement of asynchronism), the interconnection network's topology and the lengths of elementary computations and communication.

17.4.2   Synchronous implementations

We are particularly interested in coarse-grain distributed-memory computers, such as the Intel iPSC/860, nCUBE hypercubes or transputer-based machines. As we saw in Chapter 4, such computers are modelled with a graph whose vertices are processors and whose arcs are communication links. The algorithms are heavily dependent on the communication strategies described in Chapter 15. Here, we present implementation on three standard topologies: rings, toric grids and hypercubes; p is the number of processors in the network of diameter D and degree Δ. We assume a packet-switching model, with linear communication costs $(\beta c + L\tau_c)$, under the assumption of parallel, bidirectional links. The cost of an ordinary arithmetic operation is written τ_a.

Firstly, the initial vector $Z^{(0)}$ is computed by all the processors. Note that the speed of convergence depends heavily on the choice of starting points. It is therefore important to find a good approximation of the solution vector $\omega = \omega_1, ..., \omega_n$ in order to ensure fast convergence. In many cases, points equally spaced on the circumference of a circle of radius r_0 are chosen as starting points, where r_0 is found from the coefficients of the polynomial by Guggenheimer's algorithm [Gug86].

Each stage of the algorithm comprises one computation and one communication phase. For s varying from 1 to p, assume that the sets Ind(s) form a partition of $\{1, ..., n\}$. The computation of H(Z) is shared between the processors: P_s computes $H_i(Z)$ for all the indices i of Ind(s). The sets Ind(s) are chosen such that the cardinal number is close to n/p in order to balance the computations. Then, during the communication stage, the processors transmit their results using all-to-all exchange; each P_s sends $H_i(Z)$ for all the indices i of Ind(s) to all the other processors. The program stops when a convergence criterion is fulfilled, such as when the maximum of the values of the polynomial is sufficiently small or the maximum number of iterations is exceeded. Thus, a generic program is as follows:

```
{synchronous algorithm: program for processor Ps}
computation of the starting point Z
repeat
    for  i  through  Ind(s)
        Zi ← Hi(Z)
    all-to-all exchange of the Zi
to  stop(Z)
```

The algorithm is synchronous: the subsequent iteration $Z^{(k+1)}$ is computed using the components of $Z^{(k)}$. Note that the word synchronous does not refer, here, to the control mode of the machine (MIMD or SIMD) but to the structure of the algorithm. Since the cost of Guggenheimer's procedure for computing the starting points is not significant and since, by using the distributed computation of the maximum, the stop criterion can be ignored, the cost of such an implementation is the sum of the computation time unit and the communication time unit. Consequently, the algorithm's performance depends on two factors: the distribution of the computations and the communication costs.

For the two methods DK and EA, the sequential cost of the computation of H(Z) is $\Theta(n^2)\tau_a$ if the standard algorithm is used (for example, if the polynomials are evaluated with Horner's rules). For the same methods, the arithmetic cost of one stage of the parallel algorithm is $\Theta(n^2/p)\tau_a$. If an all-to-all exchange is considered as p broadcasts, we have seen that the communication costs are of the order $D(p\beta_c+\Theta((n)\tau_c))$. As a consequence, the speed-up of a parallel synchronous implementation depends asymptotically (when n increases) solely on the parallel arithmetic cost. Communications are in O(n) whereas the computations are in $\Theta(n^2)$ for a fixed number of processors.

However, if we now assume that p can be arbitrarily large, for example $p = \alpha n$, then the communication cost cannot be ignored. Since each processor receives O(n) data items on all the $\Delta(p) = \Theta(\Delta(n))$ communication links and since the diameter of the graph is $D(p) = \Theta(D(n))$, the communication time is at least:

$$\max\left\{\Omega\left(\frac{n}{\Delta(n)}\right)\tau_c, \Omega(D(n))\beta_c\right\}$$

So, the computation cost and the communication cost can be of the same order. This is the case if $\Delta(p)$ is bounded or if $D(p)$ depends linearly on p. In all cases, if $\beta_c \gg \tau_a$ or if $\tau_c \gg \tau_a$, the communication time can be a major disadvantage in parallelizing iterative methods.

More specifically, our aim is to implement these algorithms on the usual topologies: rings, toric grids and hypercubes. In this case, we can use the standard methods of broadcasting described in Chapter 15. From this, it is deduced that the above algorithm has the following cost per iteration:

$$\Theta\left(\frac{n^2}{p}\right)\tau_a + \left\lfloor\frac{p}{2}\right\rfloor\beta_c + \Theta\left(\frac{n}{2}\right)\tau_c \qquad \text{on a ring,}$$

$$\Theta\left(\frac{n^2}{p}\right)\tau_a + 2\left\lfloor\frac{\sqrt{p}}{2}\right\rfloor\beta_c + \Theta\left(\frac{n}{4}\right)\tau_c \qquad \text{on a toric grid,}$$

$$\Theta\left(\frac{n^2}{p}\right)\tau_a + \log_2(p)\beta_c + \Theta\left(\frac{n}{\log_2(p)}\right)\tau_c \qquad \text{on a hypercube.}$$

It follows that the total time per stage is expressed as:

$$T_{syn}(n,p) = \Theta\left(\frac{n^2}{p}\right)\tau_a + D\ \beta_c + \Theta\left(\frac{n}{\Delta}\right)\tau_c$$

Thus, if $p = \alpha n$:

$$T_{syn}(n,\alpha n) = \Theta(n)\tau_a + D\ \beta_c + \Theta\left(\frac{n}{\Delta}\right)\tau_c$$

and it appears that the communication cost strongly influences the total execution time.

17.4.3 Asynchronous implementations

We propose a modification to the communication strategy such that at each iteration, a processor does not have to wait at certain points. The algorithm, referred to as *asynchronous* by Beaudet [Bea78], could be constructed as follows. A processor P_s computes $z_i(k+1)$, at stage k+1, using the formula:

$$z_i^{k+1} = H_i\left(z_1^{k-r(1,k,s)}, z_2^{k-r(2,k,s)}, \ldots, z_n^{k-r(n,k,s)}\right)$$

Each component z_i is updated using the vector of the last values of the components z_j that were known by processor s at stage k. They are written $z_j^{(k-r(j, k, s))}$, where $r(j, k, s)$ is a period of time that is independent of j, k and s, which indicates that processor P_s only knows the value of z_j which was computed at stage $k-r(j, k, s)$.

Note that the word *asynchronous* refers only to the fact that, at each stage, local computations are performed by using only a part of the information as if it were the whole information. In order to ensure that asynchronous algorithms are valid, we assume that the scattering strategy of the indices satisfies the following assumptions:

1. $z_i(k+1)$ is computed by a single processor, for all $i = 1,\ldots, n$

2. $r(i, k, s) = 0$, that is, the processor that computes $z_i(k+1)$ knows $z_i^{(k)}$.

The first assumption ensures that there is no redundancy in the computations. The second implies that, at stage k, if $z_i(h)$, ($0 \le h \le k$, i in $\{1,\ldots, n\}$), is known by a set of processors, its value is the same for all processors. The validity criteria for an asynchronous algorithm can be stricter than they are for its synchronous counterpart. Moreover, as Bertsekas and Tsitsiklis observed [BeT89], determining when the algorithm stops tends to be more difficult for asynchronous algorithms than for synchronous algorithms.

In asynchronous implementation, it is hoped that communication times will decrease. However, the number of iterations can increase. The convergence conditions for the asynchronous approach are to be found in [CoF92], as well as the proof of the fact that the orders of its convergence are smaller than in the synchronous case. Specifically, it is proved that if $r = \max r(i, k)$, then the order of convergence of the DK method is the only positive root of the equation $\lambda^{r+1} - \lambda^r - 1 = 0$, which is strictly between 1 and 2, and that the order of convergence of the AE method is the only positive root of the equation $\lambda^{r+1} - 2\lambda^r - 1 = 0$, which is strictly between 2 and 3. If $r = 1$, the corresponding values are 1.62 and 2.41, which is a significant reduction. This result shows that the convergence of an asynchronous algorithm is slower than that of a synchronous algorithm. Consequently, the extent to which asynchronous implementation is advantageous depends on achieving the right balance between reducing communication cost and increasing the number of iterations.

The strategy can be implemented in many different ways, but we shall only describe the most natural one: at each step, processor P_s sends only the values that it has computed to its neighbours and the cost of one computation stage remains $\Theta(n^2/p)\tau_a$, whereas the communication cost is $\beta_c + \Theta(\frac{n}{p})\tau_c$, whatever the interconnection network's topology. The total time is thus:

$$T_{asyn}(n,p) = \Theta\left(\frac{n^2}{p}\right)\tau_a + \beta_c + \Theta\left(\frac{n}{p}\right)\tau_c$$

which represents a saving of D–1 start-up time and the reduction of the propagation time from

$$\Theta\left(\frac{n}{\Delta}\right)\tau_c \quad \text{to} \quad \Theta\left(\frac{n}{p}\right)\tau_c$$

Note that if each processor always updates the same component, then each processor knows only a section of the data. This can lead to non-convergence. The sets of indices Ind(s) must therefore change during the algorithm. The set of indices of components of Z that are processed by P_s at time k is written Ind(s, k). The set of indices of processors that are neighbours of P_s is called V(s). A sufficient condition is that, for all i, the time difference between two evaluations of the ith component by the processors of V(s) is bounded by a constant ρ. This implies that the longest of the delays is bounded by ρ. A generic program would be as follows:

```
{asynchronous algorithm: program of processor Pₛ}
computation of the starting point Z
k ← 0
repeat
    k ← k + 1
    computation of Ind(s, k)
    for i through Ind(s)
        Zᵢ ← Hᵢ(Z)
    {Zᵢ / i ∈ Ind(s, k)} sent to the processors of V(s)
    {Zᵢ / i ∈ Ind(q, k), q ∈ V(s)} received
    k ← k + 1
to  stop(Z)
```

It can be seen that the two algorithms have the same structure, except for the section concerned with communications where the all-to-all exchange is replaced by a local exchange. The stop test presents a greater difficulty for the asynchronous algorithm and therefore slightly complicates its stop algorithm. We will not provide strategies for determining the sets Ind(s, k). We will simply state that in all cases the time is necessarily greater than p/Δ.

For the two algorithms to be compared, their respective total lengths have to be evaluated, that is, the product of the number of iterations and the length of each iteration. Unfortunately, there is no theoretical result that can be used to find a bound on the number of iterations. In [CoF92], experimental results show that the asynchronous algorithm can, in some cases, perform better than those of the synchronous version.

17.5   Gustafson speed-up

Although we looked at speed-up for algorithms on shared-memory computers, we have not so far discussed the issue in this chapter; we do so here. We also provide a new definition of speed-up that is more appropriate for distributed-memory computers and discuss how to implement it.

17.5.1   Review of Amdahl's law

Speed-up was defined in Section 2.3.1, as the result of dividing the computation time of the best sequential algorithm by the computation time of the best parallel algorithm with p processors. In practice, speed-up is measured by measuring the time it takes the sequential algorithm to execute on a single processor of the p-processor computer. The measurement is performed with limited resources, especially memory. However, if a shared-memory computer is considered, the memory size is the same, whether the problem is solved with one or p processors. It is not the same if the memory is distributed since, if the algorithm is executed sequentially, the processor can only use its own memory. Let us examine the consequences of this limitation on speed-up.

To do this we refer to the proof of Amdahl's law (*see* Section 2.3.2). Consider the execution of a program in sequential and parallel modes. Suppose the program has an intrinsically sequential part S and an intrinsically parallel part P, where these are given as fractions so that S+P=1. If t_1 is the sequential time (the time for execution with one processor) we can, without any loss of generality, take $t_1=1$. With p processors, we then obtain an execution time of: $t_p = S + \frac{P}{p}$. Therefore:

$$S_p = \frac{S+P}{S+\dfrac{P}{p}} = \frac{1}{S+\dfrac{P}{p}} \leq \frac{1}{S}$$

and thus the speed-up is, whatever the value of p, lower than the proportion of sequential code. For example, if 50% of the program is sequential, speed-up is lower than 2, if it is 10%, it is lower than 10, and if it is 1%, it is lower than 100, and this applies however many processors there are. This result, known as *Amdahl's law* (1967), expresses the fact that speed-up is bounded by a constant that is independent of the number of processors and the machine's structure (*see* Figure 17.21).

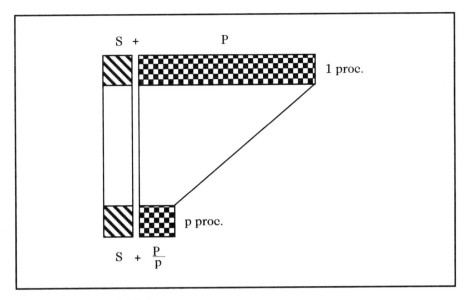

Figure 17.21   Amdahl's law

17.5.2   Definition of Gustafson speed-up

Historically, Amdahl's law is of great importance, since it led those involved in researching parallel computing to deduce that substantial increases in performance could not be achieved by implementing parallelism and that the number of processors has to be restricted to a few tens. However, since the late 1980s, machines with hundreds of processors have been constructed and users have reported considerable increases in performance. Gustafson [Gus88] studied this paradox and came up with a solution.

Let us look at the class of problems – a large class – whose execution time increases with the size of the instance under consideration. Assume that the memory space used also increases with this size. On a shared-memory machine, memory size is not relevant, since, with either one or p processors, the same instances of the problem can be solved. It can therefore be said (rather hastily, perhaps) that Amdahl's law applies. This does not hold for distributed-memory machines. If a parallel computer is used, it is in order to solve a problem more rapidly, but also, and above all, in order to solve larger problems. This point is very important for distri-buted-memory machines and is the basis of Gustafson's argument: with a distributed-memory machine, instances of larger size can be solved. Let us compare the performance of the algorithms for instances of maximum size (with p processors, memory is p times larger).

Suppose we execute our maximum-size problem with a parallel algorithm written for the p processors; the execution time will be S+P=1, since all the processors will compute simultaneously. Its sequential time is S+pP (*see* Figure 17.22). Speed-up is therefore:

$$SG_p = \frac{S+pP}{S+P} = S+pP \geq pP$$

Thus the speed-up is bounded below by an expression which increases linearly with p. If 50% of the program is sequential, speed-up is greater than 0.5p, if it is 10% it is greater than 0.9p, and if it is 1% it is greater than 0.99p. In theory, there is no bound on speed-up.

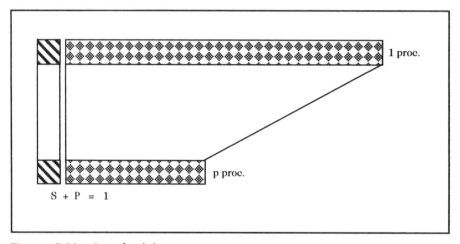

Figure 17.22   Gustafson's law

17.5.2   Computing Gustafson speed-up

This model proves to be well adapted to distributed-memory machines and explains the high performance achieved with them. However, in practice, S and P are not known. Gustafson therefore suggests obtaining speed-up by computing the time required to compute the largest instance of the problem being considered and by obtaining the quotient of the size of that instance by the size of the largest instance that can be resolved with p processors.

Another way of evaluating speed-up is to compare computation times per elementary operation. To be more precise, let $t_{max}(1)$ be the average computation time for executing an elementary operation of a sequential algorithm that solves the largest problem that can be stored on a processor and $t_{max}(p)$ the average computation time for executing an elementary operation of a parallel algorithm that solves the largest problem that can be stored on p processors. Gustafson speed-up is estimated by:

$$SG_p = \frac{t_{max}(1)}{t_{max}(p)}$$

To prove this, consider $N_{max}(1)$ and $N_{max}(p)$ to be the respective sizes of the largest problems. The problem of size $N_{max}(1)$ is executed with 1 processor in a time of $t(N_{max}(1))$ and the problem of size $N_{max}(p)$ is executed with p processors in a time of $t(N_{max}(p))$. This can be used to determine $t_{max}(1)$ and $t_{max}(p)$ since

$$t(N_{max}(1))=N_{max}(1)\,t_{max}(1) \text{ and } t(N_{max}(p))=N_{max}(p)\,t_{max}(p)$$

Assume there is enough memory available to solve the problem of size $N_{max}(p)$ with one processor. We then obtain:

$$SG_p = \frac{t_1}{t_p} = \frac{N_{max}(p)t_{max}(1)}{N_{max}(p)t_{max}(p)} = \frac{t_{max}(1)}{t_{max}(p)}$$

To illustrate the method, let us estimate Gustafson speed-up in Gaussian elimination on a pipelined ring as presented in Section 17.3.2. Its complexity is:

$$\frac{2n^3}{3p}\tau_a + (n-1)\beta_c + \frac{3n^2}{2}\tau_c$$

Let M be the size of the memory per processor. The sizes of the largest problems that can be solved are therefore N=M with 1 processor and N=pM with p processors, which yields $n=\sqrt{M}$ and $n=\sqrt{pM}$ respectively. By applying the formulae above and knowing that the amount of computation is $\frac{2n^3}{3}$ operations, a varying Gustafson speed-up, such as $O(\sqrt{p})$, is obtained, which contradicts Amdahl's law. A full description of the method can be found in [CRT89].

17.6   Conclusion

We have described techniques for designing numerical algorithms on processor networks and illustrated them with a few representative examples. In
particular, it is often fairly simple to choose a good way of initially dividing
data and to identify communication schemes for them. However, this
approach does not necessarily yield high performance. Designing efficient
algorithms entails stages where local computations and communications are
closely intertwined. From this perspective, dependency graphs may prove
to be very useful.

18

Conclusion

Competition, Cooperation, Communication.
The Coordinated Research Programme
(CNRS and French Ministry of Research)

18.1   Summary

Parallelism is relevant to all sections of information science and computing. It is causing profound changes in all the traditional areas of information science and computing and in the commercial sectors it affects. The pace at which it is progressing is extraordinarily fast, and practical and theoretical tools are being developed at a similar rate. It can be unequivocally stated that, by the end of the century, all computers – rather than just super-computers – will be parallel. This means that progress will have to be made in all fields of information science and computing, but it also means that new problems will arise and further progress will result from this.

In this book, we chose to concentrate on architectures and algorithms. Our aim was to focus on the principles and methodological aspects of the subject, rather than to describe or analyse implementations (which, generally speaking, are short-lived). Our main concern was therefore to concentrate on constructing models (which are as realistic as possible, but which, of necessity, are reductionist) and to attempt to learn as much as

517

possible from them. Of course, our aim was to enable readers to use current machines more profitably and to keep abreast of, if not actively engage in, developments that are currently taking place.

As far as architectures are concerned, we adopted a historical approach, which fits in rather well with studying progressively complex structures: starting with vector processors and moving on to shared-memory and distributed-memory multiprocessors. We described the architectural principles of each of these categories and examined their main models and theoretical developments of them; at the same time, we concentrated on the methodological aspects of these categories, so that their advantages and disadvantages could be more readily grasped. Although we cannot claim that the description was comprehensive, we nevertheless believe that the methods described in this book can be used for designing, evaluating and implementing parallel algorithms on the most commonly used architectures. The most essential issue is to optimize an algorithm's efficiency, as measured by its execution time on the architecture being used. This approach can be summarized as follows:

- analysing the main characteristics of the architecture and modelling them,
- listing the relevant efficient sequential algorithms,
- restructuring and, where required, modifying them,
- constructing a parallel algorithm,
- evaluating the algorithm's efficiency in terms of complexity,
- implementing this algorithm on the target architecture.

We described tools for automatic parallelization for several cases, including vector and, to a certain extent, shared-memory architectures.

Many architecture models were not discussed in this study: systolic networks, neural networks and data flow machines, for example. We concentrated instead on general-purpose machines, and readers who are interested in specialized machines are referred to the relevant literature.

18.2   Systems and languages

The most important of the areas that we did not cover, or covered only in part, relate to software – systems and languages in particular. There is a significant amount of both theoretical and practical literature on these topics. However, results in the commercial sector have failed to match those in hardware and parallel algorithm development.

Many avenues of software research are currently being explored with a view to remedying the chronic weaknesses of parallel machines. Basic software, tools for automatic parallelization and programming environments are the major issues facing the commercial sector. Virtualization is another major issue, and the question arises as to whether research efforts should concentrate on developing an implicit parallelism that is hidden from the user – shared virtual memory and shared virtual memory machines are important concepts in this context. In the former, a single address space is created from a set of distributed memories. The different processes use addresses in this space, and the underlying system executes the requisite message exchanges between processors and maintains the memory's global coherence. In the latter, a set of machines – either parallel or non-parallel – are considered to be a single resource, and the system is responsible for distributing tasks to various computers, according to their loads and capacity for further work. As a result, implicit languages are used.

A variety of tools is required to write parallel algorithms directly, including explicitly parallel languages, parallel control programs, program development environments, recording and display tools, performance evaluation, parallel data structures and communications and applications libraries. The diversity of models used has resulted in several types of language being developed – synchronous or asynchronous, SIMD or MIMD and sequential languages with parallel or specific tools. Fortran 90, High Performance Fortran (HPF), occam, Ada and C* are among the most well known.

As we have seen, parallel languages are far more complex than their sequential counterparts, because the former make use of multiple control flows and message exchange management between processors. As a result, obtaining high performance from programs is a laborious process, requiring many different program versions to be written – if high performance is not being sought, it is better to use sequential programs. Tools for developing and recording the execution of parallel programs help in designing and validating the different program versions. But they also create a great number of difficulties: generally, the user is dealing with a large amount of information on the status of various processes – active, inactive or communicating, communications between processors, the division of computation time between processors and so on. At run time, the information is gathered by a record collection system and can be used either online, or after the program has ended ('post-mortem'). On massively parallel machines, the amount of information can be considerable and processing it difficult.

18.3   Prospects

Parallelism is still evolving – at a very fast pace. Establishing what its long-term prospects are is difficult and risky. In this book, we attempted to analyse it, describe methods for using it and summarize the main points arising from it, rather than go into its technical details. We believe that developing models of parallelism is essential to a detailed understanding of the mechanisms involved in systems of this complexity. Whatever developments lie in store for parallelism, this approach will remain valid.

As far as architecture is concerned, massively parallel machines are set to undergo significant development. In 1995, machines with several thousand processors will be available in supercomputing centres. At the same time, integration capabilities will be such that it will be possible for slightly parallel multiprocessors to be fabricated on a single circuit. It is quite reasonable to believe that such developments will continue in the coming years.

In the more distant future, the capabilities of current technology are likely to be outstripped, as we are already approaching its physical limits. New technologies will then push the evolution of parallelism even further. Optoelectronics is particularly attractive in relation to parallelism, especially as far as interconnection networks and communication devices are concerned. As far as models are concerned, cell processor and neural networks can be seen as interesting alternatives to standard parallel models.

There is every reason for optimism – and for a bright future for parallelism.

Bibliography

[ABB92]   E. Anderson, Z. Bai, C. Bischof *et al.*, *LAPACK users' guide*, SIAM Philadelphia (1992).

[Abe73]   O. Aberth, Iteration methods for finding all zeros of a polynomial simultaneously, *Maths. Computation* 27, 122 (1973) 339–44.

[ACD74]   T.L. Adam, K.M. Chandy, J.R. Dickson, A comparison of list schedules for parallel processing systems, *Communications ACM* 17 (1974) 685–90.

[ACK87]   J.R. Allen, D. Callahan, K. Kennedy, Automatic decomposition of scientific programs for parallel execution, *Fourteenth ACM Symposium on the Principles of Programming Languages* (1987) 63–76.

[ACS90]   A. Aggarwal, A.K. Chandra, M. Snir, Communication complexity of PRAMs, *Theoretical Computer Science* 71 (1990) 3–28.

[AHU74]   A.V. Aho, J.E. Hopcroft, J.D. Ullman, *The design and analysis of computer algorithms*, Addison-Wesley, Reading (1974).

[AHU87]   A.V. Aho, J.E. Hopcroft, J.D. Ullman, *Structures de données et algorithmes*, InterEditions (1987).

[Akl85]   S. Akl, *Parallel sorting algorithms*, Academic Press, New York (1985).

[Akl89]   S. Akl, *The design and analysis of parallel algorithms*, Prentice-Hall (1989).

[AKS84]   M. Ajtai, J. Komlos, E. Szemeredi, An O(nlogn) sorting network, *Combinatorica* 3 (1984) 1–19.

[AlK87]   J.R. Allen, K. Kennedy, Automatic translation of Fortran programs to vector form, *ACM Transactions on Programming Languages and Systems* 9, 4 (1987) 491–542.

[Amd67]   G.M. Amdahl, Validity of the single processor approach of achieving large scale computing capabilities, *AFIPS Conf. Proc.* 30 (1967) 483–5.

[AnP88]   F. André, J.L. Pazat, Le placement de tâches sur des architectures parallèles, *TSI*, 7, 4 (1988) 385–401.

[AuB82]   M. Auguin, F. Boeri, Efficient multiprocessor architecture for digital signal processing, *ICASSP* (1982) 675–9.

[AuB86]   M. Auguin, F. Boeri, The OPSILA computer, in *Parallel Algorithms and Architectures*, Eds. M. Cosnard *et al.*, North-Holland (1986) 143–54.

[BaA91]   M. Baumslag, F. Annexstein, A unified framework for off-line permutation routing in parallel networks, *Mathematical Systems Theory* 24 (1991) 233–51.

[Bab87]   R.G. Babb II Jr. (Ed), *Programming parallel processors*, Addison-Wesley (1987).

[Ban88]   U. Banerjee, An introduction to a formal theory of dependence analysis, *Journal of Supercomputing* 2 (1988) 133–49.

[Bat68]   K.E. Batcher, Sorting networks and their applications, *Proc. AFIPS* (1968) 307–14.

[Bau78]   G.M. Baudet, Asynchronous iterative methods for multiprocessors, *Journal ACM* 25, 2 (1978) 226–44.

[BBK84]   A. Bojanczyk, R.P. Brent, H.T. Kung, Numerically stable solution of dense systems of linear equations using mesh-connected processors, *SIAM Journal Sci. Stat. Comput.* 5, 1 (1984) 95–104.

[BCH86]   P.W. Beame, S.A. Cook, H.J. Hoover, Log depth circuits for division and related problems, *SIAM Journal of Computing* 15, 4 (1986) 994–1003.

[BCS89]   A. Billionnet, M-C. Costa, A. Sutter, Les problèmes de placement dans les systèmes distribués, *TSI* 8, 4 (1989) 317–36.

[Bea72]   J.C. Beatty, An axiomatic approach to code optimization for expressions, *Journal of ACM* 19, 4 (1972) 613–40.

[Ben65]   V.E. Benes, *Mathematical theory of connecting networks and telephone traffic*, Academic Press, New York (1965).

[Ber83]   C. Berge, *Graphes et hypergraphes*, Bordas (1983).

[Ber92]   J-C. Bermond (Ed), Interconnection networks, *Discrete Applied Mathematics*, special issue (1992).

[BeS87]   F. Berman, L. Snyder, On mapping parallel algorithms into parallel architectures, *Journal Parallel and Distrib. Comput.,* Vol. 4, No. 5 (1987) 439–58.

[BeS92]   J-C. Bermond, M. Syska, Wormhole routing and virtual channels, in *Algorithmique Parallèle*, Eds. M. Cosnard *et al.*, Collection ERI, Masson (1992) 149–58.

[BeT89]   D.P. Bertsekas, J.N. Tsitsiklis, *Parallel and distributed computation – numerical methods*, Prentice-Hall (1989).

[BHL89]   J-C. Bermond, P. Hell, A.L. Liestman, J.G. Peters, Broadcasting in bounded degree graphs, *Technical report* 88–5, Simon Fraser University (1989).

[BKM73]   R.P. Brent, D.J. Kuck, K.M. Maruyama, The parallel evaluation of arithmetic expressions without divisions, *IEEE Transactions on Computers* 22 (1973) 532–4.

[BKT91]   E. Bampis, J-C. König, D. Trystram, Impact of communications on the complexity of the parallel Gaussian elimination, *Parallel Computing* 17 (1991) 55–61.

[BKT93]   E. Bampis, J-C. König, D. Trystram, A low overhead schedule for the 3D-grid graph, *Parallel Processing Letters* 3 (1993).

[BlT90]   J-Y. Blanc, D. Trystram, Implementation of parallel numerical routines using broadcast communication schemes, *Proceedings of the CONPAR'90 Conference, Zurich,* LNCS 457 Springer Verlag (1990) 467–78.

[BMR90]   E.W. Burton, G.P. McKeown, V.J. Rayward-Smith, Applications of UET scheduling theory to the implementation of declarative languages, *The Computer Journal,* 33, 4 (1990) 330–6.

[Bok81]   S.H. Bokhari, On the mapping problem, *IEEE Transactions on Computers,* Vol C-30, No. 3 (1981) 207–14.

[Bok88]   S.H. Bokhari, *Assignment problems in parallel and distributed computing,* Kluwer Academic Publishers, Boston (1988).

[BoM75]   A. Borodin, I. Munro, *The computational complexity of algebraic and numeric problems,* American Elsevier, New York (1975).

[BoM88]   S.W. Bollinger, S.F. Midkiff, Processor and link assignment in multicomputers using simulated annealing, *International Conference on Parallel Processing ICPP '88* (1988) 1–7.

[Bor73]   A. Borodin, On the number of arithmetics required to compute certain functions – Circa May 1973, in *Complexity of Sequential and Parallel Numerical Algorithms,* J.F. Traub Ed., Academic Press, New-York (1973) 149–80.

[Bor77]   A. Borodin, On related time and space to size and depth, *SIAM Journal on Computing,* Vol. 5 (1977) 733–44.

[BoR90]   R. Boppana, C.S. Raghavendra, Optimal self-routing of linear complement permutation in hypercubes, *International Conference on Parallel Processing* (1990) 800–8.

[BOS91]   D.P. Bertsekas, C. Ozveren, G.D. Stamoulis, P. Tseng, J.N. Tsitsiklis, Optimal communication schemes for hypercubes, *Journal of Parallel and Distributed Computing* 11 (1991) 263–75.

[Bra90]   B. Braschi, *Principes de base des algorithmes d'ordonnancement de liste et affectation de priorités aux tâches,* Thèse INP Grenoble (1990).

[Bre70]   R.P. Brent, On the addition of binary numbers, *IEEE Transactions on Computers* C-19 (1970) 758–9.

[Bre73]   R.P. Brent, The parallel evaluation of arithmetic expressions in logarithmic time, in *Complexity of Sequential and Parallel Numerical Algorithms,* J.F. Traub Ed., Academic Press, New York (1973) 83–102.

[Bre74]   R.P. Brent, The parallel evaluation of general arithmetic expressions, *Journal ACM* 21, 2 (1974) 201–6.

[BrT93]   B. Braschi, D. Trystram, A new insight into the Coffman-Graham algorithm, *SIAM Journal on Computing*.

[BTV92]   P. Bouvry, D. Trystram, F. Vincent, An automatic mapping tool for parallel task graphs, *LMC-IMAG technical report* (1992).

[Buz73]   B.L. Buzbee, A fast Poisson solver amenable to parallel computation, *IEEE Transactions on Computers* 22 (1973) 793–6.

[CaC88]   J. Carlier, P. Chrétienne, *Problèmes d'ordonnancement*, Collection ERI, Masson (1988).

[CaK87]   D. Callahan, K. Kennedy, Analysis of interprocedural side effects in a parallel programming environment, *First International Conference on Supercomputing*, Athens (1987).

[CaK88]   D. Callahan, K. Kennedy, Compiling programs for distributed memory machines, *Journal of Supercomputing* 2, 2 (1988) 151–69.

[CaK88]   T. Casavant, J.G. Kuhl, A taxonomy of scheduling in general-purpose distributed computing systems, *IEEE Transactions on Software Engineering* 14 (1988) 141–54.

[CaT93]   C. Calvin, D. Trystram, Matrix transposition on regular networks, *LMC-IMAG technical report* (1993).

[CDM86]   M. Cosnard, M. Daoudi, J.M. Muller, Y. Robert, On parallel and systolic Givens factorizations of dense matrices, in *Algorithmes et Architectures Parallèles*, Eds. M. Cosnard *et al.*, North-Holland (1986) 245–258.

[CDM93]   C. Calvin, F. Desprez, P. Michallon, D. Trystram, A fine grain pipelined scientific library for parallel computers, preprint (1993).

[CDR86]   S.A. Cook, C. Dwork, R. Reischuk, Upper and lower time bounds for parallel random access machines without simultaneous writes, *SIAM Journal of Computing* 15 (1986) 87–97.

[CDT87]   M. Cosnard, M. Daoudi, B. Tourancheau, Communication dans les réseaux de processeurs et complexité des algorithmes, *Technical report TIM3* Grenoble (1987).

[ChK75]   S.C. Chen, D.J. Kuck, Time and parallel processor bounds for linear recurrence systems, *IEEE Transactions on Computers* 24 (1975) 701–17.

[CHL80]   W. Chu, L. Holloway, M. Lan, K. Efe, Task allocation in distributed data processing, *Computer* (1980) 57–69.

[ChP92]   P. Chrétienne, C. Picouleau, The basic scheduling problem with interprocessor communication delays, *Actes de l'Ecole d'été INRIA sur l'Ordonnancement et ses Applications*, Bonas (1992) 81–100.

[Chr92]   P. Chrétienne, Ordonnancement et parallèlisme, in *Algorithmique Parallèle*, Eds. M. Cosnard *et al.*, Collection ERI, Masson (1992) 297–312.

[ChS85]   T.F. Chan, Y. Saad, Multigrid algorithms on the hypercube multiprocessor, *Research report* 368, Yale University (1985).

[ChS90]   T.C. Cheng, C.C. Sin, A state-of-the-art review of parallel-machine scheduling research, *European Journal of Operational Research*, No 47 (1990) 271–92.

[CiV87]   L. Ciminiera, A. Valenzano, *Advanced microprocessor architectures*, Electronic systems engineering series, Addison-Wesley (1987).

[Clo53]   C. Clos, A study of nonblocking switching networks, *Bell System Tech. J* 32 (1953) 408–24.

[CMR86]   M. Cosnard, J.M. Muller, Y. Robert, Parallel QR decomposition of a rectangular matrix, *Numerische Mathematik* 48, (1986) 239–49.

[CMR87]   M. Cosnard, M. Marrakchi, Y. Robert, D. Trystram, Parallel Gaussian elimination on a MIMD computer, *Parallel Computing* 6 (1987) 275–96.

[CNR92]   M. Cosnard, M. Nivat, Y. Robert, Eds. *Algorithmique parallèle*, Collection ERI, Masson (1992).

[CoC91]   J-Y. Colin, P. Chrétienne, CPM Scheduling with small interprocessor communication delays, *Operations research* Vol. 39, 3 (1991).

[CoD73]   E.G. Coffman, P.J. Denning, *Operating systems theory*, Prentice-Hall (1973).

[CoD92]   M. Cosnard, M. Daoudi, Optimal algorithms for parallel Givens factorization on a coarse grained PRAM, *Journal of ACM* (1994).

[Cof76]   E.G. Coffman, *Computer and job-shop scheduling theory*, New York, Wiley (1976).

[CoF90]   M. Cosnard, P. Fraigniaud, Finding the roots of a polynomial on a MIMD multicomputer, *Parallel Computing* 15 (1990) 75–85.

[CoF91a]   M. Cosnard, A. Ferreira, On the real power of loosely coupled parallel architectures, *Parallel Processing Letters* Vol. 1, 2 (1991) 103–12.

[CoF91b]   M. Cosnard, A. Ferreira, Designing parallel non numerical algorithms, in *Parallel Computing '91*, Eds. D.J. Evans *et al.*, North Holland (1991) 3–18.

[CoF92]   M. Cosnard, P. Fraigniaud, Analysis of asynchronous polynomial root finding methods on a distributed memory multicomputer, *LIP-IMAG research report*, ENS Lyon (1992).

[CoG72]   E.G. Coffman, R.L. Graham, Optimal scheduling for two processor systems, *Acta Informatica* 1 (1972) 200–13.

[CoL90]   C Coroyer, Z. Liu, Effectiveness of Heuristics and Simulated Annealing for the Scheduling of Concurrent Tasks – An Empirical Comparison, *INRIA research report* 1379 (1990).

[Col90]   R. Cole, Parallel merge sort, *SIAM Journal of Computing* 17, 4 (1988) 770–85.

[Coo71]   S.A. Cook, The complexity of theorem proving procedures, *Proceedings of the 3rd ACM Symposium on the Theory of Computing*, (1971) 151–8.

[CoR86a]   M. Cosnard, Y. Robert, Systolic Givens factorization of dense rectangular matrices, *Int. Journal Comp. Math.* (1986).

[CoR86b]   M. Cosnard, Y. Robert, Complexity of parallel QR factorization, *Journal ACM* 33, 4, (1986) 712–23.

[CoR87]   M. Cosnard, Y. Robert, Algorithmique parallèle: une étude de complexité, *Technique et Science Informatiques* (1987).

[CoW87]   D. Coppersmith, S. Winograd, Matrix multiplication via arithmetic progressions, *19th Annual ACM Symp. Theory Comp.* (1987) 1–6.

[CRT86]   M. Cosnard, Y. Robert, D. Trystram, Résolution parallèle de systèmes linéaires denses par diagonalisation, *Bulletin EDF*, series C 2 (1986) 67–88.

[CRT87]   M. Cosnard, Y. Robert, M. Tchuente, Matching parallel algorithms with architectures: a case study, in *Highly Parallel Computers for Numerical and Signal Processing Applications*, North Holland (1987).

[CRT89]   M. Cosnard, Y. Robert, B. Tourancheau, Evaluating speedups on distributed memory architectures, *Parallel Computing* 10 (1989) 247–53.

[Csa76]   L. Csanky, Fast parallel matrix inversion algorithms, *SIAM Journal of Computing* 5 (1976) 618–23.

[Cve87]   Z. Cvetanovic, The effect of problem partitioning, allocation, and granularity on the performance of multiple-processor systems, *IEEE Transactions on Computers*, Vol. C36, No. 4, (1987) 421–32.

[CyP90]   R. Cypher, C.G. Plaxton, Deterministic sorting in nearly logarithmic time on the hypercube and related computers, *Proceedings of ACM Symposium on the Theory of Computing* (1990).

[DalS87]   W.J. Dally, C.L. Seitz, Deadlock-free message routing in multiprocessor interconnection networks, *IEEE Transactions on Computers* Vol. C36, No. 5 (1987) 547–53.

[DaR92]   A. Darte, Y. Robert, Séquencement des nids de boucles, in *Algorithmique parallèle*, Eds. M. Cosnard *et al.*, Masson (1992) 344–68.

[DDD88]   J. Demmel, J.J. Dongarra, J. DuCroz, A. Greenbaum, S.J. Hammarling and D.C. Sorensen, A project for developing a linear algebra library for high-performance computers, in *Aspects of Computation on Asynchronous Parallel Processors*, Ed. M. Wright, 1988.

[DDH90]   J.J. Dongarra, J. DuCroz, S.J. Hammarling, I. Duff, A set of level 3 Basic Linear Algebra subprograms, *ACM Transactions on Mathematical Software*, Vol. 16, No. 1, (1990) 1–17.

[DDT92]   D. Delesalle, L. Desbat, D. Trystram, Résolution de grands systèmes linéaires creux par méthodes itératives parallèles, *RAIRO M2AN* (1993).

[Del92]   O. Delmas, Permutations parallèles 'off-line' de données sur grilles de processeurs, *DEA report, INP* Grenoble (1992).

[DGK84]   J.J. Dongarra, F.G. Gustavson, A. Karp, Implementing linear algebra algorithms for dense matrices on a vector pipeline machine, *SIAM Review* 26, 1 (1984) 91–112.

[Dig92]   Digital, *Alpha architecture handbook – Special announcement edition*, (1992).

[DII86]   J.M. Delosme, I.C.F. Ipsen, Systolic array synthesis, in *Algorithmes and Architectures Parallèles*, Eds. M. Cosnard *et al.*, North-Holland, (1986).

[DLR82]   M.A. Dempster, J.K. Lenstra, A.H. Rinnooy Kan, *Determinist and Stochastic Scheduling*, Nato Advanced Study Institutes Series, Kluwer (1982).

[DMB79]   J.J. Dongarra, C.B. Moler, J.R. Bunch, G.W. Stewart, *LINPACK users' guide*, SIAM Philadelphia (1979).

[DoE84]   J.J. Dongarra, S.C. Eisenstat, Squeezing the most out of an algorithm in CRAY Fortran, *ACM Transactions on Math. Software* 10, 3 (1984) 221–30.

[Don88]   J.J. Dongarra, The LINPACK Benchmark: an explanation, *International Conference and Supercomputing*, (1988).

[DRT92]   B. Dumitrescu, J-L. Roch, D. Trystram, Fast matrix multiplication algorithms on MIMD architectures, *LMC-IMAG research report* 87 (1992).

[DTW91]   D. Delesalle, D. Trystram, D. Wenzek, Optimal total exchange on a SIMD distributed memory hypercube, *Proc. DMCC6* Portland, Oregon (1991) 279–82.

[Dua91]   J. Duato, On the design of deadlock-free adaptive routing algorithms for multicomputers: design methodologies, *PARLE'91 Conference*, Springer Verlag (1991) 390–405.

[Dun90]   R. Duncan, A survey of parallel computer architectures, *Computer* (1990) 5–16.

[Dur60]   E. Durand, *Solutions numériques des équations algébriques*, Volume 1, Masson, Paris (1960).

[DuV91]   D. Du, G. Vidal-Naquet, Mapping communication task graph onto reconfigurable multiprocessor architectures, ISCIS VI, 6th *International Symposium on Computer and Information Sciences*, Turkey (1991).

[Ede91]   A. Edelman, Optimal matrix transposition and bit reversal on hypercubes: all-to-all personalized communication, *Journal of Parallel and Distributed Computing* 11 (1991) 328–31.

[Efe82]   K. Efe, Heuristic models of task assignment scheduling in distributed systems, *Computer* 15 (1982) 50–6.

[Ehr67]   L.W. Ehrlich, A modified Newton method for polynomials, *Communications ACM* 10, 2 (1967) 107–8.

[ErL90]   H. El Rewini, T.G. Lewis, Scheduling parallel program tasks onto arbitrary target machines, *Journal of Parallel and Distributed Computing*, Vol. 9 (1990) 138–53.

[ERS90]   F. Ercal, J. Ramanujam, P. Sadayappan, Task allocation onto a hypercube by recursive mincut bipartitioning, *Journal of Parallel and Distributed Computing* 10 (1990).

[FaP80]   S.M. Farley, A. Proskurowski, Gossip in grid graphs, *Journal of Combinatorics Information and System Sciences* 5, 2 (1980).

[FCS90]   C. Froidevaux, M.C. Gaudel, M. Soria, *Types de données et algorithmes*, McGraw-Hill (1990).

[Fea92]   P. Feautrier, Techniques de parallélisation, in *Algorithmique parallèle*, Eds. M. Cosnard *et al.*, Masson (1992) 244–257.

[FeB73]   E.B. Fernandez, B. Bussel, Bounds on the number of processors and time for multiprocessor optimal schedule, *IEEE Transactions on Computers* 22 (1973) 745–51.

[Fen81]   T.Y. Feng, A survey of interconnection networks, *Computer* 14 (1981) 12–27.

[FiO84]   J.A. Fischer, J.J. O'Donnell, VLIW machines: multiprocessors we can actually program, *COMPCON* (1984) 299–305.

[Fli90]   S. Flieller, TELMAT et le projet SUPERNODE, *La lettre du Transputer* 7 (1990) 79–86.

[Fly66]   M.J. Flynn, Very high-speed computing systems, *Proc. IEEE* 54 (1966) 1901–9.

[Fly72]   M.J. Flynn, Some computer organizations and their effectiveness, *IEEE Transactions on Computers* 21 (1972) 948–960.

[FMR90]   P. Fraigniaud, S. Miguet, Y. Robert, Scattering on a ring of processors, *Parallel Computing* 13 (1990) 377–83.

[Fra90]   P. Fraigniaud, Communications intensives dans les architectures à mémoire distribuée, *Thèse ENS* Lyon (1990).

[FrH84]   C. Fraboul, N. Hifdi, LESTAP: A Language for Expression and Synchronization of Tasks on a Multi Array Processor architecture, *Cours de Calcul parallèle de l'INRIA* (1984).

[FrL91]   P. Fraigniaud, E. Lazard, Methods and problems of communication in usual networks, *Research report* 701 LRI Université d'Orsay (1991).

[FrR87]   J.B. Frenk, A.H. Rinnooy Kan, The asymptotic optimality of the LPT rule, *Mathematics of Operations Research*, 12, 2 (1987) 241–5.

[FRS91]   C. Fraboul, J.Y. Rousselot, P. Siron, Software tools for developing programs on a reconfigurable parallel architecture, *EURO-COURSES Computing with parallel architectures: TNODE*, Kluwer Academic Publ., (1991) 101–10.

[Gab82]   H.N. Gabow, An almost-linear algorithm for two-processor scheduling, *ACM Journal* 29, 3 (1982) 766–80.

[GaJ77]   M.R. Garey, D.S. Johnson, Two-processor scheduling with start-times and deadlines, *SIAM Journal of Computing* 6 (1977) 416–26.

[GaJ79]   M.R. Garey, D.S. Johnson, *Computers and intractability – A guide to the theory of NP-completeness*, Freeman and Co. (1979).

[GaP85]   D.D. Gajski, J.K. Peir, Essential issues in multiprocessor systems, *IEEE Computer* (1985) 9–27.

[GaV84]   D. Gannon, J. Van Rosendale, On the impact of communication in the design of parallel algorithms, *IEEE Transactions on Computers* 33, 12 (1984) 1180–94.

[GeH85]   G.A. Geist and M.T. Heath, Parallel Cholesky factorization on a hypercube multiprocessor, preprint ORNL-6190 (1985).

[Gei85]   G.A. Geist, Efficient parallel LU factorization with pivoting on a hypercube multiprocessor, preprint ORNL-6211 (1985).

[GeK81]   W.M. Gentleman, H.T. Kung, Matrix triangularization by systolic arrays, *Proc SPIE* 298, *Real-time Signal Processing IV*, San Diego, California (1981).

[Gen73]   W.M. Gentleman, Least squares computations by Givens transformations without square roots, *J. Inst. Math. Appl.* 12 (1973) 329–36.

[Gen78]   W.M. Gentleman, Some complexity results for matrix computations on parallel processors, *ACM Journal* 25, 1 (1978) 112–5.

[GeN89]   A. Gerasoulis, I. Nelken, Static scheduling for linear algebra DAGs, *Proceedings of the Fourth Conference on Hypercubes*, Monterey (1989) 671–4.

[GeY92]   A. Gerasoulis, T. Yang, A comparison of clustering heuristics for scheduling DAGs on multiprocessors, *Journal of Parallel and Distributed Computing* (1992).

[GGK83]   A. Gottlieb, R. Grishman, C.P. Kruskal, K.P. McAuliffe, L. Rudolph, M. Snir, The NYU Ultracomputer – Designing a MIMD, shared-memory parallel machine, *IEEE Transactions on Computers* C-32 (1983) 75–89.

[GHS86]   J.L. Gustafson, S. Hawkinson, K. Scott, The architecture of a homogeneous vector supercomputer, *International Conference on Parallel Processing*, The Pennsylvania State University Press (1986) 649–52.

[GiR88]   A. Gibbons, W. Rytter, *Efficient parallel algorithms*, Cambridge University Press (1988).

[GIS77]   T. Gonzales, O.H. Ibarra, S. Sahni, Bounds for LPT schedules on uniform processors, *SIAM Journal of Computing* 6, 1 (1977) 155–66.

[GLL79]   R.L. Graham, E.L. Lawler, J.K. Lenstra, A.H. Rinnooy Kan, Optimization and approximation in deterministic sequencing and scheduling: A survey, *Annals of Discrete Math*. 5 (1979) 287–326.

[GLR84]   C. Gao, J.W.S. Liu, M. Railey, Load balancing algorithms in homogeneous distributed systems, *Int. Conf. Parallel Proc.* (1984) 302–6.

[GoK84]   A. Gottlieb, C.P. Kruskal, Complexity results for permuting data and other computations on parallel processors, *Journal ACM* 31 (1984) 193–209.

[GoM79]   M. Gondran, M. Minoux, *Graphes et algorithmes*, Eyrolles (1979).

[Gon77]   M.Y. Gonzales, Deterministic processor scheduling, *ACM Comp. Surveys* 9, 3 (1977) 173–204.

[GoV83]   G.H. Golub, C.E. Van Loan, *Matrix computations*, The John Hopkins University Press (1983).

[Goy77]   D.K. Goyal, Non-preemptive scheduling of unequal execution time tasks on two identical processors, CS-77-039, Comp. Sc. Dept., Washington State University, Pullman, Washington (1977).

[GPC88]   J.L. Gaudiot, J.I. Pi, M.L. Campbell, Program graph allocation in distributed multicomputers, *Parallel Computing* 7 (1988) 227–47.

[Gra69]   R.L. Graham, Bounds for multiprocessing timing anomalies, *SIAM Journal Appl. Math.* 17, 2 (1969) 416–429.

[Gug86]   H. Guggenheimer, Initial approximations in Durand-Kerner's root finding method, *BIT* 26 (1986) 537–9.

[Gui91]   F. Guinand, Ordonnancement et Placement de tâches sur architectures distribuées, *DEA report INP*, Grenoble (1991).

[Gus88]   J.L. Gustafson, Reevaluating Amdahl's law, *Communications ACM* 31, 5 (1988) 532–3.

[HaB88]   P. Haden, F. Berman, A comparative study of assignment algorithms for an automated parallel programming environment, *Tech. Rep.* CS-088, UC San Diego.

[Had89]   E.K. Haddad, Partitioned load allocation for minimum parallel processing execution time, *International Conference on Parallel Processing ICPP '89* (1989) 192–9.

[Ham74]   S. Hammerling, A note on modifications to the Givens plane rotation, *J. Inst. Math. Appl.* 13 (1974) 215–8.

[Hel74]   D. Heller, A determinant theorem with applications to parallel algorithms, *SIAM J. Num. Anal.* 11 (1974) 559–68.

[Hel78]   D. Heller, A survey of parallel algorithms in numerical linear algebra, *SIAM Review* 20 (1978) 740–77.

[Her86]   A. Herscovici, *Introduction aux grands ordinateurs scientifiques*, Eyrolles (1986).

[HHL86]   S.M. Hedetniemi, S.T. Hedetniemi, A.L. Liestman, A survey of gossiping and broadcasting networks, *Networks* 18 (1986) 319–49.

[HoJ81]   R.W. Hockney, C.R. Jesshope, *Parallel computers: Architectures, programming and algorithms*, Adam Hilger Ltd., Bristol (1981).

[HoJ88]   R.W. Hockney, C.R. Jesshope, *Parallel Computers 2: Architectures, programming and algorithms*, Adam Hilger Ltd., Bristol (1988).

[HoJ89]   C-T. Ho, L. Johnsson, Algorithms for matrix transposition on Boolean n-cube configured ensemble architectures, *International Conference on Parallel Processing* (1987) 621–9.

[HoJ89]   C-T. Ho, L. Johnsson, Optimal broadcast on hypercubes, *IEEE Transactions on Computers* 38, 9 (1989) 1249–68.

[HoZ83]   E. Horowitz, A. Zorat, Divide and conquer for parallel processing, *IEEE Transactions on Computers* 32, 6, (1983) 582–5.

[Hu 61]   T.C. Hu, Parallel sequencing and assembly line problems, *Operating Research* 9, 6, (1961) 831–40.

[HwB84]   K. Hwang, F. Briggs, *Parallel processing and computer architecture*, McGraw-Hill (1984).

[HyK77]   L. Hyafil, H.T. Kung, The complexity of parallel evaluation of linear recurrences, *Journal ACM* 24 (1977) 513–21.

[ISS85]   I.C.F. Ipsen, Y. Saad, M.H. Schultz, Complexity of dense linear system solution on a multiprocessor ring, *Research report* 389, Computer Science Dept., Yale University (1985).

[JoH91]   S.L. Johnsson, C.T. Ho, Optimal communication channel utilization for matrix transposition and related permutations on Boolean cubes, *Research report* RJ 7953 CS, IBM Almaden (1991).

[KaF90]   A.H Karp, H.P. Flatt, Measuring parallel processor performance, *Communications ACM* 33, 5 (1990) 539–43.

[KaN84]   H. Kasahara, S. Narita, Practical multiprocessor scheduling algorithms for efficient parallel processing, *IEEE Transactions on Comp.*, Vol. C33, No. 11 (1984) 1023–9.

[KaR90]   R.M. Karp, V. Ramachandran, A survey of parallel algorithms for shared memory machines, in *Handbook of Theoretical Computer Science*, Ed. Van Leeuwen, North Holland (1990) 869–942.

[KeK79]   P. Kermani, L. Kleinrock, Virtual cut-through: a new computer communication switching technique, *Computer Networks*, 3, 4 (1979) 267–86.

[Kho75]   W.H. Kholer, A preliminary evaluation of the critical path method for scheduling tasks on a multiprocessor system, *IEEE Transactions on Computers* 24, (1975) 1235–8.

[KKL80]   D.J. Kuck, R. Kuhn, B. Leasure, M. Wolfe, The structure of an advanced retargetable vectorizer, *Proceedings COMPSAC* 80 (1980) 709–15.

[KLL81]   D. Kleitman, F.T. Leighton, M. Lepley, G.L. Miller, New layouts for the shuffle-exchange graph, *Proc. of ACM 13th Ann. Symp. on Theory of Computing*, 278–92 (1981).

[KMW67]   R.M. Karp, R.E. Miller, S. Winograd, The organization of computations for uniform recurrence equations, *Journal ACM* 14, 3 (1967) 563–90.

[Knu73]   D.E. Knuth, *The Art of Computer Programming: Sorting and Searching*, Addison-Wesley, Reading (1973).

[Kog74]   P.M. Kogge, Parallel solution of recurrence problems, *IBM Journal Res. Dev.* 18 (1974) 138–48.

[Kog81]   P.M. Kogge, *The Architecture of Pipelined Computers*, Hemisphere Publishing Corporation (1981).

[KoS73]   P.M. Kogge, H.S. Stone, A parallel algorithm for the efficient solution of a general class of recurrence equations, *IEEE Transactions on Computers* 22 (1973) 786–93.

[Kos86]   S.R. Kosaraju, Parallel evaluation of division-free arithmetic expressions, *STOC* (1986) 231–9.

[KrL88]   B. Kruatrachue, T. Lewis, Grain size determination for parallel processing, *IEEE Soft.* (1988) 23–32.

[KrM89]   O. Krämer, H. Mühlenbein, Mapping strategies in message-based multiprocessor systems, *Parallel Computing* 9 (1989) 213–25.

[KrS83]   C.P. Kruskal, M. Snir, The performance of multistage interconnection networks for multiprocessors, *IEEE Transactions on Computers* C-32 (1983) 1091–8.

[Kru83]   C.P. Kruskal, Searching, merging and sorting in parallel computation, *IEEE Transactions on Computers* 32, 10 (1983) 942–6.

[Kuc73]   D.J. Kuck, Multioperation machine computational complexity, in *Complexity of Sequential and Parallel Numerical Algorithms*, J.F. Traub Ed., Academic Press, New York, (1973) 17–47.

[Kuc76]   D.J. Kuck, Parallel processing of ordinary programs, *Advances in Computers* 15 (1976) 119–79.

[Kuc78]   D.J. Kuck, *The Structure of Computers and Computations: Volume One*, Wiley & Sons (1978).

[KuL80]   H.T. Kung, C.E. Leiserson, Systolic arrays for VLSI, in *Introduction to VLSI systems*, C.A. Mead and L.A. Conway Eds., Addison-Wesley, (1980).

[KuM75]   D.J. Kuck, K. Maruyama, Time bounds for the parallel evaluation of arithmetic expressions, *SIAM Journal of Computing* 4 (1975) 147–162.

[Kum82]   S.P. Kumar, *Parallel algorithms for solving linear equations on MIMD computers*, PhD. Thesis, Washington State University (1982).

[Kun76]   H.T. Kung, New algorithms and lower bounds for parallel evaluation of certain rational expressions and recurrences, *Journal ACM* 23 (1976) 252–61.

[Kun80]   H.T. Kung, The structure of parallel algorithms, *Advances in Computers* 19 (1980) 65–112.

[Kun81]   M. Kunde, Nonpreemptive LP-scheduling on homogeneous multiprocessor systems, *SIAM Journal of Computing,* 10, 1 (1981) 151–73.

[Kun82]   H.T. Kung, Why systolic architectures?, *IEEE Computer* 15 (1982) 37–46.

[Kun88]   S.Y. Kung, *VLSI Array Processors*, Prentice-Hall (1988).

[KuS72]   D.J. Kuck, A.H. Sameh, Parallel computations of eigenvalues of real matrices, *Information Processing* 71 (1972) 1266–72.

[LaD90]   S. Lakshmivaharan, S.K. Dhall, *Analysis and Design of Parallel Algorithms*, McGraw-Hill (1990).

[LaF80]   R.E. Ladner, M.J. Fischer, Parallel prefix computation, *Journal ACM* 27 (1980) 831–8.

[Lam74]   L. Lamport, The parallel execution of do loops, *Communications ACM* 17, 2 (1974) 83–93.

[LaV75]   J.J. Lambiotte, J.R. Voigt, The solution of tridiagonal linear systems on the CDC STAR-100 computer, *ACM TOMS* 1 (1975) 308–29.

[Law75]   D.H. Lawrie, Access and alignment of data in an array processor, *IEEE Transactions on Computers* C-24 (1975) 1145–1155.

[LeA87]   S-Y. Lee, J.K. Aggarwal, A mapping strategy for parallel processing, *IEEE Transactions on Computers,* 36, 4 (1987) 433–42.

[Lee80]   R.B. Lee, Empirical results on the speed, efficiency, redundancy and quality of parallel computations, *Proc. 1980 International Conference on Parallel Processing,* (1980), 91–100.

[Lee91]   C.L. Lee, Parallel machines scheduling with non-simultaneous machine available time, *Discrete Applied Math.* 30 (1991) 53–61.

[Lei91]   F.T. Leighton, *Introduction to Parallel Algorithms and Architectures*, Morgan Kaufmann Publishers, CA (1991).

[Len82]   J. Lenfant, Mémoires parallèles et réseaux d'interconnexion, *TSI* 1, 2 (1982) 135–42.

[Len84]   J. Lenfant, Introduction aux réseaux d'interconnexion, Ecole d'été 'Calcul Vectoriel et Parallèle' CEA-EDF-INRIA (1984).

[LeS88]   I. Lee, D. Smitley, A synthesis algorithm for reconfigurable interconnection networks, *IEEE Transactions on Computers* 37, 6 (1988) 691–9.

[LGT88]   P. Laurent-Gengoux, D. Trystram, Parallel conjugate gradient algorithm with local decomposition, *Research report* #689 *TIM3-IMAG* (1988)

[LGT89]   P. Laurent-Gengoux, D. Trystram, *Comprendre l'Informatique Numérique*, Editions TEC&DOC (1989).

[LHC88]   C.Y. Lee, J.J. Hwang, Y.C. Chow, F.D. Anger, Multiprocessor with interprocessor communication delays, *Operations Research Letters* 7 (1988) 141–7.

[LiC86]   G. Li, T.F. Coleman, A parallel triangular solver for a hypercube multiprocessor, *Technical report* TR 86-787, Cornell University, New York (1986).

[Lil91]   S. L. Lillevik, The Touchstone 30 Gigaflops DELTA prototype, *Proc. DMCC*6, Portland, Oregon (1991) 671–7.

[Liu90]   Z. Liu, Graham's bound revisited, *Information Processing Letters* (1990).

[LKK83]   R.E. Lord, J.S. Kowalik, S.P. Kumar, Solving linear algebraic equations on a MIMD computer, *Journal ACM* 30 (1983) 103–17.

[Lo84]   V.M. Lo, Heuristic algorithms for task assignment in distributed systems, *4th Int. Conf. Dist. Comp. Systems* (1984) 30–9.

[Lo88]   V.M. Lo, Algorithms for static task assignment and symmetric contraction in distributed systems, *International Conference on Parallel Processing ICPP '88* (1988)

[LoN89]   M. Louter-Nool, LINPACK routines based on level 2 BLAS, *The Journal of Supercomputing* 3 (1989) 331–49.

[LoR90]   V.M. Lo, S. Rajopadhye, OREGAMI: software tools for mapping parallel computations to parallel architectures, CIS-TR-89-18, Dept. of Comp. Sc., University of Oregon (1990).

[Lub90]   A. Lubiw, Counter-example to a conjecture of Szymanski on hypercube routing, *Information Processing Letters* 35 (1990) 57–61.

[MaA86]   C.E. MacDowell, W.F. Appelbe, Processor scheduling for linearly connected parallel processors, *IEEE Transactions on Computers* 35, 7, (1986) 632–8.

[Mar73]   K.M. Maruyama, On the parallel evaluation of polynomials, *IEEE Transactions on Computers* 22, (1973) 2–5.

[Mil73]   R.E. Miller, A comparison of some theoretical models of parallel computation, *IEEE Transactions on Computers* 22, (1973) 710–17.

[Mil75]   W. Miller, Computational complexity and numerical stability, *SIAM Journal of Computing* 4 (1975) 97–107.

[Mil88]   V.M. Milutinovic (Ed.), *Computer Architecture – Concepts and Systems*, North Holland (1988).

[MiP71]   M. Minsky, S. Papert, On some associative parallel and analog computations, in *Associative Information Techniques*, E.R. Jacks Ed., Elsevier (1971).

[Mir71]   W.L. Miranker, A survey of parallelism in numerical analysis, *SIAM Review* 13, 4 (1971) 524–47.

[Mis87]   N.M. Missirlis, Scheduling parallel iterative methods on multiprocessor systems, *Parallel Computing* 5 (1987) 295–302.

[MiT90]   R. Miller, S.L. Tanimoto, Detecting repeated patterns on mesh computers, Technical report #90-11-01, University of Buffalo (1990).

[MiT93]   P. Michallon, D. Trystram, Practical experiments of broadcasting algorithms on a configurable parallel computer, *Discrete Applied Math.* special issue (1993).

[MLT82]   P-Y. Ma, E.Y.S. Lee, M. Tsuchiya, A task allocation model for distributed computing systems, *IEEE Transactions on Computers* 31, 1 (1982) 41–7.

[MoC84]   J.J. Modi, M.R.B. Clarke, An alternative Givens ordering, *Num. Math.* 43 (1984) 83–90.

[Mod88]   J.J. Modi, *Parallel Algorithms and Matrix Computation*, Clarendon Press, Oxford (1988).

[MoS90]   B. Monien, H. Sudborough, Embedding one interconnection network in another, *Computing Suppl.* 7 (1990) 257–82.

[MRK76]   N.K. Madsen, G.H. Rodrigue, J.I. Karush, Matrix multiplication by diagonals on a vector/parallel processor, *Information Processing Letters* 5 (1976) 41–45.

[MTV92]   P. Michallon, D. Trystram, G. Villard, Optimal broadcasting algorithms on torus, *LMC-IMAG technical report* Grenoble (1991).

[MuC69]   R.R. Muntz, E.G. Coffman, Optimal scheduling on two processor systems, *IEEE Transactions on Computers* 18, 11 (1969) 1014–20.

[MuK73]   Y. Muroaka, D.J. Kuck, On the time required for a sequence of matrix products, *Communications ACM* 16 (1973) 22–6.

[MuP73]   I. Munro, M. Paterson, Optimal algorithms for parallel polynomial evaluation, *Journal Comput. System Sci.* (1973) 189–98.

[MuP76]   D.E. Muller, F.P. Preparata, Restructuring of arithmetic expressions for parallel evaluation, *Journal ACM* 23 (1976) 534–43.

[Mur71]   Y. Muroaka, *Parallelism exposure and exploitation*, Ph.D. dissertation, Dept. Computer Sci., University of Illinois, Urbana (1971).

[MuW90]   T. Muntean, P. Waille, L'architecture des machines SUPERNODE, *La lettre du Transputer* 7 (1990) 11–40.

[NaS81]   D. Nassimi, S. Sahni, Data broadcasting in SIMD computers, *IEEE Transactions on Computers* 30 (1981) 101–6.

[NeT85]   B. Neta, H.M. Tai, LU factorization on parallel computers, *Comp. & Maths. with Appls.* 11, 6 (1985) 573–9.

[Nor90]   M.G. Norman, Multicomputer applications, and how to model the mapping problem, TR90-05, Edinburgh Parallel Comp. Centre (1990).

[PaS82]   C.H. Papadimitriou, K. Steiglitz, *Combinatorial Optimization, Algorithms and Complexity*, Prentice-Hall (1982).

[PaU87]   C.H. Papadimitriou, J.D. Ullman, A communication-time tradeoff, *SIAM Journal of Computing*, 16, 4, (1987) 639–46.

[PaY79]   C.H. Papadimitriou, M. Yannakakis, Scheduling interval-ordered tasks, *SIAM Journal of Computing*, 8 (1979).

[Pea67]   M.C. Pease, Matrix invariant using parallel processing, *Journal ACM* 14, 4 (1967) 757–64.

[Pea68]   M.C. Pease, An adaptation of the fast Fourier transform for parallel processing, *Journal ACM* 15, (1968) 252–64.

[Pea69]   M.C. Pease, Inversion of matrices by partitioning, *Journal ACM* 16, (1969) 302–14.

[Pea90]   J. Pearl, *Heuristique*, Cépadues (1990).

[PeC89]   J.K. Peir, R. Cytron, Minimum distance: a method for partitioning recurrences for multiprocessors, *IEEE Transactions on Computers* 38, 8 (1989) 1203–11.

[PKL80]   D.A. Padua, D.J. Kuck, D.L. Lawrie, High speed multiprocessor and compilation techniques, *IEEE Transactions on Computers* 29 (1980) 763–76.

[PlT92]   B. Plateau, D. Trystram, Optimal total exchange for a 3D torus of processors, *Information Processing Letters* 42 (1992) 95–102.

[Pol88]   C.D. Polychronopoulos, Compiler optimizations for enhancing parallelism and their impact on architecture design, *IEEE Transactions on Computers* 37, 8 (1988) 991–1004.

[PoV74]   W.G. Poole Jr., R.G. Voigt, Numerical algorithms for parallel and vector computers: an annotated bibliography, *Computing Review* 15, 10 (1974) 379–88.

[PRR92]   B. Plateau, A. Rasse, J-L. Roch, J-P. Verjus: Parallélisme, Polycopié de cours ENSIMAG Grenoble (1992).

[PrV81]   F.P. Preparata, J. Vuillemin, The cube-connected cycles: a versatile network for parallel computation, *Communications ACM* 24 (1981) 300–9.

[Qui83]   P. Quinton, *The systematic design of systolic arrays*, Research report 193, IRISA, Rennes (1983).

[Qui84]   P. Quinton, Automatic synthesis of systolic arrays from uniform recurrent equations, *11th ISCA*, IEEE Comp. Soc. Press (1984).

[Qui87]   M.J. Quinn, *Designing Efficient Algorithms for Parallel Computers*, McGraw-Hill (1987).

[QuR89]   P. Quinton, Y. Robert, *Algorithmes et architectures systoliques*, Collection ERI, Masson (1989).

[Ray87]   V.J. Rayward-Smith, UET scheduling with interprocessor communication delays, *Discrete Applied Math.* 18 (1987) 55–71.

[RCG72]   C.V. Ramamoorthy, K.M. Chandy, M.J. Gonzalez, Optimal scheduling strategies in a multiprocessor system, *IEEE Transactions on Computers* 21 (1972) 137–46.

[Rob90]   Y. Robert, *The Impact of Vector and Parallel Architectures on Gaussian Elimination Algorithms*, Manchester University Press (1990).

[RoT88]   Y. Robert, D. Trystram, Comments on scheduling parallel iterative methods on multiprocessor systems, *Parallel Computing* 7 (1988) 253–5.

[RoT89]   Y. Robert, D. Trystram, Optimal scheduling algorithms for parallel Gaussian elimination, *Theoretical Computer Science* 64 (1989) 159–73.

[RoT90]   A. Rosset, C. Tricot, Les machines VOLVOX, *La lettre du Transputer* 8 (1990) 37–44.

[Roy70]   B. Roy, *Algèbre moderne et théorie des graphes*, Dunod (1970).

[Rum92]   Rumeur, Communications dans les réseaux de processeurs, *Actes de l'Ecole d'été C3*, Cargèse (1992).

[RVV92]   J-L. Roch, A. Vermerbergen, G. Villard, Cost prediction for load-balancing: application to algebraic computations, *CONPAR'92 Lyon*, Springer Verlag LNCS 634 (1992) 467–78.

[Saa83]   Y. Saad, Practical use of polynomial preconditionings for the Conjugate Gradient Method, Research report 282, Computer Science Dept., Yale University (1983).

[Saa85]   Y. Saad, Communication complexity of the Gaussian elimination algorithm on multiprocessors, Research report 348, Computer Science Dept., Yale University (1985).

[Saa86]   Y. Saad, Gaussian elimination on hypercubes, in *Algorithmes and Architectures Parallèles*, Eds. M. Cosnard et al., North-Holland, (1986).

[SaB77]   A.H. Sameh, R.P. Brent, Solving triangular systems on a parallel computer, *SIAM Journal Num. Anal.* 14, 6 (1977) 1101–13.

[SaK77]   A.H. Sameh, D.J. Kuck, A parallel QR algorithm for symmetric tridiagonal matrices, *IEEE Transactions on Computers* 26 (1977) 147–53.

[SaK78]   A.H. Sameh, D.J. Kuck, On stable parallel linear system solvers, *Journal ACM* 25, 1 (1978) 81–91.

[Sam71]   A.H. Sameh, On Jacobi and Jacobi-like algorithms for a parallel computer, *Math. Comput.* 25 (1971) 579–90.

[Sam77]   A.H. Sameh, Numerical parallel algorithms – a survey, in *High Speed Computer and Algorithm Organization*, D. Kuck, D. Lawrie and A. Sameh Eds, Academic Press, (1977) 207–28.

[Sam82]   A.H. Sameh, Solving the linear least squares problem on a linear array of processors, *Proc. Purdue Workshop on algorithmically-specialized computer organizations*, W. Lafayette, Indiana, (1982).

[Sam83]   A.H. Sameh, An overview of parallel algorithms, *Bull. EDF*, C1 (1983) 129–34.

[Sam84]   A.H. Sameh, On some parallel algorithms on a ring of processors, *Computer Phys. Com.* 37 (1985) 159–66.

[Sar89]   V. Sarkar, *Partitioning and Scheduling Parallel Programs for Multiprocessors*, MIT Press (1989).

[SaS85]   Y. Saad, M.H. Schultz, Topological properties of hypercubes, *Research report* 389, Computer Science Dpt., Yale University (1985).

[SaS89]   Y. Saad, M.H. Schultz, Data communication in parallel architectures, *Parallel Computing* 11 (1989) 131–50.

[ScC91]   I.D. Scherson, P.F. Corbett, Communications overhead and the expected speed-up of multidimensional mesh-connected parallel processors, *Journal of Parallel and Distributed Computing* 11 (1991) 86–96.

[Sch80]   J.T. Schwartz, Ultracomputers, *ACM TOPLAS* 2, (1980) 484–521.

[Sch83]   J.T. Schwartz, A taxonomic table of parallel computers, based on 55 designs, Courant Institute, N. Y. U. (1983).

[Sch84]   U. Schendel, *Introduction to Numerical Methods for Parallel Computers*, Ellis Horwood Series, J. Wiley & Sons, New York (1984).

[SCK76]   A.H. Sameh, S.C. Chen, D.J. Kuck, Parallel Poisson and biharmonic solvers, *Computing* 17 (1976) 249–30.

[Sei85]   C.L. Seitz, The cosmic cube, *Communications ACM* 28, 1 (1985) 22–33.

[Sha78]   H.D. Shapiro, Theoretical limitations on the efficient use of parallel memories, *IEEE Transactions on Computers*, 27, 5 (1978).

[ShT85]   C-C. Shen, W-H. Tsai, A graph matching approach to optimal task assignment in distributed computing systems using a minimax criterion, *IEEE Transactions on Computers* 34, 3 (1985) 197–203.

[Sie79]   H.J. Siegel, Interconnection networks for SIMD machines, *Computer* 12 (1979) 57–65.

[Sie85]   H.J. Siegel, *Interconnection Networks for Large-scale Parallel Processing*, Lexington Books (1985).

[Sin87]   J.B. Sinclair, Efficient computation of optimal assignments for distributed tasks, *Journal of Parallel and Distributed Computing* 4 (1987) 342–62.

[SkV85]   S. Skyum, L.G. Valiant, A complexity theory based on Boolean algebra, *Journal of ACM* 32, 2 (1985) 484–502.

[Sni85]   M. Snir, On parallel searching, *SIAM Journal of Computing* 14, 3 (1985) 688–708.

[Sor84]   D.C. Sorensen, Analysis of pairwise pivoting in Gaussian elimination, *Technical report MCS* 26, Argonne National Laboratory (1984).

[Sri82]   M.A. Srinivas, Optimal parallel scheduling of Gaussian elimination DAGs, *IEEE Transactions on Computers* 32, 12 (1982) 1109–17.

[Ste73]   G.W. Stewart, *Introduction to Matrix Computations*, Academic Press, New York (1973).

[Sto71]   H.S. Stone, Parallel processing with the perfect shuffle, *IEEE Transactions on Computers,* 20 (1971) 57–65.

[Sto73a]   H.S. Stone, Problems of parallel computation, in *Complexity of Sequential and Parallel Numerical Algorithms*, J.F. Traub Ed., Academic Press, New York (1973) 1–16.

[Sto73b]   H.S. Stone, An efficient algorithm for the solution of a tridiagonal linear system of equations, *Journal ACM* 20 (1973) 27–38.

[Sto75]   H.S. Stone, Parallel tridiagonal equation solvers, *ACM TOMS* 1, 4 (1975) 289–307.

[Sto77]   H.S. Stone, Multiprocessor scheduling with the aid of network flow algorithms, *IEEE Transactions on Software Engineering* 3, 2 (1977) 85–93.

[Sto87]   H.S. Stone, *High-Performance Computer Architecture*, Addison-Wesley (1987).

[Str69]   V. Strassen, Gaussian elimination is not optimal, *Num. Math.* 13, 4 (1969) 354–6.

[StW90]   Q. Stout, B. Wagar, Intensive hypercube communication. Prearranged communication in link-bound machines, *Journal of Parallel and Distributed Computing* 10 (1990) 167–81.

[Swe74]   R.A. Sweet, A generalized cyclic reduction algorithm, *SIAM Journal Num. Anal.* 11, (1974) 1136–50.

[Sys92]   M. Syska, *Communications dans les architectures à mémoire distribuée*, Thesis at the University of Nice (1992).

[Szy89]   T. Szymanski, On the permutation capability of a circuit-switched hypercube, *International Conference on Parallel Processing* (1989) 103–10.

[Tal92]   E-G. Talbi, Etude expérimentale d'algorithmes de placement de processus, *Lettre du Transputer* 15 (1992) 7–26.

[TBH82]   P.C. Treleaven, D.R. Brownbridge, R.P. Hopkins, Data-driven and demand-driven computer architecture, *ACM Computing Surveys* 14 (1982) 93–143.

[Tra73]   J.F. Traub, Iterative solution of tridiagonal systems on parallel and vector computers, in *Complexity of Sequential and Parallel Numerical Algorithms*, J.F. Traub Ed., Academic Press, New York (1973) 49–82.

[TrW91]   A. Trew, G. Wilson, *Past, Present and Parallel*, Springer Verlag (1991).

[Try90]   D. Trystram, *Algorithmique parallèle: Analyse, Conception et Implémentation*, thèse d'habilitation à diriger des recherches INPG (1990).

[Ull75]   J.D. Ullman, NP-complete scheduling problems, *Journal of Computing System Science* 10 (1975) 384–93.

[VaB90]   E.A. Varvarigos, D.P. Bertsekas, Optimal communication algorithms for isotropic tasks in hypercubes and wrap-around meshes, Laboratory for Information and Decision Systems, Report LISD-P-1972 (1990).

[VaL90]   J. Van Leeuwen Ed., *Algorithms and Complexity*, Elsevier (1990).

[Var62]   R.S. Varga, *Matrix Iterative Analysis*, Prentice-Hall, Englewood Cliffs, NJ (1962).

[Vis83]   U. Vishkin, Implementation of simultaneous memory address access in models that forbid it, *Journal of Algorithms* 4 (1983) 45–50.

[WaK80]   Y. Wallach, V. Konrad, On block-parallel methods for solving linear equations, *IEEE Transactions on Computers* 29 (1980) 354–9.

[Wan81]   H.T. Wang, A parallel method for tridiagonal equations, *ACM TOMS* 7 (1981) 170–83.

[Wil83]   E. Williams, Assigning processes to processors in distributed systems, in *International Conference on Parallel Processing* (1983) 404–6.

[Wil83]   P. Wilson, OCCAM architecture eases system design – part 1, *Computer Design* (1983) 107–15.

[Wil85]   J.H. Wilkinson, *The Algebraic Eigenvalue Problem*, Oxford University Press, London (1985).

[Win70]   S. Winograd, On the number of multiplications to compute certain functions, *Comm. Pure and Applied Math.* 23 (1970) 165–79.

[Win73]   S. Winograd, Some remarks on fast multiplication of polynomials, in *Complexity of Sequential and Parallel Numerical Algorithms*, J.F. Traub Ed., Academic Press, New York (1973) 181–96.

[Win75]   S. Winograd, On the parallel evaluation of certain arithmetic expressions, *Journal ACM* 22, 4 (1975) 477–92.

[Wol89]   Y. Wolfstahl, Mapping parallel programs to multiprocessors: a dynamic approach, *Parallel Computing* 10 (1989) 45–50.

[Wol91]   P. Wolper, *Introduction à la calculabilité*, InterEditions (1991).

Index